Nine Lives of Neoliberalism

Nine Lives of Neoliberalism

Edited by Dieter Plehwe,
Quinn Slobodian, and Philip Mirowski

VERSO
London • New York

The publication of this book was funded by the Open Access
Publishing Fund of the Leibniz Association.

URN:ISBN:978-1-78873-253-6

First published by Verso 2020

1 3 5 7 9 10 8 6 4 2

Verso
UK: 6 Meard Street, London W1F 0EG
US: 20 Jay Street, Suite 1010, Brooklyn, NY 11201
versobooks.com

Verso is the imprint of New Left Books

ISBN-13: 978-1-78873-253-6
ISBN-13: 978-1-78873-254-3 (UK EBK)
ISBN-13: 978-1-78873-255-0 (US EBK)

British Library Cataloguing in Publication Data
A catalogue record for this book is available from the British Library

Library of Congress Cataloging-in-Publication Data

Names: Plehwe, Dieter, editor. | Slobodian, Quinn, 1978- editor. | Mirowski,
    Philip, 1951- editor.
Title: Nine lives of neoliberalism / edited by Dieter Plehwe, Quinn
    Slobodian, and Philip Mirowski.
Description: Brooklyn, NY : Verso, 2020. | Includes bibliographical
    references and index.
Identifiers: LCCN 2019017198| ISBN 9781788732536 (hardback : alk. paper) |
    ISBN 9781788732550 (US ebk)
Subjects: LCSH: Neoliberalism. | Liberalism.
Classification: LCC JC574 .N57 2020 | DDC 320.51/3–dc23
LC record available at https://lccn.loc.gov/2019017198

Typeset in Minion by Hewer Text UK Ltd, Edinburgh
Printed and bound by CPI Group (UK) Ltd, Croydon CR0 4YY

Contents

List of Figures and Tables

List of Figures

List of Tables

Acknowledgments

In March 2016, a group of thirty scholars from around the world convened at the WZB Berlin Social Science Center to discuss "more roads" to and from Mont Pèlerin. All the chapters in this volume were presented and discussed at the conference and benefited from seventy-two hours of intense debate. The four organizers of the conference (Philip Mirowski, Dieter Plehwe, Hagen Schulz-Forberg, and Quinn Slobodian) and the authors of the present volume are indebted to the other participants: Ola Innset, Jacob Jensen, Niklas Olsen, Tiago Mata, Elisabeth Winter, Fabio Masini, Andrea Franc, Merijn Oudenampsen, Bram Mellink, Karin Fischer, Lars Mjoset, Tamotsu Nishizawa, Isabella Weber, Aditya Balasubramanian, Joshua Rahtz, Holger Straßheim, and Vineet Thakur. The conference was generously funded by Schulz-Forberg's Velux "Good Society" Project at Aarhus University and the WZB Research Unit on Inequality and Social Policy, which was headed by Felix Elwert at the time. Our thanks are due to the WZB team of Stefanie Roth, Marion Obermaier, and Moritz Neujeffski.

The conference was the third international conference on the topic of neoliberalism focusing on organized neoliberal networks. The previous conference at NYU led to the publication of *The Road from Mont Pèlerin: The Making of the Neoliberal Thought Collective*, which has sparked an ongoing international debate and a wide range of research on the intellectual and social history of neoliberalism. The 2016 meeting was actually a return to the origins of the research project as the first conference took place in Berlin in 2002. It led to *Neoliberal Hegemony: A Global Critique*, edited by Dieter Plehwe, Bernhard Walpen, and Gisela Neunhöffer. Ironically, much like the present volume, the book's introduction attacked the notion of the impending demise of neoliberalism. We hope the next effort to deal with global neoliberalism, and much of the work of the other conference participants, will not require similar introduction. We thank Sebastian Budgen and Cian McCourt at Verso for shepherding the current volume to completion.

We are grateful for the spirit and support of many friends and colleagues who are living together with us in these neoliberal times, and dedicate this book to all those who struggle with and against neoliberalism. They understand that there are alternatives, and that they will certainly not be a result of purely academic declarations.

Introduction

Quinn Slobodian and Dieter Plehwe

Neoliberalism is dead again. After the election of Donald J. Trump, political economist Mark Blyth declared the "era of neoliberalism is over," intellectual historian Samuel Moyn tweeted neoliberalism "RIP," and Cornel West wrote that "the neoliberal era in the United States ended with a neofascist bang."[1] Such pronouncements recur with regularity. A quarter-century ago, a Latin American politician deemed neoliberalism "dead" after the election of another US president—Bill Clinton. Obituaries resurfaced as critiques of the Washington Consensus in the wake of the Asian Financial Crisis in 1997, returned on the crest of the Latin American pink tide (Evo Morales declared "neoliberalism is dead" in 2003), and peaked in the wake of the near-collapse of the global financial system in 2008.

One year after Trump's election, with a tax plan benefiting corporations and the country's wealthiest citizens as his only major legislative achievement, the obituarists for neoliberalism had fallen silent too. The real-estate magnate's cabinet has pursued policies openly geared to the richest members of society and done little beyond making token gestures to reverse the flight of industrial jobs from the United States. The promised infrastructure plans that had some dreaming of a second New Deal vanished without ceremony.

The standard response to what Colin Crouch called the "strange non-death of neoliberalism" has been a turn to the metaphor of the

---

1 Cornel West. "Goodbye, American neoliberalism. A new era is here." *The Guardian* (17 Nov 2016).

zombie.[2] Yet invoking the occult in the interest of reasoned analysis strikes us as self-defeating. Jamie Peck has suggested that neoliberalism lost "another of its nine lives" after the global financial crisis in 2008.[3] We adopt his metaphor in seeing neoliberalism as less like a zombie and more like a cat. Though cats are granted nine lives, this is not meant literally. There is no sorcery in their survival, simply a preternatural ability. As a body of thought and set of practices, neoliberalism too has proven agile and acrobatic, prone to escaping alive from even the most treacherous predicaments. As Peck writes, it has shown a consistent feline capacity to "fail-and-flail-forward."[4]

There are two ways of making sense of neoliberalism's longevity. One is to point to the durability of the blocs of capital and their allies in government. The other points to the expansion and adaptation of neoliberal worldviews encroaching upon the competing ideologies of conservatism and social democratic liberalism. This book has no quarrel with the former explanations, including those of neo-Gramscian International Political Economy, and finds them essential for making sense of the present.[5] To draw attention to the intellectual history of neoliberalism as in the second model is not to insist dogmatically on the primacy of ideas. It would be ironic, as some have noted, if leftist critics became fixated on the realm of ideas while the right adopted materialist explanations of the present. At the same time, proposals for social changes, whether large or small, do not emerge in a vacuum, which requires attention to the universe of ideologies and to the process of preference formation.

If neoliberalism's demise has been foretold prematurely yet again, then we still need more and better analyses of its mechanics, its morphology, and the stations of its metamorphosis. Eighty years after the term

---

2 Colin Crouch, *The Strange Non-Death of Neoliberalism* (Cambridge: Polity, 2011).

3 Jamie Peck, *Constructions of Neoliberal Reason* (New York: Oxford University Press, 2010), 277. He uses the metaphor elsewhere, including in the title of a foreword seen by this volume's editors only after its completion. We credit him with the evocative metaphor. Jamie Peck, Nik Theodore, and Neil Brenner, "Neoliberalism Resurgent? Market Rule after the Great Recession," *The South Atlantic Quarterly* 111, no. 2 (Spring 2012): 265; Jamie Peck, "Foreword: The Nine Lives of Neoliberalism," in *Urban Political Geographies: A Global Perspective*, ed. Ugo Rossi and Alberto Vanolo (London: Sage, 2012).

4 Peck, *Constructions of Neoliberal Reason*, 277.

5 See, e.g., Stephen Gill and A. Claire Cutler, eds, *New Constitutionalism and World Order* (New York: Cambridge University Press, 2014).

was coined, forty years after the Volcker shock and the victories of Thatcher and Reagan, people still do not agree on whether neoliberalism exists. Many continue to find it useful to avoid the term—preferring "advanced liberalism," distinguishing between "financialization" and neoliberalism, or insisting on neoliberalization as a verb rather than a noun.[6] The authors in this book find it perfectly acceptable to use a word with a contested definition. Rather than jettisoning the term altogether, they seek to add precision to its use, examine its conceptual background, clarify important building blocks, and observe its evolution as a result of the interplay of intellectual debate, changing circumstances, and, not least, social struggles.

The alternative narrative according to which neoliberalism is not a suitable analytical category because it changes or because it has multiple and sometimes contradictory meanings amounts to self-defeating denialism, expressing a desire for a neat and simple singular ideology with an ahistorical essence to replace the messy world of competing worldviews. Marxism, liberalism, and conservatism have experienced kaleidoscopic refraction, splintering, and recombination over the decades. We see no reason why neoliberalism would not exhibit the same diversity. Indeed, we can prove that it has. If the loose use of terms was the grounds for expungement, then "socialism," "capitalism," "conservatism," and plain "liberalism" would have long been purged. Avoiding the term does little to address the ideology it was coined to describe.

In 2009, two editors of this volume helped launch a wide-ranging conversation about neoliberalism as an intellectual movement around the Mont Pèlerin Society, or what they dubbed with Bernhard Walpen the "neoliberal thought collective," with the publication of *The Road from Mont Pèlerin*.[7] In defense of its central contention that neoliberalism could be studied as an intellectual network and not simply an agentless spirit of capitalism, the contributions to that book focused on the

---

6 See, e.g. Nikolas Rose, "Still 'Like Birds on the Wire'? Freedom after Neoliberalism," *Economy and Society*, published online November 10, 2017; Aeron Davis and Catherine Walsh, "Distinguishing Financialization from Neoliberalism," *Theory, Culture & Society* 34, nos. 5–6 (2017); Simon Springer, Kean Birch, and Julie MacLeavy, "An Introduction to Neoliberalism," in *The Handbook of Neoliberalism*, ed. Simon Springer, Kean Birch, and Julie MacLeavy (New York: Routledge, 2016), 2.

7 Philip Mirowski and Dieter Plehwe, eds, *The Road from Mont Pèlerin: The Making of the Neoliberal Thought Collective* (Cambridge, MA: Harvard University Press, 2009).

confluence of national traditions of neoliberal economic thought in the postwar moment as well as the debates on a few key issues like competition, trade unions, and development economics. The book helped accelerate a shift in the scholarship on neoliberalism. Critical studies of neoliberalism had begun in the 1990s with the basic contention that the ideology meant the rollback of the state and the return of laissez-faire: a market fundamentalism, which purportedly dictated the liberation of markets and the transformation of every member of the world's population into homo economicus. The scholarship evolved in the early 2000s to clarify that neoliberalism in both theory and practice actually meant a "strong state and free market" with a "roll-out" (Peck) of a new form of state to match its rollback.[8]

New work clarified the importance of the knowledge problem for neoliberals and outlined their project of building a counter-public to the social democratic consensus after 1945. Insights from this literature surfaced during the Eurozone crisis with repeated arguments that the European Union seemed to realize F. A. Hayek's visions for federation from decades earlier. German Finance Minister Wolfgang Schäuble cited Hayek's warnings against "the pretense of knowledge" as he clung to the precepts of austerian orthodoxy, and Chancellor Angela Merkel repeated a term coined by neoliberal Wilhelm Röpke a half-century earlier when she spoke of the need for a "market-conforming democracy." Op-ed columns, social media feeds and academic journals were suddenly alive with pronouncements of the "return of ordoliberalism."[9]

Despite—or because of—this flourishing of scholarship, the literature on neoliberalism is now at a critical juncture. Weary of the range and variety of analyses, some observers on the left propose that there is "no such thing" as neoliberalism and that "the left should abandon the concept."[10] Curiously, this is happening parallel to a moment when the IMF itself dares to speak the name of neoliberalism,[11] and when members

8 Werner Bonefeld, *The Strong State and the Free Economy* (London: Rowman & Littlefield, 2017); Jamie Peck, "Neoliberalizing States: Thin Policies/Hard Outcomes," *Progress in Human Geography* 25, no. 3 (2001): 447.

9 Werner Bonefeld, *The Strong State and the Free Economy* (London: Rowman & Littlefield, 2017); Jamie Peck, "Neoliberalizing States: Thin Policies/Hard Outcomes," *Progress in Human Geography* 25, no. 3 (2001): 447.

10 Bill Dunn, "Against Neoliberalism as a Concept," *Capital & Class* 41, no. 3 (2017); Rajesh Venugopal, "Neoliberalism as Concept," *Economy and Society* 44, no. 2 (2015).

11 Jonathan D. Ostry, Prakash Loungani, and Davide Furceri, "Neoliberalism: Oversold?" *Finance & Development* (June 2016).

of the market-right, including the venerable UK think tank, the Adam Smith Institute, have, in their own words, "come out as neoliberals."[12]

This volume contends that more is to be learned by continuing the inquiry into neoliberalism than declaring it dead, defunct, or a diversion. It follows a number of exceptional publications on this topic.[13] At the same time, it builds on this literature in ways that strike us as crucial for the development of the field. The first is its focus on institutional embeddedness. *Nine Lives of Neoliberalism* places ideas in context and follows them in action. Sites of analysis include the League of Nations' intellectual wing, the Bellagio Group of academics and central bankers, and the California tax and welfare reform movement. Against charges that critical scholars cast neoliberalism as a monolith, *Nine Lives of Neoliberalism* also emphasizes the diversity and heterogeneity of the neoliberal thought style. Attention is drawn to the deep influence of the philosophy of science on early neoliberalism, the contested nature of behavioral economics in neoliberalism, the divergent stances on the idea of intellectual property rights, and the bitter conflicts within the Mont Pélerin Society (MPS) over what might underpin a global monetary order.

Through a serious engagement with the histories of actually existing neoliberals, their ideas, discussions, battles, projects, and legacies, we can learn about the ways in which neoliberals themselves thought of the political and economic spheres as not being separate. Many critics of neoliberalism fail to acknowledge that neoliberals themselves moved beyond classical liberalism and economic naturalism. Since most critics continue to not take neoliberals seriously, they are content to equate neoliberal calls for a "free market" to neoliberalism regardless of the clear profession of all neoliberals that there is no such thing as a free market. The announcement of "the death of homo economicus" is deployed as a supposedly radical provocation despite the fact that Hayek described "economic man" as a skeleton in the closet of economics eight decades ago.[14] Against the

---

12 Sam Bowman, "Coming out as Neoliberals," *Adam Smith Institute Blog* (October 11, 2016).

13 For a state of the field, see the two impressive new handbooks: Springer, Birch, and MacLeavy, eds, *The Handbook of Neoliberalism*; Damien Cahill, Melinda Cooper, Martijn Konings, and David Primrose, eds, *The Sage Handbook of Neoliberalism* (Los Angeles: Sage, 2018).

14 F. A. Hayek, "Economics and Knowledge (1937)," in *Individualism and Economic Order*, ed. F. A. Hayek (Chicago: University of Chicago Press, 1948), 46. See Peter Fleming, *The Death of Homo Economicus: Work, Debt and the Myth of Endless Accumulation* (London: Pluto Press, 2017).

reality of nearly half a century of modifications in neoliberal doctrine, political economists continue to (re)discover the origins of neoliberalism in the US Democratic Party of the 1980s and reduce it to the idea of a "single blueprint" for deregulation and privatization.[15]

By definition, theories that postulate free or pure markets per se are not neoliberal, and it is easy for neoliberals to point to the need for the right set of institutions, politics, and nowadays even behavior to allow markets to operate relatively freely, and, more importantly, to set market forces free. The charge of "one size fits all" fails in the face of the documentable shifts in neoliberal approaches to policy problems. Our case studies show that neoliberalism is less a policy orthodoxy than a consistent approach to policy problems. To adapt the famous legal maxim of Ernst-Wolfgang Böckenförde, neoliberals hold that the market lives by prerequisites it cannot guarantee itself. Rather than operate with a belief in the "magic" of a putatively "natural" market, neoliberals are avowed interventionists of their own kind, rethinking policies according to context and showing both a capacity for improvisation and an attitude of flexible response. If the end goal remains constant—safeguarding what neoliberals call a competitive order and exposing humanity ever more to the compulsions of adjustment according to the price mechanism—the means of arriving at this goal shift with time and place. Only by understanding this flexibility do the nine lives of neoliberalism become explainable.

The contributions in this book introduce readers to lesser-known but still influential neoliberal thinkers. These include former MPS president Herbert Giersch, described as "Germany's Milton Friedman"; Fritz Machlup, coiner of the term "the knowledge economy"; the generations of German ordoliberals taught by Walter Eucken; and another former MPS president, George Stigler, who often exists in the shadow of Friedman and Hayek in histories of the Chicago School. The contributions also show how much more attention to the broader philosophical and epistemological underpinnings of neoliberal ideology and political theory is required in order to account for its influence across disciplines and professions; for the creative and innovative

---

15 Dani Rodrik, "Rescuing Economics from Neoliberalism," *Boston Review* (6 Nov 2017). On the history of supranational visions of order see Quinn Slobodian, *Globalists: The End of Empire and the Birth of Neoliberalism* (Cambridge, MA: Harvard University Press, 2018). Quinn Slobodian, "Perfect Capitalism, Imperfect Humans: Race, Migration, and the Limits of Ludwig von Mises's Globalism," *Contemporary European History* 28(2): 143–55.

development of new approaches to and theoretical understandings of economic and social theory, and the subtleties of neoliberal reasoning; for the institutional positions and embeddedness—both domestic and international—of key neoliberal intellectuals and events; and, last but not least, for the neoliberal capacities and infrastructures that influence science and society, through networks of intellectuals and think tanks, donors, and supporters.

Lifeboat Neoliberalism

This book's method can help explain some of the apparent contradictions of the present. Many observers felt that neoliberalism lost its latest life with the victory of Brexit and Trump in 2016. Political diagnoses have pitched an ascendant populism against a degenerate neoliberalism reaping the effects of the inequality and democratic disempowerment it had sown. Yet a closer look at the standard-bearers of the right throws this dichotomy into question. We find that many neoliberals are more than willing to find a middle ground between their own principles and those of an exclusionary culturalist, and even racist, right.

To offer a few examples: Antonio Martino, MPS member since 1976 and president from 1988–1990, was a founding member of Forza Italia in 1994 and a minister of foreign affairs and minister of defense in two of Silvio Berlusconi's governments. A member of the core negotiators in coalition talks for the Austrian Freedom Party (whose slogans included "Vienna must not become Istanbul") in late 2017 was president of the Friedrich Hayek Institute, Barbara Kolm. The leadership of the German far-right party, Alternative für Deutschland (AfD), for whom opposition to migration from majority Muslim countries is central, includes multiple members of the Friedrich Hayek Society, some of whom have been active in Euro-critical parties since the early 1990s. Among the AfD's founders are Joachim Starbatty, who filed a constitutional complaint against Germany joining the Euro in 1997 and helped found an anti-European party with New Right politician Manfred Brunner in 1994.[16] As early as 1993, a Brussels think tank, Centre for the New

---

16 For this history see Dieter Plehwe, "'Alternative für Deutschland,' Alternativen für Europa?" in *Europäische Identität in der Krise? Europäische Identitätsforschung und Rechtspopulismusforschung im Dialog*, ed. Gudrun Hentges, Kristina Nottbohm, and Hans-Wolfgang Platzer (Wiesbaden: Springer VS, 2017), 249–69; Quinn Slobodian and

Europe, was founded under the direction of MPS member Hardy Bouillon, criticizing EU policy. In the late 1990s, German neoliberals like Detmar Doering and Roland Vaubel were among the few to openly theorize and demand a right of secession in the EU with emphasis on the salutary nature of fragmentation and competition. Symptomatically, Doering wrote a column in 1999 attempting to rehabilitate the category of social Darwinism.[17]

Although the EU is described regularly as a neoliberal federation, there are clear forerunners to Brexit in neoliberal networks. One sees this in the European Conservatives and Reformers Group (ECR) and the affiliated Alliance of European Conservatives and Reformers, both established in 2009 and led by British Conservatives. The Prague declaration of the ECR, prepared by Tories and the Liberal Institute led by MPS member and former Czech president Václav Klaus, emphasized economic not political freedom as the foundation of individual freedom and national prosperity.[18] At the MPS meeting in South Korea in 2017, Klaus voiced typical xenophobic "populist" themes, saying that "mass migration into Europe . . . threatens to destroy European society and to create a new Europe which would be very different from the past as well as from MPS way of thinking [sic]."[19] Referring to far-right parties in France, Austria, Germany, and Italy, he said: "The people are starting to open their eyes, to look around, to speak out, to express their dissatisfaction with the brave new world without freedom and democracy, with the world heralding relativism, with the suppression of old values, traditions, customs and habits, with the world of new aristocracies."[20] Already in 2014 at an MPS meeting in Hong Kong, Klaus had made it clear that "to protect liberty . . . we need to rehabilitate the sovereign nation-state . . . We need responsible citizens anchored in domestic realities, not cosmopolitan, selfish individuals 'floating' at the surface and searching for short-term pleasures and advantages—without roots and

---

Dieter Plehwe, "Neoliberals against Europe," in William Callison and Zachary Manfredi, eds. *Mutant Neoliberalism: Market Rule and Political Ruptures* (New York: Fordham University Press, 2019).

17   Detmar Doering, "'Sozialdarwinismus' Die unterschwellige Perfidie eines Schlagwortes," *Eigentümlich Frei* 2, no. 6 (1999).

18   The declaration is available at http://ecrgroup.eu/about-us/our-history.

19   Václav Klaus, "Mont Pèlerin Society Speech in Korea" (2017), 12, available at montpelerin.org.

20   Ibid., 16.

responsibility."[21] Along with parties organized in the AECR, the far-right parties invoked by Klaus share the rejection of an ever-closer European Union and insist on a Europe of nations. Yet even as they reject free migration, they retain the other three freedoms of European integration: those of goods, services, and capital. The new variety of conservative-neoliberal perspectives combines uninhibited economic liberalism with limited mobility of people and a new attention to the sociological—and sociobiological—necessity of cultural homogeneity as a basis for order.

To understand the current convergence of far-right and neoliberal thought, it is helpful to return to the philosopher and ecologist Garrett Hardin's essay on "lifeboat ethics" from 1974, subtitled "the argument against helping the poor."[22] Hardin is best known for his idea of the "tragedy of the commons" from 1968.[23] While some take this to be a call for regulatory intervention, Hardin clarified his own understanding in collaboration with the self-professed free market environmentalist and MPS member John Baden. To be used according to economic principles, nature had to be commodified, declared the founder of so-called New Resource Economics. The solution to problems of scarcity was neither free access nor regulation but management according to property rights and price signals.[24]

Hardin proposed his system of "lifeboat ethics" in response to contemporary concerns over ecology, overpopulation and migration, including *The Limits to Growth* report published by the Club of Rome in 1972. He opposed the spaceship earth metaphor—introduced by Adlai Stevenson and developed by Barbara Ward—for implying central leadership in the form of a captain that did not exist. Against the idea of global planning, he posed nation-states trapped in a realist game of global anarchy with relations between states depending on relative strength. Given the limited resources of the lifeboat nation, stranded

---

21 Václav Klaus, "Careless Opening up of Countries (without Keeping the Anchor of the Nation-State) Leads Either to Anarchy or to Global Governance: Lessons of the European Experience," Speech at the Mont Pèlerin Society General Meeting, Hong Kong (July 23, 2014), 16, available at montpelerin.org.

22 Garrett Hardin, "Lifeboat Ethics: The Argument Against Helping the Poor," *Psychology Today* 8 (1974): 38–43.

23 Garrett Hardin, "The Tragedy of the Commons," *Science, New Series* 162, no. 3859 (1968): 1243–8.

24 Garrett Hardin and John Baden, eds, *Managing the Commons* (San Francisco: W. H. Freeman and Company, 1977).

swimmers (read: migrants) could not be taken aboard without endangering the lives of others through overtaxing limited resources. Prefiguring the later anti-immigration slogan "the boat is full," Hardin's ethics posited the inhumanity of wealthier, more economically efficient nations as a utilitarian necessity.

In his final book, Hayek referred to Hardin in a section titled "the calculus of costs is a calculus of lives." Expanding on his ideas of cultural evolutionary progress measured in the quality and quantity of lives, Hayek suggested that humans could be ranked by utility: "The good hunter or defender of the community, the fertile mother and perhaps even the wise old man may be more important than most babies and most of the aged." "The requirement of preserving the maximum number of lives," he wrote, "is not that all individual lives be regarded as equally important."[25]

The far-right strain of neoliberalism deploys a similarly dispassionate calculus of human lives. The national community is not privileged for its transcendent value (in the Herderian sense of the *Volk*) but because of the utility of cultural homogeneity for stability and the accumulated cognitive capital of the population in industrialized nations. Combining critiques of foreigners and the welfare state with calls for closed borders and private property rights has become standard fare for right-wing neoliberals in the new millennium. A case in point is Erich Weede, sociology professor, MPS member since 1992, and leader of the right wing of the German Hayek Society. In an article from 2016, Weede, who has argued for the genetic basis of differential "human capital" endowments and has correlated economic growth to IQ, called for the closing and fortification of borders to prevent the influx of refugees. Using an intergenerational zero-sum logic, he wrote that "one must not forget that governments are always dispensing other people's money—or in the case of higher and rising state debts, even the money of underage and yet unborn tax payers. Those who give governments the freedom to do good for foreigners must by necessity take freedom and property away from citizens."[26] Lifeboat neoliberalism sees empathy as feckless state spending, and openness to foreigners as a downgrading of human capital.

25 F. A. Hayek, *The Fatal Conceit: The Errors of Socialism* (Chicago: University of Chicago Press, 1988), 132.

26 Erich Weede, "Vertragen die alternden europäischen Sozialstaaten die Massenzuwanderung, die wir haben?" *Orientierungen zur Wirtschafts- und Gesellschaftspolitik* no. 143 (June 2016): 64. On the intellectual history see Quinn Slobodian, "Anti-68ers and the Racist-Libertarian Alliance: How a Schism among Austrian School Neoliberals Helped Spawn the Alt Right," *Cultural Politics* 15 no. 3 (2019): 372–86.

Rather than posing a globalist neoliberalism against a neo-nationalist and social conservative populism, we must remain mindful of the elasticity of neoliberal norms and principles. Principles of competition, private property, and consumer sovereignty can be tied to human rights, multicultural tolerance, and recognition of minorities as well as exclusionary bonds based in culture and race. Neither left nor right had much affinity to neoliberal-style individualism historically. But the advance of neoliberal worldviews expanded certain ideas at the expense of competing notions of individualism and solidarity. Social democracy has become less concerned with redistribution under the impact of advancing neoliberal understandings of social life, while conservatism has become less concerned with tradition under the impact of advancing neoliberal understandings of competitiveness. The way in which neoliberal core ideas have made inroads and been absorbed by competing worldviews is among the most important reasons for the longevity of neoliberalism in spite of the perceptions of its eternal crisis.

The task at hand is twofold: observe the historical development and expansion of neoliberal ideas, or the morphology of neoliberal worldviews in their own right, while also tracking the linkages of elements of those worldviews to competing ideologies, or the mixed morphologies of both conservative-neoliberal and progressive-neoliberal perspectives. Both more progressive and conservative fusions with neoliberalism result in patterns of exclusive solidarity: progressive neoliberals preach recognition but not redistribution, and conservative neoliberals abandon the humanitarian face of social order. Once belief and trust in mutual and comprehensive solidarity is lost, communities of competition constitute themselves against one another: core workforce against peripheral workers, rich communities against poor, and so on.

The current fusion of neoliberalism and right-wing populism is a consequence of the unleashed notion of the competition state, the competition region, and the competitive units of and within the enterprise. The social reproduction of the moral underpinnings of neoliberal order—communitarian notions of self-help and caring, social responsibility for those in close proximity—can be regarded as compensation for social redistribution and welfare, but it may not develop fast enough or at the same speed as the centrifugal notions of selfishness and competitiveness. Only time will tell when neoliberalism will use up its next—or even final—life.

Chapter Outline

The chapters of this book introduce domains of neoliberal theory unfamiliar to many and offer revisionist perspectives on supposedly well-worn truths about what neoliberalism is. The book begins with the question of knowledge itself. The limitation of human cognition is a leitmotif in neoliberal theory. The origin of the axiom that the mass of tacit human knowledge coordinated without direction by market actors trumps any attempt at centralized knowledge production, most often associated with Hayek, is rooted in debates in the philosophy of science dating before 1945. Martin Beddeleem's chapter explains the innovative character and the strength of neoliberal epistemology vis-à-vis traditional liberal epistemologies of empiricism and naturalism (based on a priori assumptions) on the one hand, and universal positivist epistemologies prevalent in both socialist and conservative Vienna Circles on the other. Faced with the scientific and rationalist optimism of the unity of science movement as well as much of Marxism, a cohort of early neoliberal philosophers of science, including Michael Polanyi, Hayek, Karl Popper, and Louis Rougier, developed a new epistemology of critical conventionalism. Separating the spheres of lawful exact knowledge from social spheres in which precise knowledge was impossible due to the dispersed, tacit, and opaque character of the subject, neoliberals intervened in the fields of both epistemology and public policy. Arguing for the unavoidability of human ignorance became an important precondition for granting the market (and, by extension, its most powerful actors) superior powers of cognition and coordination.

Abstract debates happened in concrete places. We still know remarkably little about how neoliberals reacted to changes in their own primary places of employment—universities—and what influence, if any, they had on higher education. Understanding this history is pressing in light of present-day concerns about "the neoliberal university" and the shift from permanent faculty to adjunct labor, the restructuring of funding in pursuit of patents and other marketable research outcomes, the pervasive discourses of impact, customer (student) experience, and realignment to forms of training rewarded by high post-graduate salaries. In his chapter, Edward Nik-Khah follows one such storyline through Chicago economist George Stigler. Beginning as an advocate of trustees as guardians of academic freedom against the student-as-customer, Stigler shifted after the campus unrest of the late 1960s towards a distrust of trustees themselves. He ended by advocating that research be hived off from instruction. Instead, privately funded institutes should produce knowledge directly respondent to the demands of the broader marketplace.

Neoliberalism's nine lives can only be understood as a chain of such transformations over time. In 1937, Lionel Robbins wrote that "true liberals should want more property all round, not less."[27] Mises complimented him on the line in a letter, saying he would use the sentence as a motto for the new edition of his book.[28] While such a statement may seem like a truism, paying attention to the transformations of neoliberal theory teaches one to be suspicious of eternal principles. Quinn Slobodian's chapter shows that the dictum of "more property" was far from the stance on patents and copyright taken by many neoliberals who felt that weaker rather than stronger property rights in ideas would produce better outcomes. While arguments from Chicago School thinkers like Stigler himself were central to the emerging intellectual property regime of the 1980s and beyond, Austrian and libertarian neoliberals continue to be forceful and sometimes radical critics of existing IP rights. Understanding neoliberalism requires first disaggregating the competing claims of different neoliberal factions and then asking which ideas are translated into policy and why.

One might also assume that the sphere of personal sexual freedom would be honored as sacrosanct by neoliberals on the principle of live-and-let-live as long as lifestyle choices could be commodified and marketed. In fact, as Melinda Cooper shows, neoliberal thinkers promoted various forms of intervention into the private sphere of kinship and marriage on the principle of offloading (and financializing) state responsibilities for welfare onto the family unit. Actual existing neoliberalism in the US since the Reagan era has required the parallel discourse of social conservatism. Far from simply dissolving society down to atomistic consumer-entrepreneurs, family ties and family values were necessary to substitute for the shredded social safety net.

The reduction of neoliberal theory to market fundamentalism is one of the most misleading tendencies in comprehending it as a body of

---

27 Lionel Robbins, *Economic Planning and International Order* (London: Macmillan and Co., 1937), 265.

28 Mises to Robbins, May 8, 1937. LSE Archive, Robbins Papers, Box 128.

thought. In fact, the neoliberal project from the 1930s onward was about charting a route between laissez-faire and planning, between universal scientific optimism and anti-scientific nihilism, and between a belief in the imminent collapse of capitalism and a belief in its natural stability. Dieter Plehwe traces the engagement of neoliberals with one of the most notorious prophets of capitalism's decline, Joseph A. Schumpeter. Plehwe shows how neoliberals revived and revised Schumpeter's understanding of the entrepreneur. Israel Kirzner, Herbert Giersch, and others grafted Schumpeter onto the theories of Ludwig von Mises, universalizing the concept of the entrepreneur and extending it from a discrete sociological group to each and every human.

Entrepreneurship in the new sense of entrepreneurial management of the self and others was not the only field defining the current *Zeitgeist* where neoliberals left their mark. The recent boom in behavioral economics, marked by the Nobel Memorial Prize for Richard Thaler in 2017, is often described as a refutation of the supposedly one-dimensional models of human behavior native to neoliberal thought. Yet this dichotomy relies on a false contrast and glosses over the many links between the two fields. Rüdiger Graf concentrates on the overlooked case of Günther Schmölders. As a member of the Nazi party and SS from 1933 onward, and MPS president from 1968 to 1970, Schmölders was the proponent of an idiosyncratic strain of behavioral economics in Germany. Graf shows the multiple political uses to which behavioral economic approaches can be put—to both limit state power and extend it into new domains.

If neoliberal theory shares some moments of origin with behavioral economics, it does so with the field of international relations as well. Hagen Schulz-Forberg sheds new light on the early discussion of the interrelation of national and international order by looking at the role of neoliberals in networks linked to the League of Nations, including the Walter Lippmann Colloquium, organized under the aegis of the League's International Intellectual Committees. Many of those involved in international networks in the wake of World War I and the Great Depresssion no longer believed that capitalism was a self-stabilizing system. The alleged correlation of trade and peace required rules and supranational institutions. The intellectual discussions of the 1920s and 1930s helped pave the way for the Mont Pèlerin Society effort, but also for the discipline of international relations after 1945. The guiding principle for both was not democracy as a principle in itself, but the stability of the free market order at the national and international levels.

One of the central debates that carried over from the League of Nations to the postwar period was about money and the global monetary order. Was it possible to return to a gold standard or was fiat money under systems of fixed or flexible exchange rates unavoidable? In the early twenty-first century, neoliberalism would seem to mean, if anything, the approval of the "casino capitalism" of deregulated financial markets, speculative capital flows, and floating currency exchange rates. Yet, Matthias Schmelzer shows that, while the core faith in the right of capital to move across borders was shared by all neoliberals, the debate over monetary order split the Mont Pèlerin Society into warring factions in the 1950s and 1960s as the older gold bugs faced off against the younger advocates of floating, including Milton Friedman. Far from being a merely technical discussion relevant only to experts and bankers, the choice about fixed or floating exchange rates had huge consequences for both democratic governance and the volatility of the global capitalist system.

Even as it is denigrated as the "dismal science," economics reigns supreme in the public mind as the social science with the most influence on policy. One of the signs of the authority of the discipline is the awarding of a Nobel Prize in Economics—an honor shared by no other social science. In his chapter on the "Ersatz Nobel Prize," Philip Mirowski emphasizes the relevance of cultural institutions for the rise and staying power of neoliberalism by recounting the genesis of the "Memorial Prize in Honor of Alfred Nobel" a half-century after the other prizes. He recounts a powerful confluence of contingency and purposeful strategy in the creation of the prize by a group of officials and economists of the Swedish Riksbank united in opposition to the Swedish welfare state in the 1960s. Mirowski details the Swedish push for modern American neoclassical economics and the right wing of neoliberal economics through the strategic selection of committee members and candidates. The eight "Nobels" enjoyed by organized neoliberals in the Mont Pèlerin Society, and the considerably larger number of prizes for work in the realm of neoliberal economics, testify to the way in which the institution has served to validate one perspective of many in the discipline of economics.

However significant within the field of economics, the role of the Riksbank Nobel pales in comparison to the importance of think tanks as platforms and megaphones for neoliberal ideas. While the role of think tanks has been observed by journalists and scholars since the 1980s, empirical studies of their organization and activity remain surprisingly rare. An important case in point is the Atlas Economic Foundation (later Atlas Network), started in the early 1980s by Antony Fisher, the founder of the UK's Institute of Economic Affairs. Marie-Laure Djelic and Reza Mousavi trace the development of the Atlas Network under the long-term leadership of the Argentine economist Alejandro Chafuen, from a modest network of fifteen think tanks in nine countries in the mid-1980s to a partnership of 457 in ninety-six countries. Beyond strongholds in North America and Europe (both West and East), the network is strong in Latin America and has reached significant member-ship in the Asia-Pacific Region and even Africa. In only a few decades, Atlas moved from the equivalent of small trade or handcraft to mass production, creating replicable templates for the production and diffu-sion of neoliberal ideas.

Stephan Pühringer also follows ideas in action, using empirical meth-ods to evaluate the influence of neoliberalism on policy in Germany—a connection more often asserted than proven. Pühringer tracks the insti-tutional affiliation and public impact of 800 German economists from 1945 to 1995. Comparing neoliberal to Keynesian economists, he finds an extremely uneven power structure in the discipline of economics in favor of the former.

Taken as a whole, this book seeks to move the study of neoliberalism beyond what has become a set of clichés that inhibit rather than advance understanding of the larger phenomenon. The chapters demonstrate varieties of neoliberal epistemology beyond market worship, and proposals for policy beyond a bullet-point list of edicts. They outline a vision of subjectivity beyond the atomized utility-maximizing individ-ual, and of organization beyond the shock doctrine. Grasping neoliber-alism in its complexity will help its opponents better identify their antagonist, and its advocates contend both with the departures from classical liberalism and with the absence of a unified theory. Recent splits within the neoliberal universe like the founding of the Property and Freedom Society by racialist right-wing libertarian Hans-Hermann Hoppe, or the failure of cosmopolitan neoliberals to purge the social conservative right-wing neoliberals from Germany's Hayek Society, should not be read prematurely as signs of disintegration. There has, however, certainly been a stronger dose of serious conflict in the neolib-eral camp, and we can expect more of it in the face of serious challenges to the competitive order in issues like climate change, growing inequality, and mass human mobility.

The founding neoliberal group's emphasis on the inviolability of the human and the epistemological baseline of human ignorance presents increasing difficulties for those who focus mainly if not exclusively on the maintenance of property rights, freedom of contract, and the praiseworthiness of endless competition. There are areas where neoliberalism appears to fail to reproduce the conditions on which its existence is based. Will the challenge of climate change and the depletion of natural resources lead to a modification of neoliberal thinking, or will the oscillating appeals to human ignorance and the superior wisdom of the market march capitalist civilization to its final extinction? Nine lives may be long but, at least theoretically, they are finite.

PART ONE

NEOLIBERAL SCIENCE BEYOND MARKET FUNDAMENTALISM

1

Recoding Liberalism: Philosophy and Sociology of Science against Planning

Martin Beddeleem

> Our often unconscious views on the theory of knowledge and its central
> problems ("What can we know?," "How certain is our knowledge?") are
> decisive for our attitude towards ourselves and towards politics.
>
> Karl Popper

In the wake of the global financial crisis, the resilience of contemporary
neoliberalism confounded its detractors who expected its "zombie
economics" and obsolete policy models to give way to new horizons of
expectations. Usually, these predictions focused either on a superficial
reading of the defeat of neoliberalism-qua-austerity or insisted that its
systemic flaws had ruined any remnant of its legitimacy.[1] More skeptical authors remarked that, far from suffering from a sudden collapse,
neoliberalism has never been more palpable than in times of crisis,
when it reinvents itself by metabolizing the criticisms leveled at it or by
entrenching its dominance over the policy debate.[2]

To be sure, neoliberalism owes its ideological fluidity and staying
power to a hegemonic position among economic elites. Yet this puzzling
continuity only becomes clearer once its epistemological fabric comes

---

1 Cf. Mark Blyth, *Austerity: The History of a Dangerous Idea* (Oxford: Oxford
University Press, 2013); Gérard Duménil and Dominique Lévy, *The Crisis of Neoliberalism*
(Cambridge, MA: Harvard University Press, 2011).

2 Philip Mirowski, *Never Let a Serious Crisis Go to Waste: How Neoliberalism
Survived the Financial Meltdown* (London: Verso, 2013); Colin Crouch, *The Strange
Non-Death of Neoliberalism* (Cambridge: Polity, 2011).

into view. Through recent decades, neoliberals have demonstrated an uncanny ability to forsake obsolete theories and models in order to produce seemingly fresh answers to the repeated crises they have encountered. Although the original agenda of neoliberalism has been revised many times over, its programmatic ambition and scientific reach have steadily increased. Commonly overlooked, this scientific dynamism, sponsored by private foundations, relayed by think tanks, and embedded within the "marketplace of ideas," remains at the very heart of the neoliberal project today.

Since its inception, the problem space shared by neoliberals has been spread out on a modernist canvas, one which contrasted sharply with conservatives, reactionaries and old-fashioned liberals. During the inter-war period, self-proclaimed neoliberals dismantled and recoded the unpopular laissez-faire liberalism with epistemological ideas adapted from the "new scientific spirit" of the early twentieth century.[3] Breaking with naturalism and empiricism, they espoused a research program inspired by mathematical and physical conventionalism, one that balanced a skeptical epistemology with a commitment to scientific progress and objectivity. To this end, methodological rules were pivotal to the reconstruction of a genuine *science of liberalism* which had fallen into disrepute. This agenda aimed at regaining the political ground lost to 'collectivism' in the twentieth century by tackling two sets of problems left aside by 'classical' liberals: the positive role of the state and the social question.

While laying this epistemological groundwork, neoliberals battled competing claims about the nature of science, its history, and its position in society by actively reshaping ideas about academic freedom, the discovery of knowledge, and their relationship with political institutions and social reform. Faced with the scientific and rationalist optimism of the unity of science movement as well as much of Marxism, early neoliberals demarcated and defended a *liberal science* against progressive scientists who promoted science as the midwife of social change. Crucially, they developed a new theory of knowledge-in-society which fused together philosophy of science and political economy into a single set of hypotheses. In these debates, concerns about the role of science in society linked up with the most pressing political question of the day: the rise of fascism and totalitarianism.

---

3   See Gaston Bachelard, *The New Scientific Spirit* (Boston: Beacon Press, 1984 [1934]).

Neoliberalism was thus born out of a collision between the controversial importation of the methods and authority of the experimental sciences into politics on the one hand, and the acknowledgement of the social and political conditions for the discovery and justification of knowledge on the other. It made the pursuit of knowledge and truth a political question, and gave the question of social order an epistemological answer: *what we can do depends ultimately on what we can know*. Nevertheless, this proclivity for epistemological investigations did not imply a unity of views among neoliberals, nor that their conclusions were devoid of political motivations. Moreover, in their contention to reclaiming the mantle of science, neoliberals shared many premises with progressive scientists regarding the position and "function" of science in society. This apparent paradox explains both the fluidity of neoliberal thinking and the inspiration it has drawn from its detractors at a sociological and organizational level, two dimensions still relevant today in accounting for the steadiness of neoliberalism and its success in cannibalizing competing ideas.

The first part of this chapter situates the scientific controversies in which neoliberal philosophers of science developed their intuitions. The second part revisits the socialist calculation debate as the cradle of their epistemological arguments for the superiority of the market. The third part deals with their common fight against the planning of science and the reciprocal relation they established between liberal institutions and the conduct of science.

Vienna

The early twentieth-century breakthroughs in relativity theory, quantum mechanics, and non-Euclidean geometry had in common an encounter with phenomena from premises which were counterintuitive to a natural or rational picture of the world. Unshackling foundational axioms from fitting any "realist," "naturalist" or "a priori" presuppositions unleashed extraordinary debates and ingenuity in the advancement of these disciplines. While scientists retreated from their pretension to describe the "real" world, their quest for new theories and assumptions, which combined methodological inventiveness and instrumental needs, became boundless.

Neoliberalism owes its scientific imagination to the strong contingent of philosophers of science who participated in its elaboration. Michael Polanyi, Alfred Schutz, Felix Kaufmann, Karl Popper, Ludwig von Mises, and F. A. Hayek, among others, were all refugees and exiles from Austria and Hungary who were immersed in the scientific world and volatile political situation of the interwar period. They unanimously perceived the dissolution of the Austro-Hungarian Empire as a disaster,[4] responsible for the rise of an antagonistic politics pitting nationalism and conservatism against the growing communist movement. At that time, Vienna underwent one of the most radical municipal experiments of the twentieth century with the large-scale social policies promoted by the Austrian Socialist Party. In 1919, the philosopher and socialist educator Otto Neurath, president of the Central Planning Office in the short-lived Bavarian Soviet Republic, advocated a centrally planned economy in which money would be abolished and exchange would be made in kind. Before the war, Neurath had been a participant in the seminar led by Austrian economist Eugen von Böhm-Bawerk, along with Joseph Schumpeter, Otto Bauer, Emil Lederer, and Ludwig von Mises, who remembered him, in his words, for the "nonsense" he presented with "fanatical fervor."[5]

The refutation of Neurath's scheme published in 1920 by Mises triggered the *Planwirtschaft* (planned economy) debate in Vienna, wherein Mises argued that economic calculation was naive and unmanageable without the indispensable role of prices as signals of the relative value of factors of production. Against Neurath's desire to institute a scientific management of the economy, Mises claimed that the complexity of the economic system made its apprehension in one mind or place so difficult as to be near impossible. The debate received considerable attention, in part because physics and economics had displaced theology as the main subjects for intellectual debate in Vienna. Within both disciplines, the Austrian scientific "culture of uncertainty" was unique in Europe: their embrace of probabilistic theory "was tied to a

---

4 Popper writes in his autobiography that "the breakdown of the Austrian Empire and the aftermath of the First World War, the famine, the hunger riots in Vienna, and the runaway inflation [. . .] destroyed the world in which I had grown up." Karl Popper, *Unended Quest: An Intellectual Autobiography* (London and New York: Routledge, 1992), 31.

5 See Bruce Caldwell's introduction to F. A. Hayek, *Socialism and War* (Chicago: University of Chicago Press, 1997), 5.

characteristically liberal and anticlerical rejection of absolute claims,"[6] and "philosophers who challenged certitude often led efforts for social reform and popular scientific education."[7] As a matter of fact, Austrian Marxism itself was unique in drawing heavily on the ideas of Ernst Mach as it blended socialist economics with a positivist philosophy of science in the hope of attaining a truly scientific socialism. A rare fluidity existed, then, between the new discoveries of the physical sciences, their impact upon philosophical debates, and their translation into economic theories or social reforms.

Though Mises never held a formal appointment at the University of Vienna, his *Privatseminar* became the meeting place for a new generation of liberal economists—first among them Hayek—wherein the discussions ranged from sociology and psychology to logic and epistemology, with a strong interest in the "methodological and philosophical foundations of economics."[8] Participants were kept abreast of the latest philosophical developments through the participation of Felix Kaufmann, who was a member of the Vienna Circle formed in 1924 by philosopher Moritz Schlick. In its manifesto of 1929, the Vienna Circle had expressed confidently that a scientific approach to social problems based on empiricism and logic ought to shape economic and social life in accordance with rational principles. In addition to Neurath, many of its important members like Rudolf Carnap, Hans Hahn, and Philip Frank had socialist convictions and conceived the philosophical work of the Circle as intimately connected with the rationalization of politics and progressive social change. In its early days, the logical positivist movement had a distinctly political flavor. Their unified and scientific world conception provided the philosophical and methodological basis for the integration of everyday life with politics and science, aiming at a comprehensive reform of society along egalitarian lines.

---

6 Deborah R. Coen, *Vienna in the Age of Uncertainty: Science, Liberalism and Private Life* (Chicago: University of Chicago Press, 2007), 13.

7 Malachi H. Hacohen, "Karl Popper, the Vienna Circle, and Red Vienna," *Journal of the History of Ideas* 59, no. 4 (1998): 718.

8 F. A. Hayek, *The Fortunes of Liberalism: Essays on Austrian Economics and the Ideal of Freedom* (Chicago: University of Chicago Press, 1992), 27. Hayek was also a founder of the "Geist circle" which comprised Herbert Fürth, Friedrich Engel-Janosi, Gottfried Haberler, Fritz Machlup, Oskar Morgenstern, Alfred Schutz, Felix Kaufmann, and Karl Menger. Alfred Schutz elaborated his *Phenomenology of the Social World* (1932) in discussion with Austrian social theory, as he sought to reconcile Husserlian philosophy with the subjectivist standpoint of the Austrians.

The positivist philosophy of science of the Vienna Circle became conflated, in the minds of their opponents, with socialist politics and economics. Neurath's radical politics repelled someone like Hayek, who credited the former's "extreme" and "naive" views on economics with his conversion from positivism.[9] In 1935, Karl Popper published in German *The Logic of Scientific Discovery*, his epistemological critique of the positivist premises of the Vienna Circle. Neurath and Carnap were singled out for their defense of physicalism: the view that scientific theories are little more than a formal system of signs with their corresponding rules for application—a "practical analog" to social reality. Against their "logical empiricism," Popper proposed that theory and experience constantly modify each other through criticism to such an extent that "the empirical basis of objective science has thus nothing 'absolute' about it." Instead he famously proclaimed that science did not "rest upon solid bedrock" since "the bold structure of its theories rises, as it were, above a swamp."[10] The falsification device favored by Popper to test the validity of theories did not convince the rest of the Vienna Circle, and Neurath remained adamant that Popper's view of science as a permanent revolution neither reflected scientific practice nor served it well.

Paradoxically, Neurath and Popper were much closer to each other than to some other Circle members. Both embraced a revised conventionalism, combining anti-absolutism and non-foundationalism, which discarded the view that scientific knowledge "corresponded" to reality. More importantly, Popper renounced any psychological foundation for knowledge, something which later became important for Hayek's own rupture with Mises's a priori praxeology of human action. In the cases of both Hayek and Popper, the distance they took from their initial intellectual environments entailed an epistemological argument that science could not rely on either deductive apodictic structures nor empirically derived protocols to guarantee its validity. Instead, they reckoned that truth corresponded to the result of an intersubjective process—thereby "socializing epistemology."[11] The heuristics of this process depended on three interrelated provisions: the methodology employed for discovery and justification, the design of its

---

9   Alan Ebenstein, *Friedrich Hayek: A Biography* (New York: St. Martin's Press, 2001), 157.

10   Karl Popper, *The Logic of Scientific Discovery* (London: Routledge, 2002), 93–4.

11   Jeremy Shearmur, "Epistemology Socialized?" *ETC: A Review of General Semantics* 42, no. 3 (1985): 272–82; Ian C. Jarvie, *The Republic of Science: The Emergence of Popper's Social View of Science 1935–1945* (Atlanta: Rodopi, 2001).

institutions, and the values shared by the participants. In the end, the epistemological conditions of truth and of social order ultimately shared the same foundations: that of conventional rules which could be revised and improved according to an established method.

The existence of the Vienna Circle had been equally crucial for its only French member and other major philosopher of science within early neoliberalism: Louis Rougier. Although one of its most unsung representatives, Rougier charted the clearest path among early neoliberals for an epistemological critique of rival political ideologies (on Rougier see Schulz-Forberg's chapter in this volume). His portrayal of socialism as a scientific fallacy originated in his early epistemological works in which he rejected the validity of all opodictic truths. Following Henri Poincaré, Rougier proposed that a scientific proposition, instead of being either a rational truth a priori, or an empirical truth a posteriori, could be a "hypothesis" or an "optional convention" picked for reasons of practical or theoretical convenience and tacitly accepted as such by the scientific community.[12] Poincaré's geometrical conventionalism, once extended to all disciplines, pointed to a "third way" which preserved the possibility of scientific objectivity while acknowledging the artificiality of reasoning and truth.

Rougier's real foe, however, was not so much rationalism as a philosophical system than as a political doctrine. He contended that the spirit and ideas of the French Revolution, originating in classical rationalism, had ended up "*par une sorte de logique immanente*" in egalitarian socialism.[13] For Rougier, political principles merely represented useful conventions suggested by experience. Any philosophical attempt to naturalize or rationalize these axioms must employ a metaphysical discourse that is ultimately unsubstantiated. To some extent, Rougier followed the same epistemological path as Hayek and Popper. Inspired by conventionalism, his criticism of a priori truths convinced him that the determinants of knowledge rested with the scientists themselves and the discrete but rigorous methodological rules they adopted.[14] Rougier's

---

12   Louis Rougier, *Les Paralogismes du rationalisme. Essai sur la théorie de la connaissance* (Paris: Alcan, 1920), 439. Rougier's doctoral dissertation dealt with Poincaré's geometrical conventionalism. It was published as *La philosophie géométrique de Henri Poincaré* (Paris: Alcan, 1920).

13   Rougier, *Paralogismes*, 30.

14   "Contemplating its evolution," writes Rougier, "the analysis of science now requires that we introduce historical, psychological and sociological considerations. Human science can only be interpreted, in the last instance, with the men who make it, just as the measurements of an instrument can only be interpreted through the theory

community of views with the Verein Ernst Mach in Vienna and Reichenbach's Gesellschaft für empirische Philosophie in Berlin led him to join both groups, and to attempt to create, without success, a similar society in France: la Société Henri Poincaré. Despite his close acquaintance with Neurath, with whom he organized in 1935 the First International Congress of Scientific Philosophy in Paris, Rougier's philosophy and politics were closer to the "right wing" of the Vienna Circle (Moritz Schlick, Friedrich Waismann, Felix Kaufmann) than to the left one.[15]

Rougier and his Viennese colleagues hoped to demarcate a sphere of knowledge sheltered from the metaphysics inherent to any language, and by extension, to any political ideologies. For Hayek, Rougier, and Popper, the application of the methods of empirical science to social phenomena raised methodological dilemmas, which were superimposed onto diverging political orientations. While sharing the same imperative as their Viennese counterparts of demarcating a decontested language of science, neoliberal philosophers of science became skeptical of the powers of scientific method to directly shape social reform. Instead, they aspired to emulate the creative rupture they applauded in the philosophy of physics and mathematics to the doctrine of liberalism.[16] During the interwar period, rival epistemological doctrines came to be deeply interwoven with the political visions they promised to vindicate. Most of the methodological and epistemological disagreements which came to light in 1920s Vienna would resurface as the economic crisis of the 1930s called past orthodoxies in economics and the social sciences into question.

Clarity and Opacity in the Liberal Order

The idea of a planned economy as the answer to the 'chaos of laissez-faire' circulated as early as 1929 on the fringes of all British political parties, while the Soviet Union implemented its first Five Year Plan in 1928.

---

of that instrument." Louis Rougier, "Une philosophie nouvelle: l'empirisme logique, à propos d'un Congrès récent," *La Revue de Paris* 43, no. 1 (1936): 194.

15   Mathieu Marion, "Une philosophie politique pour l'empirisme logique?" *Philosophia Scientiae* CS 7 (2007): 209–10.

16   Another crucial publication illustrating this evolution is Jacques Rueff, *From the Physical to the Social Sciences* (Baltimore, MD: The Johns Hopkins Press, 1929 [1922]).

"Planning is forced upon us," wrote one of its most vocal promoters in 1933, "not for idealistic reasons, but because the old mechanism which served us when markets were expanding naturally and spontaneously is no longer adequate when the tendency is in the opposite direction . . . The economic system is out of gear," concluded Harold Macmillan, echoing the *Zeitgeist* of post-1929 England.[17] Such was the pervasiveness of planning that it became defined as the "middle opinion" of the 1930s, paving the way for the post-World War II consensus on the British welfare state.[18] Its popularity owed to the apparent scientificity of its mechanism as well as to the promise of an engineered economy where control and reason would be restored at the hands of the state. The success of the experimental methods in the natural sciences provided a vivid case in point for reformers eager to rein in the growing complexity of the world economy, whereas the discipline of economics was seen to have failed to provide a coherent picture of the crisis or suitable remedies to cure it.

Founded in 1931, the British think tank Political and Economic Planning (PEP) aspired to design a theory of "capitalist planning" where legislative delegation, expertise oversight, and the cult of the scientific method would make economic policy a mere matter of arbitration between public and private interests. Resolutely pro-business, their proposal was also fiercely anti-free-market, testifying to how unpopular laissez-faire had become with large sections of the business world itself. Not unlike the rhetoric of the New Deal, "rational capitalism," "orderly economy," and "scientific planning" were all terms used in contraposition to the "evils of competition" or the "chaos of overproduction."[19] With the exception of Mises, few free market economists on either side of the Atlantic denied that better state controls were needed to rein in the economic crisis.[20] Confronted with the popularity of state controls,

---

17 Harold Macmillan, *Reconstruction: A Plea for a National Policy* (London: Macmillan, 1933), 18, 23.

18 Arthur Marwick, "Middle Opinion in the Thirties: Planning, Progress and Political 'Agreement'," *The English Historical Review* 79, no. 311 (1964): 285–98.

19 If a wide spectrum of politicians agreed on planning however, no one could reach an understanding as to what it meant and covered: it ranged "from capitalist-sponsored efforts to 'rationalize' industries to market socialism to Soviet-style *Gosplanning*, with Keynes-inspired fiscal 'planning' often thrown in for good measure." Ben Jackson, "At the Origins of Neo-Liberalism: The Free Economy and the Strong State, 1930–1947," *The Historical Journal* 53, no. 1 (2010): 139–40.

20 "There is now an imperative need for a sound, positive program of economic legislation," announced Chicago economist Henry Simons in the opening pages of his

F. A. Hayek and Michael Polanyi in England, and Walter Lippmann in the United States, independently reached the same conclusion: the feasibility of economic planning was not solely a technical problem, but called for a much larger understanding of the epistemological foundations of liberalism and its relationship with the market economy.

Arriving in England in 1931, Hayek did not simply apply his expertise on the German-language calculation debate of the 1920s to the English situation. Rather, his own thinking was transformed by the planning mania of the 1930s. As he emphasized in his inaugural lecture at the LSE, the way forward for liberals was to learn from the failures of free market rhetoric in order to initiate a long-term process of ideological change. He worried that the masses were deluded by the promise of reason and science to direct social reform. While the scientific economist cautioned against government interference, the layman demanded immediate change in society. The lack of legitimacy of a market economy lay precisely with the hidden nature of the economic problem—the invisibility of Adam Smith's hand.[21]

This was the spirit in which Hayek published his contribution to the socialist calculation debate in 1935. He was confident that a technical demonstration of the economic impossibility of socialism was all that was needed to undermine its political appeal, the same way that Mises's critique had discredited the Austrian socialist plan for a centrally planned economy. His goal was to bring socialism out of the ethical and political realm to wage a scientific battle against it: to subject its ideology and plans of social organization to a scientific examination of their proposed means.[22] Hayek's strategy was two-pronged. On the one hand, the signaling function of prices was reliable for economic decisions and

---

Positive Program for Laissez-faire: "in earlier periods, [our economic organization] could be expected to become increasingly strong if only protected from undue political interference. Now, however, it has reached a condition where it can be saved only through adoption of the wisest measures by the state." Henry Simons, *A Positive Program for Laissez-faire: Some Proposals for a Liberal Economic Policy*, Public Policy Pamphlet no. 15 (Chicago: University of Chicago Press, 1934), 2.

21 Hayek wrote in 1935 that "the fact that in the present order of things such economic problems are not solved by the conscious decision of anybody has the effect that most people are not conscious of their existence." Hayek, *Socialism and War*, 56.

22 Hayek states in his refutation that "on the validity of the ultimate ends science has nothing to say. They may be accepted or rejected, but they cannot be proved or disproved. All that we can rationally argue about is whether and to what extent given measures will lead to the desired results." Ibid., 62.

forecasts insofar as markets were competitive. Information, as relayed by prices, was not only carried but generated through the market—a crucial insight. On the other hand, this limited the kind of problems that economic science could solve. Widely shared among neoliberals, Hayek's critique pivoted around one single axis: the (seemingly infinite) cognitive function of markets worked hand in hand with the epistemic limitations of other disciplines and institutions aiming to correct its workings. Knowledge remained irrevocably local, dispersed, and impossible to centralize; the marketplace produced a continuous stream of new data within the confines of a radical skepticism towards intervention.

Like Hayek, Michael Polanyi perceived the obscure workings of economics as demanding both explanation and passivity. After his multiple trips to the Soviet Union as a chemist, he published a detailed study of Soviet statistics demonstrating the failure of the Communist Party to reach the objectives set by their plan. Despite its abysmal record, the genuine support of the population puzzled Polanyi, who spotted in the Soviet propaganda's displays of "public emotion" a "vivid form of social consciousness" which provided clear purpose and direction to the citizens. At the core of the desire for social revolution in Western societies, he concluded, brewed a frustration with the opacity of the market system, a lack of a refined grasp of its concealed mechanisms.[23]

Taking it upon himself to correct the situation, Polanyi produced an educational motion picture expounding the workings of a market economy which aimed at embedding in the public spirit an expert understanding of the economic mechanism.[24] Inspired by Keynes's *General Theory*, the film centered around the representation of the money belt, streaming from industries, to shops, to consumers, with a central bank regulating the flow of spending and saving. Praising the film's semiotic properties, which allowed an invisible complex structure to be seen and thus understood, Polanyi was optimistic about its educational impact on the lay masses, hoping it would turn them away from central planning and restore their confidence in a market economy. A society so transformed by this effort to publicize the coordinating virtues of markets would fulfil the "promise of liberalism": the social integration achieved

---

23   Michael Polanyi, *U.S.S.R. Economics: Fundamental Data, System and Spirit* (Manchester: Manchester University Press, 1936).

24   The final version titled "Unemployment and Money" (1940) is available at the following address: www.youtube.com/watch?v=qTMdHC_OU2w. Trivial nowadays, the use of film for economic education was entirely novel at the time.

in the Soviet Union through public emotion and propaganda could be accomplished in liberal societies through reason and public education.

Commending Polanyi as an "exceptionally gifted observer," Walter Lippmann reflected on the same theme in the opening chapters of his book *The Good Society*, published in 1937. The complexity of social life appeared to him as an invisible canvas into which our daily interactions were woven. The opacity of the individual psyche veiled a wealth of knowledge which the market artfully and efficiently coordinated. Complete planning, by bringing all the economic processes to the fore, failed to acknowledge the cognitive economy brought forth spontaneously by the division of labor. Once the intrinsic limitations of thought were established, conscious control over social orders became a delusion. "No human mind has ever understood the whole scheme of society," wrote Lippmann, "at best a mind can understand its own version of this scheme, something much thinner, which bears to reality some such relations as a silhouette to a man."[25] The opacity of society to our efforts of scientific probing had become so overwhelming that no science of society could form the basis of its conscious control.[26] Consequently, the legitimacy of the market economy relied on entrenching these invisible processes within public opinion.

Taken together, these arguments against the possibility of planning revolved around the elaboration of two key ideas. First, social knowledge is irremediably divided and dispersed. Second, it is a resource that remains largely implicit and tacit. In his seminal article on "Economics and Knowledge" from 1937, Hayek argued that the assumption of perfect knowledge in economic science was eliding the most important question that the social sciences had to address: "how knowledge is acquired and communicated."[27] Epistemic limitations deriving from the division of

---

25   Walter Lippmann, *The Good Society* (New Brunswick, NJ: Transaction Publisher, 2005 [1937]), 31.

26   Lippmann's criticism of a socialist economy, however, did not originate with the preparation of *The Good Society*. Already in 1933, he was familiar with the socialist calculation debate and pointed at the same epistemological argument which Hayek and Polanyi had exposed. Quoting the American Austrian economist Benjamin Anderson, Lippmann stated clearly in his column "Today and Tomorrow" from February 27, 1934 that the state was in no position to intervene in a detailed manner in the economy because "to regulate the business of a country as a whole and to guide and control production there is required a central brain of such vast power that no human being can be expected to supply it." Cf. Craufurd D. Goodwin, *Walter Lippmann: Public Economist* (Cambridge, MA: Harvard University Press, 2014), 149.

27   F. A. Hayek, *Individualism and Economic Order* (Chicago: University of Chicago Press, 1948), 46.

knowledge had both scientific and political consequences for just how much one (e.g. the state; the planning board; the welfare economist) was capable of knowing and thus of predicting adequately. Neoliberals shared the same critique of planning based on the impossibility of centralizing information efficiently, and the necessity of letting horizontal adjustments substitute for vertical decisions. But there existed an additional epistemological limit to planning. It was not only that social knowledge could not be centralized in one place, but also that it remained largely implicit, that is, tacitly embedded in traditions and customs.

In order to articulate a model for a liberal society, neoliberals agreed, one had to start from the complexity of existing orders wherein "we make constant use of formulas, symbols, and rules whose meaning we do not understand and through the use of which we avail ourselves of the assistance of knowledge which individually we do not possess."[28] The superiority of competitive markets did not lie only with the putatively effortless coordination of the various individual plans, but stemmed from their capacity to draw out, compute, and value the tacit knowledge carried by the participants.

As a result, the neoliberal argument about the superiority of a market economy was predicated upon an epistemology which distinguished between spheres of lawful exact knowledge, and spheres where precise knowledge was impossible because it remained dispersed, tacit, and opaque. This assumption accounted for much of the anti-positivist and anti-reductionist position shared by neoliberals, as well as their insistence upon the observation of actions rather than the sociological scanning of intentions.[29] First rolled out in the analysis of the economic order, these epistemological ground rules were later extended by analogy to all "spontaneously arising orders": common law, language, aesthetics, traditions, etc.[30] By the end of the 1930s, the socialist calculation debate had been reframed in terms of the defence of liberalism against totalitarianism, giving political leverage to epistemological arguments which had been originally devised to discredit the idea of economic planning. Far from evident at the outset, this recoding has become a hallmark of neoliberal thinking.

---

28 Ibid., 88.

29 In his lectures on *The Birth of Biopolitics* (Basingstoke and New York: Palgrave Macmillan, 2008), Michel Foucault clearly identified this core element in the neoliberal theory but attributed it mainly to the social theory of Gary Becker. The postulate of a sociological anti-reductionism within neoliberalism was instrumental from the beginning.

30 Michael Polanyi, "The Growth of Thought in Society," *Economica* 8 (1941): 432.

The Mantle of Science

Beyond economics, the 1930s also proved to be a pivotal decade in the discipline of the history of science, a period "when radical historicist messages from Central Europe and the new Soviet Union combined with local antiquarian cultures into historiographical and institutional changes."[31] The movement for the planning of science gained prominence in the United Kingdom after a Russian delegation led by Nikolai Bukharin stunned the Second International Congress for the History of Science held in London in 1931.[32] The audience, largely scientists and amateurs, had been unprepared to hear the discourse of dialectical materialism applied to the history of science. What sounded like a Martian language to some was a revelation to others. Relating scientific discovery to historical processes, Soviet scientists openly challenged the dominant internalist accounts of progress and discovery in science. These birth pangs of the externalist account of the history of science activated an intense scrutiny over the possibility and desirability of planning in science. Many left-leaning scientists and intellectuals visited the Soviet Union in the early 1930s looking for an alternate model for the organization of science and railed against the "frustration of science" felt in Europe because of its lack of coordination and planning.

This conference, remarked Edward Shils, "led an important bloc of British scientists to support the Marxist theses that all scientific work, however abstruse, is a witting or unwitting response to the practical problems confronting the society or the ruling classes of the society in which the scientists live."[33] Pure research meant nothing on its own, but constituted a preparatory step to applied science and, ultimately, social change. At the same time, many natural scientists themselves supported a wider application of science to social problems, promoting its rationality and tangibility over the dead-end of partisan shibboleths. The fact that economic planning had been infused with scientific credibility

---

31 Anna-K. Mayer, "Setting up a Discipline, II: British History of Science and 'the End of Ideology,' 1931–1948," *Studies in History and Philosophy of Science* 35, no. 1 (2004): 43.

32 The papers given by the Russian delegation were published together a couple of days after the end of the Congress and were widely disseminated. See N. I. Bukharin, ed., *Science at the Cross-Roads* (London: Frank Cass & Co., 1971 [1931]).

33 Edward Shils, "A Critique of Planning: The Society for Freedom in Science," *Bulletin of the Atomic Scientists* 3, no. 3 (1947): 80.

granted a good measure of legitimacy to sympathetic scientists. They were to be the "men of science" or "experts" in charge of rationalising the economy and the administration. In his 1933 presidential address to the British Association for the Advancement of Science (BAAS), the President of the Royal Society Frederick G. Hopkins applauded the use of science to solve social problems, adding that "the trained scientific mind must play its part" in the current debates on planning.[34]

Under the leadership of J. D. Bernal, P. M. S. Blackett, Joseph Needham, and Lancelot Hogben, the "social relations of science movement" put forward a fuller integration of society, industry, and science, in which the latter, rationally planned and emancipated from capitalism, would fulfil its natural object of serving human welfare. They adopted the conclusion of Soviet scientists that "only in a socialist society will science genuinely belong to all mankind."[35] Capitalism, they thought, had led to a scientific regression, introducing competition between researchers "when what is really needed is more science applied to the convenience of living instead of to profit-making."[36] Bernal, their most vocal spokesperson, denounced liberalism as the method of chaos, "spontaneously grown," hindering the use of knowledge in society because innovation was corrupted by private profiteering. On the contrary, communism as a political system bore the closest resemblance to the collaborative method used by researchers.[37]

The challenge of "Bernalism," and its continuous influence during World War II, vastly influenced the orientation of neoliberalism. Epistemological battles around the scientific method reverberated as a political and ideological argument over the best form of government. The formative political activities of neoliberals during the 1930s were chiefly set against natural scientists promoting socialism and planning as the logical extrapolation of a scientific worldview

34 Frederick G. Hopkins, "Some Chemical Aspects of Life," *Nature* 132, no. 3332 (1933): 394.

35 Boris Hessen, "The Social and Economic Roots of Newton's 'Principia'," in *Science at the Cross-Roads*, ed. Bukharin, 212.

36 See Daniel A. Hall, ed., *The Frustration of Science* (London: Allen & Unwin, 1935), 60.

37 "The task which the scientists have undertaken," Bernal concluded in his *Social Function of Science*, "the understanding and control of nature and of man himself, is merely the conscious expression of the task of human society . . . in its endeavour, science is communism." J. D. Bernal, *The Social Function of Science* (London: Routledge, 1939), 415.

and organization. They are set to show that the scientific community, far from embodying an archetypal communist society, represented, on the contrary, the incarnation of a liberal order guided by the scientific method.

As the 1930s progressed, it became increasingly obvious that scientific research in totalitarian countries was impaired to a large extent. The academic purge in Nazi Germany and Lysenkoism in the Soviet Union had laid bare the gradual submission of science to ideological purposes. This spectacle, Rougier admitted, had proven to him through "the absurd, the necessity and the soundness of liberalism." He portrayed the *mystique soviétique* as a new form of "state religion," "whose particularity is to present itself as . . . the highest synthesis of the totality of scientific knowledge."[38] Rougier's portrait of the state of the Soviet Union was one of complete failure in all domains, as whole areas of scientific research, notably genetics, had been deemed incompatible with orthodox Marxist-Leninism. The gradual alignment of Russian scientific research with the Soviet ideology equally disturbed Polanyi, who set chemistry aside and endeavored to write about the nature of science specifically in reaction to the Vavilov-Lysenko controversy. He condemned the corruption of Russian science, where the authority of science had been replaced "by that of the State," and advocated the self-government of science to restore the "independence of scientific opinion."[39] Polanyi argued that both science and truth were lost whenever political liberty fell, as independent thought was subjugated to temporal powers. Therefore, there existed "a common fate between independent science and political liberty."[40] A free society cultivated science as the boundless quest for new truths whose ultimate uncertainty lay at the core of the liberal values of tolerance and freedom of conscience: science under political direction was thus bound to become an instrument of propaganda.

Both Hayek and Polanyi were looking for ways to defeat the "scientism" and "scientific socialism" which they felt dominated the media and the public intelligentsia, thanks to the well-disposed editorship of *Nature*

38 Louis Rougier, "La mystique soviétique. Une scolastique nouvelle: le marxisme-léninisme," *La Revue de Paris* 41, no. 2 (April 1934): 622.

39 Michael Polanyi, *The Logic of Liberty* (Indianapolis: Liberty Fund, 1998 [1951]), 81, 78.

40 Michael Polanyi, "Congrès du Palais de la Découverte," *Nature* 140 (October 1937): 710.

and the BBC. Returning to England after the Walter Lippmann Colloquium in Paris in 1938, Hayek committed himself to his *Abuse and Decline of Reason* project in which a series of historical case studies and problems of methodology would lead to "the fundamental scientific principles of economic policy and ultimately to the consequences of socialism."[41] In parallel, his position as editor of *Economica* afforded him an outlet both to present his own views and to publish major papers by Polanyi (1941), Schutz (1943), and Popper (1943–44) which complemented his arguments. In the midst of the project, Hayek wrote to Polanyi that he attached "very great importance to these pseudo-scientific arguments on social organization being effectively met and I am getting more and more alarmed by the effects of the propaganda" of the left-wing scientists which "discredit the reputation of science by such escapades."[42] The movement for economic planning supported by socialist scientists and engineers, Hayek wrote in *Nature*, had now so "succeeded in capturing public opinion that what little opposition there is comes almost solely from a small group of economists."[43] In due course, his *Abuse of Reason* project laid the groundwork for *The Road to Serfdom* and prolonged the previous developments of his methodological views. But to a large extent, it amounted to a wartime effort against the left scientists in England who occupied vital positions within the wartime government, continued to influence the general public, and met regularly to discuss their views in the Tots & Quots discussion group.

In the meantime, Polanyi's own refutation of planning evolved from a defence of pure science towards an epistemological defence of liberalism based on the position of thought in society. The struggle for pure science had been a small but revelatory part of a much larger civilizational struggle. "The attack on science," he proclaimed, "is a secondary battlefield in a war against all human ideals, and the attack on the freedom of science is only an incident in the totalitarian assault on all freedom in society."[44] In 1941, Polanyi founded the Society for Freedom in

---

41 F. A. Hayek, Letter to Machlup, dated August 27, 1939. Cf. F. A. Hayek, *Studies in the Abuse and Decline of Reason* (Chicago: University of Chicago Press, 2010), 1.

42 F. A. Hayek, Letter to Michael Polanyi, dated July 1, 1941, Polanyi Papers, Box 4, Folder 7.

43 F. A. Hayek, "Planning, Science, and Freedom" (1941), in Hayek, *Socialism and War*, 213.

44 Polanyi, "The Growth of Thought," 454.

Science (SFS) with Oxford zoologist J. R. Baker. Like his rivals from the left, he dismissed the neutralist position as naive in the face of the "absolute state," citing the detachment of the scientist as a main cause for concern. The SFS circulated a four-page letter among scientists in May 1941 which pressed for the "defence of scientific freedom" not to be put to rest once peacetime came. Explicitly conceived as an organization to match the influence of the 'social relations of science movement', the SFS insisted that adhering to a liberal view of science was not to retreat into the high spheres of knowledge, but to serve society to the scientist's best abilities. As long as it remained free from state interference, science stood as the perfect example of liberalism in action, demonstrating how individual liberty may be seamlessly reconciled with authority, tradition, and social control.

Despite their irreconcilable political differences, Polanyi and Bernal envisaged in remarkably similar ways the operation of social norms within the scientific community and the paucity of a history of science told as the progressive evolution of intangible ideas. Each argued in their own way "for a social turn in studying the history and philosophy of science."[45] As a result, the project of recoding liberalism incorporated the growing externalist account of science that sought to reground its history within the social and economic determinants of scientific research and knowledge. Neoliberal philosophers of science largely agreed with the necessity of conceptualizing knowledge and science within their institutional conditions and not as a disembodied process, yet proposed an alternative model for the workings of science which drew its inspiration from economic liberalism: the Republic of Science.[46] In this model, the metaphor of the market played out as the epistemological engine of a largely dispersed and tacit knowledge between individuals, be they scientists, producers, lawyers, or road-users. The rule of law, market regulations, and scientific conventions were conceived as so many analogical *methods* of social coordination to achieve a liberal social order, as they ensured a variety of ends with minimum direct control. Peculiar to neoliberalism therefore is the strong epistemological bent of its social theory, one where freedom is recoded as

---

45   Mary-Jo Nye, *Michael Polanyi and his Generation: Origins of the Social Construction of Science* (Chicago: Chicago University Press, 2011), 184.

46   Michael Polanyi, "The Republic of Science: Its Political and Economic Theory," *Minerva* 1 (1962): 54–74.

instrumental to the activity of separate independent orders working according to analogous principles.

Building a Neoliberal Research Program

During the Second World War, the polemical use of the term "scientism" by Hayek complemented Popper's refutation of "historicist" doctrines, Polanyi's defense of pure science, Lippmann's call for the restoration of a "liberal science," and Rougier's dichotomy of doctrine and mystique. Each demonstrated that liberal principles were concomitant with the proper view of science while a purely instrumental conception served the goals of collectivist ideologies. Arguments once used against Viennese philosophers were recycled in a context in which preparation and planning for war had given pride of place to applied scientists and engineers. From varying angles, they all accused the application of the aims and methods of the natural sciences to power social change of usurping the mantle of science out of sheer intellectual error. The *opacity* of the "sense-data" in the social sciences made its methods and orientation different than those of the natural sciences, because it could only observe man's actions—and their undesigned results—without accessing the inner realm of consciousness. Opinions, they believed, constituted the genuine "facts" of the social sciences.[47]

On the one hand, neoliberals argued, any theory of historical development wrongfully applied lawful assumptions to the contingency of history, thereby confusing prophecy and prediction,[48] and mistaking explanation by general principles with the knowledge of deliberate direction. On the other hand, engineers and planners suffered from a "slavish imitation of the method and language of Science" which they used for the purpose of "social midwifery."[49] By denying the fundamental uncertainty in social processes, and the logical impossibility of controlling social wholes, Polanyi contended that their mentality veered towards "utopian engineering," and was the inspiration for "grandiose planning."[50] The application of statistics and mathematics to social

---

47 Hayek, *Studies*, 86ff.

48 Karl Popper, *The Poverty of Historicism* (London: Routledge, 2002), 110ff.

49 Hayek, *Studies*, 80; Popper, *Poverty*, 52.

50 Michael Polanyi, *The Contempt of Freedom: The Russian Experiment and After* (London: Watts & Co., 1940), 28.

problems was inadequate because of epistemological complications linked with the use of probabilities for predictions. To Rougier, "social engineering" and the use of econometrics amounted to a "technocratic conceit," whose method "to put everything into equations" was stimulated by a metaphysical belief in universal determinism incompatible with the fundamental indeterminacy found at the atomic level.[51]

To rescue a "liberal science" meant wresting the authority of science away from these competing projects. The polemical use of "scientism" and its analogues served precisely this purpose. This came at the cost of acknowledging that liberalism was itself an ideology, that is, a conventional doctrine that is *socially constructed* and not the logical output of abstract reason. As such, they effectively contended, there is no intrinsic relationship between objective science and a specific social philosophy. Neoliberals and social engineers alike fully embraced the scientific modernism of the twentieth century, wherein scientific arguments provided the ultimate source of authority to arbitrate political and social questions. Moreover, neoliberals and their opponents both sought to capitalize on that authority in order to make their discourse more persuasive. Like the "men of science" or the engineers they criticized, both groups believed in science as a way to gain truth and a mastery of social phenomena. Nevertheless, between pure and applied science lay the neoliberal gap: a refusal to harness the progress of knowledge to social expediency. Neoliberals believed an elective affinity endured between the rigors and complexity of economic science, the dispersed and tacit state of social knowledge, and a restrained liberal doctrine. Neoliberals alone embraced the fact that ideology and science ultimately shared the same conventional framework, whereby axiomatic rules had to be trusted by their participants to bring about optimal yet uncertain results.

The sophistication of neoliberal sociological thinking owed much to the thought and writings of fellow Hungarian exile Karl Mannheim. Between his arrival in London in 1933 and his death in 1947, Mannheim's output combined his sociology of knowledge developed in *Ideology and Utopia* with a dark assessment of the course of European history, where the safeguard of freedom could only be achieved through planning lest the masses fall for totalitarian ideologies. In the Germany of the 1920s, Mannheim's sociology of knowledge aimed at creating a scientifically

---

51 Cf. Louis Rougier, "L'impossibilité scientifique du planisme économique," *Les Écrits de Paris* (January 1948): 36.

informed politics which could overcome the irrational elements present in ideology. He proposed the "free-floating intelligentsia" as being in a privileged position to achieve the integration of the common denominator present in the various thought-models, thereby actualizing the emancipatory promise of sociology. In the England of the 1930s, however, Mannheim turned towards the idea of "planning for freedom" as a way to pre-emptively safeguard Western civilization, which meant that traditional elites ought to embrace his sociological diagnosis of their failures and apply remedies.[52] He shifted from a conception of knowledge with a catalytic function at the service of a better-informed politics towards a knowledge instrumental for control by the planning elite as a way to counter social disintegration. Liberalism could only be rescued through a positive understanding of its automatic mechanism of integration, then to be strategically reoriented towards a therapeutic reconstruction of society.

Popper, Hayek, and Polanyi all came into contact with Mannheim during his London exile. Hayek and Mannheim were colleagues at the LSE and Mannheim invited Polanyi to participate in The Moot, a Christian discussion circle initiated by J. H. Oldham and attended by T. S. Eliot.[53] They all perceived his sociology of knowledge in the service of scientific politics as deeply antagonistic to the neoliberal project which sought to sever the link between knowledge and social reform. Polanyi considered Mannheim's sociological reductionism antithetical to the restoration of dynamic orders founded in the personal knowledge of individuals.[54] Planning entailed a revaluation of the old traditional beliefs to achieve a controlled direction of the masses. Polanyi, on the other hand, valued the continuity of Western intellectual custom, where dedicated communities of practitioners were guided by tradition and

---

52 See Karl Mannheim, *Man and Society in an Age of Reconstruction* (New York: Harcourt, Brace & Co., 1940).

53 Phil Mullins and Struan Jacobs, "T. S. Eliot's Idea of the Clerisy, and its Discussion by Karl Mannheim and Michael Polanyi in the Context of J. H. Oldham's Moot," *Journal of Classical Sociology* 6, no. 2 (2006): 147.

54 Polanyi wrote personally to Mannheim: "As regards the social analysis of the development of ideas, suffice it to say that I reject all social analysis of history which makes social conditions anything more than opportunities for a development of thought. You seem inclined to consider moral judgments on history as ludicrous, believing apparently that thought is not merely conditioned, but determined by a social or technical situation. I cannot tell you how strongly I reject such a view." Michael Polanyi, Letter to Karl Mannheim, dated April 19, 1944, Polanyi Papers, Box 4, Folder 13.

faith. Equally for Popper, uncovering the "social determination of scientific knowledge" annihilated the basis of free discussion and controversy and the quest for scientific objectivity.[55] The goal of a higher synthesis of dormant elements by an intelligentsia contradicted the process of scientific discovery, which remained always incomplete and subject to modification. Popper identified Mannheim's utopian vision with that of a closed society which was fundamentally hostile to his own open society based on conjectures and refutations. Equally mistaken in Popper's view was Mannheim's conception of knowledge: like Polanyi, Popper emphasized the personal elements of scientific knowledge and discovery. "What the 'sociology of knowledge' overlooks," he wrote in *Poverty of Historicism*, "is . . . the fact that it is the public character of science and of its institutions which imposes a mental discipline upon the individual scientist, and which preserves the objectivity of science and its tradition of critically discussing new ideas."[56]

Similarly for Hayek, Mannheim's sociology of knowledge was the latest avatar of "scientism" where the comprehension of the mechanisms of thought would allow the theoretician to predict its development. The "constitutional limitations of the individual mind" proposed by Hayek as the foundation of spontaneous orders solved the problem of coordination and integration that Mannheim was hinting at with his scientific planning. "Those who hold these views," Hayek wrote, "have indeed regularly some special theory which exempts their own views from the same sort of explanation and which credits them, as a specially favoured class, or simply as the 'free-floating intelligentsia', with the possession of absolute knowledge."[57] All three effectively argued that scientific knowledge was a socially determined process, yet an intersubjective and rational one, and not the result of social conditioning. Their philosophy of science, valuing the social process of science within dedicated institutions as independent from the scientist's social position, was, in effect, an answer to any materialist sociology of knowledge.

Mannheim represented one of the most potent intellectual adversaries of early neoliberals because he advertised planning not as a rejection of liberalism but as its most advanced stage, in line with scientific

55 Karl Popper, *The Open Society and its Enemies* (London: Routledge, 2013 [1945]), 420.

56 Popper, *Poverty*, 144.

57 Hayek, *Studies*, 150–3.

modernity. Like the neoliberals, Mannheim argued against objectivism and scientific detachment and attempted to save a scientifically valid knowledge beyond relativism.[58] While their political conclusions radically diverged, neoliberals shared a substantial number of commitments with Mannheim. First among them was the acknowledgment that knowledge is socially produced and disseminated. Furthermore, Mannheim also advocated environmental interventions—or indirect methods of social control—to orient society from the top, and acknowledged the functional role of the elite above the masses. While criticizing Mannheim's sociology of knowledge, neoliberals would come to build their own "neoliberal" model for the production and diffusion of knowledge in society. From Hayek's intention to found the Mont Pèlerin Society as a closed group of like-minded individuals to his 1949 article on "Intellectuals and Socialism," neoliberals embraced a sociology of knowledge at the service of their ideological project. What Hayek identified as the hubris of the sociologist would ironically be the position he aimed at occupying with the Mont Pèlerin Society.

Conclusion

This chapter has shown how the production of a neoliberal epistemology supported the ideological project of revamping liberalism on a new scientific basis. Many of the subsequent theoretical elaborations within neoliberalism derived from the common epistemological framework drawn here. On the theoretical level, early neoliberals sought to distance themselves from the rationalism, empiricism, and naturalism which prevailed in classical liberalism, and to adopt a critical conventionalism, where knowledge and truths were established intersubjectively in a constant process of exchange between theories and the test of experience. As a result, neoliberal thinkers devised a skeptical view of the reach of the social sciences as their prime angle from which to attack competing ideologies promoting an instrumentalist view of knowledge. Paradoxically, they also came to share many premises with the most sophisticated of their adversaries.

The science of liberalism that neoliberals attempted to mend overlapped with the construction of a liberal view of science as these two strands became intimately conjoined in the shadow of totalitarianism.

---

58 Nye, *Michael Polanyi*, 282.

Through their publications and correspondence, neoliberals fortified their epistemological insights and complementary social theory. This was one in which the method of freedom was bound by conventional rules which had to be adopted as articles of faith, that is, as a constitution. Nonetheless, when neoliberalism started taking institutional shape, many of the latent divergences became manifest and its scientific and ideological turf fissured. The first decades of the Mont Pèlerin Society can be seen retrospectively as the impossible attempt to reconcile these diverging views. Many of the polymaths, including Polanyi, left the Society during the first decade of its existence as it relinquished its role as a multidisciplinary intellectual center for the growth of an alternative theory of liberalism venturing beyond economic freedom. The disappearance of self-proclaimed neoliberals, and the fortune of "neoliberalism" as a critical concept, prove beyond doubt the discontinuities between its many lives.

Since its inception, neoliberalism has hinged on two forces tugging in opposite directions: a scientific program based on a strict respect for the scientific method, and strategic appeals to morals and values when results did not point to an agreeable consensus. As a consequence, the neoliberal attempt to recode liberalism left an ambiguous legacy. On the one hand, the neoliberal discourse of the superiority of the market, the rule of law, and the rejection of economic intervention became firmly anchored in a coherent research program. On the other hand, the project to redefine liberalism along the lines of a liberal science collapsed because of its contradictions with the ideological goal of controlling the production and diffusion of theoretical knowledge. Accordingly, the neoliberal *ideological* project superseded the *scientific* intuitions advanced by its early promoters. From a critical program designed to contest the opportunity of economic intervention, it had progressed through an epistemological recoding of liberalism. Following the success of *The Road to Serfdom*, Hayek further elaborated an ideological strategy in which a closed circle of intellectual producers feed their ideas to the public through strategically placed intermediaries.[59] As well as their democratic aspirations, the cognitive capacity of the masses was deemed trivial compared with the intellectual influence of the elites, which neoliberals began to purposefully target.

---

59 F. A. Hayek, "The Intellectuals and Socialism" (1949), in Hayek, *Socialism and War*, 221–37.

As a result, neoliberals developed a sociology of knowledge wherein discourses enunciated at different levels preserved the critical philosophy of uncertainty which had been developed in the late 1930s at the core, while frankly embracing an instrumentalist and positivist view of knowledge at the lower end of its channels of distribution. If the epistemological agility afforded by conventionalism eroded some of its founding principles, it nurtured the *think tank* ideological machines and their capture of the marketplace of ideas. Largely imperceptible, these deliberate epistemic inconsistencies paved the way for the long-term resilience and success of neoliberalism as a social and political ideology.

2

On Skinning a Cat: George Stigler on the Marketplace of Ideas

Edward Nik-Khah

The great majority of Americans would not dream of abandoning the important regulatory policies . . . [but] what is not commonly realized is that there are several ways to skin even a reforming cat.

George Stigler, 1973[1]

It seems that those wishing to grapple with neoliberalism face a nearly irresistible temptation to reduce a complex and heterogeneous collective movement to the ideas of a single charismatic individual.[2] Or, perhaps two of them. Take, for example, one of the most celebrated histories of the Mont Pèlerin Society, Angus Burgin's *The Great Persuasion*.[3] In his history, Burgin portrays neoliberalism as comprised of two periods, and identifies each period with an exemplary individual.

---

1 George Stigler, "The Confusion of Means and Ends," in *Regulating New Drugs*, ed. Richard Landau (Chicago: University of Chicago Center for Policy Study, 1973), 10–12.

2 This chapter draws from and expands upon portions of "The 'Marketplace of Ideas' and the Centrality of Science to Neoliberalism," in *The Routledge Handbook of the Political Economy of Science*, ed. David Tyfield, Rebecca Lave, Samuel Randalls, and Charles Thorpe (New York: Routledge, 2017), 32–42. I wish to thank Stephen Stigler for his permission to access the George J. Stigler Papers, Anna Yeatman for helpful comments in improving a previous draft, and Quinn Slobodian for editorial suggestions in improving the present one. Archival materials from the George J. Stigler Papers (Special Collections Research Center, Regenstein Library, University of Chicago) are quoted with permission.

3 Angus Burgin, *The Great Persuasion* (Cambridge, MA: Harvard University Press, 2012).

The first, lasting from the founding of the MPS until the early 1960s, was the "Age of Hayek," which in Burgin's telling was characterized by a wide-ranging discussion of pro-market principles, aimed at creating a moderate social philosophy. But the possibilities for such moderation were foreclosed during the "Age of Friedman," ushered in by the ascension to the leadership of the MPS of the cruder and economistic Milton Friedman, and reflecting in part the movement of the center of gravity from Europe to the US. One takes from Burgin's history a sense that we are still well within Friedman's Age. His hope seems to be that we reject the cruder Friedman and set to the Hayekian task of developing a more sophisticated market philosophy.

At first glance, the choice to portray Hayek and Friedman as central protagonists in the neoliberal program seems understandable. If the central purpose of a history concerns the persuasion of the masses into pro-market thinking, it makes a certain sense to focus on instantly recognizable Big Names. Yet, for those familiar with the figures in question, the resulting history seems too coarse—and this is true even if we follow Burgin in confining most of our attention to the US. At the University of Chicago, figures other than Friedman were at least as responsible (and arguably more so) for its ascendance to the most influential neoliberal outpost in the US.[4] By the 1980s those who were at Chicago acknowledged that Friedman's views about markets had been eclipsed by George Stigler's, which were in some important respects opposed to Friedman's, as we will see below.[5] To the general public, Stigler was not nearly as well-known as Friedman, and the same could be said of other neoliberals in close proximity (such as Aaron Director and Allen Wallis), pointing to a second curiosity. Many of the most influential neoliberals had little patience for "persuasion," and hence carried out their activities well outside the public eye. Indeed, one might

---

4 Robert Van Horn and Philip Mirowski, "The Rise of the Chicago School of Economics and the Birth of Neoliberalism," and Robert Van Horn, "Reinventing Monopoly and the Role of Corporations," both in *The Road from Mont Pèlerin*, ed. Philip Mirowski and Dieter Plehwe (Cambridge, MA: Harvard University Press, 2009); Edward Nik-Khah, "George Stigler, the Graduate School of Business, and the Pillars of the Chicago School," in *Building Chicago Economics*, ed. Robert Van Horn, Philip Mirowski, and Tom Stapleford (New York: Cambridge, 2011); Edward Nik Khah and Robert Van Horn, "The Ascendancy of Chicago Neoliberalism," in *The Handbook of Neoliberalism*, ed. Simon Springer, Kean Birch, and Julie MacLeavy (New York: Routledge, 2016).

5 Melvin Reder, "Chicago Economics: Permanence and Change," *Journal of Economic Literature* 20, no. 1 (1982); Nik-Khah, "George Stigler."

attribute the very existence of the MPS precisely to the wish to carry out a political program to which the public could not be reconciled, at least in the foreseeable future.

Within the confines of the MPS meetings, debates erupted concerning the best way to bring about an ideal market society under these unfavorable conditions. As the movement matured, neoliberals sought to reconcile the various aspects of their program to a shared commitment to the market as an information processor of unsurpassable power.[6] Increasingly, neoliberals considered their own roles as intellectuals in light of a "marketplace of ideas," and advanced the distinctive positions they arrived at in terms of how they understood its operation.

Importantly, the person who most doggedly pursued the implications of the concept of the marketplace of ideas for the neoliberal project was *not* Milton Friedman, but his Chicago colleague (who would also serve as president of the MPS), George Stigler. Stigler's views did not emerge fully formed like Athena from Zeus's head, but developed over time as he questioned whether and under what circumstances the university upheld the epistemic virtues of the marketplace. He would eventually relinquish an early hope that existing institutions devoted to producing and ratifying knowledge (universities—or, more precisely, an elite subset of them, such as Chicago) could be reconciled to the proper functioning of the marketplace of ideas, in favor of the more hard-edged position that this would require them to undergo radical reorganization. So, too, would Stigler challenge the most prominent activities of his fellow neoliberals: he would *reject* Friedman's approach to dealing directly with an obstinate public, and urged his fellow neoliberals to do the same. Popularizing neoliberal economics was at best useless, at worst dangerous.

Viewing neoliberalism through the lens of Friedman has the effect of considering only one possible approach to the neoliberal problem of the public, and thereby introducing a grave misunderstanding about how neoliberalism works. There was, as Stigler argued, more than one way to skin this cat, more than one strategy to triumph over the will of the

---

6 Philip Mirowski, *Science-Mart* (Cambridge, MA: Harvard University Press, 2011) and *Never Let a Serious Crisis Go to Waste* (New York: Verso, 2013); Edward Nik-Khah, "Neoliberal Pharmaceutical Science and the Chicago School of Economics," *Social Studies of Science* 44, no. 4 (2014); David Tyfield, "Science, Innovation, and Neoliberalism," in Springer et al., eds, *The Handbook of Neoliberalism*.

public. By understanding these strategies we may come to better appreciate the reason neoliberalism itself has had "nine lives."

Science Contra Democracy

When Friedrich Hayek intervened in the socialist calculation controversy by reconceptualizing the economy from a system of allocation to a system of communications, this brought knowledge and information under the purview of economics for the first time.[7] Markets would now be praised for their epistemic virtues. But for neoliberals, this would raise thorny questions: how could the market—the best method of organizing and disseminating knowledge hitherto known to humankind—give rise to knowledge that was hostile to its very operation? Why had the intellectual tide moved against them?

Hence, neoliberals felt compelled to contemplate organizing intellectual life in such a way that would respect their developing pro-market creed. They did so in a variety of ways, too many to discuss here. One of the most significant concerned the appropriation of the "marketplace of ideas," a metaphor previously used by their political enemies to support robust democratic discussion, but now repurposed by neoliberals to rebut an ambition they increasingly regarded as dangerous.[8] Beginning with Aaron Director, MPS members would with increasing frequency place intellectual, political, and trade concepts side by side in their work.[9] Consequently, they came to explore the implications of the metaphor for organizing intellectual life more closely.

No single way of understanding these implications commanded the assent of all neoliberals. This was due in part to a previous unwillingness to nail down exactly what the real-world equivalent to the market was

---

7   Philip Mirowski and Edward Nik-Khah, *The Knowledge We Have Lost in Information* (New York: Cambridge University Press, 2017).

8   Edward Nik-Khah, "What is 'Freedom' in the Marketplace of Ideas?" in *Neoliberalism and the Crisis of Public Institutions*, ed. Anna Yeatman (Rydalmere, NSW: Whitlam Institute within Western Sydney University, 2015).

9   Director first unveiled this argument in 1953, though it remained unpublished for over a decade. Aaron Director, "The Parity of the Economic Market Place," *Journal of Law and Economics* 7 (1964). On Director, see also Robert Van Horn and Ross Emmett, "Two Trajectories of Democratic Capitalism in the Post-War Chicago School: Frank Knight versus Aaron Director," *Cambridge Journal of Economics* 35, no. 5 (2014); Nik-Khah and Van Horn, "The Ascendancy."

and how it gave rise to the desired commodity (presumably "knowledge," though this was not always made entirely clear). This issue first surfaced in a 1957 MPS session entitled "Egalitarianism and 'Democratisation' in Education," which turned out to be a wide-ranging traverse over history, philosophy, education theory, and economics. In what seemed at first glance to be a narrowly "economic" contribution, Benjamin Rogge delivered a paper on the financing of higher education.[10] Rogge argued that the appropriate way to respect the pro-market creed in the organization of colleges and universities would be to finance all their operations out of student tuition fees. Rogge decried the subsidization of student education on the grounds that it served as an unnecessary and unwarranted intervention into the education market. He found it especially objectionable that people routinely denied the principle of consumers' sovereignty in this market on the grounds that those seeking education were uneducated. Contrariwise, he held that having students pay the full cost of education would force professors to more faithfully attend to the instruction of their students. To subsidize students' education, colleges and universities placed themselves in the position of needing funds from the government, alumni, the wealthy, and corporations. But relying on these groups for funding gave them undue sway over the curriculum, stifling intellectual diversity. Rogge noted, "he who pays the piper will call the tune."[11] He did not begrudge funders for seeking to "call the tune," but he sought to diffuse such power among many more, and diverse rather than organized, tune-callers (the students themselves). A full-cost pricing method would achieve this because the consumers of education—the students—were, in his view, many and diverse. Consequently, full-cost pricing would also supposedly promote *intellectual* diversity. Specifically, by eliminating the state's funding of professors' activities, full-cost pricing would help to combat "collectivism."

The person assigned as discussant for Rogge's paper was the Chicago economist and founding MPS member George Stigler. Stigler would come to occupy an unusual position within the intellectual and political crosscurrents of the Cold War economics profession—we might even characterize his position as unique. He was able to combine an interest

---

10 Rogge was at that time serving as dean of Wabash College, a US private liberal arts college. The paper he presented at the MPS meetings, "Financing Higher Education in the United States," was later published in his *Can Capitalism Survive?* (Indianapolis: Liberty Fund, 1979).

11 Rogge, *Can Capitalism Survive?*, 255.

in formal models of information, orthodox economics, pro-market politics, and the role of the intellectual in capitalism into something approaching a coherent set of views and practices that he then deployed both inside and outside economics—indeed, inside and outside the academy—all the while claiming to uphold the best traditions of science, and gaining a reputation among even his intellectual antagonists for doing just this.

Stigler rejected Rogge's argument. First, he denied that full-cost pricing would necessarily attract a variety of funders and promote intellectual diversity. Research funding already utilized it, he argued; nevertheless, the US federal government and the Ford Foundation managed to exert tremendous influence over research priorities.[12] Second, Stigler objected to the proposal to promote student sovereignty over higher education. He argued that students lacked the qualifications to judge either the quality of a course or the quality of research. He noted dryly: "At Minnesota, 2 Mt. Pèlerin Members [were] at [the] bottom in 1946."[13] At that time, the University of Minnesota's Department of Economics employed three MPS members: Rogge, Stigler, and Milton Friedman.

Stigler then attacked the metaphor of the democratic diffusion of power that underpinned Rogge's consumer sovereignty argument:

In general in intell[ectual] affairs democracy is not a proper system of organizing. The best econ[omics] in the US is not the one the public would elect; a science must impose the standards of an elite upon a profession . . . Affairs of science, and intellectual life generally, are not to be conducted on democratic procedures. One cannot establish a mathem[atical] theorem by a vote, even a vote of mathematicians. An elite must emerge and instill higher standards than the public or the profession instinctively desire.[14]

Here Stigler expressed a deep suspicion about the knowledge of the public. The preferences of the patrons of science might indeed triumph,

---

12 Stigler often decried the influence of the Ford Foundation, despite its instrumental role in establishing Chicago's Graduate School of Business as a "center of excellence." See Nik-Khah, "George Stigler."

13 George Stigler, "Comments on Rogge's 'Financing Higher Education in the United States,'" George J. Stigler Papers, Regenstein Library, University of Chicago (hereafter, GSRL), Box 26, File: Mont Pèlerin Society 10th Anniversary Meeting.

14 Ibid.

but their sovereignty over the knowledge produced was nothing necessarily to celebrate. Unless, that is, they were the right kind of patrons.

Stigler elaborated on his views in his 1963 publication *The Intellectual and the Market Place*. In the title essay, Stigler announced an intention to persuade intellectuals to reexamine their attitudes towards markets:

> The intellectual has never felt kindly toward the marketplace. Whether this intellectual be an ancient Greek philosopher, who viewed economic life as an unpleasant necessity that should never be allowed to become obtrusive or dominant, or whether this intellectual be a modern man, who focuses his scorn on gadgets and Madison Avenue, the basic similarity of view has been pronounced.[15]

Roughly contemporaneously, Stigler complained: "social problems are the creation of the 'intellectual.' The intrinsic importance of a complaint against a social system, as judged by later opinion, has little to do with its effectiveness in shifting opinion. If enough able and determined men . . . denounce and denounce a deficiency, that deficiency becomes grave."[16] Lurking was a question about what role, if any, economics could play in preventing or at least counteracting the intellectuals' monstrous creations. Although Stigler is well-known for arguing that the study of economics may make one "conservative," he held that in practice this conversion would rarely happen.[17] It would require people to acquaint themselves with economics at a very high level. But, more importantly, even for the persistent student who undertook such a regimen, the baleful effects of culture could never be entirely wiped away:

> I cannot believe that any amount of economic training would wholly eliminate the instinctive dislike of a system of organizing economic life through the search for profits. It will still appear to many intellectuals that a system in which men were driven by a reasonably selfless devotion to the welfare of other men would appear superior to one in

---

15 George Stigler, *The Intellectual and the Market Place* (New York: Free Press of Glencoe, 1963), 85.

16 George Stigler, *Essays in the History of Economics* (Chicago: University of Chicago Press, 1965), 285–6.

17 Ibid., 56.

which they sought to their own preferment. This ethic is deeply imbedded in the major religions.[18]

In Stigler's view, the study of economics had little effect in eliminating collectivist policies. Additionally, there were features of the academic community that further entrenched such harmful views.

Stigler argued that state universities were inhospitable to freedom of inquiry. Only an elite few truly promoted it:

> Not only have the productive achievements of the marketplace supported a much enlarged intellectual class, but also the leaders of the marketplace have personally been strong supporters of intellectuals, and in particular those in the academic world. If one asks where, in the Western university world, the freedom of inquiry of professors has been most staunchly defended and energetically promoted, my answer is this: not in the politically controlled universities . . . and not in the self-perpetuating faculties . . . No, inquiry has been most free in the college whose trustees are a group of top-quality leaders of the marketplace, men who, experience shows, are remarkably tolerant of almost anything except a mediocre and complacent faculty.[19]

One may be reminded of Schumpeter's *Capitalism, Socialism, and Democracy*, wherein he argues that markets produced the conditions that allowed intellectuals to thrive.[20] But Stigler is going further than Schumpeter. Intellectuals should show greater appreciation for those who make their living in the marketplace, not only because their actions have provided for the material progress necessary to support them, but also because by their oversight of elite private universities they have *personally* safeguarded freedom of inquiry. In his private correspondences, he was candid:

> A college community—faculty, and their disciples, the students—is a cohesive group, sharing to remarkable degree a common cultural life, similar educational backgrounds, and even fairly similar political

---

18 Stigler, *The Intellectual*, 94–5.
19 Ibid., 87.
20 Joseph Schumpeter, *Capitalism, Socialism, and Democracy* (New York: Harper & Brothers, 1942).

views. If this community were to govern the college exclusively (as was true at Oxford and Cambridge for several centuries), the college sooner or later would become "academic" in some undesirable senses—precious, narrow, removed from unpleasant realities, and downright lazy. The trustees are men of affairs, and bring to the college decisions an element of the virility and realism of the non-college world.[21]

In arguing for the superiority of the "leaders of the market place," Stigler effectively dismissed Rogge's concern that a small group of people would stifle inquiry—so long as the group is composed of the right kind of people. In the elite private universities, freedom of inquiry would flourish. Their trustees would see to that.

If bringing the good deeds of businesspeople to the attention of intellectuals was insufficient to convince them to reexamine their attitudes, then perhaps closer scrutiny of the deep similarities between the marketplace and the intellectual world would do the trick: "The organizing principles of [the marketplace and intellectual world] are the same . . . Just as real markets have some fraud and monopoly, which impair the claims for the marketplace, so the intellectual world has its instances of coercion and deception, with the coercion exercised by claques and fashion. But again these deviants are outside the logic of the system."[22] Stigler continued, "the analogies could be pursued much further," and so one should not read too much into his apparent distinction between "real" markets and the intellectual world.[23] Of course, one could certainly dispute his characterization of monopoly as ruled out by some universal "logic of the [market] system"—many economists of his day would have. Nevertheless, for Stigler, the rationality of science and the effectiveness of the market for goods and services were due to the same organizational principles. Hence, intellectuals should regard the marketplace favorably.

---

21 George Stigler, Letter to Robert F. Leach, dated May 23, 1969, GSRL Box 22, File: 1969 Student Aid. As he was then serving on the board of Carleton College, it was an observation Stigler surely believed he was well-positioned to make.

22 Stigler, *The Intellectual*, 87–8.

23 This was, after all, one who in completing a foray into science policy portrayed scientific labor as no different from any other type of labor. See David Blank and George Stigler, *The Demand and Supply of Scientific Personnel* (New York: NBER, 1957). He would later explicate this theme, presenting economics as offering a different model for the scientific occupations than those who view science as a vocation.

On the surface, Stigler's appeal to a marketplace of ideas may seem to suggest a view of science as "self-regulating."[24] However, Stigler had already argued that one should *not* trust the academy to regulate itself. Absent some jolt from the outside, a faculty would become "mediocre and complacent." But this raised a perplexing question. If the organizing principles of intellectual life and markets really were the same, then how could one reasonably hold—as Stigler did—that there was something persistently wrong with the kind of knowledge it produced? Stigler's answer is worthy of close scrutiny. Markets *did* give people what they wanted. But this was nothing to celebrate, because most people are instinctively predisposed to hold the wrong views about them. Markets produced the wrong kind of knowledge *because* they gave people what they wanted.

After all, there was something to be said for coercion. An elite could potentially countervail such views. But larger political forces hampered its ability to do so. Stigler complained that the demand expressed by government for science as channeled through the system of publicly funded universities and grant programs had become intertwined with a set of egalitarian concerns, encouraging "diffusion" of talent, leading ultimately to a decrease in the quality of research, entrenching professional consensus.[25] Estate taxes eliminated the possibility of a future Rockefeller, and therefore the establishment of another University of Chicago was out of the question. States had diverted resources to the system of public universities that otherwise would have gone to a Harvard or, better yet, a Chicago. Overall, Stigler was skeptical of the prospects for US higher education, but he held out limited hope that a small set of institutions might yet help to impose the higher standards that he so desired.

---

24 James Wible (mistakenly, in my view) picks up on this aspect of Stigler's account, and identifies Stigler as an advocate of the position that science is self-regulating. See James Wible, *The Economics of Science* (New York: Routledge, 1998).

25 Such diffusion was a disaster, since science was properly an elite activity: "there are at most fourteen really first class men in any field, and more commonly there are about six." See Stigler, *The Intellectual*, 37. This followed straightforwardly from his elitist views about human abilities: "there are natural differences in the quality of both men and acres, unlikely to be eliminated under any social system." See Stigler, *Essays*, 280. Egalitarianism was a sin against nature, and a sin against science.

Intellectual Freedom Contra Academic Freedom

Clearly, Stigler and his fellow neoliberals expressed concern for "freedom of inquiry"—particularly the freedom to promote their views of
the marketplace within the academy, which they felt to be implacably
opposed to their aims. This raised the question about whether it would
be possible to promote their interests within existing academic structures, or whether this called for a more radical response.

The question would surface as neoliberals considered the appropriate
attitude to take towards established principles of academic freedom.[26] At the
MPS, the president of Brooklyn College (and later the New School of Social
Research) Harry Gideonse became the standard-bearer for the position that
an imminent communist threat rendered principles of academic freedom
quaint.[27] He argued for suspending tenure protection for communists and
purging them from the professorate. On the other hand, MPS members
were keenly aware that they themselves were an intellectual minority. Did
rules supporting academic freedom help or hinder neoliberal aims?

In 1964, the Austrian economist and founding MPS member, Fritz
Machlup, delivered a defense of academic freedom, and in particular its
tenure protection (on Machlup see Slobodian's contribution to this
volume). At that time, Machlup was serving as president of the American
Association of University Professors. In his talk, he focused specifically
on how tenure helped "to secure the great benefit of academic freedom
and of the fruit it bears."[28] Machlup viewed the professor as playing a
crucial role in the advancement of knowledge:

---

26 In 1940, the American Association of University Professors had approved its
"Statement of Principles on Academic Freedom and Tenure"; subsequently, many US
institutions of higher education and professional bodies endorsed this statement (the
American Economic Association eventually did so in 1962).

27 It boggles the mind to realize that Gideonse previously found himself as one of the
accused during the hearings into communism at the University of Chicago. See John Boyer, *A
Twentieth-Century Cosmos* (Chicago: The College of the University of Chicago, 2007). These
hearings set into motion a sequence of events that led decades later to George Stigler assuming
the Walgreen Chair. See Nik-Khah, "George Stigler." One full session at the 1950 MPS
meetings was devoted to discussing Gideonse's "The Moral Basis of Academic Freedom." For
Gideonse's published work on academic freedom, see Harry Gideonse, "Changing Issues in
Academic Freedom in the United States Today," *Proceedings of the American Philosophical
Society* 94, no. 2 (1950); "Academic Freedom: A Decade of Challenge and Clarification,"
Annals of the American Academy of Political and Social Science 301, no. 1 (1955).

28 Fritz Machlup, "In Defense of Academic Tenure," *AAUP Bulletin* 50, no. 2 (1964),
119.

One incident during my term of office has, more than anything else, reinforced my belief in the importance of tenure. It had to do with a young
medical researcher in the last year of his probationary period, who had
discovered toxic qualities of a drug distributed by a company which was
supporting his university with generous research grants. Should he
publish the report of his findings? Would he risk nonrenewal of his
appointment if his publication angered the donor and the chairman of
the department? As it was, or as I was told, the young man decided to
publish and he lost his post . . . Just think how easy it would have been for
this scientist to postpone publication by just one year; and what consequences for the health, perhaps the lives, of many could have been
entailed by postponement of such publications by as little as a month.[29]

In order for them to play this important role, professors have to personally sacrifice: "[T]he free competitive market for higher learning would
not guarantee all the academic freedom which society ought to provide
in the interest of progress; without the interference through the universal tenure system the degree of academic freedom would be only that
which professors would be willing to pay for, and this would be much
less than what is socially desirable."[30] Machlup portrayed the intellectual marketplace as beset by "externalities." For Machlup, professors
produced the fruits of academic freedom. The problem was that they did
not reap the full benefits of such freedom, while at the same time they
solely bore the costs of it. In forging a binding commitment amongst
professors, trustees, and administrators, tenure operated as a corrective
for this "market failure."

The central question was whether tenure could be squared with
developing notions of the intellectual marketplace. There were a variety
of reasons that Machlup's position on its operation would eventually be
viewed as intolerable to Chicago neoliberals. His statement came at
almost precisely the same time as the advent of the "Coase Theorem."
Stigler interpreted and promulgated the Coase Theorem (a term Stigler
claims to have "christened"), which effectively denied that externalities
posed any significant problem for economies.[31] For Stigler, the inability

29 Ibid., 124.
30 Ibid., 119–20.
31 On Stigler's invention of the Coase Theorem, see Steven Medema, "A Case of
Mistaken Identity: George Stigler, 'The Problem of Social Cost,' and the Coase Theorem,"
European Journal of Law and Economics 31, no. 1 (2011).

to appropriate the fruits of academic freedom would suggest at most rejiggering the property rights associated with intellectual activities— for example by the expansion of intellectual property.[32]

But Stigler had an additional reason for rejecting Machlup's argument. Stigler wrote Machlup in 1969 with the following objection:

> [T]he censorship of professors is more severe than that of either trustees or the market. Could you conceive of Princeton appointing an economist who actively professed racist views? I cannot. Indeed I am impressed that Allen Wallis has yet to receive his first L.L.D.—I would welcome an explanation other than his association with Nixon in 1959–60. Professors are highly conformist and make very poor custodians of intellectual freedom when it conflicts with the academy's beliefs.[33]

One finds in this letter a similar praise of the role of non-academics in stimulating intellectual innovation as that offered in *The Intellectual and the Market Place*. But whereas Stigler earlier argued that the coercive power of intellectual "claques and fashions" was much exaggerated, here he expresses doubts. The faculty had control of the university and intellectual freedom had suffered. What had happened?

The short answer is: the student movement. The intervening years between *The Intellectual and the Market Place* and Stigler's correspondence with Machlup had been a turbulent time in US higher education, and the University of Chicago was not spared. In 1967 the Chicago campus was roiled by a series of disruptive student protests.[34] Reasons for the unrest included the administration deciding to comply with

---

32 For his part, Machlup had expressed considerable doubt about the role of patents in spurring innovation. See Fritz Machlup, "Patents and Inventive Effort," *Science* 111, no. 3463 (1961).

33 George Stigler, Letter to Fritz Machlup, dated April 14, 1969, GSRL Box 10, File: Machlup. Allen Wallis attended the University of Chicago as a graduate student at the same time as Stigler and was a member of the MPS; later (as dean of the Graduate School of Business) Wallis hired Stigler to Chicago from Columbia and arranged for him to receive the Walgreen Chair. See Nik-Khah, "George Stigler." In the US, an L.L.D. (Doctor of Laws) is awarded as an honorary degree.

34 The following two paragraphs draw from Terry Anderson, *The Movement and the Sixties* (New York: Oxford University Press, 1995), and Marina Fang, "Born Amidst '60s Protests, Kalven Report Remains Controversial," *The Chicago Maroon*, February 21, 2013.

Selective Service requirements to share student transcript information with draft boards (this meant that students with low grades might then find themselves reclassified by the draft board as eligible for military service) and the University's partnership with Continental Illinois Bank (which held investments in South Africa). Students held several rallies on campus; a group of 400 students staged a sit-in within the administration building.

In response to the student protests, University of Chicago president George Beadle appointed a group of luminaries to craft a university policy and to carry this out. It met during 1967, and after a period of study and internal debate produced a final report in June.[35] That same month, members of the Chicago faculty senate unanimously approved the principles established in that report.[36] George Stigler was a member of this group.[37]

The Kalven Report was one of the most famous statements on academic freedom produced during that era, and many at the University of Chicago still regard it as authoritative.[38] In light of this, it is revealing that Stigler felt the need to issue a dissenting statement. He took exception with a passage in the report which allowed that, "in the exceptional circumstance," the university might need to consider the compatibility

35 University of Chicago Kalven Committee, "Report on the University's Role and Social Action," *University of Chicago Record* 1, no. 1 (1967).

36 Richard Shweder has summarized the report as having established two principles. The first obligated the university to defend the autonomy of its faculty and students "in the discovery, improvement, and dissemination of knowledge." The second principle was that the university should maintain a position of "institutional neutrality" on matters of public import. See Richard Shweder, "Protecting Human Subjects and Preserving Academic Freedom: Prospects at the University of Chicago," *American Ethnologist* 33, no. 4 (2006), 511.

37 The other members were John Hope Franklin, Gwin Kolb, Jacob Getzels, Julian Goldsmith, Gilbert White, and Harry Kalven, who would serve as chair of what would henceforth be known as the Kalven Committee.

38 In recent years the Kalven Report has been cited in support of divestment from companies conducting business with Sudan, in a proposal to change university policy towards research on human subjects (Shweder, "Protecting Human Subjects"), and, interestingly, in opposition to the establishment of the Milton Friedman Institute. See Jamie Kalven, "Unfinished Business of the Kalven Report," *The Chicago Maroon*, November 28, 2006; Shweder, "Protecting Human Subjects"; Bruce Lincoln, "Address to the University Senate," October 15, 2008. For a discussion of the contretemps over the establishment of the Milton Friedman Institute, see Edward Nik-Khah, "Chicago Neoliberalism and the Genesis of the Milton Friedman Institute (2006–2009)," in *Building Chicago Economics*, ed. Robert Van Horn, Philip Mirowski, and Tom Stapleford (New York: Cambridge University Press, 2011).

of its business dealings with "paramount social values." Stigler, in
dissenting, argued: "The university should not use [its] corporate activities to foster any moral or political values because such use of its facili-
ties will impair its integrity as the home of intellectual freedom."[39]

Stigler was coming around to the position that matters had become
dire. Students' demands for greater say in administering the university
had disturbed him. But the decisions of some faculty to support them in
their demands had shaken him even more. And by now his experience
had tempered his admiration of the trustees, to say the least: "[T]he
trustees have been as craven and irresponsible as the faculties. The trustees have not led the movement towards the political college or university, but they have hastened along in the rearguard—dutifully repenting
to themselves that academic freedom includes the freedom to abandon
academic standards and to smash academic windows."[40] Once the great
hope for the private university, these "top-quality leaders of the marketplace" were now, when they were most needed, missing in action.

By Stigler's reckoning, even some of his most trusted colleagues had
abandoned their posts. In 1968, Edward Levi—who participated in the
Free Market Study and the Antitrust Project, programs of crucial importance to the development of the Chicago School of Economics and
Chicago Law and Economics—assumed the presidency of the University
of Chicago.[41] Initially, Stigler's praise of Levi was extravagant. But Stigler
quickly became disenchanted:

> President Levi has read the trends of our times, and concludes that
> they are irresistible. What then can he do to preserve his beloved
> university? Since he cannot preserve it as a premier intellectual insti-
> tution, he will minimize the travail in its accommodation to those
> forces which have brought down Columbia, Harvard, and in fact in

39 Kalven Committee, "Report." Stigler's full statement can be found in a manuscript
entitled "The University in Political and Social Movements," GSRL Box 22. In 1970,
when the Kalven Committee was reconvened, Stigler took the opportunity to amplify on
his dissent: "Disengagement and specialization are a sane man's—and a sane
university's—way of living in an infinitely complex world." "Supplementary Statement"
(to Kalven Committee Report), dated May 1, 1970, GSRL Box 22.
40 George Stigler, "Do Trustees Have a Place in Education?" GSRL Box 22.
41 On the Free Market Study and Antitrust Project, See Van Horn, "Reinventing
Monopoly"; Edward Nik-Khah and Robert Van Horn, "Inland Empire: Economics
Imperialism as an Imperative of Chicago Neoliberalism," *Journal of Economic
Methodology* 19, no. 3 (2012).

some measure every premier university in our nation . . . The alternative view makes a different reckoning of prospects for one university, ours. A few universities can oppose the trends toward making the university a social welfare mission operated by a miniature democracy, on this view . . . The difficulty is that the Levi policy has never given this alternative a hearing.[42]

The number of academics whom Stigler trusted to carry forth the university's proper mission was now vanishingly small. In a 1969 letter, Stigler admitted, "I am becoming increasingly more critical of present-day higher education."[43] Students had taken to acting as "barbarians"; the president and trustees had fiddled while Rome burned; and the faculty had given the hordes military training. In a paper intended for Irving Kristol's *The Public Interest*, Stigler blamed the behavior of the students on the system of higher education: "There are many complaints today about our turbulent college students: should they not be directed instead at an educational system that offers so little to the ambitious and energetic young?"[44] Even after the issues of the day had been resolved, fundamental problems would remain: "The forces politicizing the university, and turning it into a sort of faculty-student guild socialism, are not going to end the day the last infantryman limps out of Viet Nam . . ."[45] The prospects were dim: "Who will dedicate his life to seeking to reverse the most powerful, most intelligent, most unrelenting, most sinuous university president in America—a man who does not even lack high purpose?"[46] Stigler answered his own question: "I know that I shall not."

Hence, by the time of his 1969 correspondence with Machlup, Stigler would not have accepted his argument that an agreement between trustees, regents, administrators, scholars, and teachers would foster intellectual freedom. He would have been skeptical that any one of those groups could be trusted to do so.

Stigler began to contemplate radically reorganizing the dissemination and ratification of knowledge. He came around to Rogge's position

---

42 George Stigler, "Whither Mr. Levi's University?" GSRL Box 22.

43 Stigler, Letter to Leach, dated May 23, 1969.

44 See George Stigler, "The Academic Featherbed," GSRL Box 22. Kristol rejected Stigler's paper, objecting to its tone.

45 Stigler, "Whither Mr. Levi's University?"

46 Ibid.

of supporting professors' salaries by student fees, but not because he
now had more confidence in students' judgments. If anything, he was
even more dubious: "Students—even college graduates—are poorly
informed judges of teachers and universities."[47] Instead, it was because
he was anxious to spin off teaching from research. This would leave
most schools in the position of catering entirely to undergraduate
instruction: "In a few schools the research function is paramount; in
nearly a thousand others teaching is the dominant or exclusive
function."[48] This was as it should be. Because undergraduate teaching
distracted from both graduate instruction and research, it would be
necessary to free elite scientists from such teaching responsibilities. As
for the lowly undergraduate professors, they would be subject to the
whims of the market—and possibly eliminated by it: "Instruction by
direct fore-to-fore methods is an anachronism, left over from the days
before books were available. Now the professor is an inspirational guide
to the literature—a task which requires few class hours—and can
usefully perform this task at numerous universities simultaneously."[49]
Following Stigler's blueprint, professors would be uprooted from their
home universities, forced to bid for teaching space, and hence would
cobble together a full-time teaching load across institutions. Stigler did
throw out a suggestion for a nationwide standardized test, to make
students more serious about "hiring" quality professors, but he did not
devote a great deal of attention to it: undergraduate instruction was
mostly a distraction, and so improving it did not concern him.

Recall, he believed in a science advanced by imposing the standards
of an elite on a profession and, ultimately, a society. But the class was
small:

> The faculty of American colleges and universities are composed of
> two classes. One class are the teachers: they engage in little research,
> seldom if ever publish, and spend the overwhelming portion of their
> days on the campus, in the classroom and the committee room. They
> constitute perhaps 96 percent of the faculty members. The second
> class is composed of the productive scholars and the academic entre-
> preneurs. They receive most of the research money, publish almost all

---

47 George Stigler, "Higher and Higher Education," GSRL Box 22.
48 George Stigler, "The Economic Structure of Universities," GSRL Box 22.
49 George Stigler, "Are There Any Professors Left?" GSRL Box 22

the serious research, manage and staff all the major conferences, and hold the offices of the professional societies. They are the other 4 percent.[50]

Academic elites needed to be protected from coercion by students, the state, and the *faculty*. Stigler regarded the university as unreliable in doing so. Stigler then proceeded to imagine how to leave aside the unproductive 96 percent and provide "care and banqueting" for the productive 4 percent. He posed the question: "Is the university a sensible base of operations for the research scholars?"[51]

Stigler Contra Friedman

On October 20 and 21, 1972, a conference was held at the University of Virginia in honor of Milton Friedman's sixtieth birthday. It coincided with the tenth anniversary of the publication of *Capitalism and Freedom*, and so the conference was framed as an exploration of the issues raised by that book—of its "Problems and Prospects." George Stigler took the occasion to express his concern about one troubling feature of the work of his old friend and close colleague:

> As I mentally review Milton's work, I recall no important occasion on which he has told businessmen how to behave ... Yet Milton has shown no comparable reticence in advising Congress and public on monetary policy, tariffs, schooling, minimum wages, the tax benefits of establishing a ménage without benefit of clergy, and several other subjects ... Why should businessmen—and customers and lenders and other economic agents—know and foster their own interests, but voters and political coalitions be so much in need of his and our lucid and enlightened instruction?[52]

Stigler took exception to what he believed to be the confused image of the marketplace for ideas that was implicit in *Capitalism and Freedom*.

50 George Stigler, "The Care and Banqueting of Scholars," GSRL Box 22.
51 Ibid.
52 George Stigler, "The Intellectual and His Society," in *Capitalism and Freedom: Problems and Prospects*, ed. Richard Selden (Charlottesville, VA: University of Virginia Press, 1975), 312.

If Friedman's popularization of Chicago neoclassical economics in his advice to the public was effective, this would imply that the public "underinvests" in knowledge—a market failure. But if agents maximize in collecting information (since his 1961 paper "The Economics of Information," Stigler argued that they did), they will already have gathered all the information that it was appropriate for them to have. Friedman's efforts at popularization would be of no use to them.[53] Worse still, Stigler believed any reference to market failure tended to provide intellectual support for objectionable efforts to expand regulation, and so popularizations of neoliberal views might turn out to be politically dangerous.

Stigler posed a provocative question: If markets generally work, then why should this not be the case for the marketplace of ideas? And if the marketplace of ideas works, then why should the public need a Milton Friedman? Or, for that matter, a George Stigler? It was a threatening question for an economist, and Stigler knew it. He had titled one article "Do Economists Matter?" Within it, Stigler insisted that the demand of the community of scholars for science was negligible: "[T]o a scientist educated hands make more melodious applause than ignorant hands, but too often the educated hands seem to be sat upon by educated asses."[54] This memorably advanced a point that Stigler had made in a number of other published and unpublished papers.[55]

Stigler answered the question affirmatively by adopting something akin to the commonsense view of science as rational and reflecting nature (or, in this case, society), and expressing it in the language of commodity exchange: "A rational society must accept tested scientific findings because they reveal a portion of the inescapable external world. Scientific knowledge must be accepted by men of all parties."[56] Science

---

53 He later repeated this specific criticism: "[Average people] lead useful lives, and they buy the amount of economic information that's appropriate for them to have. And they don't go home every night and say, 'I wonder what Friedman wrote today that I can read.'" See Thomas Hazlett, "Interview with George Stigler," *Reason*, January 1984.

54 George Stigler, "Do Economists Matter?" *Southern Economic Journal* 42, no. 3 (1976), 354.

55 The problem was not confined to economics: "What would be the use of intellectuals—meaning people who strongly prefer talking and writing to physical exertion—in a world where men knew their interests and efficiently pursued them?" See Stigler, *The Intellectual*, 313.

56 Ibid., 316.

was a very special kind of commodity, differing from other information-commodities in its *effects*. Science is rational, and so is society (albeit in a different way), and therefore a rational society must make use of science. Society *did* need Friedman's work—not his popularizations, but his economic science. It needed his *Monetary History of the United States*, but not his *Free to Choose*. It needed his scientific work, but it did not need to agree with it, much less comprehend it.

But "society" doesn't purchase knowledge. People do, and for specific purposes. Students decide from which college or university to purchase knowledge. Patrons of research do much the same: in an unpublished 1977 lecture whose title "To What Tune Does Science Dance?" clearly echoed Rogge, Stigler observed: "[the] huge area of antitrust & I[ndustrial] O[rganization economics] in [the] US [was] generated by both public policy and business defenses against it."[57] Stigler was in an excellent position to make such an observation. He played an important role in developing a distinctive Chicago approach to industrial organization, and had consulted for firms facing antitrust action. Economists develop ideas in response to consumer demand for them. In Stigler's words, the economist was a "customer's man."

The argument led Stigler to state what he himself called a "paradoxical" conclusion: economists are truly influential only when they work on technical matters for an audience of technical economists and not when they speak directly to society. (Here we encounter yet another expression of the belief that the teaching of economics is mostly inconsequential.) Only in the former case will economists achieve the fundamental effect of changing the platform upon which policy debates take place, a change due to the special reception given by the public and polity to science.[58]

Stigler believed the university was beset by serious problems. He set out to construct an institution exempt from them. He would substitute contract research for tenure, thereby providing a director with clear lines of control in assigning research tasks to junior economists. This private research institute would provide "an authoritarian structure

---

57 George Stigler, "To What Tune Does Science Dance?" GSRL Box 20. The economic field of industrial organization had traditionally concerned itself with assessing the competitiveness of market structures; work in this field was often used in adjudicating antitrust cases in the US, and economists, Stigler included, often served as expert witnesses.

58 Stigler, "Do Economists Matter?" 351.

which is appropriate for contract research: there is authority over junior members (more than in the university) and hence a capacity for maintaining and discharging promises."[59] To view science as thriving on the curiosity of fresh minds called to science as a vocation was for Stigler misguided. Junior scholars would provide the "semi-skilled labor of research." The best method of producing research would concentrate scholars in a setting freed from teaching obligations, removed from the inconvenient protection of tenure, and placed under the watchful supervision of an "authoritarian" master. In this way, Stigler hoped to impose the standards of an elite upon his profession.[60]

To do so, it would be necessary to find a set of patrons uncontaminated by the egalitarian views of the government and the public at large. Stigler found them in corporations and pro-market foundations. Such patrons had funded the rise of Chicago Law and Economics and the development of a Chicago neoliberal version of Industrial Organization. Stigler heeded his own advice; so did those in his orbit. The topics Stigler settled on, studies of the economy and the state, had the virtue of appealing to a paying clientele. He believed that economists and political scientists held unrealistically optimistic views about the ability of democracy to address social problems, and that these views tainted their studies of democracy and regulation. Stigler held that studies of the "capacities of democracy" could counteract prevailing beliefs about the way the political system functions, beliefs that supported the expansion of what he called "governmental control of economic life."

Stigler was keen to persuade his newfound patrons that science's effects truly were special. In an unpublished 1971 memo proposing a privately funded research institute, he insisted: "The relevance of this work to public policy will be both indirect and decisive . . . It is essentially and exclusively scientific work, and is intended to work its effects upon the appropriate disciplines (economics and political science) rather directly than on public opinion. The work will often shatter the fond hopes of the scholarly professions."[61] Stigler argued that using

---

59 Stigler, "The Care and Banqueting of Scholars."

60 Hence, I cannot accept Arthur Diamond's characterization that Stigler harbored an "aversion to institutional reform" of science and refused to draw any direct lessons for the organization of science. See Arthur Diamond, "Measurement, Incentives, and Constraints in Stigler's Economics of Science," *European Journal of the History of Economic Thought* 12, no. 4 (2005), 641–2.

61 George Stigler, "A Research Institute in Economics," GSRL Box 21.

science was the best—indeed, the *only*—way to achieve the influence that patrons might desire. He proposed using two types of studies to deliver this influence. The first would study the effects of past economic policies to develop techniques for auditing and guiding, and therefore controlling, administrative bodies. The second would study and test hypotheses on the nature of the political process, for the purpose of counteracting the attitudes of political scientists and economists within those academic disciplines. Together, these studies would impose the standards of an economic elite on the social sciences.

Three Ways to Skin a Cat

By the 1970s, Milton Friedman was surely the most famous US exponent of neoliberalism. He popularized Chicago neoliberal analysis, though sometimes crudely and ineffectively, as when he called for eliminating regulatory agencies. In urging that there were "several ways to skin even a reforming cat," Stigler hoped to draw his fellow neoliberals' attention to that fact that there were alternative means of advancing neoliberal aims. Notwithstanding Friedman's public claims, it was perfectly possible to do so by keeping regulatory agencies in place so long as regulators were forced to follow cost-benefit procedures and neoliberal scholars had identified the relevant costs and benefits for them:

> The appraisal of the achievements of a regulatory body is not impossible: a whole series of such appraisals is gradually developing an arsenal of techniques for measurement. I may cite . . . a large number of economic studies, many of which have appeared in the *Journal of Law and Economics*. It would at least be a minor improvement of our world if once a decade each major regulator was reviewed by a committee appointed by the appropriate scientific body, with funds and subpoena powers provided by the OMB.[62]

The *Journal of Law and Economics* was the house organ for the neoliberal law and economics movement. The most important use of the arsenal of "measurement" techniques was not necessarily to persuade anyone of anything—but instead to redirect state policy. No longer would

---

62 Stigler, "The Confusion of Means and Ends," 16.

regulation be conceived as inevitably bad or inefficacious, but instead as improvable; econometric method was to be deployed not merely for convincing fellow economists, but for effecting this improvement. Through these newly developed neoliberal techniques of auditing, with the promise of more to come, Stigler sought to impose the views of an economic elite on the social sciences, and ultimately regulators.

In short order, his ideas took root. At the University of Chicago, Stigler opened the Center for the Study of the Economy and the State, which dedicated itself to pursuing the plan he outlined in his 1971 memo to achieve "decisive influence" over the conduct of government. Outside of Chicago, Stigler, his students, and those in their close orbit developed relationships with scientists, resulting in a variety of interlinked and coordinated research institutes spanning economics, politics, and even the biomedical sciences.[63] These efforts were significant enough to draw the attention of Michel Foucault who, in his *Birth of Biopolitics*, not only mentions Stigler's research by name, but also singles out the work of the American Enterprise Institute's Center for Health Policy Research as an exemplary instance of the "permanent criticism of governmental policy" so characteristic of neoliberalism.[64]

In the decades following Foucault's prescient observations, neoliberals solidified their connections with scientists. They pioneered arguments that science must endorse the epistemic superiority of the marketplace; if it fails to do so, it is illegitimate. Neoliberals denied that the scientific community could access knowledge apart from the marketplace. Such efforts gave rise to what amounted to a third skinning strategy: the science used by regulatory bodies should *itself* be regulated by the marketplace. Neoliberals would now actively encourage the commercialization of science; they also begin to engage in direct intervention into the conduct of science itself, thereby introducing multitudinous ways for regulated industries to harness it.[65] Machlup's position

63 Nik-Khah, "Neoliberal Pharmaceutical Science."

64 Michel Foucault, *The Birth of Biopolitics* (New York: Palgrave Macmillan, 2008), 246–7. The first director of the Center for Health Policy Research was Robert Helms, Sam Peltzman's PhD student at UCLA; its first publication was a book-length treatment of Peltzman's work on pharmaceutical regulation.

65 Nik-Khah, "Neoliberal Pharmaceutical Science"; Edward Nik-Khah, "Neoliberalism on Drugs: Genomics and the Political Economy of Medicine," in *Routledge Handbook of Genomics, Health and Society*, ed. Sahra Gibbon, Barbara Prainsack, Stephen Hilgartner, and Janelle Lamoreaux (New York: Routledge, 2018).

on academic freedom—both in general, and in the specific case of drugs—had been thoroughly repudiated.

Well in advance of these developments, Stigler had provided a blueprint for the emerging epistemic regime. A market-governed science should utilize contract research and be conducted outside the structure of academic departments, under close supervision of one empowered to deliver on promises made to patrons. The purpose was not merely to produce "more" science, and certainly not to ensure the freedom of the individual scientist to pursue independent inquiry. Far from it. Instead, it was to free elite scientists from the need to satisfy their students and fellow faculty. If it worked to plan, it would free them from the need to persuade most anyone of anything. Anyone, that is, apart from their patrons, who demanded they produce the "right" kind of knowledge, and justifiably so. Stigler's vision, although ahead of its time, anticipated the private funding of economics imperialism and neoliberal governmentality that has transformed the academy and science in the four decades since.

3

The Law of the Sea of Ignorance: F. A. Hayek, Fritz Machlup, and other Neoliberals Confront the Intellectual Property Problem

Quinn Slobodian

Neoliberalism is often presented as a set of solutions: a ten-point plan to destroy solidarity and the welfare state. John Williamson's Washington Consensus is the most famous example with its edicts to privatize, liberalize, and deregulate. Neoliberals are often said to offer a laundry list, a recipe book, a panacea and a one-size-fits-all rostrum. Such totalizing and apparently final descriptions have accorded well with the subjective sense of many on the left in Europe and the US from the 1990s onward that we are effectively "post-democracy."[1] Governments are now left "ruling the void," where an impotent *Staatsvolk* is left open to the vagaries of a *Marktvolk* comprising the transnational investor class.[2] Neoliberals have imposed a "worldwide institutional grid that offers transnational capital multiple exit options" and "locks in" a "market-disciplinary agenda."[3]

Resistance, it seems, might be futile. Wendy Brown, an important tone-setter for the discussion, wrote an article in 2003 titled "neoliberalism and the end of liberal democracy."[4] The last section of her 2015

---

1 Colin Crouch, *Post-Democracy* (London: Polity, 2004).

2 Peter Mair, *Ruling the Void: The Hollowing of Western Democracy* (New York: Verso, 2013). For the latter description see Wolfgang Streeck, *Buying Time: The Delayed Crisis of Democratic Capitalism* (New York: Verso, 2014).

3 Neil Brenner, Jamie Peck, and Nik Theodore, "New Constitutionalism and Variegated Neo-Liberalization," in *New Constitutionalism and World Order*, ed. Stephen Gill and A. Claire Cutler (New York: Cambridge University Press, 2014), 127, 29.

4 Wendy Brown, "Neo-Liberalism and the End of Liberal Democracy," *Theory & Event* 7, no. 1 (2003).

book on "neoliberalism's stealth revolution" was titled simply "despair."[5] Examples from the right would be equally easy to find with the sentiment that the rule of the "globalists" and an international elite have left nations powerless and stripped of their strength. The Alt Right itself, despite the large number of libertarians in its ranks, has taken up the claim of being critics of neoliberalism in a racist register.[6]

Like other authors in this volume, I suggest that we might better understand neoliberalism not as a collection of foregone conclusions and formulae, let alone as the final chapter in human history, but as a set of open-ended problems and questions. Among the unresolved questions faced by neoliberals are those of culture (are all populations equally capable of rational market activity?), of design (can institutions and laws be made or must they grow?), of legitimacy (how can markets survive despite their frequent cruelty?), of leadership (can judges, autocrats, central bankers, or businesspeople offer reliable guardians of order?), and of democracy (can it be contained and directed or must it be escaped?). While the final goal of creating a competitive order immunized from popular demands for social justice remains constant over time, neoliberal strategies for arriving at the goal change considerably. A historical approach is necessary to avoid misidentifying the object of critique.

This chapter concentrates on one of the best examples of a neoliberal problem—that of intellectual property (IP). Since the 1980s, IP rights have moved from the periphery to the center of conflicts over the shape and future of the world economy. The shift of the US economy's competitive edge from manufacturing to entertainment, apparel, pharmaceuticals, and information technology has led policy-makers and corporate interests to seek globally enforceable protection of the often intangible and easily reproducible recipes for drugs or sequences of bits that become movies or software as well as trademarks, designs, circuit board layouts, and other lucrative pieces of information. The last change of the thirty companies in the Dow Jones Industrial Index reflects the ongoing shift in the US economy as the aluminum company Alcoa and telecom giant AT&T made way for Apple and Nike in 2015.

---

5 Wendy Brown, *Undoing the Demos: Neoliberalism's Stealth Revolution* (New York: Zone Books, 2015), 220.

6 See, e.g. Ahab, "Neoliberalism Is Hell-Bent on Destroying the White World," Altright.com (May 29, 2017).

In an epochal transformation occurring within the last generation, IP rights have become binding international economic law with the passage of the Agreement on Trade-Related International Property Rights (TRIPS) as part of the WTO Agreement signed in 1994 and coming into force the following year. IP rights have been extremely controversial, especially around the issues of patenting lifeforms, the prohibitive pricing of potentially life-saving drugs in the Global South, and, less existentially, infringements on cultural and intellectual liberty represented by prohibitions on sharing, adapting, and "remixing" data of text, music, images, and code.

Aggressive IP rights are often assumed to be one feature of the global neoliberal regime snapping into place since the 1970s. According to the dominant reading, because property rights are central to neoliberalism, then IP rights must be too. Yet, as this chapter shows, neoliberals themselves have been far from unanimous on the question of when, how, and even *if* ideas can be treated as property. If neoliberalism is synonymous with hardline intellectual property rights, what to make of the signatures of MPS members Milton Friedman, James Buchanan, and Ronald Coase on a friend-of-the-court brief opposing the Copyright Extension Act of 1998? How to explain the fact that Richard Posner, the leading figure of the Law and Economics movement and a member of the Mont Pèlerin Society, has not only suggested that there are "too many patents in America" but cites Hayek in his authoritative work on IP law to the effect that "a slavish application of the concept of property as it has been developed for material things has done a great deal to foster the growth of monopoly and . . . here drastic reforms may be required if competition is to be made to work"?[7] The text is not marginal—it comes from one of Hayek's addresses at the founding MPS meeting in 1947.[8]

Neoliberals were—and are—far from IP fundamentalists in the sense of propagating a reflexive extension of property rights in perpetuity to intangible entities. The overarching goal of securing a capitalist competitive order has sometimes led them to support property rights in ideas and sometimes to oppose them. While a host of Chicago School

---

7 Richard A. Posner, "Why There Are Too Many Patents in America," *The Atlantic* (July 12, 2012); Hayek quoted in William M. Landes and Richard A. Posner, *The Economic Structure of Intellectual Property Law* (Cambridge, MA: Belknap Press of Harvard University Press, 2003), 415.

8 F. A. Hayek, "'Free' Enterprise and Competitive Order (1947)," in *Individualism and Economic Order*, ed. F. A. Hayek (Chicago: University of Chicago Press, 1948), 107.

economists and MPS members including Harold Demsetz, Steven Cheung, and Richard A. Epstein were indeed key figures in shifting the US legal consensus away from antitrust since the 1980s, not all neoliberals took the "shift on patents" tracked by scholars.[9] As alternatives, this chapter looks at the heterodox Austrian approaches of Hayek and his contemporary Fritz Machlup, coiner of both the terms "knowledge economy" and "production of knowledge" and an understudied member of the Mont Pèlerin cohort.

Through the case of IP, this chapter also makes three methodological points for the study of neoliberalism writ large. First, scholars need to differentiate more systematically between the utterances of those individuals defined as neoliberals and the developments in global capitalism since the 1970s as a whole. Second, even the rough heuristic of defining neoliberal status through affiliation with the MPS does not allow for generalizing statements about anything resembling a neoliberal party line. The case of IP shows diversity within the MPS cohort and, thus, within neoliberal thought itself. Last, appreciating the heterogeneity of neoliberal thought encourages us to revisit the so-called political power of economic ideas.[10] If what scholars call "neoliberalization" is clearly not "a unidirectional process of enacting a master plan cooked up by Hayek and friends at their mountain resort in Mont Pèlerin," we must ask which ideas eventually become policy and why.[11] The case of IP suggests that it is those neoliberal ideas most compatible with corporate interests that have been transmuted into law. Neoliberal theory is an intellectual reservoir drawn on selectively rather than as a readymade blueprint for later realization.

---

9   Robert Van Horn and Matthias Klaes, "Intervening in Laissez-Faire Liberalism: Chicago's Shift on Patents," in *Building Chicago Economics: New Perspectives on the History of America's Most Powerful Economics Program*, ed. Robert Van Horn, Philip Mirowski, and Thomas A. Stapleford (New York: Cambridge University Press, 2011). See also William Davies, "Economics and the 'Nonsense' of the Law: The Case of the Chicago Antitrust Revolution," *Economy and Society* 39, no. 1 (2010): 64–83; Robert Pitofsky, ed., *How the Chicago School Overshot the Mark: The Effect of Conservative Economic Analysis on US Antitrust* (Oxford: Oxford University Press, 2008).

10   Peter A. Hall, ed., *The Political Power of Economic Ideas: Keynesianism across Nations* (Princeton: Princeton University Press, 1989).

11   Jamie Peck, "Explaining (with) Neoliberalism," *Territory, Politics, Governance* 1, no. 2 (2013): 145.

F. A. Hayek and the Knowledge Problem

To understand why intellectual property is such a confounding problem within neoliberal theory, it helps to revisit Hayek's idea of what an economy is and the centrality of what has been called the knowledge problem.[12] As many have pointed out, Hayek rethought the problem of capitalism from one of labor, commodities, or even value, to one of knowledge and information.[13] The world's knowledge was strewn across the globe's diverse populations and individual actors. In Hayek's retelling, the story of capitalism becomes one of how this so-called distributed knowledge was recombined in ways productive for the human race's survival, propagation and ongoing expansion on the planet. As Hayek wrote in 1973,

> Economics has long stressed the 'division of labor' . . . But it has laid much less stress on the fragmentation of knowledge, on the fact that each member of society can have only a small fraction of the knowledge possessed by all, and that each is therefore ignorant of most of the facts on which the working of society rests. Yet it is the utilization of much more knowledge than anyone can possess . . . that constitutes the distinctive feature of all advanced civilizations.[14]

To bring home the link between tacit knowledge and productive action, Hayek quoted the Enlightenment philosopher Giambattista Vico to the effect that "man unknowingly makes all things."

Following his mentor Ludwig von Mises's idea of the "division of knowledge," Hayek's narrative of civilization was one of innovating new means for putting the knowledge of person A into productive contact with persons B through Z and from person B to persons A through Z and

---

12   See Lynne Kiesling, "The Knowledge Problem," in *The Oxford Handbook of Austrian Economics*, ed. Peter J. Boettke and Christopher J. Coyne (New York: Oxford University Press, 2015). Don Lavoie, "The Market as a Procedure for Discovery and Conveyance of Inarticulate Knowledge," *Comparative Economic Studies* 28 (Spring 1986).

13   See Philip Mirowski and Edward Nik-Khah, *The Knowledge We Have Lost in Information: The History of Information in Modern Economics* (Oxford: Oxford University Press, 2017).

14   F. A. Hayek, *Rules and Order: A New Statement of the Liberal Principles of Justice and Political Economy*, vol. 1, *Law, Legislation, and Liberty* (London: Routledge & Kegan Paul, 1973), 14.

so on in an endless, unmappable, and indeed unrepresentable series of branching, splitting and star-bursting nodes and networks. Philip Mirowski has insisted correctly that Hayek saw the market as a "uniquely omnipotent information processor"—but even this metaphor is too concrete, conjuring up the image of an actual piece of hardware as it does—a supercomputer that one can look at.[15] Hayek's metaphors are more evanescent. The example he uses are the reconfiguration of neurons in the brain or a system of leaky tubes set into a pliable material so that pressure from the tubes creates new channels and rivulets in a constantly shifting and undulating arrangement. This vision of the economy differed starkly from that of Keynesianism visualized in the MONIAC machine designed by the economist Arthur Philips in 1949 to portray the econ-omy as a self-contained hydraulic system of neat reservoirs and volumes responsive to the fine-tuning of the enlightened policy-maker.

In the Keynesian vision, the national economy is contained and money moves through it in broadly predictable and indeed plannable ways. Hayek conceded that his own vision of tubes failed for being too mechanical: it is not one substance that moves through neutral channels but energy, or knowledge, which is released in neurons at every node of connection, or the unlocking of the local knowledge of the "man on the spot" about conditions that perhaps even he could not put into words. Among his favored metaphors were the crystals formed inside of a petri dish or the constellations of iron filings responding to a magnet. As he wrote, such "physical examples of spontaneous orders . . . are instructive because they show that the rules which the elements follow need of course not be 'known' to them." In the same way, "man does not know most of the rules on which he acts; and even what we call his intelligence is largely a system of rules which operate on him but which he does not know."[16]

The error that Hayek spent his life diagnosing and denouncing was what he called "the synoptic delusion," the belief that humans could gain an overview of the economy adequate to plan it effectively. The means to solve the resultant calculation or coordination problem was the combi-nation of laws and prices. Private property rights here were key. Through

15 Philip Mirowski, *Never Let a Serious Crisis Go to Waste: How Neoliberalism Survived the Financial Meltdown* (New York: Verso, 2013), 141.
16 F. A. Hayek, "Kinds of Order in Society," *New Individualist Review* 3, no. 2 (1964): 461.

what he calls the institutions of *meum* and *teum*, mine and yours, combined with the free movement of prices, packets of knowledge would find their way to the most productive users. What he calls the "constitutional ignorance" of humans meant that we could only surrender the task to the market. Given an adequate legal framework, we could let the market effectively think for us.

While some scholars sympathetic to Hayek have celebrated the subtle and even mystical quality of these insights, others have condemned their implicit "agnotology" or reliance on a benighted and uneducated set of consumers and producers.[17] What neither side has delved into, however, is the delicacy of the question of *intellectual* property within Hayek's framework. If the economy is knowledge before it is property, then the question of how much of that knowledge should be made into property is of critical importance. Private property is not an end in itself. Hayek's was not an argument based on natural law or Lockean just desert for labor spent. Private property was a means not an end—a means to coordinate dispersed knowledge in conjunction with contracts and the price mechanism.

It follows from a commonsense understanding of neoliberalism that state ownership of property would be inefficient, but it is also true from within neoliberal thought that if you *privatize* too much or incorrectly, knowledge could also be misallocated, blocked, or left stagnant. MPS president and Bank of Sweden Prize winner James M. Buchanan suggested that expansion of patents on basic scientific research, for example, could lead to a "tragedy of the anti-commons"—where too many competing property claims impeded efficiency and innovation.[18] As scholars point out, there is the danger, even from a utility-maximizing perspective, of "too much property."[19]

Hayek's own position shifted little over the decades. In *The Road to Serfdom*, he suggested that patent law had been one of the measures that

17 Philip Mirowski, *Science-Mart: Privatizing American Science* (Cambridge, MA: Harvard University Press, 2011), chapter 7.

18 James M. Buchanan and Yong J. Yoon, "Symmetric Tragedies: Commons and Anticommons," *Journal of Law and Economics* 43 (April 2000). This idea was also cited in the friend-of-the-court brief mentioned above. See George A. Akerlof et al., "The Copyright Term Extension Act of 1998: An Economic Analysis" (May 2002): 13, available at brookings.edu.

19 Lawrence Becker quoted in Robert P. Merges, "One Hundred Years of Solicitude: Intellectual Property Law, 1900–2000," *California Law Review* 88, no. 6 (December 2000): 2240.

had "led to the destruction of competition in many spheres," and he repeated the statement almost verbatim twenty-five years later.[20] IP law was a specific case because of its potential to block the flow of knowledge. As Hayek wrote in 1960, "Knowledge, once achieved, becomes gratuitously available for the benefit of all. It is through this free gift of the knowledge acquired by the experiments of some members of society that general progress is made possible, that the achievements of those who have gone before facilitate the advance of those who follow."[21] Obstructing the dissemination of knowledge threatened the very mechanism of advancing civilization itself. For Hayek, patents and copyrights could be a particularly pernicious form of legally sanctioned monopoly. His skepticism towards IP in the 1940s reflected a consensus both within early neoliberal circles and indeed in the larger economic discourse and even the US Supreme Court in the "antitrust moment" from the New Deal to the 1950s.[22] Yet, it is striking that, even within this overall climate, some of the arguments against strong IP rights that continue to be cited by scholars come from early neoliberals and MPS members.

The first of these is Arnold Plant, Hayek's close friend and colleague and a founding member of the MPS.[23] Plant, who began his career at the University of Cape Town (alongside later MPS member William H. Hutt from 1928) before moving to the LSE in 1930, later credited conversations with Hayek for influencing his own theories of intellectual property law.[24] Lionel Robbins, a colleague of Plant and Hayek at the LSE, offered the most lasting twentieth-century definition of economics in

---

20 F. A. Hayek, *The Road to Serfdom* (London: George Routledge & Sons, 1944), 39; "Liberalism (1973)," in Hayek, *New Studies in Philosophy, Politics, Economics and the History of Ideas* (Chicago: University of Chicago Press, 1978).

21 F. A. Hayek, *The Constitution of Liberty* (Chicago: University of Chicago Press, 2011 [1960]), 97.

22 Horn and Klaes, "Intervening," 184.

23 On Plant as one of Hayek's "closest friends" see Stephen Kresge and Leif Wenar, eds, *Hayek on Hayek: An Autobiographical Dialogue* (London: Routledge, 1994), 68. Although Plant did not attend the early MPS meetings, Hayek remained in contact with him and invited him unsuccessfully to speak on the topics of development policy and property in the early 1950s. Hayek, Letter to Plant, dated April 1, 1951. Hayek, Letter to Plant, dated April 4, 1954. Both in Stanford University, Hoover Institution Archives, Hayek Papers (hereafter Hayek Papers), Box 78, Folder 33. Plant left the MPS with Robbins in the 1950s. Philip Plickert, *Wandlungen des Neoliberalismus. Eine Studie zu Entwicklung und Ausstrahlung der 'Mont Pèlerin Society'* (Stuttgart: Lucius & Lucius, 2008), 166.

24 Quoted in John Gray, *Hayek on Liberty* (New York: Routledge, 1984), 168.

1932 when he said that it was "the science which studies human behaviour as a relationship between ends and scarce means which have alternative uses." An idea, once thought, or knowledge once discovered, was no longer scarce. In two articles on copyrights and patents from 1934, Plant made what has now become a standard argument that ideas are not like other property. Rather, they are non-rivalrous and non-excludable. As he pointed out, property rights in ideas created scarcity artificially through statute law and thus resembled monopolies.[25] Present-day libertarians continue to appeal to Plant to criticize IP rights.[26] MPS members William M. Landes and Richard A. Posner begin their authoritative economic analysis of IP rights with reference to his "pathbreaking" work.[27]

Another of the most strident critics of patents was MPS member, chemist, and Karl's brother, Michael Polanyi (on Polanyi see Beddellem's contribution to this volume). He wrote in 1944 that patent law

> tries to parcel up a stream of creative thought into a series of distinct claims, each of which is to constitute the basis of a separately owned monopoly. But the growth of human knowledge cannot be divided up into such sharply circumscribed phases . . . Mental progress interacts at every stage with the whole network of human knowledge and draws at every moment on the most varied and dispersed stimuli. Invention is a drama enacted on a crowded stage.[28]

Polanyi's suggestions went beyond compulsory licensing for new products and towards the socialization of all research—a direction consonant with his own openness to social democratic planning that led to Wilhelm Röpke's later call for his expulsion from the MPS.[29]

25 Keith Tribe, "Liberalism and Neoliberalism in Britain, 1930–1980," in *The Road from Mont Pèlerin*, ed. Philip Mirowski and Dieter Plehwe (Cambridge, MA: Harvard University Press, 2009), 80.

26 Aaron Steelman, "Intellectual Property," in *The Encyclopedia of Libertarianism*, ed. Ronald Hamoy (London: Sage, 2008), 250.

27 Landes and Posner, *The Economic Structure of Intellectual Property Law*, 2.

28 Quoted in Fritz Machlup, *An Economic Review of the Patent System* (Washington, DC: United States Government Printing Office, 1958), 103–4. For the original see Michael Polanyi, "Patent Reform," *The Review of Economic Studies* 11, no. 2 (1944).

29 Adrian Johns, "Intellectual Property and the Nature of Science," *Cultural Studies* 20, nos. 2–3 (March/May 2006): 153; Victor L. Shammas, "Burying Mont Pèlerin: Milton Friedman and Neoliberal Vanguardism," *Constellations* 25, no. 1 (2018).

The ideas of Plant and Polanyi were echoed in the work of neoliberals from the 1930s to the 1950s. As cited by Landes and Posner, Hayek singled out patents at the first meeting of the MPS as a case where state intervention was needed to encourage competition.[30] Here he followed the leaders of the Freiburg School of ordoliberalism, Walter Eucken and Alexander Rüstow, who held a similar position on patents.[31] In a book from 1942, Röpke cited Plant to write that "the modern patent system has developed into a weapon of the big against the small."[32] Like many after him, he advocated a shortened patent protection and compulsory licensing "which would permit everyone to make free use of the invention on payment of a fee." The assumption that neoliberals were skeptics of IP was widespread from the 1940s to the 1960s. In 1952, later MPS president Herbert Giersch described "transformation of association and patent law" as one of the "instruments of competition policy ... discussed in neoliberal circles."[33] An American article on "German neoliberalism" from 1960 identified patent-law reform as one of the pillars of their anti-monopolism, including shortening patent protection, preventing misuse of patent law, and generally including it as part of their anti-monopoly vision.[34]

Fritz Machlup and the Invention of the Knowledge Economy

Perhaps the most influential critic of IP from the neoliberal world—and one who did not take the later turn on patents that Chicago School economists did—was the Austrian economist Fritz Machlup, a fellow member of Mises's seminar with Hayek in 1920s Vienna and also a founding member of the MPS. Born in 1902, Machlup emigrated to the US in the 1930s and taught at the University of Buffalo, Johns Hopkins University, Princeton University, and New York University before his death in 1983. Beginning in 1950, Machlup wrote sympathetically with

30 Hayek, " 'Free' Enterprise and Competitive Order," 113.
31 The core of the proposal was compulsory licensing. See Hans Otto Lenel, "Alexander Rüstows Wirtschafts- Und Sozialpolitische Konzeption," *Ordo* 37 (1986): 50.
32 Wilhelm Röpke, *The Social Crisis of Our Time* (Chicago: University of Chicago Press, 1950), 250.
33 Herbert Giersch, "Das Beste aus beiden Welten: Planung und Preismechanismus," *Weltwirtschaftliches Archiv*, no. 69 (1952): 227.
34 Henry M. Oliver Jr., "German Neoliberalism," *Quarterly Journal of Economics* 74, no. 1 (February 1960): 142.

his student, the economist Edith Penrose, about the tradition of what he called "patent abolitionism" among free trade liberals in the nineteenth century.[35] By harking back to this earlier period of anti-patent activism, Machlup found forebears for his own skepticism towards arguments about the need for patents related to natural law ideas of property as well as incentivizing invention and disclosure.

In 1958, Machlup spoke before a US congressional subcommittee considering the question of what was then called "industrial property" as often as intellectual property. In calling patents into question, he cited MPS neoliberals from Mises and Hayek to Plant and Robbins. A striking absence in his discussion was the notion that property rights could apply in a commonsense way to ideas as they did to things. As he wrote in 1962, "If a public or social good is defined as one that can be used by additional persons without causing any additional cost, then knowledge is such a good of the purest type. To seek knowledge, to create, acquire, transmit, or retrieve knowledge—all these activities are ordinarily associated with effort or sacrifice of some sort; that is, they are not without cost. To use existing knowledge, however, may be costless."[36] Machlup's appearance before Congress led to a fight with fellow MPS member John Van Sickle for what was interpreted as his call to eliminate patents altogether.[37] Although this misrepresents Machlup's view, he did demand the shortening of patent protection as well as schemes for compulsory licensing. The guiding belief was that economic actors did not have to be incentivized to innovate as competition would do the incentivizing for them. Keeping or gaining the lead in a crowded field would compel companies onward to fund research and development. In the case of patents, it was weaker rather than stronger property rights that would serve the higher interests of the competitive order.

From 1958 to 1968, Machlup received nearly $400,000 in funding (nearly $3 million in 2017 values) from a series of foundations including the National Science Foundation to investigate the question of technology,

---

35 Fritz Machlup and Edith Penrose, "The Patent Controversy in the Nineteenth Century," The Journal of Economic History 10, no. 1 (1950).

36 Fritz Machlup, The Economics of Information and Human Capital, vol. 3, Knowledge, Its Creation, Distribution, and Economic Significance (Princeton: Princeton University Press, 1984), 159.

37 Albert Hunold, Letter to Wilhelm Röpke, March 5, 1962. Röpke Archive, File 238.

including patent protection, and copyrights.[38] The gist of the research was skeptical about IP rights. Among the project's products was a talk by German economics student Gerhard Prosi at the Caracas, Venezuela, regional meeting of the MPS in 1969 on "patents and copyrights as obstacles to development." Prosi argued forthrightly that "no economic justification for the protection of foreign inventions in developing countries can be derived from traditional theories."[39] Machlup has remained an inspiration to later critics. The most radical opponents of IP in recent years, the economists Michele Boldrin and David K. Levine, frame their book as a long dialogue with the Austrian neoliberal.[40]

While his work on patents was influential, Machlup's place alongside Hayek as the leading thinker on the knowledge question in neoliberal circles was cemented, above all, with his 1962 book on *The Production and Distribution of Knowledge in the United States*, where he popularized the terms "production of knowledge," "the knowledge economy," and "the knowledge industry" and introduced a means of quantifying knowledge that is used by the OECD up until the present.[41] Machlup's framework reimagined the economy as a whole, attempting to displace the idea of a three-sector economy—of raw materials, manufacturing, and services—developed in the 1930s, for one with only two sectors: knowledge-producing and non-knowledge producing.[42] In the process he came to the startling conclusion that 29 percent of the US GNP sat in the knowledge industry. Machlup was a pioneer of the epistemic shift, which would follow structural change, from a focus in the US on manufacturing objects to manufacturing—and collecting rent on—ideas.

---

38   See Folder 4702, Box, 550, ser. 200, RG 1.2, Rockefeller Foundation records, Rockefeller Archive Center.

39   Gerhard Prosi, "Patents and Copy-Right as Obstacles to Development," Caracas Conference, 1969, Hayek Papers, Box 86, Folder 4.

40   Michele Boldrin and David K. Levine, *Against Intellectual Monopoly* (Cambridge: Cambridge University Press, 2008), 243.

41   Fritz Machlup, *The Production and Distribution of Knowledge in the United States* (Princeton: Princeton University Press, 1962); Dominique Foray, *Economics of Knowledge* (Cambridge, MA: MIT Press, 2004), 25. For a thorough analysis see Benoît Godin, "The Knowledge Economy: Fritz Machlup's Construction of a Synthetic Concept," *Project on the History and Sociology of S&T Statistics Working Paper*, no. 37 (2008).

42   On the intellectual origins of the "three-sector" model see Rüdiger Graf and Kim Christian Priemel, "Zeitgeschichte in der Welt der Sozialwissenschaften. Legitimität und Originalität einer Disziplin," *Vierteljahrshefte für Zeitgeschichte* 59, no. 4 (October 2011): 497–9.

Although the terms "knowledge worker" and the "production of knowledge" are now standbys of left-leaning academics, the first response from the left to Machlup's terminology was revolt. When University of California president Clark Kerr used Machlup's terms, he created some of the first sparks to the fire of the Berkeley Free Speech Movement as young students protested against what they misheard as the "knowledge factory" and its apparent reduction of learning to economic incentives and standardizing conformity.[43] Machlup insisted in response that he meant the analogy not as a pejorative "in any sense demeaning intellectual and humanistic knowledge" but as praise.[44]

Daniel Bell noted later that Machlup's figure of nearly 30 percent of GNP was extremely high.[45] How did he arrive at this figure? We can see some of the specifically "Austrian" features of his framework through closer examination. Machlup began by measuring what he called the "stocks of knowledge." He attempted to tabulate what he called a "universal library" of all books and scientific journals ever published before conceding that, in fact, " 'living knowledge,' or what living people know, may be the relevant stock of knowledge in society."[46] Before despairing at how one might measure this reservoir, he determined that it made more sense to measure instead "flows of information." Because the final reference point was GNP, these flows would include everything that was priced.

In measuring the flows of information, Machlup's emphasis was not on invention or the creation of new knowledge but on the communication of existing knowledge. As he put it, "the 'knowledge-producing' occupations include all workers engaged in communication or in any other kind of endeavor related to knowledge transmission: analyzers, interpreters, processors, transformers and transporters of knowledge, as well as original creators."[47] In this sense, apparent craftspeople like

---

43   Fred Turner, *From Counterculture to Cyberculture: Stewart Brand, the Whole Earth Network, and the Rise of Digital Utopianism* (Chicago: University of Chicago Press, 2006), 12; Clark Kerr, *The Gold and the Blue: A Personal Memoir of the University of California, 1949–1967*, vol. 1 (Berkeley: University of California Press, 2001), 153.

44   Fritz Machlup, *Knowledge and Knowledge Production*, vol. 1, *Knowledge, Its Creation, Distribution, and Economic Significance* (Princeton: Princeton University Press, 1980), xxiv.

45   Daniel Bell, *The Coming of Post-Industrial Society: A Venture in Social Forecasting* (New York: Basic Books, 1973), 212.

46   Machlup, *Knowledge and Knowledge Production*, 1, 162–7.

47   Fritz Machlup and Trude Kronwinkler, "Workers Who Produce Knowledge: A Steady Increase, 1900 to 1970," *Weltwirtschaftliches Archiv* 111, no. 4 (1975): 756.

lithographers and typesetters were "knowledge producers" or, as he called them elsewhere, "brain workers." In Machlup's model, new knowledge is appended almost as an afterthought. The emphasis is on the extension of the network or the system of knowledge transmission rather than the conditions for knowledge creation. His resistance to strong IP laws becomes legible in this light. The point was not to protect knowledge for its initial producer but to expand its use and circulation in the aggregate.

Machlup's approach was consistent with his background in Austrian marginalism, where the focus is not on the worker supposedly producing value by her labor but on the price-setters and price-takers, that is the entrepreneurs and the consumers. Machlup's "knowledge industry" dissolved work into a form of exchange. It moved from a labor theory of value to a knowledge theory of labor. The Machlup model of the knowledge economy displaced the laboring body and dissolved economics into information. He offered a vision of the economy as a flat network, where work was synonymous with communication.

Hayek cited Machlup on patents and copyrights until his final book published in 1988, and Machlup cited Hayek on knowledge in his three volumes of a planned ten-volume "Knowledge Project" cut short by his death in 1983.[48] These two leading neoliberals were united by a skeptical attitude towards intellectual property premised first on their faith in competition and suspicion of monopoly and second on their epistemological belief in distributed knowledge composed of both "known knowns" and "unknown knowns," or to use Michael Polanyi's category, tacit knowledge.[49] Because of the importance of the latter, IP becomes relatively less important as the use of knowledge always relies on a certain locally embedded set of understandings and inherited practices to be made operational. The benefits of free knowledge-flow generally outweighed the supposedly incentivizing traits of IP rights.

Hayek and Machlup represent a tradition of IP critique within neoliberal theory. The tension was never resolved. As economist and MPS member Peter Lewin puts it, "the status of IP in an Austrian worldview is

---

48 Richard N. Langlois, "From the Knowledge of Economics to the Economics of Knowledge: Fritz Machlup on Methodology and on the 'Knowledge Society'," *Research in the History of Economic Thought and Methodology* 3 (1985).

49 Michael Polanyi, *The Tacit Dimension* (Chicago: University of Chicago Press, 2009).

not unambiguous. It is a difficult question."[50] Hayek and Machlup's skepticism was seconded by other thinkers in the self-described libertarian tradition, who question the capacity of state actors to make efficient allotments of monopoly—leading, as it often does, to outright rent-seeking—and who sometimes object to IP rights by doubling down on property rights. Libertarian economist Stephen Kinsella argues, for example, that if someone owns a piece of software, they should be able to distribute and copy it to whoever they want.[51] To stop them would infringe on their own property rights in the object purchased. Yet even Ayn Rand, who appeared to take a fundamentalist position on IP rights as "a man's right to the product of his mind," nonetheless conceded the need for time limits on patent and copyright protection to prevent "parasitism."[52] The Cato Institute's suggestions to Congress in the early 2000s recommend "balancing artistic and entrepreneurial incentives to create with the interests of the larger community of users in an unhindered exchange of ideas and products."[53]

The choice of most neoliberals, especially within the Law and Economics tradition, has been to take a "consequentialist" rather than an "axiomatic" position, working from a pragmatic evaluation of outcomes rather than inflexible first principles.[54] Led by Posner, these economists use both modeling and historical observation to advocate policy based on the conclusion that well-designed patent rights incentivize innovation. This is also the stance taken by latter-day ordoliberals, including the former director of the Kiel Institute, Horst Siebert, and in the pages of *Ordo* journal, founded by the IP-skeptical Walter Eucken.[55]

50   Peter Lewin, "Review: Dina Kallay, the Law and Economics of Antitrust and Intellectual Property," *Review of Austrian Economics* 18, nos. 3/4 (2005): 344.

51   See, e.g., Boudewijn Bouckaert, "What Is Property?" *Harvard Journal of Law & Public Policy* 13 (1990). N. Stephan Kinsella, *Against Intellectual Property* (Auburn: Ludwig von Mises Institute, 2008).

52   Ayn Rand, *Capitalism: The Unknown Ideal* (New York: Signet, 1967), 130–1.

53   Cato Institute, *Cato Handbook for Congress: Policy Recommendations for the 108th Congress* (Washington, DC: Cato Institute, 2003), 411.

54   Peter Lewin, "Creativity or Coercion: Alternative Perspectives on Rights to Intellectual Property," *Journal of Business Ethics* 71 (2007). See Landes and Posner, *The Economic Structure of Intellectual Property Law*.

55   Horst Siebert, *The World Economy: A Global Analysis*, 3rd edition (London: Routledge, 2007), 259. For a distortion of Hayek's own take on IP see Gerard Radnitzky, "An Economic Theory of the Rise of Civilization and Its Policy Implications: Hayek's Account Generalized," *Ordo* 38 (1987): 59. Thomas Oppermann and Jutta Baumann, "Handelsbezogener Schutz geistigen Eigentums ('TRIPS') im GATT: Ein neues Stück Weltmarktwirtschaft durch die GATT-Uruguay-Runde?" *Ordo* 44 (1993): 134.

The neoliberal discourse on IP is nonetheless contextual and internally heterogeneous. Even the consensus around the so-called Posnerian utilitarian position is not absolute.[56] As mentioned above, Posner himself has argued that there might be too many patents in America. The writings of one-time MPS member Douglass C. North, winner of the Bank of Sweden Nobel Memorial Prize in 1993, offers a further example. While North argued himself for the centrality of patents to innovation, he also suggested that the system that had developed in the US failed to provide adequate incentives.[57] In 2009, he argued that "most of what patents and copyrights are about is the protection of monopolies, not the encouragement of more rapid development."[58] Referring to Hayek on the importance of cognitive psychology, he also put the edict of flexible adaptation programmatically: "The world is evolving. What made sense and structured the game yesterday does not necessarily work today and tomorrow."[59]

We are far from the one-size-fits-all recipe that neoliberals are often accused of wielding. One need look no further than Hayek's first MPS speech when he said that "Patents, in particular, are specially interesting from our point of view because they provide so clear an illustration of how it is necessary in all such instances *not to apply a ready-made formula* but to go back to the rationale of the market system and to decide for each class what the precise rights are to be which the government ought to protect."[60] One thinks here also of Milton Friedman's description of economics as "a body of tentatively accepted generalizations" rather than ironclad laws of nature (and the neoliberal rejection of naturalism described in Beddeleem's contribution to this volume).[61] By this understanding, the attitude of the neoliberal intellectual is not

---

56   For a critique of Posner from a Hayekian perspective by current MPS member, senior fellow at Cato and vice-president of the Atlas Network, see Tom G. Palmer, "Intellectual Property: A Non-Posnerian Law and Economics Approach," *Hamline Law Review* 12, no. 2 (Spring 1989): 261–304.

57   See, e.g., Douglass C. North, *Institutions, Institutional Change and Economic Performance* (New York: Cambridge University Press, 1990), 75.

58   "A Recommendation on How to Intelligently Approach Emerging Problems in Intellectual Property Systems," *Review of Law & Economics* 5, no. 3 (December 2009): 1131.

59   Ibid., 1133.

60   Hayek, "'Free' Enterprise and Competitive Order," 114.

61   Milton Friedman, "The Methodology of Positive Economics (1953)," in *Essays in Positive Economics* (Chicago: University of Chicago Press, 1966), 39.

that of dogmatist but shares some of the traits of alertness they themselves attribute to the entrepreneur (see Plehwe's contribution to this volume). The open-endedness of the evolutionary process of capitalism meant that the devising of new frameworks of incentives was also never-ending. For most neoliberals, it is not property itself that is the absolute value but the fluctuating set of human-made laws required to encase the competitive order.

Explaining the Global Enclosure of Ideas: TRIPS against the NIEO

Speaking at the Walter Eucken Institute in Freiburg in 1967, F. A. Hayek spoke of the need for rules and law in "the sea of ignorance in which we move." Fifteen years later, a literal Law of the Sea was signed at the United Nations, a non-binding agreement to manage the resources of the world's oceans collectively. Though seemingly unrelated, the two invocations of the sea point to a problem central to both neoliberal thought and twentieth-century global political economy at large. Given the unknowability of both the totality of human knowledge and the totality of the world's resources, how much of both must be left in the commons as part of what has been called the common heritage of mankind?

Linking knowledge and natural resources is not only a poetic choice. In 1974, the UN General Assembly passed a declaration on the New International Economic Order (NIEO) proposed by the G77 coalition of developing nations, approving an ambitious set of demands for global redistribution, increased aid, stabilization of commodity prices, and permanent sovereignty over natural resources.[62] The G77 made demands for collective management and ownership of the seabed, the moon, and Antarctica alongside those for central management of the world's information. Third World demands for rents for the airspace used by Western satellites circling overhead was only one of the ways that the materiality of information infrastructure met the spaces of the so-called natural world.

The origins of the current global regime of IP rights can only be discerned by tracking the counter-mobilization to Global South demands alongside the contributions of neoliberal theory. In the late

---

62 On the NIEO see the special issue of *Humanity* 6.1 (2015).

1970s, the G77 extended its demands to a New International Information Order, focusing on news production and, fatefully, the question of copyrights and patents. In the early 1980s, they began to push for revision of patent and copyright conventions in the main responsible agency, the World Intellectual Property Organization (WIPO), which became an agency of the UN in 1974.[63] As the NIEO ramped up, US industrial associations began to lobby Washington to tighten IP protections, relying on a negative rhetoric of "piracy" in the Third World contrasted with the positive rhetoric of the natural rights of patent and copyright holders.

While, as shown above, the received economic analysis was about finding the balance between rewarding innovation and throttling it, campaigners for global IP protection wrapped themselves "in the mantle of property rights."[64] The new language of IP in the 1980s figured it as "a system to protect and exclude, rather than one based on competition and diffusion."[65] National competitive*ness* rather than the competitive order was the watchword, a shift signaled by the Presidential Commission on Industrial Competitiveness created in 1984 and the rise of both competitiveness indices and the competitiveness advice industry.[66]

. While neoliberal economists did not follow natural law IP arguments as a group, neoliberal-affiliated think tanks including the Cato Institute (founded by MPS members Charles Koch, Ed Crane, and Murray Rothbard) and the Heritage Foundation (founded by MPS member and president Edward Feulner) lent their weight to the corporate campaign. MPS member and Cato senior fellow Douglas Bandow, special assistant to Reagan at the Third UN Conference on the Law of the Sea (and later disgraced in the Abramoff scandal), linked the Law of the Sea and the New International Information Order (with efforts to "limit trademark and patent rights") as a common campaign of "totalitarian global management."[67] He applauded the US for its refusal to sign the Law of the Sea Treaty in 1982 and its withdrawal from UNESCO two years later

63 Christopher May, *A Global Political Economy of Intellectual Property Rights: The New Enclosures?* (London: Routledge, 2000), 68, 83.

64 Susan K. Sell, *Private Power, Public Law: The Globalization of Intellectual Property Rights* (Cambridge: Cambridge University Press, 2003), 51.

65 Ibid., 75.

66 See William Davies, *The Limits of Neoliberalism: Authority, Sovereignty and the Logic of Competition* (London: Sage, 2014), chapter 4.

67 Doug Bandow, "Totalitarian Global Management: The UN's War on the Liberal International Economic Order," *Cato Institute Policy Analysis* no. 61 (October 24, 1985).

as the body joined the push for a New International Information Order. An author for the Heritage Foundation denounced the "war on patents" and recommended creating "specific counter-proposals to the developing nations—particularly G77's—proposals."[68] Counter-attack is what the industrial associations did in their campaign to have IP included in the Uruguay Round of GATT negotiations, which commenced in 1985 and culminated in the creation of the WTO in 1995. The outcome was not good for the developing world. The WTO's "grand bargain" by which the Global South conceded to trade disciplines in IP and services in exchange for reciprocity on agriculture and textiles ended up favoring the Global North disproportionately.[69]

The NIEO had made the radical claim that much of the world's knowledge was an inalienable part of the common heritage of mankind.[70] Corporate advocates of IP responded with a claim that was equally radical and equally at odds with mainstream and neoliberal economic discourse: that IP rights were simple analogues of other property rights. Vulgarized economic discourse was used to serve private interests. The only academic economist with a starring role in the global IP story, Jacques Gorlin, by his own confession, acted as a lobbyist representing a client and relied on no sophisticated argumentation. In his account, TRIPS was not an economic document nor even a legal document: "It is a political document. The decision to bring cases is a political decision. The decision to push a case in terms of supporting a certain interpretation is a political decision."[71] While the shift of Chicago School economists towards a more charitable perspective on market concentration and monopolies helped lay the intellectual groundwork for the new policies, the global enclosure of ideas took place without consulting the

68 Roger A. Brooks, "At the UN, a Mounting War on Patents," *The Heritage Foundation Backgrounder*, (October 4, 1982); Roger A. Brooks, "Multinationals: First Victim of the UN War on Free Enterprise," *The Heritage Foundation Backgrounder*, (November 16, 1982). See also Thomas E. L. Dewey, "At WIPO, New Threats to Intellectual Property Rights," *The Heritage Foundation Backgrounder*, (September 11, 1987).

69 See Sylvia Ostry, "The Uruguay Round North-South Grand Bargain: Implications for Future Negotiations," in *The Political Economy of International Trade Law*, ed. Daniel M. Kennedy and James D. Southwick (New York: Cambridge University Press, 2002).

70 Peter Drahos and John Braithwaite, *Information Feudalism* (London: Earthscan, 2002), 112.

71 Jacques J. Gorlin, "US Industries, Trade Associations and Intellectual Property Lawmaking," *Cardozo Journal of International Comparative Law* 10 no. 1 (2002): 11.

original theorists of the knowledge economy.[72] Under TRIPS, Hayek's sea of ignorance was parceled off into real estate.

Conclusion: Three Ways of Historicizing Neoliberalism

Where does the story of intellectual property leave us? The mismatch between the divisive discussion of IP within neoliberal circles and the bluntness of its application in foreign economic policy should not lead us to throw our hands up in despair at the incoherence of neoliberalism as a category of analysis. Rather, the neoliberal confrontation with the intellectual problem can help to distinguish between three ways of historicizing neoliberalism that have surfaced in recent scholarship.

The first mode of explanation is ideational. In this model, based on the political power of economic ideas, neoliberal theory incubates in think tanks before being transformed into policy. We can think of a range of examples tracking the diffusion of policy models, from the Laffer Curve to central bank independence, austerity, formalization of property in the Global South, the move to floating exchange rates, and the globalization of all manner of "zones." This conception of intellectual mobilization reflects the discourse of neoliberals themselves. In 1986, Edwin Feulner spoke of the "war of ideas."[73] The Institute of Economic Affairs, founded by MPS member Antony Fisher, also takes this framing as their own, subtitling a recent collection on think tanks "Waging the War of Ideas around the World" (on Fisher see Djelic and Mousavi's contribution to this volume; on flexible exchange rates see Schmelzer's contribution).[74]

A second form of scholarly explanation, favored in the field of International Political Economy, uses the language of capture. Critics from both sides of the political spectrum use this category to criticize the current global IP regime.[75] Here special interests, usually the wealthiest

---

72 On Chicago School influence see Sell, *Private Power, Public Law,* 72; Horn and Klaes, "Intervening," 204.

73 Edwin J. Feulner, "Waging and Winning the War of Ideas," *The Heritage Lectures,* no. 84 (1986).

74 Colleen Dyble, ed., *Taming Leviathan: Waging the War of Ideas around the World* (London: Institute of Economic Affairs, 2008).

75 Amy Kapczynski, "Intellectual Property's Leviathan," *Law and Contemporary Problems* 131 (Fall 2014).

sectors of society—but also specific industry interest groups, nations, or even individuals such as Charles and David Koch—capture policy through proactive lobbying efforts. The think tank is part of the story but in a supplemental role. Against the political power of economic ideas, this could be called the political power of economic power. Examples of this storyline include studies of the creation of international trade treaties, international investment law, the WTO, and other international financial institutions, including the creation of TRIPS, where the Cato Institute and Heritage Foundation play a supporting but not a crucial role. Neoliberalism is seen in this analysis primarily as the restoration of class power; ideas take a back seat to market forces.

A last mode of explanation follows a methodology emerging, in part, as a backlash against what is seen as an excessive emphasis on the power of ideas. This is a historicization of the rise of neoliberalism based on contingency. Here it is less the political power of economic ideas or economic power but the accumulation of political decisions of ad hoc governance. These scholars suggest that it is a fool's errand to look for theoretical coherence or consistency in historical developments such as the Reagan tax cuts, the fiscal crisis of New York in the 1970s, or the decisions to deregulate financial industry or to build the European Monetary Union. These were all decisions made by harried politicians under acute pressures of management and not according to preconceived plans.[76]

In some cases, the backlash against ideational explanations arguably goes too far. Kim Phillips-Fein, for example, writes in her excellent book that New York's civic leaders did not think of ways of managing debt through austerity "because they had read the free-market critiques of economist Milton Friedman or the antigovernment philosophizing of University of Virginia professor James Buchanan."[77] Yet the crux of her narrative is the dogged refusal of Gerald Ford, William Simon, and Alan Greenspan to bail out the city's debt. A story of contingency hits a

---

76 See Monica Prasad, "The Popular Origins of Neoliberalism in the Reagan Tax Cut of 1981," *Journal of Policy History* 24, no. 3 (2012); Jan-Otmar Hesse, "Wissenschaftliche Beratung der Wirtschaftspolitik," in *Das Bundeswirtschaftsminsterium in der Ära der Sozialen Marktwirtschaft*, ed. Werner Abelshauser (Berlin: De Gruyter, 2016); Greta R. Krippner, *Capitalizing on Crisis: The Political Origins of the Rise of Finance* (Cambridge, MA: Harvard University Press, 2012); Harold James, *Making the European Monetary Union* (Cambridge, MA: Belknap, 2012).

77 Kim Phillips-Fein, *Fear City: New York City's Fiscal Crisis and the Rise of Austerity Politics* (New York: Metropolitan, 2017), 161.

three-person wall which included a long-time devotee of Ayn Rand in Greenspan and, in Simon, an MPS member who wrote a neoliberal tract with a foreword written by Hayek himself.[78] We need not choose between contingency, materialist forces, and the influence of ideas—the forms of explanation can and must work together.

The story of intellectual property offers evidence that there is no trans-historical set of policy prescriptions within neoliberal thought prone to summary in the Washington Consensus or any other bullet-point list. In fact, the end goal of a competitive order requires flexibility by its very nature. Part of the capacity of neoliberalism to survive a series of what should have been existential crises must be credited to the adaptability of its basic policy prescriptions. Because neoliberals believe that markets are not natural but made possible through human intervention, they also believe that different circumstances require different solutions. Precisely because the unpredictability of capitalist evolution is an article of faith for neoliberals of the Hayekian variety, there can be no final blueprint.

Neoliberals frequently appeal to Hayek's idea of the limits of knowledge to justify their adherence to rules prohibiting solutions to problems of inequality through redistribution, progressive taxation, or tighter regulation of corporate power. Because our knowledge is limited, so their argument goes, we must respect the wisdom of private actors in the market. Such pieties have their obvious hypocrisies as in the series of bailouts that have encouraged the financial boom-and-bust cycle of the last half century and repeatedly socialized private debt. Yet the idea of the sea of ignorance is also a genuine constraint on arriving at a final prescription. To take the sea of ignorance seriously means that its law is, at least potentially, always open to revision.

---

78 Philips-Fein noted this herself in her previous book. Kim Phillips-Fein, *Invisible Hands: The Making of the Conservative Movement from the New Deal to Reagan* (New York: W. W. Norton & Company, 2009), 246.

PART TWO

NEOLIBERAL SUBJECTIVITY BEYOND HOMO ECONOMICUS

4

Neoliberalism's Family Values: Welfare, Human Capital, and Kinship

Melinda Cooper

Writing at the end of the 1970s, the Chicago School neoliberal econo-mist Gary Becker remarked that the "family in the Western world has been radically altered—some claim almost destroyed—by events of the last three decades."[1] He went on to list a familiar series of ills, from the rapid rise in divorce and female-headed families, to the decline in birth rates and the growing labor force participation of married women, which he claimed had "reduced the contact between children and their mothers and contributed to the conflict between the sexes in employ-ment as well as in marriage." Becker believed that such dramatic changes in the structure of the family had more to do with the expansion of the welfare state in the postwar era than with feminism per se—which could be considered a consequence rather than an instigator of these dynam-ics. Like many of his contemporaries, both neoliberals and neoconserv-atives, Becker singled out AFDC (Aid to Families with Dependent Children)—the "poor woman's alimony"—as one of the primary causes of the breakdown of the family.[2]

Fifteen years later, we find Becker congratulating President Bill Clinton on his efforts to "end welfare as we know it."[3] These efforts would soon bear fruit with the passage of Clinton's monumental welfare

---

1   Gary S. Becker, *A Treatise on the Family*, enlarged edition (Cambridge, MA: Harvard University Press, 1993 [1981]), 1.

2   Becker, "Altruism in the Family," in ibid., 357.

3   Gary S. Becker, "Unleash the Bill Collectors on Deadbeat Dads," Bloomberg, July 18, 1994, available at bloomberg.com.

reform act of 1996—the Personal Responsibility and Work Opportunity Reconciliation Act (PRWORA)—a piece of legislation that dramatically restricted the scope of AFDC.[4] Clinton's welfare reform act is infamous for installing both workfare and marriage promotion at the heart of American social policy. It is less well known that PRWORA essentially federalized a principle of poor relief dating right back to the old poor law tradition—the principle, that is, of *private family responsibility* for the welfare of dependents. Even less well known is the fact that Ronald Reagan first initiated this project as Governor of California in the 1970s, when he sought to revive the state's old poor law rules for compelling family members to look after impoverished relatives.[5]

As defenders of the competitive free market order, neoliberals may not have cared much for the active promotion of marriage, responsible fatherhood programs, and faith-based provision of services, all of which were supported by communitarians and social conservatives and included within Clinton's welfare reform. But neoliberals were certainly in favor of efforts to enforce kinship obligations as an alternative to the redistribution of income by the state. When welfare recipients refused to take care of themselves within the proper structure of the family, neoliberals believed that the state had every right to leverage (or indeed to *create*) these relationships by force, just as it had every right to compel the long-term unemployed to work. Unmarried mothers who sought welfare from the state should first be obliged to seek support from an "absent father," via child support orders, before the state disbursed any funds.

Becker's abiding concern with the destructive effects of public spending on the family represents a key element of his microeconomics—but one that is consistently overlooked by the critical literature. At different times and in different contexts, each of the key figures of American neoliberalism can be found invoking the idea that the "natural obligations" of family should serve as a substitute for the welfare state, indeed that the "altruism" of the family represents a kind of primitive mutual insurance contract that we would do well to revive today.[6] From here

---

4 Personal Responsibility and Work Opportunity Reconciliation Act of 1996, H.R. 3734 104th Cong. (1995–1996).

5 Governor of California (Ronald Reagan), *California's Blueprint for National Welfare Reform: Proposals for the Nation's Food Stamp and Aid to Families with Dependent Children Programs* (Sacramento, CA: Office of the Governor, 1974).

6 Richard Posner refers to the "insurance function of marriage," pointing to the fact that marriage is expected to serve as a form of risk protection in those social contexts

derives the notion, now pervasive in American welfare practice, that the state has the right to identify and enforce legal obligations of marital support and child custody even when the parties concerned do not consent to or recognize this relationship. In the absence of a suitable family structure, the state is authorized to enforce the sexual contract just as it is authorized to enforce work.

What are we to make of the fact that the same neoliberal thinkers who extolled the virtues of the free market order were also prepared to defend the legal and economic bonds of kinship as inescapable, noncontractual obligations? And should we be surprised to learn that the American neoliberals were stridently opposed to the sexual privacy jurisprudence of the 1970s which turned sexual freedom into a constitutional right and ushered in the so-called sexual revolution in family law? Or that Gary Becker and Richard Posner were opposed to no-fault divorce? Only, I would argue, if we neglect the necessary role of family responsibility within the neoliberal vision of a free market order and only if we forget the historical relationship between economic liberalism and the poor law tradition—a tradition which, in the words of one historian, confounds the "moral and economic functions of the family."[7]

"where kinship has receded but market and social insurance is not yet common" (or, we might add, has significantly diminished). The "insurance function" of marriage, he writes, "arises from the fact that the correlation of spouses' health and other welfare factors is less than one, so given a mutual obligation of support and assistance, marriage serves as a form of health, hunger, and life insurance." Richard A. Posner, *The Economics of Justice* (Cambridge, MA: Harvard University Press, 1981), 190. On the family as a natural insurance mechanism, see also Becker, "Altruism in the Family." For Richard Epstein, the rules of social welfare should "follow the basic pattern of natural obligation as it is perceived to arise within families." The task of neoliberal welfare reform is "to transform [this] inclination into duty" and thus to "derive an 'is' from an 'ought.'" Richard Epstein, *Principles for a Free Society* (New York: Basic Books, 1998), 23. For the argument that "family responsibility and solidarity" have been weakened by the welfare state, see James M. Buchanan, *The Public Finances* (Homewood, Illinois: Richard D. Irwin, Inc. 1960), 399. On the link between the destruction of the family, declining morality and the welfare state, see James M. Buchanan, "The Samaritan's Dilemma," in *Altruism, Morality, and Economic Theory*, ed. E. S. Phelps (New York: Russell Sage Foundation, 1975), 71–85; James M. Buchanan, "Methods and Morals in Economics: The Ayres-Knight Discussion," in *Science and Ceremony: The Institutional Economics of C. E. Ayres*, ed. W. Breit and J. William Patton Culbertson (Austin: University of Texas Press, 1976), 163–74.

   7 M. A. Crowther, "Family Responsibility and State Responsibility in Britain before the Welfare State," *The Historical Journal* 25, no. 1 (1982): 135. Crowther is referring specifically to the English New Poor Law of 1834, which inspired America's post-bellum system of public relief.

I have argued elsewhere that American neoliberalism, as it matured in the 1970s, must be understood as an attempt to revive and reinvent the poor law tradition as a wholesale alternative to the mid-twentieth-century welfare state. This was not a project that was self-evident in the Chicago School of American neoliberalism at its starting point in the 1930s, and indeed it was far from evident as late as 1970, when Milton Friedman could be found collaborating with President Nixon on the project of a basic guaranteed income.[8] Rather, it crystallized in the mid-1970s—a turning point in American politics, when the perfect storm of inflation, unemployment, and the rising militancy of the new left convinced neoliberals they must articulate a much more potent critique of the expansion of welfare under President Johnson's Great Society. It is at this point that American neoliberals perfected their signature critique of the welfare state and that American neoliberalism per se acquired its mature form, in many ways distinct from the early Chicago School neoliberalism of the 1930s. And it is at this point that someone like Friedman completely abandoned any attempt to reform the welfare state in its existing form. Instead, the American neoliberals now turned back to the much older poor law tradition of relief to find inspiration for their welfare reform initiatives. This is a tradition that dates right back to the Elizabethan poor laws and last flourished in the late nineteenth century, in what is referred to as the Gilded Age of American capitalism. A guiding principle of this poor law tradition was the notion of family responsibility.

Family Responsibility and the American Poor Laws

What is family responsibility? And what is the relevance of the poor law tradition to the history of American social welfare? The principle of family responsibility for welfare has deep roots in the British and North American traditions of public relief and can be traced back to the Elizabethan poor laws of 1601, where it is stated that "the father and grandfather, and the mother and grandmother, and the children of every poor, old, blind, lame and important person, or other person not able to work, being of a sufficient ability, shall, at their own charges, relieve and

---

8 Marisa Chappell, *The War on Welfare: Family, Poverty and Politics in Modern America* (Philadelphia: University of Pennsylvania Press, 2010).

maintain every such poor person."[9] The poor laws distinguished between the impotent poor, unable to work and eligible for care in an almshouse; the able-bodied poor, who must be compelled to work in a poorhouse; and the idle poor or vagrants, who could be imprisoned or confined in a House of Correction. But before any recourse to forced labor or incarceration could be activated, all three of these populations were subject to the principle of familial responsibility. In other words, before the parish took any action, family members would be compelled to provide as much support as they could.

The early American colonies imported the poor laws virtually verbatim and they were later incorporated into state legal systems during the early American Republic. These laws were continually reinvigorated and embellished to adapt to what we might call periodic episodes of sexual revolution. That is, at each historical juncture where the legal obligations of family were somehow weakened or threatened by the generalization of divorce, the waning importance of marriage, or the liberation of slaves who had never been married, the poor laws would be reinforced to punish those who threatened to transfer the costs of their welfare onto the state.[10] As divorce became more common in the nineteenth century, the poor laws were modified to require post-divorce child support.[11] When slaves were enfranchised in the 1860s, they were immediately encouraged to enter formal marriages and were subsequently subject to new legal rules of family support and mutual dependence.[12] In many instances, those who failed to comply with family responsibility rules of economic obligation were subject to criminal sanctions such as forced labor or imprisonment. The poor laws helped the state to contain the costs of evolving sexual mores by imposing marital and familial support as an economic obligation.

If the poor were unwilling to enter into binding agreements of

---

9 43 Eliz. 1, ch.2, § VI (1601) (as amended).

10 Daniel R. Mandelker, "Family Responsibility under the American Poor Laws I," *Michigan Law Review* 54, no. 4 (1956): 497–532; Daniel R. Mandelker, "Family Responsibility under the American Poor Laws II," *Michigan Law Review* 54, no. 5 (1956): 607–32.

11 Drew D. Hansen, "The American Invention of Child Support: Dependency and Punishment in Early American Child Support," *Yale Law Journal* 108, No. 5 (1999): 1123–53.

12 Katherine Franke, "Becoming a Citizen: Reconstruction Era Regulation of African American Marriages," *Yale Journal of Law and the Humanities* 11 (1999): 251–309.

marriage and kinship by consent, then the state was quite happy to conjure up these unions out of thin air and impose them as a legal obligation of mutual support. If a male servant refused to pay for the support of his presumptive bastard child, then he would be called upon to perform unpaid labor to pay off his debts to the parish.[13] If recently freed slaves continued to live together outside of wedlock, the state would compel them to marry and threaten them with forced labor if they refused to comply.[14] These laws remained very much in vigor right up until the mid-twentieth century, when they came into conflict with the principles of state-managed social insurance championed by New Deal reformers. In many instances, they were never completely overridden.

From Private Family Responsibility to Public Responsibility for the Family

The comprehensive forms of social insurance that had been implemented in Germany under Otto von Bismarck as early as the 1880s, and in other European states throughout the following decades, were much slower to be accepted in the United States, where they had to overcome both elite and popular attachment to notions of personal and family responsibility.[15] Throughout the early twentieth century, opponents of social welfare argued that the socialization of risk would destroy the family as a moral institution by displacing economic solidarity among kin. Even public assistance to noncontributing dependents such as widows and the aged was attacked as a threat to the values of family responsibility and self-support.

With the passage of the Social Security Act in 1935, the advocates of social insurance claimed a decisive victory. The New Deal introduced comprehensive forms of social insurance against workplace accidents, unemployment, and aging and definitively removed one class of workers (standard, white, male workers) from the poor law system of family

---

13 Mary Ann Mason, *From Father's Property to Children's Rights: The History of Child Custody in the United States* (New York: Columbia University Press, 1994).

14 Franke, "Becoming a Citizen."

15 For a comparative account of social insurance in Bismarck's Germany, other European states, and the United States, see John Fabian Witt, *The Accidental Republic: Crippled Workingmen, Destitute Widows, and the Remaking of American Law* (Cambridge, MA: Harvard University Press, 2004), 71–102.

responsibility. Hoping to capitalize on this victory, federal administrators on the Social Security Board launched a vigorous assault on state poor laws over the following years and sought as far as possible to limit their use.[16] Yet, many states resisted these intrusions and continued to enforce family responsibility in public assistance programs for the nonworking and noncontributing poor—including, most notably, Aid to Dependent Children or ADC (later renamed AFDC).[17]

The dividing line between federal social insurance programs and state-governed public assistance became increasingly meaningful in this period. At a time when the government was assuming full social responsibility for standard male workers and their dependents, public assistance claimants were relegated to an older tradition of private (albeit state-enforced) family obligations.[18] When single mothers, the blind, the disabled, the mentally ill, or the indigent claimed public assistance, state welfare departments were authorized to investigate and enforce private family obligations before disbursing any public funds. An adult child could be brought to court to pay for an elderly parent's nursing home costs; aunts and uncles held accountable for the costs of housing and educating a blind relative; and parents forced to contribute to the care of an insane child. In some states, the welfare department could claim retrospective compensation for benefits paid or seize the estate of a deceased claimant to reimburse the public purse.

During this period of rapid liberalization, the much-maligned AFDC program remained firmly embedded in the poor law tradition. Far from phasing out the family responsibility provisions of AFDC, state legislatures continued to strengthen them after World War II, reinforcing the idea that impoverished women should look to individual men and not the state as sources of support. So-called "substitute father" or "man-in-the-house" rules had been imposed on welfare mothers since the beginning of the program, serving to create a de jure relationship of paternal and marital responsibility where none had been consented to by the parties concerned. From the 1950s onward, many states, including California, extended their family responsibility laws to include "absent fathers"—the

---

16 Alvin Louis Schorr, *Filial Responsibility in the Modern American Family. US 96. Department of Health, Education and Welfare, Division of Program Research* (Washington, DC: US Government Printing Office, 1960), 23; R. Shep Melnick, *Between the Lines: Interpreting Welfare Rights* (Washington, DC: Brookings Institution Press, 1994), 67–8.

17 Schorr, *Filial Responsibility*, p. 23; Melnick, *Between the Lines*, 69–70.

18 Mandelker, "Family Responsibility under the American Poor Laws II," 626.

former husbands of women who had been separated or divorced or the biological fathers of children who had been born out of wedlock.[19] Now more than ever, women were reminded that their economic welfare depended primarily on their legal connection to a man.

Yet the fortunes of AFDC changed dramatically around 1965, thanks in large part to the rise of a new kind of public-interest lawyer working in close collaboration with the nascent welfare rights movement.[20] In mounting their case against public assistance laws, these lawyers looked to recent changes in family law as a model of the kinds of freedoms that might also be extended to those on welfare. Family law was effectively undergoing an extraordinary process of liberalization during this period. After more than a century of little change at all, laws that limited divorce, stigmatized non-marital unions, and discriminated against illegitimate children were repealed or ceased to be enforced within the space of a decade or so.[21] Alongside the marginalization of older, status-based rules governing sexual relationships, a new jurisprudence came into being that explicitly recognized "sexual freedom" as a constitutionally protected right. In two landmark decisions, *Griswold v. Connecticut* (1965) and *Eisenstadt v. Baird* (1972), the Supreme Court fashioned a new "right to privacy" that limited the power of the state to police intimate, sexual relationships in the home. Yet none of these innovations extended to impoverished women on welfare who were regularly subject to salacious investigations into their sexual histories, unannounced home visits, and strict moral policing under state law. As the field of family law entered a new age of relative sexual freedoms, welfare law— aptly dubbed the "family law of the poor" by legal scholar Jacobus tenBroek[22]—continued to reflect the punitive moral conservatism of the poor law tradition.

Relaying the most radical voices in the welfare rights movement, progressive public-interest lawyers questioned why recipients of public assistance and public housing were still subject to such intrusive forms

---

19 Melnick, *Between the Lines*, 96.

20 Martha F. Davis, *Brutal Need: Lawyers and the Welfare Rights Movement, 1960–1973* (New Haven: Yale University Press, 1993); Mark Neal Aaronson, "Representing the Poor: Legal Advocacy and Welfare Reform during Reagan's Gubernatorial Years," *Hastings Law Journal* 64 (2013), 992.

21 Jana B. Singer, "The Privatization of Family Law," *Wisconsin Law Review* 5 (1992): 1443–568.

22 Jacobus tenBroek, "California's Dual System of Family Law: Its Origin, Development, and Present Status: Part I," *Stanford Law Review* 16, No. 2 (1964): 257–84.

of moral surveillance. If the Supreme Court now recognized a constitutional right to sexual privacy, why would this right not be extended to women on welfare? If middle-class women were now free to dissolve marriages at will and had increasing power to earn an independent wage in the labor market, why should poor women remain imprisoned within the private bonds of economic dependence? If marriage no longer counted in determining the legal status of middle-class children, why would the children of welfare mothers still be classified as illegitimate and punished for the sins of the parents?[23] In short, poverty lawyers were looking to the liberalization of family law to argue against the continuing enforcement of private familial obligations in the realm of welfare.

The institutional and judicial environment of the 1960s was extraordinarily conducive to such ambitious social reform agendas. Public-interest litigators who sought to reform welfare found an unusually receptive audience in the progressive Warren Court and the even more liberal California Supreme Court. Their strategy of test-case litigation turned state public assistance into a federal issue, forcing the Supreme Court to pass judgment on matters it would rarely have encountered in the past. The outcome of these decisions was both to federalize (and thus liberalize) control of welfare and to align its provisions with recent changes in family law. In the *King v. Smith* case of 1968, Chief Justice Earl Warren ruled that Alabama's substitute father rule violated the terms of the Social Security Act and was out of touch with family law, which no longer sought to punish extramarital relations and no longer recognized any valid status distinction between legitimate and illegitimate children.[24] In another decision, Justice Brennan opposed child support enforcement as an invasion of privacy.[25] As a result of these rulings, the number of welfare applicants who refused to cooperate with district attorneys in child support matters rose dramatically.[26]

By placing welfare benefits on a more secure footing and ridding them of punitive behavioral rules, the federal court decisions of this era

---

23 These arguments were lucidly outlined by Yale law professor Charles A. Reich in "Individual Rights and Social Welfare: The Emerging Legal Issues," *Yale Law Journal* 74, No. 7 (1965): 1245–57, and "Social Welfare in the Public-Private State," *University of Pennsylvania Law Review* 114, No. 4 (1966): 487–93.

24 Melnick, *Between the Lines*, 84.

25 Ibid., 103.

26 Governor of California, *California's Blueprint for National Welfare Reform*, vii.

had the effect of liberating women from the confines of private family dependence. The overall message conveyed by these rulings was that the welfare of poor women was a public responsibility on a par with that of standard male workers. Whatever their marital status, sexual history, or race, impoverished women were just as deserving of a social wage as any other citizen. At a time when middle-class women were entering the workforce in growing numbers and achieving some degree of economic independence from men, unmarried women on welfare also appeared to be in reach of a social wage that was no longer mediated through a "substitute husband."

Public assistance benefits, however menial, were functioning like a social wage for unmarried women—a configuration that had not been envisaged in the Social Security Act, and one that many perceived as a perversion of its original intent. As Stephanie Coontz points out, it was not so much women's *dependence* on the state that turned a generation of social reformers against the welfare state tout court; it was rather the growing realization that welfare was making women *independent* of individual men and freeing them from the obligations of the private family.[27]

This particular challenge to the Fordist family wage system was profoundly unsettling to people from right across the political spectrum, and it is fair to say that it crystallized the enormous welfare backlash of the 1970s. It is in this period that you begin to hear the argument—echoed by both neoliberals such as Gary Becker and neoconservatives such as Daniel Bell and Daniel Patrick Moynihan—that public spending on welfare was making women too independent of presumptive husbands and fathers and thus effectively subsidizing the breakdown of the family. Neoliberals and neoconservatives were united in their opposition to the expansion of the welfare state under the sign of "sexual freedom," although their motivations were very different. Neoconservatives feared that the subsidization of non-normative lifestyle choices by the welfare state would undermine the moral foundations of social order. Neoliberals were primarily motivated by economic concerns: if growing numbers of women were now claiming both equal wages and an independent social wage, the resulting expansion of claims on the state threatened to exacerbate the problem of inflation.

---

27 Stephanie Coontz, *The Way We Never Were: American Families and the Nostalgia Trap* (New York: Basic Books, 2000), 59.

Neoliberalism and the Revival of Family Responsibility

Milton Friedman's evolving position on welfare is exemplary of this shift. Up until 1970, Friedman was a pragmatic supporter of at least some of the elements of the New Deal welfare state and indeed was actively involved in efforts to extend public assistance to families with dependent children under Nixon. His pragmatism was in keeping with the bipartisan consensus on the basic premise of redistributive social welfare which existed up until the late 1960s. Until this time, Democrats and Republicans alike were committed to the redistributive policies of the family wage, although they were divided on the question of whether or not it should be extended to African American men. By 1969, however, even the Republican President Nixon was convinced that the public assistance program, AFDC, should be made more inclusive and secured on a firmer, federal basis. His proposed new program—the Family Assistance Plan or FAP—promised to extend basic income guarantees to men, to two-parent families, and to those engaged in low-waged work.[28] It also promised to include African American men within welfare benefits for the very first time. The reform responded to both progressive and conservative critics of the old AFDC program: tarred with the brush of subsidizing the immoral lives of single mothers, welfare support would now function as an extension of the Fordist family wage and seek to buttress normative kinship structures by prioritizing intact families and unemployed fathers; at the same time, the normative family wage structure would be extended to African American men also.

When it was first proposed, Nixon's Family Assistance Plan attracted an extraordinarily broad alliance of supporters—embracing the Republican president and moderate conservative Richard Nixon, the neoliberal Milton Friedman, the Democrat Moynihan, the liberals and leftists of the National Welfare Rights Movement, and liberal economists such as John Kenneth Galbraith and James Tobin. There were of course clear differences of opinion among those who supported the plan—Friedman, for example, envisaged a more frugal form of welfare redistribution than that favored by liberals or leftists (in private

---

28 There are several excellent historical accounts of the FAP and the welfare rights movement. See Chappell, *The War on Welfare*; Felicia Kornbluh, *The Battle for Welfare Rights* (Philadelphia: University of Pennsylvania Press, 2007); and Premilla Nadesan, *Welfare Warriors: The Welfare Rights Movement in the United States* (London: Routledge, 2005).

correspondence, he conceded that he saw the negative income tax as a pragmatic step towards the elimination of all social welfare programs).[29] But with the exception of a few dissident, feminist voices in the National Welfare Rights Movement, all agreed that welfare in its existing form undermined the traditional family. And all converged on the necessity of maintaining some kind of redistributive welfare system. In the 1960s, even Friedman recognized the need for a basic income redistribution program to ameliorate the inevitable market failures of private charity.

In its broad conception, the plan was inspired by the work of the Catholic Democrat (and future neoconservative) Daniel Patrick Moynihan, who in his *The Negro Family: The Case for National Action* had denounced the corrosive effects of welfare benefits to single mothers on black masculinity and the black family.[30] By extending welfare entitlements to African American husbands and fathers, Moynihan hoped to include them within the stabilizing norms of the family and to undo the moral damage inflicted by the old AFDC program.[31]

In its practical details however, the Family Assistance Plan was based on the idea of a negative income tax first proposed by Friedman in 1962.[32] Friedman conceived of the negative income tax as a way of channeling income redistribution through the federal tax system, thereby eliminating the excessive administrative costs associated with dedicated welfare programs. With each annual tax submission, those whose income fell below a certain threshold would receive a sum of money in return, guaranteeing them an annual basic living wage. By replacing in-kind welfare with the most liquid form of benefit—cash— Friedman thought that the negative income tax would encourage the poor to behave as responsible free market actors. With its minimal but efficient system of redistribution, the negative income tax would bypass the disabling paternalism of the welfare state and undermine the

---

29 Milton Friedman, Letter to Patrick Buchanan, dated October 25, 1973, Box 22, Folder 11, Friedman Papers. Cited in Angus Burgin, *The Great Persuasion: Reinventing Free Markets Since the Depression* (Cambridge, MA: Harvard University Press, 2012), 197.

30 Daniel Patrick Moynihan, "The Moynihan Report. The Negro Family: The Case for National Action," *The Moynihan Report and the Politics of Controversy*, ed. Lee Rainwater and William L. Yancey (Cambridge, MA: MIT Press, 1967 [1966]), 39–124.

31 Kornbluh, *The Battle for Welfare Rights*, 148.

32 Milton Friedman and Rose Friedman, *Capitalism and Freedom* (Chicago: University of Chicago Press, 1962), 192–5.

entrenched power base of liberal welfare bureaucrats.[33] It would also eliminate the moral hazards embedded in the old AFDC program—that of promoting nonwork and family breakdown—by extending subsidies to those in low-wage work and intact families.

In 1970, the Democratic Party-controlled House of Representatives approved Nixon's recommendations by a large majority. The success of the Family Assistance Plan was short-lived, however. Later that year, the plan was roundly defeated by a coalition of Republicans and Democrats in the Senate, presaging a long-term reshuffling of left and right in the American political landscape. Designed to suit all stakeholders, the final version of the Family Assistance Plan ended up disappointing everyone. Welfare rights activists objected that the plan would reduce benefits to well below the poverty line for most welfare recipients, would eliminate the right to a fair hearing, and would reintroduce arbitrary powers of surveillance.[34] Free market economists such as Friedman thought the plan ended up complicating rather than streamlining the current welfare bureaucracy and did not sufficiently remove disincentives to work.[35]

What defeated the plan, however, was not so much these specific objections as Nixon's own decision to abandon the politics of consensus on welfare in a context of rising inflation.[36] In the first year of his presidency, Nixon had surrounded himself with policy advisors such as Moynihan and Robert Finch, who convinced him that an expansion of the family wage was the best way to placate racial tensions while simultaneously allowing him to wrest the white working class from its traditional allegiance to the Democratic party. By his second year in government, the economic outlook had soured and Nixon was less convinced that this strategy would work. Instead, he decided, behind closed doors, to abandon any attempt to reform AFDC while simultaneously overseeing some of the most generous expansions to Social Security in the program's history.[37] Social Security was (and still is) one of the New Deal's less contentious social insurance programs precisely because it

33 Milton Friedman and Rose Friedman, *Free to Choose: A Personal Statement* (New York: Harcourt Brace Jovanovich, 1980), 120, 123.

34 Chappell, *The War on Welfare*, 90–1.

35 William Ruger, *Milton Friedman* (London: Bloomsbury Academic, 2011), 120–1.

36 Nixon's change of tack on the black family wage presaged a more general turn to the right within his administration. See Kornbluh, *The Battle for Welfare Rights*, 148–50.

37 Jill Quadagno, *The Color of Welfare: How Racism Undermined the War on Poverty* (Oxford: Oxford University Press, 1994), 158.

remains relatively untouched by the normative issues of race, gender, and family formation that intersect in programs such as AFDC.

When Nixon retreated from the agenda of reforming AFDC then, the extraordinary consensus that had formed around the project of the expanded family wage came apart and reshuffled into distinct political positions. As the expanding economy of the mid-1960s gave way to the soaring inflation of the 1970s, AFDC became the touchstone for increasingly acrimonious debates about the very feasibility of welfare redistribution. In particular, the rising demands of the welfare rights movement—along with its successes in the federal courts—convinced many former pragmatic supporters of the New Deal welfare state that a crisis point had been reached. The importation of "sexual freedom" arguments into welfare rights law opened up the distinct possibility that the federal government would now be compelled to subsidize the existence of women who wantonly chose to live without the support of a man, thereby greatly increasing the burdens on state coffers. In this regard, the phenomenon of stagflation (combining inflation and unemployment) began to be understood as much more than a macroeconomic problem in the conventional sense of the term—what it reflected was a breakdown of moral order itself, an unsustainable inflation of monetary and libidinal demands beyond the limits established by the Keynesian consensus. If one could imagine an expansion of welfare state spending to include nonwhite men within the category of breadwinner, one could not question the normative premise of the male breadwinner family itself without completely defeating the arithmetic of restrained public spending—and thus generating runaway inflation.

In this new economic context, free market neoliberals such as Friedman who had once accepted the pragmatic necessity of a state-subsidized family wage began to formulate a distinct new political philosophy of non-redistributive family values. They now perceived the "perverse incentives" of the Great Society welfare state as responsible for both a breakdown in family values and an unsustainable inflation of monetary demands. Turning against the New Deal welfare state tout court, they now called for the strategic reinvention of a much older, poor law tradition of private family responsibility, using the combined instruments of welfare reform, changes to taxation, and monetary policy.

In 1980, for instance, Friedman, who had been so instrumental in the campaign for an expanded family wage, could be found reiterating the arguments of early twentieth-century opponents of social insurance, that social welfare was fundamentally inimical to the bonds of family responsibility. Pointing to the example of Social Security, he observed that the natural obligations of kinship that had once compelled children to look after their parents in old age had now been supplanted by an impersonal system of social insurance whose long-term effect was to usurp the place of the family:

> the difference between Social Security and earlier arrangements is that Social Security is compulsory and impersonal—earlier arrangements were voluntary and personal. Moral responsibility is an individual matter, not a social matter. Children helped their parents out of love or duty. They now contribute to the support of someone else's parents out of compulsion and fear. The earlier transfers strengthened the bonds of the family; the compulsory transfers weakened them.[38]

Much like Friedman, Gary Becker credits AFDC (along with social insurance programs and public services such as state education) with weakening the bonds of familial obligation. For Becker, the family in its equilibrium state or free market state could be understood as serving a kind of natural insurance function that was fatally disturbed when the welfare state socialized insurance.[39] Writing in the early 1980s, Becker credits the postwar welfare state with destroying the natural altruism of the family, but surmises that the decline in welfare initiated by Reagan will ultimately compel the poor to restore the bonds of kinship as a source of privatized welfare.[40]

Once we restore the question of family to its central place within the neoliberal critique of social welfare, we are in a much better position to understand the nuance of the neoliberal position on sexual freedom. It is almost universally assumed that neoliberal legal scholars were sympathetic to—perhaps even ultimately responsible for—the jurisprudence of privacy that transformed sexual freedom into a (limited) constitutional right in the late 1960s and 1970s. Thus, a certain kind of left-wing critique of neoliberalism sees it as having inspired the individualist ethics of sexual choice informing such landmark cases as the *Roe v.*

---

38 Friedman and Friedman, *Free to Choose*, 106.

39 On the family as a natural insurance mechanism, see Becker, "Altruism in the Family," 281–2.

40 Becker, "The Evolution of the Family," in *A Treatise on the Family*, 360.

Wade decision of 1973 and by extension all other cases involving the recognition of a constitutional right to sexual liberty.[41] In fact, the opposite is true: a scholar such as Richard Posner who otherwise supported the extension of the private commercial contract (in such areas as the trade in drugs, sex and babies) was unequivocally hostile to the idea of a constitutional right to sexual freedom, for the simple reason that it might impose an obligation on the state to actively enable and subsidize the freedoms in question.[42] This was precisely what occurred when sexual privacy jurisprudence was extended to welfare recipients in the 1970s. Instead, neoliberals support the more limited notion that private contractual freedom (as opposed to a constitutional right to freedom) should be extended to all arenas of social and intimate life, on the proviso that the associated costs are fully internalized by the contracting parties. Failing this, neoliberals are no less willing than social conservatives to invoke the necessity of noncontractual obligations in marriage and parenthood and are more than prepared to call on their enforcement by the state.

Posner and Becker were adamantly opposed to no-fault divorce, not out of any overt moral concern with the decline of family life (the rising divorce rates of the late twentieth century were inevitable, Becker insists) but because of the potential social costs involved in supporting dependent women and children.[43] When women and men fail to privatize the costs of their sexual behavior, instead transferring these costs to the state, neoliberals make an exceptional case for the imposition of noncontractual obligations. In cases of marital dissolution then, the legal responsibilities of marital and child support must take precedence over the wishes of the parties involved. As noted by the Chicago School legal

---

41 This assumption is widespread in the critical literature on neoliberalism. See, for instance, Anne Alstott, "Neoliberalism in US Family Law: Negative Liberty and Laissez-Faire Markets in the Minimal State," *Law and Contemporary Problems* 77, No. 4 (2014): 25–42. For a detailed rebuttal of this position with respect to Richard Posner, see Jean L. Cohen, *Regulating Intimacy: A New Legal Paradigm* (Princeton: Princeton University Press, 2004), 77–124.

42 In Posner's words, the "Supreme Court's decisions on sexual privacy are not only poorly reasoned but poorly informed." Richard A. Posner, *Sex and Reason* (Cambridge, MA: Harvard University Press, 1994), 7.

43 Ibid., 181–9, and Gary S. Becker, "Finding Fault with No-Fault Divorce (1992)," in *The Economics of Life: From Baseball to Affirmative Action to Immigration, How Real-World Issues Affect Our Everyday Life*, ed. Gary S. Becker and Guity Nashat Becker (New York: McGraw Hill Education, 1998), 98–100.

scholar, Richard A. Epstein, the rules of social welfare should "follow the basic pattern of natural obligation as it is perceived to arise within families."[44] The task of neoliberal welfare reform is "to transform [this] inclination into duty" and thus to "derive an 'is' from an 'ought'"—a precise translation of the poor law philosophy of natural charity within the family.[45]

The Revival of Family Responsibility in Practice: From Reagan to Clinton

The neoliberal critique of welfare had a profound influence on the subsequent history of American social policy and informed both direct efforts to revive the poor laws and much more general interventions into the realm of fiscal and monetary policy, all of which had the effect of transferring economic responsibility to the family. As Governor of California in the late 1960s and 1970s, Ronald Reagan was one of the first to implement the desiderata of the neoliberals with respect to welfare reform. In 1971, he pushed a comprehensive Welfare Reform Act through the Californian legislature with the intent of reactivating the state's poor law provisions. In the words of Reagan's task force on welfare reform, the intervention was designed to

> enforce the principle that family members are responsible for the support of relatives. In its simplest form, the argument was that every dollar contributed by the relative of a person on the welfare rolls was a dollar saved the taxpayer. However, the welfare reform goals went further and identified the family as the basic unit in society, emphasizing increased dependence upon the family and eliminating aspects of the welfare system that constitute incentives to break up the family.[46]

---

44 Richard Epstein, *Principles for a Free Society* (New York: Basic Books, 1998), 23.

45 Epstein's wording closely follows that of a famous family responsibility judgment made by the Illinois Supreme Court in 1896, *People v. James W. Hill*, 163 Ill. 186 (1896). Here it was stated that the object of both the original Elizabethan poor laws and those enacted by the state of Illinois was "to protect the public from loss occasioned by the neglect of a moral or natural duty imposed on individuals, and to do this by transforming the imperfect moral duty into a statutory and legal liability."

46 Ronald A. Zumbrun, Raymond M. Momboisse, and John H. Findley, "Welfare Reform: California Meets the Challenge," *Pacific Law Journal* 4 (1973): 769.

With recommendations extending to all of the state's public assistance programs, Reagan's welfare reform ended up reinstating family responsibility rules covering relationships between adult children and aged parents; grandparents, aunts, uncles, and impoverished children; parents and unwed minor mothers; as well as stepfathers and nonadoptive children—with most attention focusing on single mothers and their "absent husbands."[47]

As president, Reagan attempted to translate his Californian project in welfare reform onto the federal stage, without success. Instead Reagan's project was brought to final fruition by President Clinton, whose monumental welfare reform of 1996 effectively federalized the poor law tradition, turning America's welfare bureaucracy into an immense national apparatus for policing and enforcing child support obligations amongst the welfare poor.

Beyond these direct efforts to revive state poor laws of family responsibility, however, the influence of the poor law tradition can be observed in many other aspects of the neoliberal campaign to reform fiscal and monetary policy. It can be seen in efforts to repeal the estate tax on inherited wealth, a campaign that was loudly supported by neoliberal thinkers in the 1970s; in the local and state tax revolts that began in California in the late 1970s and then spread throughout the country, placing permanent limits on the power of the state to spend, tax, and most importantly, redistribute wealth; in the war of attrition to replace Social Security and work-based health insurance with private asset accumulation strategies; and in efforts to promote home ownership as a form of "asset-based welfare" under Clinton and George W. Bush. We tend to forget how central the problematic of the family was to each of these campaigns, but it was always front and foremost in the eyes of neoliberal policy-makers, who saw asset-based welfare as a way of replacing the "impersonal bonds" of social insurance with family-based forms of wealth accumulation and transmission.[48]

We can also observe multiple ways in which cuts to public funding in healthcare, education, and welfare have pushed more and more people back towards kinship-based forms of self-care and mutual support and

47 Ibid.
48 For a more detailed account of the role of the family in these various campaigns, see my *Family Values: Between Neoliberalism and the New Social Conservatism* (New York: Zone Books, 2017).

how the expansion of consumer credit has turned household deficit-spending into a substitute for state deficit-spending. Today, family responsibility very often takes the form of intergenerational debt where parents and other family members are actively enrolled in the debt obligations of children, signed up as guarantors or required to post their housing wealth as collateral to fund the social mobility (or simply stasis) of younger generations. Here too neoliberal policy prescriptions have played an important role, as Friedman and Becker were among the first to suggest that investment in "human capital" such as education should be the responsibility of the family, aided and abetted by private credit markets, not the state. Their policy prescriptions have had a profound influence on higher education funding in the United States, as the federal government and states have progressively chipped away at public funding and private credit markets have expanded to fill the gap—with parents often acting as co-signors or guarantors of student debt. I now turn to the issue of higher education funding in more detail, with the aim of showing just how central the concept of family responsibility was to neoliberal thinking on human capital theory.

Human Capital, Household Debt, and Family Responsibility

Today, human capital theory is almost synonymous with Chicago School neoliberalism, thanks in large part to the publication of Foucault's seminars at the Collège de France.[49] In the late 1950s and 1960s, however, the concept of human capital was much more closely associated with the name of Theodore Schultz, an economist who worked alongside Friedman and Becker at the University of Chicago but who would be more accurately described as a neo-Keynesian of the likes of Paul Samuelson, Robert Solow, and Richard Musgrave. It was Schultz who first popularized the idea that spending on human services such as education should be considered an investment rather than an act of consumption—and therefore that education itself should be considered a form of capital or interest-bearing asset.

Specifically, Schultz believed that investment in education could

---

49 See Foucault's discussion of Gary Becker's theory of human capital in Michel Foucault, *The Birth of Biopolitics: Lectures at the Collège de France, 1978–1979*, ed. Frédéric Gros (London: Palgrave Macmillan, 2008), 215–37.

help explain a hitherto perplexing problem in the calculation of national economic growth, one that had been identified by the founding figure of neoclassical growth economics, Solow. In two seminal articles in the field, Solow reported that only a small part of the rapid economic growth of the United States in the early twentieth century could be attributed to increases in the size of the labor force or physical capital—the sources of investment traditionally thought to account for GDP growth.[50] Schultz thought that the problem could be resolved if one took into account the sustained increase in private and public investments in education that had occurred over this period, an increase that was not the result of any conscious policy decision but that nevertheless had had the desirable effect of greatly improving GDP. Human capital investment, then, was the missing production factor in growth economics.

Schultz's insights led him to a number of practical conclusions regarding the role of public investment in education. First, he reasoned that if haphazard investment in higher education had been responsible for such a large portion of national economic growth, then the federal government would be well advised to adopt an active policy of sustained investment in the sector. Second, he argued that selective underinvestment in the education of the working class, African Americans, and women could account for the labor market discrimination experienced by these demographics.[51] Underinvestment in education was not only a source of economic, racial, and gender inequality; it was also a waste of national human resources that could have greatly increased GDP had they been deployed. When Friedman, commenting on one of Schultz's drafts, asked him the critical question of whether returns to investment in education accrued primarily to the individual or the collective, Schultz replied that such investment raised national income and was therefore in the interests of the public as a whole. The public provision of free education, moreover, enabled rich and poor to attend college, independently of family wealth; the corresponding increase in wages for

---

50 Robert M. Solow, "Technical Change and the Aggregate Production Function," *The Review of Economics and Statistics* 39 (1957): 312–20; and Robert M. Solow, "Technical Progress, Capital Formation, and Economic Growth," *The American Economic Review* 52 (1962): 76–86.

51 Theodore W. Schultz, "Investment in Human Capital," *The American Economic Review* 51, No. 1 (1961): 13–14; Theodore W. Schultz, "Woman's New Economic Commandments," *Bulletin of the Atomic Scientists* XXVIII, No. 2 (1972), 29–32.

poor students could be justified in the same way as progressive taxation.[52]

Theodore Schultz's human capital theory can be said to have inspired the Higher Education Act of 1965, a piece of legislation that doubled the federal budget for the sector, increased the number of grants available to low-income students and created a program of guaranteed student loans to be subsidized by the federal government. In 1972, Congress supplemented this act by approving a program of grants for low-income students (later renamed Pell grants). These policies had the effect of welcoming unprecedented numbers of low-income, black, Latino/a and women students into colleges and universities, a demographic shift that would soon be reflected in the political and pedagogical demands of the student movement. As Schultz had foreseen, sustained federal investment in higher education functioned much like an "inheritance tax":[53] by redistributing the costs of education through the tax base, President Johnson had made it possible for students without family wealth to access an institution that had once been a major conduit of class reproduction. During the 1970s, Pell grants were generous enough to cover both tuition fees and living costs, liberating students from the need to rely on the contributions of their parents.[54]

From the beginning, Schultz had his critics. Friedman and Becker in particular developed a perspective on human capital which highlighted the value of private as opposed to public returns to investment and led to policy recommendations at complete variance with those of Schultz. In their 1962 publication, *Capitalism and Freedom*, Rose and Milton Friedman pronounced themselves decisively in favor of private investment in human capital. Here they argued that the returns to investment in education accrued entirely to the individual student and that any ostensible social benefits were merely the summation of private wage gains.[55] The individual student should therefore be held responsible for the costs of his education. The Friedmans concurred with Schultz that there had been massive underinvestment in higher education, but unlike Schultz, believed that this failure could best be remedied through the liberalization of credit. The fact that low-income students were unable

---

52 Schultz, "Investment in Human Capital," 15.

53 Ibid.

54 Suzanne Mettler, *Degrees of Inequality: How the Politics of Higher Education Sabotaged the American Dream* (New York: Basic Books, 2014), 53.

55 Friedman and Friedman, *Capitalism and Freedom*, 100–1.

to pay for a degree and thus discriminated against in the labor market could be attributed to "imperfections in the capital market," that is, the absence of a liquid market in private student loans.[56] At best, the Friedmans conceded that the state might play a minimal role in remedying this state of affairs by providing loans repayable through the tax system and contingent on future earnings.[57] But they clearly saw the private credit market as the most efficient source of funding for student loans and thought that government incentives to banks were the best way of stimulating this market.

Becker had a very similar position to Friedman but as a microeconomist was always much more attentive to the intimate, domestic underpinnings of human capital investment and therefore has the merit of rendering explicit what remains unsaid in the work of the other neoliberals. Free public education, Becker argued, could be critiqued on the same grounds as the progressive income tax, which (in his words) "initially narrows inequality" but ends up raising the "equilibrium level of inequality . . . because families reduce their investments in descendants."[58] If we could only turn off the spigots of government spending, then families would spontaneously rediscover their natural altruism and start investing in their children again. The argument was improbable and at odds with the evidence but it enabled Becker to identify private credit markets as a logical alternative.[59] In Becker's ideal world, students would once again look to the family as a source of economic support, and yet the old stratifications of family wealth would simultaneously be deferred and elasticized by expanding opportunities for private debt.

Becker's microeconomic perspective on human capital investment was a mirror image of the more familiar theories of the Chicago and Virginia School neoliberals, who famously argued that public deficit spending and the resulting national debt had the unfortunate effect of "crowding out" private credit markets and discouraging private investment. But whereas Friedman and James M. Buchanan were primarily referring to business investment, what Becker meant by private investment was intergenerational, family investment. If the government would

56 Ibid., 107.
57 Ibid., 102–5. Friedman's vision of a federally administered student loan program tied to the tax system was formalized as the "income-contingent loan" and implemented in Australia in 1989.
58 Becker, "Inequality and Intergenerational Mobility," in *A Treatise on the Family*, 222.
59 Ibid.

only scale back on its investments in public goods, Becker surmised, then the family would resume its proper role of investing in children.[60] Further than this, the family's traditional economic responsibility in ensuring the welfare of its members would be greatly expanded by the stimulation of appropriate credit markets. With a little help from government, *the old poor law tradition of family responsibility could be reinvented in the form of an infinitely elastic intergenerational debt.*

Friedman in particular had a direct influence on this trajectory of higher education funding in America. Reagan, a vocal opponent of the Berkeley student movement, invoked Friedman's version of human capital theory to attack the funding structures of the University of California system as Governor of California in the late 1960s.[61] Free tuition, he believed, had destroyed the incentive structures of private family responsibility and in the process stoked the anti-authoritarianism of the student movement. Only a return to private, parental investment in the education of children, he thought, could resolve the fiscal and moral problems associated with public education.[62] A few short days after his swearing in as governor of the state of California in 1967, Reagan seized the opportunity to announce a 10 percent cut to the annual budget of the UC and state colleges and, more controversially, put forward a plan to introduce tuition fees as a way of covering the shortfall.[63]

Reagan's plan to introduce tuition fees was ultimately defeated by the regents in August 1967, although they did allow him to raise the revenue he wanted by increasing existing administrative charges.[64] In economic terms, the difference between Reagan's plan and the regents' eventual compromise solution was minimal. Yet the idea of introducing tuition fees was understood as a devastating symbolic attack on the tradition of

---

60 Ibid.

61 Ronald Reagan, "The Perils of Government-Sponsored Higher Education," in *The Creative Society: Some Comments on Problems Facing America* (New York: Devin-Adair Company, 1968), 109–17; Milton Friedman, "'Free' Education," *Newsweek* (February 14, 1967), 86.

62 Reagan, "The Generation Gap," in *The Creative Society*, 63.

63 Ray Zeman, "Reagan Pledges to Squeeze, Cut and Trim State Spending: Reagan Pledges Strict Government Economy," *Los Angeles Times* (January 6, 1967), 1 and 20. The UC budget for 1967–8 was eventually cut by $20 million.

64 Gladwin Hill, "Reagan Defeated on Tuition Plans: Regents Vote, 14–7, to Bar Fees at the University," *New York Times* (September 1, 1967), 13. The existing administrative fees were minimal and could be spent on noninstructional expenses only, such as administration, health services, and counselling.

free college education. Once tuition was accepted in principle, how could one remain committed to the ideal of free education? And what limits would be placed on annual increases? Reagan's state-level experiment in education reform subsequently served as the blueprint for the massive overhaul of higher education which he undertook as president.[65]

When we look at the subsequent history of higher education funding in the United States, it is astounding how closely neoliberal reforms of the sector have followed the prescriptions set out by Friedman and Becker. Since Reagan's reforms of higher education in 1980, federal policy has tended to diminish the spending power of Pell grants and to push instead for the expansion of federal and private student loans. At the same time, state governments have been chipping away at their investments in public universities so that institutions that were free for state residents before the 1980s have now become effectively private. The effect of this policy drift, as few would be unaware, has been rapidly inflating tuition costs and an enormous expansion in student debt. As movements such as Strike Debt have explained so well, inequality now tends to manifest in the form of differing degrees of debt servitude rather than outright exclusion.

What Strike Debt fails to take into account, however, is the fact that so-called private or personal debt is very often intergenerational, familial debt. As tuition fees have skyrocketed and lending thresholds have been raised, both the federal government and private lenders have pushed students towards loans that are signed by parents in the name of their children and where the obligations between parent and child serve as a kind of substitute for secure collateral.[66] It is not the case then that we might undermine the debt obligations of high finance by valorizing our "debts . . . to our friends, families, and communities," as Strike Debt advises us, since the global market in securitized household debt is entirely dependent on our intimate obligations to each other, particularly at the level of the family.[67] The fact that we are unwilling to abandon such obligations serves a highly useful anchoring role for the market in

---

65 Michael Mumper, *Removing College Price Barriers: What Government Has Done and Why It Hasn't Worked* (Albany: SUNY Press, 1996), 94.

66 Marian Wang, Beckie Supiano, and Andrea Fuller, "No Income? No Problem! How the Government is Saddling Parents with College Loans They Can't Afford," *Propublica* (October 4, 2012), at propublica.org.

67 "We want an economy where our debts are to our friends, families, and communities—and not to the 1%" (homepage of strikedebt.org).

securitized credit, ensuring that consumer debtors will typically remain wedded to a contract much longer than professional market players.

The key figures in American neoliberalism cannot of course be held responsible for the enormous liberalization of financial markets that took place from the 1980s onward. But they were certainly some of the first to advocate private over public deficit spending as a way of financing investment in "human capital," and the first to call for the subsidization of private credit markets as a way of satisfying the minority desires unleashed by the 1960s' social revolution. Friedman and Becker could not have foreseen how dramatically consumer credit markets would expand in the following decades, nor could they have anticipated how closely the student loan market would approximate their policy prescriptions. Yet they understood very clearly how private credit markets could perform democratic inclusion without disturbing the economic structures of private family wealth.

Today the effects of this shift in public finance are experientially self-evident. The Federal Reserve recently published a report seeking to explain the fact that a growing number of young adults are living at home with their parents well into their twenties and even thirties—a demographic trend it attributes first and foremost to college debt.[68] The shift from public to private investment in so-called human capital has forcefully reinvigorated the importance of family debt networks and inherited wealth in the shaping of social destinies. The effect of more than three decades of neoliberal economic reform has been to reinstate the legal and economic function of the private family as the first-line provider of welfare, very much in keeping with the policy prescriptions of neoliberals themselves.

---

68 Zachary Bleemer, Meta Brown, Donghoon Lee, and Wilbert van der Klaauw, *Debt, Jobs, or Housing: What's Keeping Millennials at Home?* Federal Reserve Bank of New York Staff Reports (November 1, 2014), at newyorkfed.org.

5

Schumpeter Revival? How Neoliberals Revised the Image of the Entrepreneur

Dieter Plehwe

Connecting neoliberalism and entrepreneurship has become a scholarly commonplace. Expanding on Michel Foucault, Wendy Brown has elaborated on the replacement of political man by economic man: a universalized notion of entrepreneurship dedicated to the self-maximization of one's human capital.[1] While acknowledging the neoliberal traditions of German ordoliberalism and Austrian economics, Brown's analysis is limited to the Chicago School, with a focus on Gary Becker. William Davies, in turn, bases his thesis on the divergent arguments of Mont Pèlerin Society (MPS) member Ronald Coase and the critic of the MPS, Joseph Schumpeter. Both Coase and Schumpeter justified imperfect competition and replaced institutional with psychological formats for competition.[2]

Although Davies links Coase and Schumpeter to the contextual changes in competition policies that have been employed since the late 1970s, he remains silent on the paradox of the Schumpeter revival. After all, Schumpeter foresaw the *end* of capitalism due to the inevitable decline of entrepreneurship in managerial capitalism. Davies reports on Schumpeter's pessimism regarding the sociological decline of the class of true entrepreneurs. Yet he follows by giving precedence to Schumpeter's

---

1 Wendy Brown, *Undoing the Demos: Neoliberalism's Stealth Revolution* (New York: Zone Books, 2015), 17f.

2 William Davies, *The Limits of Neoliberalism: Authority, Sovereignty and the Logic of Competition* (Thousand Oaks: SAGE Publications, 2014), 54.

visionary mindset in his chapter on "competitive psychologies" beyond the economic sphere.[3]

Schumpeter's essentialist concept of small groups of entrepreneurial elites has been resurrected well beyond the confines of business leadership. Allegedly "Schumpeterian" explanations of the driving forces of economic development have been universalized by management gurus and consultants to advance competitiveness strategies of nations and regions. The small-elite concept has been extended to political and cultural leadership responsible for human development at large.[4]

If the ubiquity of entrepreneurship discourse is impossible to miss, scholarly explanations of its origins have been more elusive. Neither Brown nor Davies deal with the shift of attention by neoliberals to questions of institutional and political context since the 1970s, which contributed decisively to overcoming essentialist versions of entrepreneurship. Nor do they trace important conversations among neoliberals on the topic of entrepreneurship that took place from the late 1940s onward, which is necessary to shed light on the neoliberal effort to revive entrepreneurship. Schumpeter played a central but variegated and changing role in these conversations. He was the nemesis for those who tried to prevent the seemingly inevitable decline of entrepreneurship and also acted as the expert economist in need of correction against whom to pitch an alternative neoliberal theory of entrepreneurship.[5] Ultimately, Schumpeter was enlisted as the crown witness for capitalism's revival in direct opposition to his own theory of decline.

The failure to untangle the process of reviving and revising Schumpeter means that diverse and even contradictory entrepreneurship theories are now presented under the common banner of neoliberalism,[6] although "[t]here is not much left of Schumpeter's entrepreneur in the post-Schumpeterian entrepreneurial theories. Only

---

3   Ibid., 51–4.

4   Ibid., 113.

5   Max Hartwell, *A History of the Mont Pèlerin Society* (Indianapolis: Liberty Fund, 1995), 102. Johannes Großmann, *Die Internationale der Konservativen. Transnationale Elitenzirkel und private Außenpolitik in Westeuropa seit 1945* (Berlin: De Gruyter Oldenbourg, 2014), 409–16.

6   Matthew Eagleton-Pierce, *Neoliberalism: The Key Concepts* (London: Routledge, 2016), 56f. For an instructive effort to distinguish expansive entrepreneurship concepts across a) actor groups, b) social and institutional contexts, and c) management levels and functions (innovation systems) see Richard Sturn, *Varianten des Unternehmertums in der Österreichischen Schule* (Graz: GSC Discussion Paper No. 18, 2017).

the conception that the entrepreneur need not be the owner has survived."[7] Critics of neoliberalism are thereby unwittingly complicit in covering up important dimensions of the intellectual history of entrepreneurship and they miss the crux of the matter.

The purpose of the entrepreneurship revival was not only to postulate allegedly universal characteristics of economic humankind. It also morphed into an effort to induce a far-reaching conceptual change in the understanding of both private and public management. Lost in what amounts to a whitewashing of the history of entrepreneurship theory are the ambiguities of Schumpeter's own daimonic understanding of the entrepreneur.[8] The successful integration of Schumpeter in the neoliberal narrative of entrepreneurial management indicates a steadily increasing neoliberal self-confidence. Schumpeter was first defeated symbolically to create room for neoliberal perspectives before the prestige of his name was integrated in a reinvigorated neoliberal perspective on economics, politics, and society.

This chapter explains the apparent Schumpeter paradox by tracing the postwar evolution of the entrepreneurship revival in neoliberal discussions. Alongside Schumpeter, another Austrian émigré economist, Ludwig von Mises, is central to the story. I show how Austrian economists like Mises and his British-born student at NYU, Israel Kirzner, alongside German economists like Günter Schmölders and Herbert Giersch, as well as a slate of other neoliberal scholars, rebutted, revived, and revised Schumpeter's theory of the entrepreneur from the 1950s to the 1980s. Apart from what must be considered a pseudo-Schumpeter revival and the important shift of attention to internal causes of economic development, innovation, and growth by the Kiel School of neoliberal economic geographers,[9] for example, students of Mises like Kirzner helped resurrect a functional and contextual entrepreneurship theory, which needs far greater attention in the effort to explain the rise of the entrepreneurial self. Beyond intellectual history,

---

7 Peter Swoboda, "Schumpeter's Entrepreneur in Modern Economic Theory," in *Lectures on Schumpeterian Economics: Schumpeter Centenary Memorial Lectures Graz 1983*, ed. Christian Seidl (Berlin: Springer, 1984), 17–28, 24.

8 Robert Fredona and Sophus A. Reinert, "The Harvard Research Center in Entrepreneurial History and the Daimonic Entrepreneur," *History of Political Economy* 49, no. 2 (2017): 268–314.

9 Dieter Plehwe and Quinn Slobodian, "Landscapes of Unrest," *Modern Intellectual History* (August 2017): 1–31; Swoboda, "Schumpeter's Entrepreneur", 24.

a diverse group of neoliberal authors and businessmen—many of them MPS members—contributed decisively to moving entrepreneurship from the wings of economic theory and economic policy-making onto center stage.

Entrepreneurship's Underdog: Ludwig von Mises

The central figure in the neoliberal discourse of entrepreneurship is not Schumpeter but Ludwig von Mises. As opposed to Schumpeter, who has become synonymous with entrepreneurship, Mises has little if any place in the mainstream intellectual history of the topic. This may be because his signature book *Human Action*,[10] published in 1949, "was already considered a closed chapter in the history of thought"[11] when it first appeared, according to his followers. His monetary and business cycle theory had been buried by John Maynard Keynes. He was seen to have lost the socialist calculation debate to the followers of Leon Walras, and his price theory was replaced by the competing Austrian tradition of Friedrich von Wieser. Mises's failure to win a permanent professional position in either Vienna or the United States left him ostracized in the academic world. Compared to Schumpeter, employed at Harvard since 1932, Mises was an outsider in the US educational field with only an adjunct position at New York University alongside paid consulting work for the Foundation of Economic Education and the National Association of Manufacturers.

Despite his professional marginality, Mises's theories had a formative influence on the revival of the Austrian School in the US and in Latin America after the 1970s.[12] Part of what made him marginal in the 1940s—and attractive to Austrian revivalists later—was the grandiosity of his scholarly goals. His large and heterodox claim was to have clarified not only economic activities, but human action in general. His

10 Ludwig von Mises, *Human Action. The Scholarly Edition* (Auburn: Ludwig von Mises Institute 1998) [German: *Nationalökonomie: Theorie des Handelns und Wirtschaften* (Genf: Union, 1940)].

11 Jeffrey M. Herbener, Hans-Hermann Hoppe, and Josef T. Salerno, "Introduction to the Scholarly Edition," in Mises, *Human Action*, v.

12 Floyd A. Harper, Henry Hazlitt, Leonard Read, Gustavo R. Velasco, and F. A. Hayek, eds, *Toward Liberty: Essays in Honor of Ludwig von Mises* (Menlo Park: Institute for Humane Studies, 1971).

central book, *Human Action*, if professionally ignored, has enjoyed popular success, having been translated into eight languages with over 500,000 copies sold.

A comparison between Mises and Schumpeter on the topic of entrepreneurship is instructive. Schumpeter pointed to the decline of a particular class of entrepreneurs. This reflected a change in the structure of global capitalism, and especially American capitalism, in the 1930s and 1940s. Partly as a result of the advance of socialist planning and the ideological conflict between socialism and capitalism, there was a growing consensus around large-scale, macroeconomic management and planning. Expanding bureaucracies in both the public and the private sector undermined the previous role of individual entrepreneurship and family firms, which Schumpeter had originally led to expect society to become more entrepreneurial.[13] At the microeconomic level, the modernization theme was mirrored by the new theory of the firm in the discipline of management and economics. Replacing the individualism of entrepreneurship, scholars pointed to the largescale organizational dimension and complex management requirements of the multi-divisional business organization, or what Alfred Chandler in 1962 called the "M form."[14] In line with a view to the distribution of responsibility, the secret of economic progress lay not in individualism and entrepreneurship but in management coordination and the cooperation of employees.

The rise of giant corporations and bureaucratic management led Schumpeter to predict the end of capitalism.[15] According to him, individual entrepreneurs who were capable of relevant innovations and pushing through new combinations in the marketplace in the face of resistance (due to the inevitable destruction of previously existing market relations) were the true cause of *macro*economic progress. The successful entrepreneur would thereby also yield considerable profit (temporary monopoly), enabling, eventually, the

---

13 Joseph Alois Schumpeter, *Theory of Economic Development: An Inquiry into Profits, Capital, Credit, Interest, and the Business Cycle*, trans. Redvers Opie (London: Routledge, 1984 [based on original material published by Harvard University Press, 1934]), 127f.

14 Alfred D. Chandler, *Strategy and Structure: Chapters in the History of the American Industrial Enterprise* (Cambridge, MA: MIT Press, 1962), 42.

15 Joseph Schumpeter, *Capitalism, Socialism, and Democracy* (New York: Harper & Brothers, 1942), chapter XII.

building of lasting (family capital) empires. Too easily forgotten is Schumpeter's reserved attitude about the role of entrepreneurs in society at large. While considered agents of change, they were neither considered initiators of economic progress per se nor heroes of the Ayn Rand variety.[16]

If Schumpeter came to see entrepreneurs as a doomed class, Mises saw entrepreneurship as a general feature of human behavior due to the need to make choices under conditions of unavoidable uncertainty. For Mises, the entrepreneur was literally everyone. In *Human Action*, Mises defined the entrepreneur as "acting man in regard to the changes occurring in the data of the market."[17] At the center of his entrepreneurial function is the anticipation of the future demand of the consumer. Unlike Schumpeter's focus on innovation and change, for Mises the entrepreneur needs nothing but market relations to perform his or her role in the economy and society. The performance earns profit for the entrepreneur, which is nothing but the acknowledgment of the capacity for making the price function work. This is why Mises reacted with hostility when profits were considered expressions of malfunctioning markets to be overcome by equilibrium. He saw the defense of profit (and loss) opportunity as central to a free economy and society.[18]

Mises's theory was marginal, if not totally foreign, to the Marshallian-Keynesian academic mainstream of the neoclassical synthesis in the postwar United States. Yet beyond a rather significant afterlife with a popular readership, Mises's theory also offered later neoliberals a source for their theory of a general economic system that stood in stark contrast to neoclassical equilibrium theory, Marxist historical materialism, and other historicist approaches in economics like that of Schumpeter. Notwithstanding its limited reception in the discipline of economics proper, and the widespread belief in his lack of importance within Mont Pèlerin circles, the work of von Mises ended up contributing to one of the most important and lasting neoliberal projects of the 1960s and 1970s: the revival of the concept of entrepreneurship.

---

16   Fredona and Reinert, "The Harvard Research Center," 289.
17   Mises, *Human Action*, 255.
18   Ibid.

Building on Mises: Kirzner Confronts Schumpeter

The topic of entrepreneurship arrived rather slowly at the meetings of the Mont Pèlerin Society.[19] It was not discussed explicitly until the Vichy general meeting in 1967, when Israel Kirzner drew on Mises and Hayek in his important paper on "Methodological Individualism, Market Equilibrium and the Market Process" in a session on "The Teaching of Economics at the Present." Kirzner drew a distinction between "Anglo-American price theory" interested in conditions of equilibrium and "Austrian price theory" interested in the market process. Kirzner suggested that, in contrast to the purely calculating and economizing role of the individual in the Anglo-American equilibrium world, there was an additional entrepreneurial element in the Austrian world of market processes due to the fact that individuals operate under conditions characterized by a lack of knowledge necessary to calculate and economize. "It is the entrepreneur," he wrote, "who is the prime mover in the market process."[20]

It is notable that entrepreneurship entered the business school curriculum precisely at the time when some of the key exponents of the new entrepreneurship literature, and Kirzner in particular, started talking about teaching economics. The first entrepreneurship courses in the United States were offered at Stanford and New York Universities in the second half of the 1960s. The first entrepreneurship MBA program in the United States was offered in the early 1970s at the University of Southern California. A decade later, several hundred undergraduate schools and universities featured entrepreneurship courses if not programs in the United States alone.[21] (Fifty years later, Marroquin University in Guatemala would name its own entrepreneurship center after Kirzner himself).

---

19 For earlier work of Mont Pèlerin members Otto von Habsburg, president of the Centre Europèenne de Documentation et d'Information, and Arvid Fredborg, head of the Institut d'Etitudes Politiques Vaduz in Liechtenstein in the 1960s, including efforts to establish a "Free Enterprise University" and an organization in defense of free entrepreneurship see Johannes Großmann, *Die Internationale*, 412.

20 Israel Kirzner, "Methodological Individualism, Market Equilibrium, and Market Process," *Il Politico* 32, no. 1 (1967), 788.

21 G. T. Solomon and L. W. Fernald, Jr., "Trends in Small Business Management and Entrepreneurship Education in the United States," *Entrepreneurship Theory and Practice* 15 (1991), 25–39. Compare the "Entrepreneurship Education Chronology" offered by Saint Louis University, at slu.edu.

Following the Vichy meeting, Kirzner also gave a paper on "Entrepreneurship and the Market Approach to Development" at the regional meeting of the MPS in Caracas, Venezuela, in 1969. In this paper, Kirzner tackled Schumpeter's concept of innovation entrepreneurship. According to him, Schumpeter's failure to recognize the entrepreneur as a decision-maker, and his exclusive emphasis on disruptive innovation, left market-correcting policies to planners. Kirzner's own concept considered entrepreneurship decisive to explain the equilibrating adjustments over time, replacing static equilibrium by intertemporal equilibrium. Kirzner distinguished two entrepreneurship issues: a) the discovery of the best way of action, and b) actually carrying out activities no matter if best or second or third best. According to him, the focus of the existing entrepreneurship discussion was on the first—calculative—dimension whereas he conceived of the need to recognize the second dimension as the real entrepreneurial function.[22] Kirzner felt that the difference mattered because Schumpeter and all the other *abstract* calculation experts failed to recognize the most important *concrete* dimension of development, namely taking advantage of opportunities presented by the market process.[23]

Kirzner's observations about real-life entrepreneurs were foreshadowed by neoliberal interventions in the debate over international development. Since the end of the 1950s, development economist and MPS member Peter Bauer had used a sociological perspective akin to Schumpeter to decry the notion of a lack of entrepreneurs in developing countries—a view also shared by important Mont Pèlerin members like Wilhelm Röpke.[24] Ignoring progressive critics who emphasized a shortage of (domestic) capital rather than a lack of entrepreneurs, Bauer's emphasis on the market process and entrepreneurship in the South sought to advance a universal neoliberal economic perspective in the field of development economics.

While Kirzner attacked the eminent economist Schumpeter, he was also eager to stress how close Schumpeter's emphasis on "dynamic

22 Israel Kirzner, "Entrepreneurship and the Market Approach to Development," in *Toward Liberty: Essays in Honor of Ludwig von Mises*, ed. Floyd A. Harper et al. (Menlo Park: Institute for Humane Studies, 1971), 201.

23 Ibid., 203.

24 Dieter Plehwe, "The Origins of the Neoliberal Economic Development Discourse," in *The Road from Mont Pèlerin*, ed. Philip Mirowski and Dieter Plehwe (Cambridge, MA: Harvard University Press, 2009), 249.

disequilibrium"[25] and innovation were to his own concept of "alertness" and to the independence of entrepreneurship from the factors of production.[26] According to Schumpeter, only the owners of capital were bearing risk, which set his reasoning apart from the contributions on uncertainty of Frank Knight at the University of Chicago, for example. Yet unlike Schumpeter, Kirzner emphasized the market process in which the entrepreneur takes a role, rather than the innovative contribution of the entrepreneur himself. He did so for a reason: Schumpeter's wartime observations regarding the decline of heroic, innovative entrepreneurship and, correspondingly, family firms, led him to expect the rise of a version of elite socialism that was difficult to counter in the age of monopoly capital, large organizations, and managerialism. The central weakness of Schumpeter's sociology of entrepreneurship, however, was a tendency to naturalize entrepreneurial talent and quality (the substantive capacity of the class of innovative individuals and the macroeconomic relevance of innovations, respectively). This was no longer needed if the entrepreneur merely reacts to market opportunities rather than having to create them. Kirzner's shift of attention to the simple individual quality of "alertness" and the primacy of market processes which present opportunities redirected the argument to the general system of thought of Ludwig von Mises.

No macroeconomic dimension of innovation was required to meet his threshold of abundant entrepreneurship, and the market process trumped market structure in what became a contingency theory of more or less restricted entrepreneurship. Following this shift, Mont Pèlerin members increasingly directed their attention to the wide range of *restrictions on entrepreneurship*. Instead of the traditional focus on the monopoly power of firms as an impediment to the market, the subtle move towards market practice enabled the shift of attention to state-related policy issues like taxation and regulation, and trade-union-related collective action, as the primary targets of critique.

25 Harald Hagemann, "Capitalist Development, Innovations, Business Cycles and Unemployment: Joseph Alois Schumpeter and Emil Hans Lederer," *Journal of Evolutionary Economics* 25, no. 1 (January 2015): 117.

26 Israel Kirzner, *Competition and Entrepreneurship* (Chicago: University of Chicago Press 1973), 80.

Günter Schmölders and the Image of the Entrepreneur

The topic of entrepreneurship arrived at the Mont Pèlerin Society in earnest in 1970 when the German economist Günter Schmölders opened the conference on the "image of the entrepreneur" which took place from August 30 to September 5 (on Schmölders and his early contribution to behavioral economics, see Graf in this volume). The content of the Munich MPS conference papers was not a purely academic matter.[27] The focus on the entrepreneur was also part of a strategic agenda-setting effort on the part of neoliberal intellectual circles in close interaction and collaboration with corporate leaders from industry and banking. West Germany's leading technology company, Siemens, provided office space and logistics. A wide range of medium and large German enterprises provided funding. Schmölders used the Aktionsgemeinschaft Soziale Marktwirtschaft (Action Group for a Social Market Economy) and the Arbeitsgemeinschaft Selbständiger Unternehmer (Association of Independent Entrepreneurs) to obtain funding. The former is a think tank financed by corporate members, which had been originally founded in 1953 to support Ludwig Erhard's neoliberal version of a social market economy.[28] The latter is a business association of family firms, which had contributed heavily to think tanks.[29] The support from big corporations and family firms suggested cross-sectoral interest in the entrepreneurship theme in Germany. Instead of an opposition between big-firm management and family-firm entrepreneurship, there was an emerging consensus on the need for a common approach to entrepreneurship and entrepreneurial management.[30] The conference served to showcase the value and the use of entrepreneurship research and education in Germany and internationally. Unsurprisingly, many if not all contributions to the conference defended entrepreneurs against critics and aimed at advancing entrepreneurship from a normative perspective.[31]

---

27 The papers were pubished as Günter Schmölders, ed., *Der Unternehmer im Ansehen der Welt* (Bergisch Gladbach: Gustav Lübbe Verlag, 1971).

28 Ralf Ptak, "Neoliberalism in Germany: Revisiting the Ordoliberal Foundations of the Social Market Economy," in *The Road from Mont Pèlerin*, ed. Mirowski and Plehwe, 98–138.

29 Hartwig Pautz, "Revisiting the Think-tank Phenomenon," *Public Policy and Administration* 26 (2011): 419–35.

30 *Unternehmer und Bildung. Festschrift zum 60. Geburtstag von Ludwig Vaubel* (Cologne: Westdeutscher Verlag, 1968).

31 Only B. R. Shenoy from India told his audience that corporate tax evasion was a real problem and not just a fantasy of socialist propaganda. His chapter arguably comes

In his opening address, Schmölders made three points to undergird the new focus on entrepreneurs. First, postwar capitalism had been hugely successful, but its very success obscured the foundations of the market system, which were considered old-fashioned or even reactionary by much of the public. This required a new effort to examine the functioning of the system, with entrepreneurs as one of the critical aspects. Second, this effort could help to atone for the longstanding sin of omission, namely the missing focus on entrepreneurs and entrepreneurship in economics. Much like Kirzner, Schmölders argued that attention needed to shift from abstractions like capital or economic laws to the real actors. Third, the public opinion of entrepreneurs was as important as the role of the entrepreneur in the functioning of the economy. Only the deep knowledge of "opinions on facts" allowed responsible politicians and their advisors to develop an understanding of preference formation processes in economic and economic policy questions.[32]

Schmölders thus set the double task of pursuing both research on entrepreneurs as critical agents and research on opinions of entrepreneurship in general. The lineup for the conference followed the dual purpose spelled out by the MPS president. A first group of speakers addressed the relevance and image of the entrepreneur in different countries, and a second group examined particular groups in society and how to improve the image of entrepreneurs. Schmölders himself covered Germany, Lawrence Fertig the United States, Francois Bilger France, Ralph Horwitz the UK, Chiaki Nishiyama Japan, B. R. Shenoy India (complemented by Peter Bauer on developing countries). James Buchanan and G. M. Wattles discussed education in the United States. The roster of speakers on the second theme included Gilbert Tixier on the perspective of French tax collectors, Götz Briefs on trade unions, Jean-Pierre Hamilius on intellectuals, and Erich Streissler on the left. Last but not least, we find Franz Böhm, Milton Friedman and Christian Gandil discussing how to improve the image of the entrepreneur. The

---

closest to Schumpeter's interest in business history. Shenoy offered insight into the historical impact of the caste system and the institutional restrictions on entrepreneurship for members of castes that did not belong to the designated commercial class (Vaishya). B. R. Shenoy, "Das Bild vom Unternehmer in Indien," in *Der Unternehmer im Ansehen der Welt*, ed. Schmölders, 156–71.

32 Günter Schmölders, "Eröffnungsansprache zur Tagung der Mont Pèlerin Society am 31. August 1970 in München," in ibid., 7–11.

1970 meeting thus placed entrepreneurship firmly on the agenda of the neoliberal intellectual movement both as subject of analytical research and as object of popular promotion efforts.

The unfolding revival agenda at this point in time can be best summarized as an exercise in defensive optimism. Speakers at the 1970 MPS conference observed a decline of owner-entrepreneurs along the lines expected by Schumpeter. Contrasting the concerns and fears voiced in conservative and neoliberal circles during the 1950s and 1960s,[33] the speakers in Munich highlighted surprising sources of optimism with regard to the future of the market economy. Authors pointed to considerable entrepreneurship in large corporations and to the changing behavior of average citizens. Fertig observed that 12 percent of Americans owned shares, for example, and reported a strong increase in the volume of investment funds. The former read like a preview of the "intrapreneurship" and innovation system discourse to be further discussed below, and the latter pointed to the impending expansion of scope of the entrepreneurship discussion.

While the familiar neoliberal mood of tragedy is quite present, the contributors were also eager to point out bright spots. Schmölders emphasized an improving approval rate for the role of entrepreneurs in Germany, although other professions were clearly held in higher esteem. Compared to the relatively positive accounts of Germany and the United States, the British perspectives offered by Hamilius and Fisher were bleak. Negative stereotypes of "Mammonism" were blamed on the politics of nationalization of industries like coal and steel. The French picture presented in turn was more positive again. A first wave of opinion surveys on the topic (like in Germany), did not display the expected stereotypes of French entrepreneurs (nationalist, protectionist). The assessment of the role and functioning of enterprises and owners was mixed, but Bilger suggested the biggest obstacle was a lack of intimate knowledge of French companies. He found old resentments based on class struggle to be in decline, while new objections against efficiency under the keyword of "Americanism" seemed to be fashionable. Tixier also pointed to a lack of employer ideology in France, which left entrepreneurs feeling helpless in the face of animosities. Japan, in turn, was held to suffer from a serious decline in the number of entrepreneurs, and the increasing relevance of large enterprises. Kiuchi's comments

---

33 Großmann, *Die Internationale der Konservativen*, 406f.

once again lent support to an expanded entrepreneurship perspective within the corporate sector.

The sociological perspective presented focused on the perceived sources of negative public opinion: intellectuals, educators, tax authorities, trade unions, and the left (though Erich Streissler explicitly defended Karl Marx and blamed Rousseau instead for the hostility of the New Left towards entrepreneurship). In a wide-ranging chapter on intellectuals and entrepreneurs, Hamilius argued that intellectuals were sawing off the branch on which they were sitting by turning against entrepreneurs. Böhm suggested that the effort to support entrepreneurs needed to be concentrated on the image of the market order. He offered three reasons for the intellectual opposition to entrepreneurs and the market: resentment, utopian ideas, and lack of knowledge. Hamilius summarized the challenges that entrepreneurs faced in a graphical display (Figure 5.1). In the face of manifold and comprehensive challenges, and the anti-intellectual alternative of totalitarianism, Hamilius demanded that the entrepreneur turn himself into an intellectual. One can easily interpret this as a recommendation for entrepreneurs to strengthen their own corps of organic intellectuals represented by the very group assembled at the MPS meeting in Munich.

Figure 5.1 Many Hounds Soon Catch the Hare

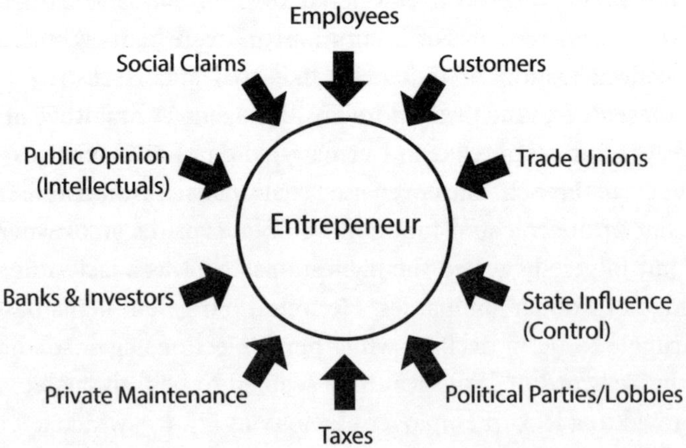

After 1970, entrepreneurship was no longer considered doomed due to an inevitable decline of the class of individual entrepreneurs. The essentialist perspective of Schumpeter was increasingly replaced by the political contingency perspective of Mises. True, the end of the 1960s and early 1970s are usually considered a very dark time for neoliberals. Student revolts and working-class collective action reached unprecedented levels in many countries, constituting the illiberal tendencies neoliberals bemoaned. Reading the papers of the Munich conference, however, one sees not just concern but also a clear sense of direction as to how to strategically address the challenges.

Firstly, neoliberal scholars used survey studies in different countries to direct attention to challenges and to offer solutions to contrast negative images. Secondly, they developed clarity about the need to defend economic freedom and the market system as a whole rather than the individual entrepreneur; the entrepreneurship function rather than the particular person. Thirdly, they clarified the sources of negative images of entrepreneurs, ranging from educators, trade unions, tax officials to intellectuals, which served also to develop agendas adequate to address particular audiences (e.g. teachers, journalists) in addition to the general public. This job was given to the growing army of neoliberal think tanks.[34] Fourthly, authors ascertained the positive roles and functions of entrepreneurs and entrepreneurship both at the micro and at the macroeconomic level. In line with the unambiguous endorsement of entrepreneurship, ever more attention was directed at the constraints entrepreneurs faced from various sides.

The 1970 MPS conference thus marked the end of Schumpeterian essentialism and pessimism and a shift in focus to the conditions of economic freedom and entrepreneurship. Apart from delivering clarity about the need for lowering constraints on business transactions, the conference also marked the beginning of revisionism with regard to Schumpeter's innovation entrepreneurship and a new perspective on corporate management. Such revisionism arguably culminated in the work of Herbert Giersch, Mont Pèlerin Society president from 1986–88, when he announced a new age of Schumpeter in 1984.

---

34 Richard Cockett, *Thinking the Unthinkable: Think-Tanks and the Economic Counter-Revolution, 1931–83* (London: Harper Collins, 1994); Lee Edwards, *The Power of Ideas: The Heritage Foundation at 25 Years* (Ottawa, IL: Jameson Books, 1997); Arthur Seldon, ed., *The Prime Mover of Progress: The Entrepreneur in Capitalism and Socialism* (London: Institute of Economic Affairs, 1980). Quite a number of think tanks even reflect the task in their name. Among those founded in the orbit of the Mont Pèlerin Society are the Competitive Enterprise Institute (US, 1984), the Centro de Investigaciones Sobre la Libre Empresa (Mexico, 1984), the Instituto de Estudos Empresariais (Brazil, 1984), and the Institut für Unternehmerische Freiheit (Germany, 2006), for example.

Incorporating Schumpeter: Herbert Giersch's Unification of Schumpeter and Mises

Herbert Giersch's work marks the reversal of previous approaches of neoliberals to issues of entrepreneurship. While Mises, Kirzner, Schmölders, and many others scrutinized the different constraints faced by entrepreneurs, Giersch turned the tables to emphasize the constraints that entrepreneurs themselves presented to regulators and other enemies of economic freedom at and beyond the scale of the region and nation. The long-time president of the Kiel Institute for the World Economy was at the center of a newfound interest in global competitiveness, innovation, and locational dynamics. Unlike well-known figures such as Michael Porter, Jeffrey Sachs, and Paul Krugman, Giersch has been unjustly forgotten in the Anglo-Saxon discussion of new growth economics and new economic geography.[35] He and his students and colleagues were at the forefront of the development of a new—and in Giersch's case, decidedly neoliberal—economic geography. They are also at the center of the intellectual history of the entrepreneurship revival of the 1980s.

Giersch's work completes the circle described above. Schumpeter's original perspective was on innovation as disruption coupled with a pessimism regarding the future of capitalism. Kirzner refuted Schumpeter's belief in the equilibrating function of entrepreneurship and argued that the future of capitalism depended on removing market restrictions. Finally, with Giersch, we see the invocation of Schumpeterian innovation as the inevitable fate of all economic regions due to globalized competition and the realities of technological innovation in communication.[36] The world economy as an "object of experience" requires the replacement of nationalist ideology with a "cosmopolitan welfare function (in the sense of Meade . . .)"[37] wrote Giersch, suggesting the rise of a new version of cosmopolitan capitalism. It was not capitalism in general that was doomed due to the lack of a capable class of entrepreneurs, but only those regions and nations unwilling or incapable of

---

35 Karl-Heinz Paqué, "Die Welt als Kegel und Vulkan," in *Das Zeitalter von Herbert Giersch. Wirtschaftspolitik für eine offene Welt*, ed. Lars P. Feld, Karen Horn, and Karl-Heinz Paqué (Tübingen: Mohr Siebeck, 2013).

36 Herbert Giersch, "Anmerkungen zum weltwirtschaftlichen Denkansatz," *Weltwirtschaftliches Archiv* 125, no. 1 (1989): 13.

37 ibid., 15.

enabling innovation-oriented competition and advancing the competitiveness of their local economic entities.

Giersch has been considered a modern Keynesian economist in
Germany, but his work displayed a decisive swerve towards supply-
side economics and Austrian perspectives from the 1970s onward.
Even before this redirection he was personally close to Hayek and
maintained a friendship with him throughout his life. For example,
Giersch's wife, Friederike, herself a PhD in economics, reported in a
personal letter that the Gierschs and Hayek met in January 1978 at
the European Management Forum in Davos.[38] In 1983, Giersch
presented at the Davos Forum again, this time on the topic of
Europessimism. He was soon to publish his famous diagnosis of
"Eurosclerosis,"[39] demanding and supporting deregulation and the
European liberalization required to enable cross-border competition
and the passage to a more complete single European market.
Notwithstanding his faith in the moving force of globalization,
Giersch was an important neoliberal agenda-setter in European inte-
gration and global trade politics.

Giersch published his seminal text on the new age of Schumpeter in
1984,[40] which marked the end of the age of merely defensive optimism
within MPS neoliberalism. Now relying on a selective reading of
Schumpeter, neoliberals like Giersch proudly professed a new confidence in greatly expanded notions of entrepreneurship. The age of
Keynes and macroeconomic steering had come to an end according to
Giersch. Keynes is presented as the pessimist instead of Schumpeter,
who is turned into a trusting supporter of capitalist revival right after
World War II.

> This point about "regenerative creeds"—made in 1946 [by Schumpeter
> against Keynes]—highlights Schumpeter's postwar optimism. The
> point is gaining more and more relevance in our present phase of slow
> world economic growth, a phase with cumulating pains of delayed
> adjustment. In such a phase, the faith in the regenerative forces of a

---

38 Friederike Giersch, Letter to Hayek, December 31, 1977. I thank the estate of F.
A. Hayek for permission to quote from his correspondence.

39 Herbert Giersch, "Eurosclerosis: The Malaise that Threatens Prosperity,"
Financial Times, January 2, 1985.

40 Herbert Giersch, "The Age of Schumpeter," *The American Economic Review* 74,
no. 2 (1984), 103–9.

decentralized market system has once more become critical for the choice of the appropriate socioeconomic paradigm.[41]

Giersch's research focus from the second half of the 1970s onward was on structural change in the world economy. This positioned him to address supply-side conditions in general and entrepreneurial activity in particular. He merged the German tradition of marginalist locational economics of Thünen and Lösch with the dynamic evolutionary economics of Schumpeter.

At the heart of Giersch's new economic geography was what he called the "Schumpeter volcano," a center of innovation in a specific location, which would provide the innovating company or business unit with a temporary monopoly. Once the innovation "lava" flowed downward and cooled, competitive advantage was lost. The volcano thus must continue producing new innovations (new technologies) or move to the margins in the process of locational competition (*Standortwettbewerb*). While established "volcanoes" can maintain their position due to incumbency effects, the framework allows for imitation and the possibility of new centers to emerge and successfully compete with existing firms, business units, and regions.

In line with Mises, innovation thus became a function of enabling factors and actively jumping at chances rather than an essential and rare ingredient of the economic process. The entrepreneurial mindset has to function perpetually or else miss opportunities and pass the command on to others. Giersch quite obviously follows Kirzner without explicit reference to his notion of alertness. To this end, local, regional, and national entities can align policies in favor of competitive practices. Successful entrepreneurship is seen to require complementary public and private initiative and resolve. While trade economists and new economic geographers like Krugman would challenge free trade on a similar basis, Giersch was adamant about unrestricted movements of capital, goods, and to a certain extent, labor. Support for innovative regions and companies would need to combine open markets and enabling policies for market participants.[42]

In reaction to the slow growth patterns of the late 1970s and early 1980s, Giersch directly opposed Keynesian economics in his nine-point program allegedly based on Schumpeter. His third point noted:

41   Ibid., 105.
42   Paqué, "Die Welt als Kegel und Vulkan."

What matters most in present circumstances are the driving forces of economic development. Emphasis, therefore, is on the growth and dissemination of knowledge, on path breaking entrepreneurs and eager imitators, on credit creation for the supply of venture capital, and on Schumpeterian competition (i.e. on innovative monopolistic competition rather than sterile perfect competition, on oligopolistic rivalry rather than collusive equilibria and on aggressive trading rather than arbitrage transactions). In the international economy, which Schumpeter mostly neglected [sic!], emphasis is on free trade rather than fair trade (trade minus competition) and on export orientation rather than import substitution.[43]

Giersch's last point number nine reads: "Entrepreneurial talent is in almost unlimited supply, but it often finds productive outlets only abroad, or less productive (or even counterproductive) use in politics and government, in public and private bureaucracies or in the military."[44] Giersch evidently took his page from Mises. Entrepreneurs are everywhere, both in the public and the private sector: in human action hampered or enabled by the institutional make-up of society. Once decision-makers embrace this understanding, society can be moved towards productive entrepreneurship. Otherwise society will have to live with an exodus of talent to better locations and with sub-optimal application of the remaining talent.

In the 1980s, Giersch divided the world into advanced innovative (Schumpeterian) regions—at the time US and Japan—and less developed Schumpeterian regions like Taiwan and Singapore, and advanced Keynesian and less developed Keynesian regions, which hampered entrepreneurship. Additional regions were categorized as Ricardian, Malthusian, or Marxist. Progressive change was on the way in the Keynesian regions (of Europe) due to disillusionment with the welfare state and increasing sensibility for the fiscal crisis, the growth of the shadow economy, mass unemployment and the spectacular growth of self-employed and employees in new businesses, and, last but not least, the decentralization potential of new telecommunication technologies.[45]

---

43 Giersch, "The Age of Schumpeter," 105. Emphasis added.
44 Ibid., 106.
45 Ibid., 108.

Giersch's dynamic reasoning has subsequently been vindicated by the collapse of the Soviet Union and the ongoing and massive neoliberal transformation of welfare state capitalism in the OECD world. Dynamics of structural change unsettled most national and regional economies, which ironically became increasingly subject to strategic planning, both public and private, precipitating the neo-nationalist rise of right-wing populism following the global financial crisis. Contrary to anti-statist rhetoric, the (competition) state has been charged with advancing the neo- and post-Schumpeterian notions of entrepreneurship through regional, educational, economic, and even social policies. Giersch himself speaks of a post-Schumpeterian approach because of the limits and problematic ambiguities of the original. While older welfare state institutions were and are shrinking, new public management and public-private governance institutions are advancing at all levels of government, supranational, national, regional, and local. Competitiveness has become the universal buzzword for all kinds of "market units," individual, companies, regions, states, and world regions.[46]

With regard to the new economic geography based on neo- and post-Schumpeterian (Gierschian) insights it is important to emphasize both the political dimension and the openness or non-local dimensions. Unlike Porter, Giersch did not perceive competitive advantages in terms of a local or national combination and allocation of resources. The world market was the key referent, attracting mobile factors of production to the most competitive region: capital and knowledge. Flexible regions are upwardly mobile, and regions marked by rigidity are prone to decline. Local endowments can be more or less favorable to local development, but they do not explain the trajectory.

Contrary to Kirzner's effort to de-emphasize innovation and the resulting disruption, Giersch reinstated the innovator-entrepreneur without reinstating the small social class of Schumpeter's elite entrepreneurs. Instead, Giersch adopted the far-and-wide approach to risk and responsibility carrying entrepreneurship offered by Knight and Mises, and the special ability entrepreneur offered by Kirzner, all fellow MPS members. All these elements of an individualist entrepreneurial mindset fed the new perspective of entrepreneurial management, collaboration in innovation systems and "intrapreneurship," or "Schumpeter

46 See Davies, *The Limits of Neoliberalism.*

Mark 2."[47] Creative destruction would no longer require the boom and bust of the firm. Giersch raised the question: Is there "enough good entrepreneurial talent and if not . . . can [we] produce more of it by forming teams?" His "tentative" answer was "there is no shortage of entrepreneurial talent, but institutional resistances and technical requirements may create so complicated situations that no single person, but only a combination of persons, can successfully perform the entrepreneurial role.[48]

Herbert Giersch's entrepreneurship amounts to the paradox of individualism. The complexity of contemporary capitalism requires a collective effort disguised by a language of entrepreneurship. Individual entrepreneurial behavior aside, the discussion is focused on the firm, on capital, on technological knowledge, and on managerial skill for the entrepreneurial talent to work out. Since it is probably "easier for a person to acquire managerial skills than to accumulate capital, it appears evident that capitalists will normally hire entrepreneurs. In this case, capital becomes the limiting factor and the barrier to entry," writes Giersch.[49] Note that the person hires managerial skills suddenly rather than entrepreneurial talent. Entrepreneurial management of companies and regions is not considered in contrast to economic and political intervention and planning. Entrepreneurship criteria simply replace the traditional socioeconomic criteria (e.g. GDP per capita) for regional and national development. Weaker regions are no longer treated as equal. Deserving regions are those that support entrepreneurial initiative and forge an ever-closer alliance of public and private actors to this end.

In any case Giersch declined the invitation offered by several authors to integrate entrepreneurship into the realm of macroeconomic neoclassical equilibrium thinking. The important link between Schumpeter, Mises, Kirzner, Schmölders, and Giersch is the emphasis on market process, dynamic, and change. The vastly expanded vision of individual entrepreneurship we already found in the writing of Mises and expressed by some of the speakers at the 1970 MPS conference was thereby consolidated in a theoretical position, and was ready to be projected to ever

---

47 Sturn, *Varianten des Unternehmertums*, 10.
48 Herbert Giersch, "The Role of Entrepreneurship in the 1980s," *Kiel Discussion Papers* (August 1982): 5.
49 Ibid., 6.

wider classes of citizens within corporations (intrapreneurship) and outside. The underemployed and unemployed are turned into self-employed, provided the political institutions are adequately reformed and the incentives are right. Giersch calls this the demand side for entrepreneurship, "the demand permitted, induced or actively provoked by the socio-economic structure and the political and cultural environment."[50] The demand for entrepreneurship, in other words, depends on the social arrangements in support of economic freedom. "The central question is . . . What institutional frameworks are best-suited to tap the reservoir of entrepreneurial alertness which is certainly present among the members of society? The answer is that entrepreneurial talent is 'switched on' by the prospect of 'pure gain'—broadly defined to include fame, prestige, even the opportunity to serve a cause or to help others."[51] Progress in favor of entrepreneurship can thus be measured by reforms dedicated to enabling the prospect of pure gain, to advance economic freedom broadly conceived, and reaching far into the nonprofit sector to advance social entrepreneurship and civic engagement. Restrictions on economic freedom included the welfare state and the whole range of legal regulatory measures that compromise price signals.[52]

Conclusion

Excavating and reconstructing the entrepreneurship discourse from the 1960s to the 1980s complements the existing narrative about the rise of shareholder-value ideas in the United States. Apart from the American students of Ludwig von Mises like Israel Kirzner, many of the key actors were located in Europe. The rise of the German-language literature on the entrepreneurship topic (*Unternehmertum*) during the 1970s and

---

50 Ibid., 15.

51 Israel Kirzner, "The Primacy of Entrepreneurial Discovery," in *The Prime Mover of Progress*, ed. Seldon, Summary / Extracts 1–2.

52 The history of the institutionalization of policy instruments in support of entrepreneurship—such as the Economic Freedom Index, developed by the Canadian Fraser Institute with funding from the Liberty Fund (Indianapolis) during the second half of the 1980s and the early 1990s—remains to be written. See Steve H. Hanke and Stephen J. K. Walters, "Economic Freedom, Prosperity, and Equality: A Survey," *Cato Journal* 17, no. 2 (Fall 1997): 117–46, and Jim Stanford, *Economic Freedom for the Rest of Us* (Halifax: Canadian Autoworkers Union, 1999), at www.csls.ca.

1980s was arguably due to the challenges emanating from institutional restrictions like co-determination and corporatist arrangements. Paradoxically, arm's-length-type market relations gave rise to managerialism and planning in the United States, whereas institutions of coordinated capitalism generated a strong sensibility for the role and relevance of entrepreneurs.

But the new entrepreneurial behavior was certainly not just left as a choice for individuals. All kinds of state and private institutions involved in regional and business development, education, and even unemployment insurance and labor exchanges were involved in crafting the new entrepreneurship agendas quite in line with the thinking and advice of neoliberal intellectuals like Herbert Giersch. Take Germany as an example: transfer payments for economic development are no longer distributed evenly across space and population. They are redirected to promising locations and firms.[53] Private companies in turn provide incentives for intrapreneurship: most company units are now organized according to the cost-center principle to simulate market relations within corporations. The meaning and practice of managerialism has changed significantly as a result. Public sector universities receive additional funding specifically for the establishment of entrepreneurship chairs, and both public and an increasing number of private business schools and universities engage in entrepreneurship education and support for start-ups.[54]

Following the Hartz reforms of social security and unemployment insurance, long-term unemployed people in Germany are offered monthly payments to start their own business for up to three years. Hundreds of thousands of new small businesses dubbed Ich-AG (I-corporation) have been funded, albeit with mixed success. In any case it is clear that entrepreneurship and entrepreneurial behavior is not left to natural development or chance. There is a common and clear understanding across the mainstream political parties now to transform public and private institutions in support of entrepreneurship. Only a

---

53 Neil Brenner, "Building 'Euro-Regions': Locational Politics and the Political Geography of Neoliberalism in Post-Unification Germany," *European Urban and Regional Studies* 7, no. 4 (2000): 319–45.

54 Jasmina Haus, *Förderung von Unternehmertum und Unternehmensgründungen an deutschen Hochschulen* (Lohmar: Josef Eul Verlag, 2006). By 2017, German universities counted 133 entrepreneurship chairs. Although the United States had already reached the number of 400 chairs in 2004, the number of chairs per capita are now approximately even in the US and Germany. Compare the tables and statistics supplied by FGF e.V. online at fgf-ev.de.

lack of political initiative and stamina gives reason for pessimism, pace Schumpeter.

While Mises is not invoked nearly as frequently in the ongoing revival as Schumpeter, it is the former who can be seen smiling. Following the general theory of *Human Action*, neoliberals subscribe to the axiomatic statement according to which the *potential* supply of entrepreneurship is unlimited. Demand can be raised, according to Giersch, by ending the growth of restrictive rules and regulations, by way of overcoming the "domestic imperialism of the welfare state," by stopping "the growth of bureaucracy within industry, greatly but only partly induced by government bureaucracy," and by ending "excessive wage pressures from organized labor."[55] Freedom of action thus becomes freedom of profit-oriented management, and the entrepreneurial self is shrinking to self-reliance and individual responsibility of those not fortunate enough to forge a liaison with capital owners.

---

55 Giersch, "Role of Entrepreneurship," 12.

6

Human Behavior as a Limit to and a Means of State Intervention: Günter Schmölders and Behavioral Economics

Rüdiger Graf

Over the last fifteen years, behavioral economists have increasingly provided policy-makers with the expertise to use the heuristics and biases of people's decision-making processes in order to influence or, in the words of Richard Thaler and Cass Sunstein, "nudge" them in the spirit of what they call "libertarian paternalism."[1] Criticizing this approach, the French economist Gilles Saint-Paul argues that the growing influence of the behavioral and social sciences on policy-making might lead to a "tyranny of utility."[2] Referring to F. A. Hayek's *The Road to Serfdom*, he describes economics as the guardian of individual liberty and the values of the Enlightenment. Recent developments, he suggests, threaten these ideals: "If current trends continue, I foresee a gradual elimination of individual freedom as 'social science' makes progress in documenting behavioral biases, measuring happiness, and evaluating the effects of coercive policies."[3] Whereas Hayek feared social democracy, communism, and National Socialism, Saint-Paul sees tyranny lurking in present-day behavioral policy. Neoliberal critics of state

---

1 Richard H. Thaler and Cass R. Sunstein, "Libertarian Paternalism," *The American Economic Review* 93, no. 2 (2003); Richard H. Thaler and Cass R. Sunstein, *Nudge: Improving Decisions About Health, Wealth and Happiness* (London: Penguin Books, 2009). I would like to thank Ralf Ahrens, Dieter Plehwe, and Quinn Slobodian for their helpful suggestions and critical comments on this chapter.

2 Gilles Saint-Paul, *The Tyranny of Utility: Behavioral Social Science and the Rise of Paternalism* (Princeton: Princeton University Press, 2011); Thaler and Sunstein, *Nudge*.

3 Saint-Paul, *The Tyranny of Utility*, 4.

interventionism echo this rejection. In 2014, for example, when Angela Merkel announced the creation of a government unit on behavioral policy (catching up on a development that had already taken place in most other Western countries),[4] Mont Pèlerin Society member Philip Plickert immediately rejected the idea as driven by a paternalistic intrusion into private lives.[5]

The source of the conflict between behavioral economics—or, more broadly, behavioral public policy—and neoliberalism, seems evident at first glance. After all, behavioral economists reject the homo economicus of neoclassical economics upon which neoliberals are assumed to make their claims.[6] Behavioral economists contend that individuals possess only a limited or "bounded rationality" that restricts their capacity to act freely as their decision-making processes are influenced by irrelevant factors. Systematically and predictably, people fail to choose what is in their best interest. If human capacities to appreciate costs and benefits, evaluate probabilities or exercise self-control are severely limited by behavioral principles beyond individual control, people are only "free to choose"—as Milton and Rose Friedman entitled their popular book and TV series—in a restricted sense of the word freedom.[7]

Yet closer examination reveals a more complex relationship, demonstrating that the gap between behavioral economics and neoliberal thought may not be as wide as it seems. Hayek, the founding father of the MPS, rejected the abstraction of homo economicus in favor of a subjectivism characteristic of Austrian economics. He also thought it was impossible to achieve full knowledge and saw the imperfections of human rationality as reasons to advocate the market as a clearing mechanism between competing perspectives and interests.[8] Hence, in

---

4 Mark Whitehead et al., "Nudging all over the World: Assessing the Global Impact of the Behavioral Sciences on Public Policy," at changingbehaviours.files.wordpress.com.

5 Philip Plickert, "Paternalisten," *Frankfurter Allgemeine Zeitung*, August 27, 2014.

6 S. Mullainathan and Richard H. Thaler, "Behavioral Economics," in *International Encyclopedia of the Social & Behavioral Sciences*, N. J. Smelser and P. B. Baltes, eds. vol. 2 (Amsterdam: Elsevier Science, 2001), 2, 1095.

7 Sören Brandes, "'Free to Choose': Die Popularisierung des Neoliberalismus in Milton Friedmans Fernsehserie (1980/90)," *Zeithistorische Forschungen/Studies in Contemporary History* 12, no. 3 (2015).

8 F. A. Hayek, "Economics and Knowledge" (London Economic Club, November 10, 1936), in *Individualism and Economic Order* (Chicago: University of Chicago Press, 1948); Hayek, "Individualism: True and False" (Twelfth Finlay Lecture, Dublin, December 17, 1945), in ibid.; Hayek, "The Overrated Reason," *Journal of the History of Economic Thought* 35, no. 2 (2013).

1986 the editors of the first handbook on behavioral economics quoted
Hayek approvingly.[9] More recently, he has even been described as a
first-generation behavioral economist in line with Herbert Simon,
George Katona, Harvey Leibenstein, Richard Nelson, and Sidney
Winter.[10]

This chapter offers a further contribution to the study of the ambivalent relationship between neoliberalism and behavioral economics by
examining the lesser-known German finance and taxation expert
Günter Schmölders, who served as president of the MPS from 1968 to
1970. As a professor in Cologne in the 1950s, Schmölders founded his
own research institute on "empirical socioeconomics" or "economic
behavioral research," trying to integrate findings from the social and
anthropological sciences into economic reasoning and developing an
early and now largely forgotten version of behavioral economics.[11]
Analyzing Schmölders's extensive writings on economics under three
different political regimes, I will try to answer the question of how he
reconciled the rejection of homo economicus and the emphasis on the
need for behavioral research with an approach to economics that made
him a prominent member of what has been described as the neoliberal
thought collective.[12] On the one hand, I will argue that, in the vein of
German ordoliberalism, Schmölders criticized certain forms of state
intervention but, in general, favored a strong state to guarantee functioning markets. On the other hand, it will turn out that acknowledging
behavioral biases and rejecting a rational, self-interested decision-maker
can serve as a reason for both restricting and enhancing state intervention. Therefore, behavioral economics can promiscuously serve various
economic policies.

9   Benjamin Gilad and Stanley Kaish, eds, *Handbook of Behavioral Economics:
Behavioral Microeconomics* (Greenwich, CT: Jai Press, 1986), xx–xxi: "As early as 1945,
Hayek's famous essay, 'The Use of Knowledge in Society,' contended that the most
important function of the market system is 'the utilization of knowledge which is not
given to anyone in its totality.'"

10   Roger Frantz, "Frederick [*sic*] Hayek's Behavioral Economics in Historical
Context," in *Hayek and Behavioral Economics*, ed. Roger Frantz and Robert Leeson
(Basingstoke: Palgrave Macmillan, 2013), 1.

11   Floris Heukelom's history of behavioral economics does not even mention
Schmölders, who had only limited reception in the Anglophone world. Floris Heukelom,
Behavioral Economics: A History (Cambridge: Cambridge University Press, 2014).

12   Philip Mirowski, "Postface: Defining Neoliberalism," in *The Road from Mont
Pèlerin*, ed. Philip Mirowski and Dieter Plehwe (Cambridge, MA: Harvard University
Press, 2009).

After outlining Schmölders's academic upbringing in Weimar Germany and his early career under National Socialism, I analyze why and how he developed his theory of behavioral economics, comparing it with the simultaneous, yet largely independent, emergence of Herbert A. Simon's conception of "bounded rationality" in the United States.[13] After that, I will examine to what extent Schmölders's analysis of human behavior that drew on results from neighboring disciplines informed his economic expertise and policy advice in the Federal Republic of Germany. In conclusion, I will try to assess both Schmölders's specific version of behavioral neoliberalism as well as the relationship between neoliberalism and behavioral economics more generally.

Alcohol, Taxation, and Price Policy—Schmölders in Weimar and the Third Reich

Günter Schmölders was born in 1903, the son of a lawyer and grandson of the Breslau orientalist August Franz Schmölders. In Berlin and Tübingen he studied political economics (*Staatswissenschaften*), receiving his doctorate in 1926 with a study of different systems of prohibition in Northern Europe. Six years later, Schmölders wrote his habilitation thesis on the fiscal potential of alcoholic beverage taxation, before becoming a professor of political economy at the University of Breslau. In 1940, he assumed the prestigious chair for political economy at the University of Cologne, now focusing on finance. A member of the National Socialist German Workers' Party (NSDAP) since May 1933, as well as of the *Schutzstaffel* SS from 1933 to 1937, he served in various functions as an economic advisor during the Third Reich. Yet, during the war, Schmölders also drafted an economic program for European postwar recovery for the oppositional Kreisauer Kreis. After 1945, Schmölders resumed his position in Cologne, heading the Financial Research Institute from 1950, founding the Research Center for Empirical Socioeconomics (*Forschungsstelle für empirische Sozialökonomik*) in 1958, and becoming the university's president in 1965 and 1966. He remained in Cologne until his retirement in 1973, served as a member of the Scientific Advisory Board of the German

---

13 Herbert A. Simon, "Behavioral Model of Rational Choice," *Journal of Economics* 69 (1955).

Federal Ministry of Finance from 1949 to 1972 and of the directorate of the Federation of German Tax Payers from 1951 to 1991. On Hayek's invitation, he presented a paper on progressive taxation at the Mont Pèlerin Society's meeting at Seelisberg in 1953 and became a member.[14] At its seventh conference in Aviemore, Scotland, in 1968, Schmölders was elected president and organized the following meeting in Munich in 1970 which, on his suggestion, was dedicated to the "entrepreneur in modern economy and society."[15]

In his early works in Weimar Germany, Schmölders examined the economic and fiscal as well as general political and social effects of the prohibition and taxation of alcoholic beverages, touching upon themes that would occupy him for the rest of his life as an economist, political advisor, and public intellectual.[16] Schmölders criticized prohibition because it failed to reduce alcohol abuse and had negative side effects, undermining state authority, harming the economy, and decreasing state revenues. In particular, the "massive sociological experiment" in the United States had failed to change the "deeply rooted habits of the whole of humanity."[17] Comparing the taxation of alcoholic beverages in various countries in his habilitation thesis, Schmölders concluded that taxes could not effectively reduce alcohol consumption but only help to increase state revenues.[18] In general, Schmölders maintained that it was paradoxical to use taxation to influence consumption patterns and improve public health, because reaching the non-fiscal goal simultaneously diminished the fiscal effect. Even worse, taxation for non-fiscal purposes would undermine people's willingness to pay taxes as well as their loyalty to the state.[19] In his inaugural lecture at Berlin University in January 1932, Schmölders generalized these findings further, arguing

---

14   Communication and paper in: Hoover Institution, Stanford CA, Schmölders (Günter) papers 1940-1985, 85017 [hereafter: Hoover Institution, Schmölders papers], Box-folder 179.

15   On the meeting see Plehwe's contribution to this volume.

16   Günter Schmölders, *Prohibition im Norden: Die staatliche Bekämpfung des Alkoholismus in den nordischen Ländern* (Berlin: Unger, 1926).

17   Günter Schmölders, *Die Prohibition in den Vereinigten Staaten: Triebkräfte und Auswirkungen des amerikanischen Alkoholverbots* (Leipzig: C. L. Hirschfeld, 1930), v.

18   Günter Schmölders, *Die Ertragsfähigkeit der Getränkesteuern: Vergleichende Übersicht über die Voraussetzungen der Alkoholbesteuerung im Deutschen Reich, in Großbritannien, Frankreich, der Schweiz, Dänemark und den Vereinigten Staaten: ein Beitrag zur deutschen Finanzreform* (Jena: Fischer, 1932), 4–5.

19   Ibid., 2–4 and 232–4.

that there was a specific tax morale that differed from conceptions of morality in other fields.[20] This tax morale could easily be undermined if people felt overburdened or treated unfairly or even if the state spent tax revenues unwisely. These beliefs—which Schmölders developed in the second half of his twenties while the legitimacy of the Weimar Republic eroded due to attacks from left- and right-wing extremists as well as the growing discontent among conservative elites with the parliamentary system—continued to guide his academic research and political interventions in the Federal Republic of Germany.

In the meantime, like many other academics of his generation, Schmölders eagerly offered his expertise to the construction of the National Socialist state and economic order. He joined the NSDAP in May 1933 and the SS in November of the same year. Moreover, he became a member of the Association of National Socialist Lawyers (NS-Rechtswahrerbund), the National Socialist Lecturers' League (NS-Dozentenbund), the Academy for German Law (Akademie für Deutsches Recht) in 1938, worked for the *Deutsche Arbeitsfront* (DAF), and functioned as an advisor to the *Gauleiter* of Silesia Josef Wagner.[21] After Schmölders had sent a card announcing the birth of his first daughter to the SS-journal *Das Schwarze Korps* in 1936, an investigation followed because the SS *Rasse- und Siedlungshauptamt* had no records of having granted him permission to marry. Schmölders defended himself vigorously, claiming that he had asked for and received permission, after having obtained an expert opinion from a race researcher at the Department of the Interior on his wife because, being born in France, she lacked documentation about her ancestors.[22] Before the issue was settled, however, Schmölders left the SS voluntarily, allegedly for health reasons.

Schmölders gained influence during the war as an economic adviser in Jens Jessen's class at the Academy for German Law, heading the working group on price policy. The group assembled central figures of German ordoliberalism, such as Walter Eucken and Franz Böhm, who were critical of the controlled war economy. After the war, Schmölders

20 Günter Schmölders, *Steuermoral und Steuerbelastung* (Berlin: C. Heymann, 1932).

21   Bundesarchiv, Berlin-Lichterfelde (hereafter BArch), Sammlung Berlin Document Center: PK/Parteikorrespondenz, VBS 1/1170012440, Q 0065.

22 BArch, Sammlung Berlin Document Center: Personenbezogene Unterlagen der SS und SA, R 9361-III/180670, F 0473.

repeatedly described the workings of this group as resistance against the Third Reich, especially referring to a conference at which a future conspirator against Hitler, Peter Graf Yorck von Wartenburg, was present.[23] The publication of the proceedings as "Competition as a Means to Enhance Economic Performance and Selection," which argued that the market mechanism was superior to price controls and state monopolies in stimulating economic performance, was indeed courageous, as any critique was under the conditions of the National Socialist dictatorship. Yet, the contributions hardly amounted to resistance against the Third Reich, as the National Socialists had few fixed views on economic policy, and the book offered suggestions on how to improve it, focusing in particular on the postwar economic order.[24]

Carefully calibrating his suggestions with National Socialist ideas, in 1941 Schmölders even declared at a public lecture celebrating the National Socialist seizure of power that the current "elastic administration of the price stop" was best suited to fulfill Hitler's demand of "wage price stability."[25] In the same speech, Schmölders praised National Socialist economic policy, acknowledging the Führer's demand that economics had to serve politics. He claimed that the first four-year plan had been the most magnificent example of economic policy ever conducted, and encouraged its further study because it had revolutionized existing theories of business cycles.[26] According to Schmölders, National Socialist economic policy was superior because the authoritarian state offered greater opportunities for technocracy. In contrast to democratic and parliamentary systems, Schmölders argued, there was no need to accommodate politicians and interest groups in a dictatorship as the government could rely solely on the advice of economic

23 Günter Schmölders, *Lebenserinnerungen: "Gut durchgekommen?"* (Berlin: Duncker & Humblot, 1988), 1, 64—82; Hoover Institution, Schmölders papers, Box-folder 127.

24 Ludolf Herbst, *Der Totale Krieg und die Ordnung der Wirtschaft: Die Kriegswirtschaft im Spannungsfeld von Politik, Ideologie und Propaganda 1939–1945* (Stuttgart: Deutsche Verlags-Anstalt, 1982); Ralf Ptak, *Vom Ordoliberalismus zur Sozialen Marktwirtschaft: Stationen des Neoliberalismus in Deutschland* (Wiesbaden: VS Verlag für Sozialwissenschaften, 2004), 61–2.

25 Günter Schmölders, *Wirtschaftslenkung als angewandte Wirtschaftswissenschaft: Festrede gehalten bei der Feier des Tages der nationalen Erhebung verbunden mit der feierlichen Immatrikulation für das Trimester 1941 am 29. Januar 1941* (Cologne: Oskar Müller Verlag, 1941).

26 Ibid., 16.

experts.[27] In Schmölders's view, German economic experts were superior to those populating Franklin D. Roosevelt's "Brains Trust" because they could rely on the "creative powers of the German spirit with its sense for thorough and systematic planning" and organization.[28]

It would overlook the nature of the National Socialist dictatorship to take Schmölders's public utterances at face value and conclude that he was an illiberal advocate of central planning. On the contrary, he was critical of monopolistic and collectivistic tendencies and preferred a market-oriented economic system, as his 1942/43 memorandum for the Kreisauer Kreis on "The Economy and Economic Leadership in a European Bloc after the War" shows.[29] Economic competition in a market economy, Schmölders argued, was ideally suited to increase efficiency and stimulate growth as the price mechanism awarded the best and punished the worst product better than any planning institution.[30] While Schmölders considered it necessary to stimulate and enhance individual economic performance, he rejected plans, orders, and other external incentives. Rather, the innate desire to gain money and achieve social recognition should be set free. While competition was the fundamental principle to engender economic prosperity, Schmölders acknowledged that it could produce inefficiencies and injustice and, therefore, needed a strong state, setting a legal order to guarantee its functioning. In this respect, his vision of the future economic order was in line with fellow ordoliberals like Ludwig Erhard, Alexander Müller-Armack, and the Freiburg School, who later helped to create the "social market economy" in the Federal Republic.[31] For some time after the war, Schmölders even saw the "necessity of some steering of production" at least in "parts of the economy." This should be done by means of subsidies and benefits that would not disturb the price mechanism in principle.[32] In sum, Schmölders's early writings exhibit both an adherence to the core principles of ordoliberalism (superiority of markets;

27 Ibid., 23.
28 Ibid., 26.
29 Günter Schmölders, "Wirtschaft und Wirtschaftsführung in einem Europa-Block nach dem Kriege," in *Personalistischer Sozialismus: Die Wirtschaftsordnungskonzeption des Kreisauer Kreises der deutschen Widerstandsbewegung* (Cologne: Westdeutscher Verlag, 1969), 67–91; similar statements in Hoover Institution, Schmölders papers, Box-folders 21-23.
30 Ibid., 76.
31 Ptak, *Ordoliberalismus*, 90–132.
32 Schmölders, *Wirtschaft und Wirtschaftsführung*, 88.

need for a strong state to secure economic competition) and a flexibility to adapt them to changing political circumstances. His economic liberalism had apparently no intrinsic connection to civil liberties and democratic political institutions, as will also become clear in his later interventions as a public intellectual.

Economic Behavioral Research and Empirical Socioeconomics in Cologne

Staying in his position as a professor in Cologne and becoming the director of the university's Financial Research Institute in the 1950s, Schmölders pursued two different but closely interconnected research interests. On the one hand, he scrutinized different methods of taxation in order to offer political advice for the reform of the German taxation system. On the other hand, he set out to develop a new academic field that he called "economic behavioral research" (ökonomische Verhaltensforschung) or, later, "empirical socioeconomics" (empirische Sozialökonomik). Comparing taxation systems in various countries, Schmölders developed a "General Theory of Taxation" that was supposed to offer scientific guidance for the "Great" or "Organic Tax Reform" in the Federal Republic. According to Schmölders and many of his colleagues, a general overhaul of the German taxation system was necessary because the taxation levels that resulted from "dictatorship and the war economy" impeded rationalization and risk-taking.[33] In their report for the German Ministry of Finance, most taxation experts agreed that exceedingly high taxes would undermine the market economy itself.[34] While there were some dissenting voices, arguing that the potential to change the wealth distribution by means of taxation was higher, most experts assumed that above a rather low "psychological breaking point" (using the English term in their report), tax resistance would intensify and tax morale decrease.[35]

---

33 Günter Schmölders, Die große Steuerreform (Bad Nauheim: Vita-Verlag, 1953), 5–6.

34 Wissenschaftlicher Beirat beim Bundesministerium der Finanzen, ed., Organische Steuerreform: Bericht an den Herrn Bundesminister der Finanzen (Bonn, 1953), 12. Fritz Terhalle was head of the advisory council and Günter Schmölders among those members who drafted the final report.

35 Ibid., 12.

When Arthur Laffer was still a child, Schmölders's primary research interest was to locate this psychological breaking point and, thereby, deduce the ideal level of taxation. In his "General Theory of Taxation," he argued that the essential purpose of taxation was to provide the state with financial resources to fulfill its basic functions, namely, to guarantee the freedom and security of its population and to offer a stable legal framework for economic and social activity to take place.[36] In line with German ordoliberalism, he did not deny the necessity and legitimacy of taxation in order to sustain these vital state functions. At the same time, however, he vigorously criticized taxes for "non-fiscal purposes," especially those that were supposed to influence people's behavior. Coming back to the theme of his inaugural lecture and drawing on earlier works by Wilhelm Gerloff and others, Schmölders emphasized that the "economic and psychological preconditions on which every taxation depended" would prevent the production of state revenues if non-fiscal purposes dominated.[37] If the burden of taxation increased, people's "taxation morale" would decrease and they would try to avoid paying taxes. Having studied the Swedish tax-payers' movement already in the 1920s, Schmölders became one of the founding fathers of its German counterpart, the German Taxpayers Federation.[38] Simultaneously, he broadened the scope of his research on "taxation psychology" towards a general financial psychology.[39]

In order to understand people's financial and economic activity, Schmölders argued, it was inadequate to conceptualize them as rational utility maximizers presuming a "primitive hedonism." In his view, developments in psychology in the twentieth century had rendered such an understanding of human beings obsolete.[40] Moreover, Schmölders criticized the "eclectic psychologisms" put forward by other economists, in particular by John Maynard Keynes, who used concepts like "liquidity preference," "saving propensity," "inducement

36 Günter Schmölders, *Allgemeine Steuerlehre* (Stuttgart: Humboldt-Verlag, 1951).
37 Ibid., 44.
38 Günter Schmölders, *Ursprung und Entwicklung der Steuerzahlerbewegung*, 2nd edition (Bad Wörishofen: Holzmann, 1977).
39 Günter Schmölders, "Das neue Finanzwissenschaftliche Forschungsinstitut," in *Finanzwissenschaftliche Forschung und Lehre an der Universität zu Köln 1927–1967*, ed. Wilhelm von Menges (Berlin: Duncker & Humblot, 1967), 41.
40 Günter Schmölders, "Finanzpsychologie," *FinanzArchiv/Public Finance Analysis*, New Series 133, no. 1 (1951/52), 2; Günter Schmölders, *Das Irrationale in der öffentlichen Finanzwirtschaft: Probleme der Finanzpsychologie* (Hamburg: Rowohlt, 1960).

to invest/save," or "propensity to consume."[41] Rather, economists should take the full spectrum of emotional attitudes and psychological motivations into account, making use of the most advanced sophisticated psychological techniques they could find in interdisciplinary exchanges.[42] According to Schmölders, depth psychology rendered the idea of the rational homo economicus absurd. He remarked ironically that it was even more absurd to assume a "gladly giving" or a "stupid" human being, a "homo libenter contribuens" or a "homo stultus," as some policy-makers apparently did.[43] Against these idealizations or even caricatures, Schmölders emphasized the need for empirical research on the actual behavior of economic actors in real-world situations, as was conducted at his Research Center on Empirical Socioeconomics.

In 1953, Schmölders published a first programmatic paper on "economic behavioral research" in the journal *Ordo*, which Walter Eucken and Franz Böhm had founded after World War II, giving German ordoliberalism its name.[44] Publication in *Ordo*, however, did not mean that other ordoliberals endorsed his ideas. On the contrary, Fritz W. Meyer and Hans Otto Lenel—who had both studied with Walter Eucken in Freiburg and now functioned as *Ordo's* editors, with Meyer also being a member of the Mont Pèlerin Society—explicitly distanced themselves from Schmölders's article in their preface: "One paper in this volume calls for an economic behavioral research. We have to admit that we do not agree with the author on essential points but we hope that the article may stimulate discussion on this special topic."[45]

In contrast to the editors' assessment, Schmölders had not intended to write a treatise on a specialized topic. Rather, he proposed a thorough reorientation of economics as it was commonly researched and taught in academia. In no other field of knowledge, according to Schmölders, was the gap between theory and practice wider than between economic research and economic policy, since economists had withdrawn into an "ivory tower of mathematical abstractions and hypothetical logicisms."[46]

---

41 Schmölders, "Finanzpsychologie," 2.

42 Ibid., 2.

43 Ibid., S. 22.

44 Günter Schmölders, "Ökonomische Verhaltensforschung," *Ordo. Jahrbuch für die Ordnung von Wirtschaft und Gesellschaft* 5 (1953).

45 Fritz W. Meyer and Hans O. Lenel, "Vorwort," *Ordo. Jahrbuch für die Ordnung von Wirtschaft und Gesellschaft* 5 (1953), IX.

46 Schmölders, "Ökonomische Verhaltensforschung," 204.

Economic behavioral research was Schmölders's attempt to bridge the
gap and overcome the predicament. He carefully distinguished his
approach from a narrower understanding of traditional behaviorism.
Economists should make use of all "anthropological sciences" that
offered insights into the motives, incentives, and impetuses of economic
activity: "psychology of the conscious and unconscious (including its
behavioristic branches), biology and brain science, . . . as well as sociology, history, social anthropology, linguistics and comparative animal
ethology and sociology."[47]

For Schmölders, the Archimedean point that economics had lacked
thus far was to be found in the "laws of human nature," the invariant
elements of economic behavior.[48] The first victim of such a "realistic"
approach to economic phenomena was the figure of the homo
economicus. It was not only modern psychology that rendered it
implausible for Schmölders. Ethnographic research also suggested
that the variety of economic exchanges in different cultures could be
captured more adequately with the assumption of a "homo institu-
tionalis" governed by unwritten customary laws of morality.[49] Close
but without reference to Hayek's ideas about the evolutionary primacy
of customs and habits over reason,[50] Schmölders even referred to
animal ethologists whose experiments allegedly proved that certain
apes exhibited forms of economic behavior commonly ascribed to
human beings.[51] Therefore, drawing on Arnold Gehlen's conservative
philosophical anthropology, Schmölders suggested that economics
should neither postulate an idealized decision-maker nor start with
the individual economic choice act. In contrast to Hayek, he did not
make the argument that economists could "derive from the knowledge of our own mind in an 'a priori' or 'deductive' or 'analytic' fashion an (at least in principle) exhaustive classification of all the possible forms of intelligible behavior."[52] Rather, Schmölders suggested
that economists should use the means of the neighboring social

47 Ibid., 205.
48 Ibid., 206.
49 Ibid., 221.
50 Hayek, "The Overrated Reason"; see also Hayek, "Individualism."
51 Günter Schmölders, *Der verlorene Untertan: Verhaltensforschung enthüllt die
Krise zwischen Staatsbürger und Obrigkeit* (Düsseldorf: ECON, 1971), 14–15.
52 F. A. Hayek, "The Facts of the Social Sciences" (Cambridge, November 19, 1942),
in *Individualism and Economic Order*, 68, fn. 8; see also Frantz, "Frederick Hayek's
Behavioral Economics," 15.

sciences in order to empirically scrutinize the "predictable, regular, and to a certain degree evocable behavior that may be called quasi-instinctive or quasi-automatic."[53]

The paradigmatic cases for Schmölders's plea to introduce psychological and behavioral insights into economic reasoning came from the realm of public and private finance, focusing on tax morale, trust in money, and the psychology of saving. While these fields formed the core of its research agenda, the Research Center for Empirical Socioeconomics also ventured into other areas. Ten years after the presentation of his research program, Schmölders presented the institute's achievements again in *Ordo*.[54] Acknowledging that his previous article had failed to spark a debate in the journal, Schmölders proudly presented fifty-seven publications on what he now called "socioeconomic behavioral research" (*sozialökonomische Verhaltensforschung*) that had been produced in Cologne. Working together with renowned public opinion and market research institutes, such as Emnid and Allensbach, as well as with the Institute for Applied Mathematics, Schmölders's research center had conducted numerous surveys. They analyzed people's attitudes towards taxation and the state, political decision-makers' knowledge and views on taxation, and, more generally, how individual households spent their money, and their attitudes towards consumption and savings.

With his non-behavioristic approach to the analysis of empirically observable behavior, Schmölders was a rather solitary figure in the German academic economics of his time.[55] Yet, he was part of a broader international trend of the 1950s to naturalize behavior and analyze it by social scientific means. Especially in the United States, a funding scheme initiated by the Ford Foundation launched a "behavioral revolution," re-organizing large parts of the social and human sciences under the label "behavioral sciences" in order to improve the understanding of all aspects of human behavior.[56] Neoclassical economists,

---

53 Schmölders, "Ökonomische Verhaltensforschung," 214.

54 Günter Schmölders, "10 Jahre sozialökonomische Verhaltensforschung in Köln," *Ordo. Jahrbuch für die Ordnung von Wirtschaft und Gesellschaft* 14 (1963).

55 Hayek was equally careful in distinguishing his approach from classical behaviorism. Hayek, "The Facts of the Social Sciences," 65.

56 Bernard R. Berelson, "Behavioral Sciences," in *International Encyclopedia of the Social Sciences*, vol. 2 (1968), 2; Jefferson Pooley, "A 'Not Particularly Felicitous' Phrase: A History of the 'Behavioral Sciences' Label," *Serendipities* 1 (2016).

however, generally shied away from interdisciplinary collaboration on human behavior.[57] An exception to the rule were members of the Cowles Commission at the University of Chicago and protagonists of early consumers' research, such as George Katona.[58] Having already advised the Ford Foundation on its program for the behavioral sciences in particular, Herbert A. Simon formulated a research agenda that resembled Schmölders's economic behavioral research. Having worked on theories of organization and administration, in 1955 Simon suggested to "substitute for 'economic man' or 'administrative man' a choosing organism of limited knowledge and ability. This organism's simplifications of the real world for purposes of choice introduce discrepancies between the simplified model and the reality; and these discrepancies, in turn, serve to explain many of the phenomena of organizational behavior."[59] Simon wanted to develop a theoretical model of "rational behavior that is compatible with the access to information and the computational capacities that are actually possessed by organisms, including man, in the kinds of environments in which they exist."[60] While this idea of a "bounded rationality" became influential for the ascendency of behavioral economics in the 1980s, Schmölders was not that successful and his empirical socioeconomics appear rather as an episode in the history of German economics.[61]

Schmölders claimed that he had been unaware of Simon and the efforts of the Ford Foundation before the publication of his programmatic piece in *Ordo*. Yet, afterwards he saw it as a boon to his position.[62] Despite their differences in intellectual scope, theoretical ambition, and style, there were salient commonalities between Schmölders's and Simon's early attempts to establish a research program in behavioral

57 Jefferson Pooley and Mark Solovey, "Marginal to the Revolution: The Curious Relationship between Economics and the Behavioral Sciences Movement in Mid-Twentieth-Century America," *History of Political Economy* 42 (annual supplement) (2010), 200.

58 Heukelom, *Behavioral Economics*, 48–82; Esther-Mirjam Sent, "Behavioral Economics: How Psychology Made Its (limited) Way Back into Economics," *History of Political Economy* 36, no. 4 (2004); Philip Mirowski, *Machine Dreams: Economics Becomes a Cyborg Science* (Cambridge: Cambridge University Press, 2002), 242–55, 266.

59 Simon, "Behavioral Model of Rational Choice," 114.

60 Ibid., 99.

61 Matthias Klaes and Esther-Mirjam Sent, "A Conceptual History of the Emergence of Bounded Rationality," *History of Political Economy* 37, no. 1 (2005).

62 Günter Schmölders, *Ökonomische Verhaltensforschung* (Cologne & Opladen: Westdeutscher Verlag, 1957), 41.

economics. To begin with, both rejected the ideal of the homo economicus as inadequate, while advocating the empirical analysis of the decisions of real people in actual situations. Moreover, deviating from methodological individualism that focused on the individual choice act, they
looked for patterns of choice or principles of behavior in larger groups
that made individual actions predictable. In addition, they did not
consider these behavioral patterns specific to human beings; some of
them allegedly were also found in apes or, as Simon would suggest,
construed in machines. Characteristically, Simon spoke of "choosing
organisms."[63] Finally, both looked at neighboring disciplines for methodological help and theoretical inspiration in order to understand the
principles of human behavior, demanding the interdisciplinary opening
up of economics. In particular, they advocated the reintroduction of
psychology into economics. In contrast to the earlier subjective value
theory, however, psychological motives of economic behavior should
not be determined by means of introspection but through the most
advanced methods of the social and behavioral sciences.[64]

Behavioral Limits to State Intervention

As Günter Schmölders's political statements and interventions clearly
show, the assumption of the homo economicus, or rather of rational and
self-interested actors, is not a necessary condition for the neoliberal
advocacy of market mechanisms. On the contrary, Hayek himself had
emphasized repeatedly that the limits to individual knowledge made
market mechanisms necessary to allocate knowledge and negotiate
supply and demand.[65] Economics, for Hayek, tried to answer the question that he considered central to all social sciences, namely "how can
the combination of fragments of knowledge existing in different minds
bring about results which, if they were to be brought about deliberately,

---

63 Simon, "Behavioral Model of Rational Choice," 114; Mirowski, *Machine Dreams*,
argues that Simon "was simulating the operation of a number of problem-solving tasks
as though they were the manipulation of symbols on something very nearly
approximating a serial von Neumann architecture" (464).

64 Sent, "Behavioral Economics."

65 F. A. Hayek, "The Pretense of Knowledge" (Nobel Memorial Lecture, Stockholm,
December 11, 1974), in *New Studies in Philosophy, Politics, Economics and the History of
Ideas* (Chicago: University of Chicago Press, 1978).

would require a knowledge on the part of the directing mind which no single person can possess?"[66] Focusing not on the economy as a whole but on individual economic actors, Schmölders argued that irrational factors influenced their economic choices, circumscribing their freedom to choose what was in their best interest.[67] Whereas other neoliberals, like Gary Becker, maintained that predictions assuming behavior in line with the homo economicus could still produce valid results,[68] Schmölders argued that explanations could only rarely confine themselves to the hypothesis of economic rationality alone but had to integrate sociological and psychological factors.[69] For Schmölders these non-economic principles of human behavior not only influenced individual economic activity but also, and more importantly, established boundaries for state intervention into the economy.

The argument concerning the behavioral limits of state intervention, which Schmölders used repeatedly as a political advisor and public intellectual, had already been implied in his early research on the prohibition or taxation of alcoholic beverages. Here, Schmölders had tried to show that people's customs and habits were stronger than the state's means of influence. Generalizing this position in his financial psychology, Schmölders argued that politicians could not and should not impose taxes that ignored or contradicted the basic principles of "human nature."[70] High taxes would necessarily result in tax evasion, effectively reduce state revenues, and even undermine the citizens' loyalty to state institutions. In an imperfect world, the state and its officials had to consider the "human, all too human" factors, Schmölders argued in Nietzschean terms. He declared that it was a mistake to view citizens only as tax payers whose behavior could easily be changed by setting financial incentives.[71] Referring to the German sociologist Hans Freyer, who had advocated a "revolution from the right" in Weimar Germany and turned conservative again after his disillusionment with National Socialism, Schmölders rejected the belief in the "malleability of everything" (die

---

66 Hayek, "Economics and Knowledge," 54.

67 Schmölders, Das Irrationale in der öffentlichen Finanzwirtschaft, 9.

68 Gary S. Becker, "Irrational Behavior and Economic Theory," Journal of Political Economy 70, no. 1 (1962).

69 Schmölders, "10 Jahre sozialökonomische Verhaltensforschung in Köln," 265.

70 Schmölders, "Finanzpsychologie," 8.

71 Günter Schmölders, "Der Staatsbürger als Steuerzahler: Wandlungen des Menschenbildes in Finanzwissenschaft und Steuerpraxis," FinanzArchiv/Public Finance Analysis 27, no. 1/2 (1968), 121.

Machbarkeit aller Dinge). He considered it wrong to conceive of citizens as the mere material of political designs.[72] On the contrary, Schmölders argued that human nature set the boundaries for political interventions into society and economy. His socioeconomic behavioral research, in turn, was the means to establish the fundamental principles of human behavior and thus the limits to interventionism.

In the 1950s and 1960s, Schmölders's institute conducted surveys on consumption and savings behavior of workers as well as lower- and middle-class clerks in order to assess the viability of state programs to encourage private savings. He did not generally oppose these programs but established significant differences in their effects on the accumulation of personal wealth among workers and employees. While both low-income and white-collar workers behaved similarly, spending wage increases for immediate consumption, above a certain level of income they differed. Whereas workers still consumed more, employees started to save money and build up personal savings. Thus, Schmölders concluded that global wage increases would not lead to a buildup of wealth among workers. Accordingly, state policies to encourage the accumulation of private property and savings could only address the middle-income employees because "the masses of the workers and lower employees today do not have the necessary inner prerequisites that would empower them to build up capital; they naturally spend income increases on consumption."[73] It was impossible, Schmölders maintained, to instill a behavior that had no support in the life worlds of the strata of society in question. Despite looking at the upper classes for behavioral orientation, workers adopted only the openly visible markers of success but not savings behavior. Moreover, according to Schmölders, the many additional benefits such as Christmas or sickness allowances systematically discouraged "responsible savings behavior."[74] Thus, he argued, a mixture of natural, political, social, and cultural factors was responsible for the impossibility of encouraging the accumulation of wealth among workers. "Well-intended" measures neglecting people's behavioral patterns could not succeed in "imposing a certain behavior."[75]

---

72 Ibid., 138.

73 Günter Schmölders, "Zur Psychologie der Vermögensbildung in Arbeiterhand," *Kyklos: International Review for Social Sciences* 15 (1962), 179.

74 Ibid., 180. His arguments against state subsidies that allegedly produced a "subsidy mentality" and had to be countered by "subsidy pedagogy" were similar; Schmölders, "Das neue Finanzwissenschaftliche Forschungsinstitut," 41.

75 Schmölders, "Zur Psychologie der Vermögensbildung," 175.

Whereas most of his studies concentrated on economic behavior in the Federal Republic of Germany, Schmölders reached similar conclusions concerning theories of economic development. By the late 1950s, experiences in development policy had clearly established that the injection of capital and technology was not sufficient to instill economic growth. Publicly, Schmölders rejected attempts to explain differences in economic development by theories of race and climate, and acknowledged that talents were equally distributed across different peoples.[76] Yet he claimed that, in analogy to the personal character, there was also a "people's character" (*Volkscharakter*), consisting of attitudes, norms, customs, and values that could be ascertained by means of socioeconomic behavioral research.[77] This people's character could explain the differences in economic development since it determined the "willingness of a majority to leave their accustomed ways of life for more lucrative ones," to work more and relocate, as well as the ability to appropriate new technologies.[78]

Whereas Schmölders had seen no possibility to influence workers' savings behavior effectively, he formulated a more ambitious goal for development policy. Behavioral research was supposed to develop methods to "effectively and responsibly influence the motives and attitudes of economic actors."[79] Besides development policy, Schmölders also advocated further international comparisons of financial psychology in order to distinguish different tax mentalities that would determine the acceptance and effectiveness of various taxes.[80] In his view, there were constant aspects of human behavior that could not be altered at all, and variable parts that were formed and influenced by political, social, and cultural factors that were subject to change and could be changed intentionally.[81]

---

76   His lecture notes suggest that he was more open to these ideas. Hoover Institution, Schmölders Papers, Box-folder 70.

77   Günter Schmölders, "Der Beitrag der Verhaltensforschung zur Theorie der wirtschaftlichen Entwicklung," in *Systeme und Methoden in den Wirtschafts- und Sozialwissenschaften: Erwin von Beckerath zum 75. Geburtstag*, ed. Norbert Kloten et al. (Tübingen: Mohr, 1964), 371.

78   Ibid., 368–70.

79   Ibid., 385.

80   Günter Schmölders and Burkhard Strümpel, *Vergleichende Finanzpsychologie: Besteuerung und Steuermentalität in einigen europäischen Ländern* (Wiesbaden: Akademie der Wissenschaften und der Literatur, 1968).

81   Schmölders, "10 Jahre sozialökonomische Verhaltensforschung in Köln," 260.

As noted earlier, as president of the Mont Pèlerin Society, Schmölders suggested the "entrepreneur in modern economy and society" as the theme for the conference he organized in Munich in 1970. Vigorously raising financial support from German companies for the ambitious conference program, Schmölders saw the meeting of the "neoliberal thought collective" as an opportunity to present his research agenda in empirical socioeconomics to an international audience. It was not sufficient to analyze the real function of the entrepreneur within the economy, Schmölders explained in his opening address, but also public opinion, which influenced economic decision-making processes and economic policy.[82] Starting with the findings of Schmölders's institute, presenters on the first day thus reported on the "image of the entrepreneur" in Germany, the United States, France, Great Britain, Japan, India, South Africa and in "Underdeveloped (Poor) Countries," before others concentrated particularly on the entrepreneur's image among certain groups. Schmölders's success in convincing his fellow neoliberals to follow his research agenda, however, was rather limited.

With the end of his university career in sight, in the early 1970s Schmölders became an increasingly vocal public intellectual, spreading his ideas in publications written for broader audiences. His behavioral research should illuminate what he, like many other conservatives of the time, considered a fundamental "crisis between citizens and authorities."[83] This alleged crisis derived from the lawmakers' neglect of their citizens' nature. Schmölders remarked ironically that they seemed to be making laws for "superhumans" (*Übermenschen*), entertaining a boundless trust in the people's wisdom and strength of will.[84] With the expansion of the welfare state, the number of laws and rules had increased and, in his view, they severely restricted the citizens' freedom of action. The authorities either overestimated or overburdened their citizens and sometimes even tried to dupe them. As a result, people became cunning rascals (*schlitzohrige Staatsbürger*) or defected by transferring their money abroad (*abtrünnige Staatsbürger*). In Schmölders's view, these despicable behaviors resulted

---

82 See Plehwe's contribution to this volume.

83 Schmölders, *Der verlorene Untertan*; Michel Crozier, Jōji Watanuki, and Samuel P. Huntington, *The Crisis of Democracy: Report on the Governability of Democracies to the Trilateral Commission* (New York: University Press, 1975); Johannes Großmann, *Die Internationale der Konservativen: Transnationale Elitenzirkel und private Außenpolitik in Westeuropa seit 1945* (Munich: De Gruyter Oldenbourg, 2014).

84 Schmölders, *Der verlorene Untertan*, 10.

from the government's neglect of human nature which limited its influence. Behavioral research was supposed to define these limits.[85]

If the state did not take the basic principles of human behavior into account, Schmölders argued, it undermined its very foundations. Even before inflation spiked after 1973, Schmölders suggested that increasing taxes while not guaranteeing the stability of the money's value would necessarily weaken tax morale.[86] In line with the emerging monetarist orthodoxy in the 1970s, he reasoned that inflation was the central problem that modern industrialized economies had to control.[87] He maintained that, in contrast to the tenets of Keynesianism, unemployment and inflation were not alternatives but mutually reinforcing evils stemming from the same source.[88] Above all, he asserted, Keynesianism had failed because of its overly simplistic assumptions about human behavior and psychology. Even if democratic states rejected Keynesianism, however, Schmölders was skeptical that they were capable of conducting the necessary economic reforms. Re-invoking a critique that ordoliberals had voiced already against the Weimar Republic, Schmölders maintained that West Germany and other industrialized countries were "complacency democracies" (Gefälligkeitsdemokratien), being inherently corrupt in their attempts to please interest groups.[89]

Schmölders understood the dictatorial overthrow of democracies with high inflation rates by military juntas as indicating that democracies were simply not capable of conducting the harsh reforms necessary to return to a hard currency. Travelling to Chile in 1981, he published an enthusiastic report in the conservative International Background about the "restoration of order" after "the liquidation of the communist-dominated dictatorship of Salvador Allende." Relying on the expertise of the so-called "Chicago Boys," the military junta had managed to set the conditions for an economic development that Schmölders compared to the economic miracle in West Germany under the guidance of Ludwig Erhard.[90] Behind Schmölders's praise of Pinochet's Chile lurked his

---

85 Ibid.

86 Ibid., 11.

87 Günter Schmölders, Die Inflation: Ein Kernproblem in Wirtschaft und Gesellschaft (Paderborn: Schöningh, 1976).

88 Ibid., 28.

89 Ibid. See also Ptak, Ordoliberalismus, 36–7.

90 Günter Schmölders, "A Visit to Santiago de Chile," International Background 8, no. 6 (1981).

fascination for the technocratic potential of dictatorships expressed in his early writings under National Socialism. Issues of finance and currency were too complex for representatives in the parliaments to understand, Schmölders maintained, so it was better if experts set the rules for the economy.[91]

At the beginning of the 1980s, Schmölders saw the modern welfare state at a fatal impasse because governments had lived beyond their economic means. The Social Democrats especially had been dominated by a "childlike belief" in the malleability of everything, neglecting alleged economic realities.[92] Publicly Schmölders supported the so-called Lambsdorff Paper that called for neoliberal economic measures and contributed to the breakdown of the social-liberal coalition government in West Germany in 1982. However, he attributed the crisis not only to the expansion of the welfare state and Keynesian fiscal policy that had produced ever-larger public deficits over the preceding decade. Rather, at the bottom, lay a more general discontent with the intrusion of the regulatory state into public and private life. In all areas, Schmölders criticized, the state overburdened its citizens with an increasing number of rules and behavioral norms that contradicted allegedly natural ways of behavior. Apparently, he saw his freedom restricted and felt almost personally humiliated and insulted by the rules that surrounded him everywhere:

Crossing the street is allowed only at crossroads and crosswalks. Blinking red and green, traffic lights breathe the same monotonous rhythm during the whole day and often even night. Orders and rules everywhere. In the event of a traffic jam, their purpose easily turns into nonsense. Shrugging his shoulders, the citizen accepts that he has to obey robots under the threat of fines while the machines are not flexible enough to adjust to the changing traffic conditions; he has learned to obey.[93]

Whereas freedom is commonly described as the highest neoliberal value, Schmölders's advocacy of freedom was apparently very selective. Visiting

---

91 Günter Schmölders, *Einführung in die Geld- und Finanzpsychologie* (Darmstadt: Wissenschaftliche Buchgesellschaft, 1975), 154.

92 Günter Schmölders, *Der Wohlfahrtsstaat am Ende: Adam Riese schlägt zurück*, 3rd edition (Munich: Langen-Müller/Herbig, 1983), 9. That is fully in line with Hayek, "The Pretense of Knowledge."

93 Schmölders, *Der Wohlfahrtsstaat am Ende*, 150.

Santiago de Chile he had only witnessed "many police regulating traffic and guaranteeing public order," but not heard any "cries of those tortured . . . penetrating the thick walls of the prison" as media reports would have suggested.[94] Yet, at home, even traffic regulation seemed to be too burdensome to endure. Despite sharing Hayek's critique of the Keynesian "pretense of knowledge," Schmölders was still very confident of being able to offer the right recipes for national economic policy.

Conclusion: Behavioral Economics and Neoliberalism

Research in behavioral economics has boomed since the second half of the 1970s. The boom was initiated largely by the studies of Daniel Kahneman and Amos Tversky on the "heuristics and biases" of human decision-making under conditions of uncertainty. Using mostly classroom surveys with simple decision problems, Kahneman and Tversky argued that people's decisions systematically deviate from the expectations of economic rationality, and not because of mere carelessness.[95] While behavioral economists generally acknowledge Herbert A. Simon as an early precursor, and some even claim that his concept of bounded rationality is superior to the Kahneman/Tversky approach, there are no references to Günter Schmölders's earlier work. Even in Germany, the recent surge of behavioral economics traces its roots to Reinhard Selten's reception of American experimental economics and Simon's concept of bounded rationality.[96] In many ways, the newly emerging form of behavioral economics differs significantly from Schmölders's approach. While Schmölders tried to describe normal behavior of people in specific economic circumstances, the school originating with Kahneman and Tversky has a specific interest in producing counter-intuitive insights into the deviations from the model of the homo economicus.[97] The latter school applies a stricter mathematical calculus with the aim of

---

94 Schmölders, "A Visit to Santiago de Chile," 183f.

95 Amos Tversky and Daniel Kahneman, "Judgment Under Uncertainty: Heuristics and Biases," *Science* 185 (1974).

96 Gerd Gigerenzer and Reinhard Selten, eds, *Bounded Rationality: The Adaptive Toolbox* (Cambridge, MA: MIT Press, 2001); Axel Ockenfels and Abdolkarim Sadrieh, eds, *The Selten School of Behavioral Economics: A Collection of Essays in Honor of Reinhard Selten* (Berlin/Heidelberg/New York: Springer, 2010).

97 Floris Heukelom, "Three Explanations for the Kahneman-Tversky Programme of the 1970s," *The European Journal of the History of Economic Thought* 19, no. 5 (2012).

conducting basic research on the principles of human decision-making as such. By contrast, Schmölders's research was much less theoretically ambitious and much more policy-oriented.

Yet, from its beginnings in the 1970s and 1980s, proponents of behavioral economics stressed the relevance of their research for policy-making—not the least to secure funding. In 1986, the editors of the first handbook of behavioral economics claimed that "several studies suggest a new rationale for government intervention in the economy, given the failure of markets to promote a classical optimization due to individual judgment bias."[98] The acknowledgment that markets might fail to provide for the common good because individuals were unable to act in accordance with the rules of economic logic and their own well-understood interests is remarkable in an age of deregulation when marketization and neoliberalism allegedly triumphed.[99] Simultaneously, behavioral economists promised to offer the means to use and overcome people's judgment biases by designing the choice architecture of the marketplace. Thus, at a time of increasing welfare costs and shrinking state financial capacities to conduct economic policy, they offered a low-cost and allegedly non-intrusive way to enlarge government intervention. Despite Thaler and Sunstein's efforts to describe their political program as *libertarian* paternalism, not diminishing people's freedom of choice but only rearranging the choice architecture and behavioral environment, to many neoliberals it smacks of old-school paternalism. Whereas for Hayek the limits to individual knowledge offered a reason to assume that only market interaction can produce a desirable outcome, behavioral economists generally accept the government's capacity to define the desirable outcome and arrange the market accordingly. As P. W. Zuidhof describes the conflict, neoliberals want to secure and govern through markets, while behavioral economists try to offer means to govern markets by directly influencing the actors' choices.[100]

In recent debates, the application of behavioral insights to public policy appears mostly as a means to widen and strengthen the capacity for state regulation, sparking fears of manipulation and control. As the

---

98 Gilad and Kaish, *Handbook of Behavioral Economics*, xx.

99 Daniel T. Rodgers, *Age of Fracture* (Cambridge, MA: Belknap Press of Harvard University Press, 2011), 41–76.

100 Peter-Wim Zuidhoff, "Behaviouralizing Europe: Behavioural Economics Enters EU Policy-making" in *Handbook of Behavioral Change and Public Policy*, ed. Holger Strassheim and Silke Beck (Cheltenham UK: Edward Elgar Publishing 2019).

case of Günter Schmölders shows, however, behavioral economics, or socioeconomic behavioral research/empirical socioeconomics as Schmölders called it, is not necessarily at odds with a neoliberal project. The empirical analysis of economic behavior can serve both as a means to increase state intervention into areas of individual choice that had formerly been considered impenetrable in liberal democracies or as an attempt to define the limits of state intervention. Schmölders intended to empirically establish the principles of human behavior that could not be changed and, therefore, also not be the object of economic policy. In this approach, he was in line with the older German ordoliberals who did not believe in the abstraction of a homo economicus but rather held the view that competitive markets produced the best economic outcomes given the limitations of human knowledge and rationality. Thus, a behavioral approach to economics is politically polyvalent with appeal across the political spectrum, which is one of the major reasons for its recent success in political consulting.

PART THREE

NEOLIBERAL INTERNATIONALISM BEYOND THE WASHINGTON CONSENSUS

7

Embedded Early Neoliberalism: Transnational Origins of the Agenda of Liberalism Reconsidered

Hagen Schulz-Forberg

Introduction: The Walter Lippmann Colloquium and Early Neoliberalism

The Walter Lippmann Colloquium (WLC) in Paris in 1938 is widely recognized as the birthplace of neoliberalism as an intellectual and political project. Participants at the WLC included figures who later joined the Mont Pèlerin Society (MPS), including F. A. Hayek, Wilhelm Röpke, Ludwig von Mises, Michael Polanyi, Alexander Rüstow, Michael Heilperin, and Jacques Rueff. It also included actors more prominent in the postwar era and aligned with different organizations, such as Walter Lippmann (Ford Foundation), Stefan Possony (life-long Pentagon advisor, fellow and director at the Hoover Institution in the 1970s), Robert Marjolin (OEEC, EC), and Raymond Aron (who joined MPS in 1951, but left in 1956). The roster was filled out with industrialists, bankers, and assorted experts, from Ernest Mercier and Louis Marlio to Alfred Schütz and John Bell Condliffe. Despite their range of backgrounds and starting points, the participants agreed at the workshop's conclusion on an "Agenda of Liberalism" that summarized the essential features of their shared approach. Over the protests of some, they settled on the label of "neoliberalism."[1]

---

1 On the Walter Lippmann Colloquium see, for example: François Denord, *Néo-libéralisme version française. Histoire d'une idéologie politique* (Paris: Demopolis, 2007), 112–25; Serge Audier, *Néo-libéralisme(s). Une archéologie intellectuelle* (Paris: Grasset, 2012), 59–164, and Serge Audier, *Le Colloque Lippmann. Aux origines de*

As we know, however, birth is preceded by pregnancy and midwifes are usually involved. This article deals with the time before delivery, long overlooked by scholars. While neoliberalism might have been named at the WLC, its early features had been worked out and argued for before within an elite transnational network of intellectuals and institutions related to the League of Nations. Early neoliberals were part of a larger effort at shaping core concepts for a new liberal order, both nationally and globally. Core concepts, in Reinhart Koselleck's sense, serve as fundamental points of reference in any political system, their interpretation providing legitimacy for political action. Because of their role as normative points of reference, core concepts are contested, their interpretations are fought over and change over time. Core concepts are characterised by their ability to create timelessness, or, in other words, they make claims of universal truths.[2] At the same time, their contested character creates the urge to produce value judgments as meanings are negotiated.[3] The new conceptualization of liberal concepts during the 1930s included such semantic negotiations and an active announcement of what early neoliberals (and their international interlocutors) called "values."

What kind of values should the new liberal order represent? The formation of neoliberal core concepts still needs to be understood more completely. A set of questions facilitating such understanding

---

néo-libéralisme (Lormont: Editions Bord de l'Eau, 2008). See also the English translation of the verbatim protocol recently published by Jurgen Reinhoudt and Serge Audier, *The Walter Lippmann Colloquium: The Birth of Neo-Liberalism* (London: Palgrave, 2017). For a first effort at contextualization, see Hagen Schulz-Forberg, "Laying the Groundwork: The Semantics of Neoliberalism in the 1930s," in *Re-Inventing Western Civilisation: Transnational Reconstructions of Liberalism in Europe in the Twentieth Century,* ed. Hagen Schulz-Forberg and Niklas Olsen (Newcastle Upon Tyne: Cambridge Scholars Press, 2014), 13–39. Walter Lippmann, *Die Gesellschaft freier Menschen,* trans. E. Schneider (Bern: A. Francke Verlag, 1945), "Einführung" by Wilhelm Röpke, 25–33, 28. See also "Centre International d'études pour la rénovation du libéralisme, Le néo-libéralisme," Inaugural discussion on March 8, 1939, reprinted in *Les Essais. Cahiers bimestriels* (Nancy: Didry and Varcollier, 1961), 86–108, 94.

2 See Reinhart Koselleck, *Critique and Crisis: Enlightenment and the Pathogenesis of Modern Society* (Cambridge MA: MIT Press, 1988); *Futures Past: On the Semantics of Historical Time* (New York: Columbia University Press, 2004); *Sediments of Time: On Possible Histories,* trans. Sean Franzel and Stefan-Ludwig Hoffmann (Stanford: Stanford University Press, 2018).

3 See Walter Bryce Gallie, "Essentially Contested Concepts," *Proceedings of the Aristotelian Society* 56 (1955–56): 167–98.

might be raised regarding the semantics of neoliberal core concepts in the 1930s and the network of actors and institutions in which these concepts matured. In this chapter I look at the normative content neoliberals associated with a "good society"[4] and explore how far the WLC was part of a larger debate. In a second step, the institutional embeddedness of the WLC is highlighted through biographical aspects of its participants and an illustration of the League of Nations' impressive knowledge- and policy-making network built around the International Committee of Intellectual Cooperation (ICIC) and the International Institute of Intellectual Cooperation (IIIC). In a third step, I focus on the particular expertise of early neoliberals in business cycle research, understood as a broad program of studying cyclical and structural change. Finally, some concluding thoughts and questions will raise points relevant for future research on the evolution of neoliberalism in general and on the role and founding of the MPS in particular.

Early Neoliberalism Before and After the Walter Lippmann Colloquium

According to the agenda of neoliberalism agreed on in 1938, the normative "good society" comprised five elements, most of which concerned the role of the state. Beyond its responsibility to, first, protect the *price mechanism*, the state must, second, put in place and guarantee a *legal order* to safeguard the market's development and legally justify any intervention. Third, *political liberalism* must embrace law as the cornerstone of legitimacy, and the codification of law must be based on representative debates capable of establishing general norms. Fourth, such a legal regime constitutes the liberal method to "*control the social*"; and fifth, a liberal state is responsible for continuously providing society with five essential elements, for which taxes could be imposed: *national defence, social insurance, social services, education, and scientific research.*[5]

4 The research behind this chapter was made possible through the generous funding of the VELUX Foundation, Denmark, of a larger research project entitled *Towards Good Society: Constructing the Social through the Economic since the 1930s.*

5 Lippmann at the WLC, in Reinhoudt and Audier, *The Walter Lippmann Colloquium*, 177–9.

Although it did not appear on their agenda, early neoliberals also placed the concepts of the "human person" and "human dignity" at the heart of the matter. For many, these were the fundamental concepts and "freedom" was the best means to achieve them, particularly in times of authoritarian regimes and war. Others, like Hayek, saw in "freedom" a fundamental concept in its own right. Hayek surely thought that the dignity of the individual was fundamental, but he rejected—as always— fixed prescriptions about how to secure it or about what freedom should serve exactly. Freedom needed to be seen as a fundamental concept, not as a way to implement other fundamental concepts, he would maintain, for in a free society one also has the choice to act wrongly.[6] More in tune with other early neoliberals he argued that certain values form the basis of a moral order, which a legal order represents and maintains. As he asked in the discussion on liberalism and Christianity during the first MPS meeting in 1947: "Does liberalism presuppose some set of values which are commonly accepted as a faith and in themselves not capable of rational demonstration?" Hayek and the other discussants agreed. Hayek then strategically argued that "there is no chance of any extensive support for a liberal program unless the opposition between liberals and Christians can somehow be bridged. This antagonism is an accidental accretion of liberalism, rather than one of the essentials to liberalism."[7]

Yet for Hayek the concept of freedom was central, rather than the dignity of man on its own. Hayek suspected that without the concept of freedom as the cornerstone of a liberal value system, efforts at defining sound moral behavior in a top-down manner are likely to take place. Others were less cautious and saw in human dignity an end to strive for during dire times. Marjolin, for example, saw freedom as the best method to reach human dignity.[8] Baudin, too, thought that "freedom, however, is only a means whereas the end is a certain notion of the development of the human personality."[9]

---

6 F. A. Hayek, *The Constitution of Liberty* (Chicago: University of Chicago Press, 1960), 142–3.

7 Hayek during the discussion on "Liberalism and Christianity," 1947, Liberaal Archief, Folder 01–1-08–14–01.

8 Marjolin at the WLC, in Reinhoudt and Audier, *The Walter Lippmann Colloquium*, 113.

9 Baudin at the WLC, in Reinhoudt and Audier, *The Walter Lippmann Colloquium*, 111.

In general, early neoliberals would follow the trend of the time and embrace the concepts of Man, of "human dignity," of the "human person" and its "inviolability," a position developed in international law particularly by Hans Kelsen with his concept of the "basic norm," and also by Christian thought.[10] In 1942, Pope Pius XII put the concept at the center of his Christmas address,[11] but it already had an ascending usage by that time. The German sociologist Alexander Rüstow summarized the general position developed at the WLC when he said that

> discussions have led to the common conviction that, of all possible economic systems, it is the system of liberalism, of the economy of the free market, that combines the following advantages: 1. It is a system that is durable on its own because it is in stable equilibrium. 2. It ensures the maximum degree of productivity and the highest standard of living. 3. It alone is reconcilable with freedom and with the dignity of man.[12]

Rüstow had developed his position regarding the concept of the human person in a critical dialogue with Carl Schmitt, the legal philosopher who had erected an anti-liberal edifice of thought throughout the 1920s and whom Rüstow had admired for some time. In a letter to Schmitt from July 4, 1930, Rüstow remarked on the relation between a value-based rule of law and a self-limiting notion of "the political." "It seems to me," he wrote, "that the idea of a democratic state based on the concept of humanity represents not only a possible, but in a certain way an unavoidable utopia."[13] Other early neoliberals followed similar arguments, particularly Röpke, who built his "Civitas *Humana*" on the same

---

10 Hans Kelsen, *General Theory of Law and State* (Cambridge MA: Harvard University Press, 1949), 110–22; Hans Kelsen, *Pure Theory of Law* (Berkeley CA: University of California Press, 1969 [1934]). Hayek is an exception here again. For an elaboration of the opposing views of Hayek and Kelsen, see Richard A. Posner, *Law, Pragmatism and Democracy* (Cambridge MA: Harvard University Press, 2003), 275–84.

11 See Samuel Moyn, *Christian Human Rights* (Philadelphia: University of Pennsylvania Press, 2015).

12 Rüstow at the WLC, in Reinhoudt and Audier, *The Walter Lippmann Colloquium*, 157.

13 Rüstow, Letter to Schmitt, dated July 4, 1930, Carl Schmitt Papers, Federal State Archive of North Rhine-Wesphalia, Duisburg, RW 265–11879/3.

fundamental concept, calling it at times "economic humanism" or
"humane economy."[14] Aron argued in his work on the philosophy of
history from 1938 that there "is no comprehension of the future without
a doctrine of Man."[15]

Closer to the WLC, Lippmann's *Good Society* resonates with the
concepts of human dignity and the human person, positing them as the
foundation of civilization and what in the end constitutes the West and
needed to be re-made. He insisted that "[i]t is just here, that the ultimate
issue is joined, on the question whether men shall be treated as inviola-
ble persons or as things to be disposed of."[16] In his opening speech at
the WLC Lippmann stressed again that

> Civilized men will have to submit the conceptions they found novel
> before the war to new scrutiny, determined as they will be to discover
> those that are and those that are not compatible with the vital needs
> and the permanent ideal of humanity. It is to these vital needs and to
> this permanent ideal, and not to the doctrines of the nineteenth
> century, that one should refer to, so as to undertake the reconstruc-
> tion of liberalism.[17]

Rougier probably summarized best what that reconstructed liberalism
should be: "it is being an activist, it is fighting for the safeguard and the
renovation of the only economic and political system compatible with
*spiritual life, human dignity, the common good, the peace of peoples, and
the progress of civilization: liberalism.*"[18]

Early neoliberals were unanimous that fundamental values representing a moral order needed to be embraced and placed at the origins

---

14 Wilhelm Röpke, *Civitas Humana. Grundfragen der Gesellschafts- und
Wirtschaftsreform* (Zurich: Eugen Rentsch, 1944); *Mass und Mitte* (Zurich: Eugen
Rentsch, 1950); *Jenseits von Angebot und Nachfrage* (Zurich: Eugen Rentsch, 1958).

15 Raymond Aron, *Introduction à la philosophie de l'histoire* (Paris: Gallimard, 1986
[1938]), 14.

16 Walter Lippmann, *An Inquiry into the Principles of the Good Society* (Boston:
Little, Brown & Co., 1937), 375.

17 Lippmann at WLC, in Reinhoudt and Audier, *The Walter Lippmann Colloquium*,
105.

18 Louis Rougier at the WLC, in Reinhoudt and Audier, *The Walter Lippmann
Colloquium*, 102. See also Röpke, *Civitas Humana*; see also discussions at the
foundational meeting of the Mont Pèlerin Society on liberalism in relation to Christianity,
Liberaal Archief, Folder 01-1-08-14-01.

of a liberal society. There was disagreement over whether or not the concept of freedom was already a fundamental value or whether it was a means to an end, namely the realization of the fundamental concept of human dignity and the human person, the way in which man can, possibly, live up to his full potential. Hayek would agree on the very construction of society and its basic norms: "Like all other values, our morals are not a product but a presupposition of reason, part of the ends which the instrument of our intellect has been developed to serve. At any one stage of our evolution, the system of values into which we are born supplies the ends which our reason must serve."[19] He was also deeply impressed by the Catholic liberal philosopher and historian, Lord Acton, who placed human dignity at the heart of his thought. Hayek also defined "true individualism" as being based on the concept of man as a social being rather than a purely self-sufficient and isolated individual.[20] Yet, Hayek did not call his 1960 book *The Constitution of Human Dignity*, but *The Constitution of Liberty*. Wary of what proactive jurists might do with the concept—namely, prescribe and spell out what human dignity supposedly was—Hayek always stressed the weight of the concept of freedom as fundamental, not only as a means to an end as it was for many of his fellow early neoliberals.

The human person, its inviolability and dignity, was, however, the dominating global concept at the time, particularly in international law.[21] Any positive law, any constitution, is ultimately based on basic moral presuppositions. Early neoliberalism built its economic and political ideology on the same basic norm. Röpke explicitly said the economy was of "second rank," the first rank being the imposition of a moral authority.[22] Jacques Rueff could not have agreed more, for, he argued, if

19 In 1960, Hayek has grown more critical of a certain way of using the concept of human dignity. See Hayek, *Constitution of Liberty*, 365.

20 F. A. Hayek, "Wahrer und falscher Individualismus," *Ordo* 1 (1948): 23.

21 See Moyn, *Christian Human Rights*; Martti Koskenniemi, "International Law as Political Theology: How to Read *Nomos der Erde*?" *Constellations* 11, no. 4 (2004): 492–511; "International Law and Hegemony: A Reconfiguration," *Cambridge Review of International Affairs* 17, no. 2 (2004): 197–218; Patrick Capps, *Human Dignity and the Foundations of International Law* (Oxford: Hart, 2009); Stephen Riley, *Human Dignity and Law: Legal and Philosophical Investigations* (Oxford: Routledge, 2017).

22 Röpke in discussion with Rueff, Rougier, and Baudin at a meeting with French employer representatives in Avignon, April 1–3, 1948, explaining what the gist of the first MPS meeting was all about. "Le Colloque d'Avignon," Rougier Papers, Chateau de Lourmarin, Box R3, Annex.

man did not impose a moral authority he would not be civilized.[23] To avoid political catastrophes and too much arbitrary political will, the rule of law was conceptualized as a check on politics, taming it and keeping it within a set frame of norms and red lines. The rule of law was seen as the best way to guarantee the inviolability of the human person.[24] Early neoliberals added the price mechanism to the formula: its smooth, unhampered running was the benchmark for the liberal society and economy.

What I call "early neoliberalism" captures the period of self-declared neoliberalism from the 1930s to the 1960s. It is quite different semantically to what one would today associate with the concept when it serves as a critical term pointing at others or at certain conditions and policies as being neoliberal. Yet, at its birth and during its adolescence, neoliberalism was self-referential. Between the 1930s and the 1960s one can follow its proponents in various forums and debates and one still finds the label actively mentioned and defended.[25] As Louis Baudin reminded Röpke and Rueff in 1948 during yet another colloquium, the term was known in the world and one could not take it back.[26]

In order to realize the agenda of liberalism, early neoliberalism rejected the notion of laissez-faire as the preferred means to serve the human individual. Rather, the competitive order, a man-made moral and legal framework within which markets would be as free as possible, was identified as the new means to the end.[27] In addition, early neoliberalism was conscious of social concerns and tasked the state with social responsibilities as well as the protection of the free market

23 Jacques Rueff, *L'Ordre Social* (Paris: Librairie de Médicis, 1949), 563.

24 See Ben Jackson, "Freedom, the Common Good, and the Rule of Law: Lippmann and Hayek on Economic Planning," *Journal of the History of Ideas* 73, no. 1 (2012): 47–68.

25 See the proceedings the Oostende Colloquium in 1957, and Alexander Rüstow, "Paläoliberalismus, Kollektivismus und Neoliberalismus," in *Wirtschaft, Gesellschaft und Kultur. Festgabe für Alfred Müller-Armack*, ed. Franz Greiß and Fritz W. Meyer (Berlin: Duncker & Humblot, 1961), 61–70.

26 Baudin at the Colloque d'Avignon in discussion with Röpke and Rougier about the term "neoliberal."

27 See the discussion following Hayek's introductory paper at the Mont Pèlerin Society, April 1, 1947, Liberaal Archief, Folder 01-1-08-14-01; also Milton Friedman, "Neo-Liberalism and its Prospects," *Farmand* (February 1951): 1–4; for the German case of ordoliberalism as competitive order see Eucken's remarks at the first session of the Mont Pèlerin Society and Franz Böhm, *Die Ordnung der Wirtschaft als geschichtliche Aufgabe und rechtsschöpferische Leistung* (Stuttgart and Berlin: Kohlhammer, 1937).

order. As the WLC participants argued in a discussion following the agreement on the five essential points of the agenda of liberalism, "maximum utility is a social good, but is not necessarily the only one that must be sought."[28] Admitting that the economy was shaped to build a society of a certain kind, early neoliberals were engaged in the conscious construction of a state to safeguard the so-called competitive order in both its internal setup and its relations to other states. This competitive order could well be run according to certain social goals and based on certain social convictions, but the operationalization needed to be carried out according to a liberal script. Any state agency had to be based on liberal interventionism, avoiding arbitrary political decisions and case-by-case action. The call was for principled legal and market-conforming intervention that would not endanger the price mechanism.

Embedding the Walter Lippmann Colloquium

It is important to emphasize that the main ideas of the Agenda of Liberalism were not originally worked out just at the WLC. The WLC was part of a large, transnational institutional landscape that was erected by and for the League of Nations after the First World War. The workshop itself took place at the International Institute of Intellectual Cooperation (IIIC), a transnational organization and League of Nations consultative body bringing together leading researchers and research institutions dealing with questions of global order and peace.[29] Within

---

28   Lippmann at the WLC, in Reinhoudt and Audier, *The Walter Lippmann Colloquium*, 178.

29   Akira Iriye, *Cultural Internationalism and World Order* (Baltimore: The Johns Hopkins University Press, 2000); Daniel Laqua, "Transnational Intellectual Cooperation, the League of Nations, and the Problem of Order," *Journal of Global History* 6 no. 2 (2011): 223–47; Michael Riemens, "International Academic Cooperation on International Relations in the Interwar Period: the International Studies Conference," *Review of International Studies*, no. 37/2 (2011), 911–28; Katharina Rietzler, "Experts for Peace: Structures and Motivations of Philanthropic Internationalism in the Interwar Years," in *Internationalism Reconfigured: Transnational Ideas and Movements between the World Wars*, ed. Daniel Laqua (London: I. B. Tauris, 2011), 45–65; Jo-Anne Pemberton, "The Changing Shape of Intellectual Cooperation: From the League of Nations to UNESCO," *Australian Journal of Politics and History* 58, no. 1 (March 2012): 34–50; Schulz-Forberg, "Laying the Groundwork."

the IIIC's permanent International Studies Conference (ISC), the relation between state and economy in view of its global function was the
central topic of the 1930s. The groundwork for the Agenda of Liberalism
was prepared within the universe of the IIIC/ISC.

Existing histories of neoliberalism have either struggled to explain
the composition of the WLC or focused on a handful of participants,
usually the better-known intellectuals and economists.[30] Yet what about
the others? What about José Castillejo, a Spanish lawyer? What about a
group of French industrialists, bankers, and young scholars like Etienne
Mantoux and Robert Marjolin, the latter known for his spell at the
OEEC and the European Commission, but less for his neoliberalism?
Unable to account for the presence of most participants, existing histories either ignore or simply enumerate them. But if the Agenda of
Liberalism represents early neoliberalism, then who were all the other
participants besides the well-known protagonists? Were they not neoliberals? After all, they all agreed on the same agenda. I will follow their
paths through the transnational network of the IIIC and the ISC in this
section.

The Walter Lippmann Colloquium bore both resemblances and
concrete connections to the International Studies Conferences developed by the International Committee on Intellectual Cooperation
(ICIC), established in January 1922, and the IIIC, established in Paris in
1926 as the ICIC's executive branch. From 1931 onward, ISC study
groups worked on a chosen topic over a cycle of two years. The chosen
study cycles were: "The State and Economic Life" (1932–33), "Collective
Security" (34–35), "Peaceful Change" (36–37) and "Economic Policies
in Relation to World Peace" (38–39). At the 1939 meeting in Bergen,
held at the precise time that Nazi Germany invaded Poland, "International
Organization" was the theme agreed upon for the 1940–41 cycle. The
WLC was also planned originally to initiate a larger, international
conference on the same topic in 1939.[31]

By 1937, thirty-eight National Committees of Intellectual Cooperation
(NCICs) were in place.[32] The reach of the system itself was global, as

---

30   Angus Burgin, *The Great Persuasion. Reinventing Free Markets since the
Depression* (Cambridge MA: Harvard University Press, 2012), 71.

31   Rougier, the organizer of the WLC, mentioned this plan in his letter of invitation.
See Audier, *Le Colloque Lippmann*, 140.

32   League of Nations, *National Committees on Intellectual Co-operation* (Geneva,
1937).

NCICs sprouted in Argentina, China, Cuba, India, Iran, Japan, Mexico, South Africa, and Syria. Experts from affiliated institutions were commissioned to write memoranda on assigned themes and questions. Once the memoranda had all been submitted (they were often quite voluminous) a general rapporteur, appointed by the ISC and funded by the Rockefeller Foundation, would summarize the main points of view in a kick-off lecture setting the stage for the discussions during the conference.[33]

By the late 1930s, the IIIC and the ISC had gained significant experience and grown into a large knowledge- and policy-making institutional arrangement. The tenth ISC conference from 1937, for example, needed ten preliminary meetings on specific sub-topics held in Geneva, London, Paris, and Vienna. The conference then had to digest more than 100 memoranda from Australia, Canada, the United States, and thirteen European countries. Overall, 142 participants came to Paris from June 27 to July 3, representing twenty national research institutes and national coordinating committees. They came mostly from Europe, but also from Australia, Brazil, Canada, and the US. Five countries sent invited experts or observers: China, Germany, Italy, Japan, and Mexico. Furthermore, organizations the IIIC grouped under the headline "international" also participated or sent experts: the Carnegie Endowment, the Rockefeller Foundation, the Pacific Institute of International Affairs, the Graduate Institute of International Studies in Geneva, the Academy of International Law, the New Commonwealth Institute (which published Hayek's essay on the effect of inter-state federation on the economy seen by many as an original script for contemporary neoliberalism[34]) and the International Labour Organization came to the ISCs.[35]

The culture of the meetings was one of open discussion without expectation of unanimity. Dialogue and contestation were expected.

---

33 League of Nations Sixth International Studies Conference, *A Record of a Second Study Conference on the State and Economic Life* (Paris: IIIC, 1934), xiv–xv.

34 See Wolfgang Streeck, *Gekaufte Zeit. Die vertagte Krise des demokratischen Kapitalismus* (Berlin: Suhrkamp, 2013), 141; similarly, Lars Magnusson and Bo Stråth, *A Brief History of Political Economy: Tales of Marx, Keynes and Hayek* (Cheltenham: Edward Elgar, 2016), 119–21.

35 Emanuel Moresco, *Peaceful Change International Studies Conference, Vol. III, Colonial Questions and Peace* (Paris: IIIC, 1939).

The fact that there was agreement on the new "Agenda of Liberalism" at the WLC actually surprised Louis Rougier, the WLC's organizer, even if its substance was less than novel. The question of legitimate state intervention, in particular, had been mulled over many times before the WLC. At the ISC's London meeting in 1933, for example, sessions dealt extensively with various "philosophical aspects of state intervention" as well as "practical aspects of state intervention."[36] Among the WLC participants, Baudin, Condliffe, Heilperin, Mises, and Piatier worked as expert authors for the IIIC on other occasions.[37] Additionally, the Graduate Institute of International Studies (from where Baudin, Heilperin, Röpke, and Mises were recruited for the WLC) acted as a reliable source of much commissioned research.

Today, when interpretations of the WLC try to connect the different individuals attending the Paris colloquium of 1938 and make sense of the heterogeneous group of participants, they have failed to look at the institutional framework within which the WLC was realized.[38] The list of participants in Paris included the international mix of experts characteristic of the IIIC who had already been involved with the League in one way or another, including representatives from knowledge- and policy-making institutions and practitioners from banks or large industries. When the list of invitees is broadened to include all those who were not able (or did not want) to attend the colloquium, the weight of the League's IIIC and the Rockefeller Foundation becomes even more obvious. For the WLC, Rougier sent invitations to Luigi Einaudi, Johan Huizinga, Tracy Kittredge, Francesco Nitti, José Ortega y Gasset, William Rappard, Charles Rist, and Lionel Robbins (these names provide

36   IIIC, *Second Study Conference on the State and Economic Life*, 181–263.

37   Louis Baudin, *Free Trade and Peace* (Paris: IIIC, 1939); Condliffe's first report from 1930 was about *International Collaboration in the Study of International Relations* (Archives of the IIIC, Paris, FR PUNES AG 1-IICI-C-88); Michael Heilperin, *International Monetary Organisation* (Paris: IIIC, 1939); Heilperin had already written for the tenth ISC in 1937 on Peaceful Change, this time on *Les Aspects Monétaires du Problèmes des Matières Premières* (Paris: IIIC, 1937); André Piatier, *Report on the Study of Exchange Control* (Archives of the IIIC, Paris, FR PUNES AG 1-IICI-K-XII-12.a).

38   The most recent presentation of the WLC again avoids any institutional reflection on the origins of neoliberalism. See the introductory essay by Reinhoudt and Audier, *The Walter Lippmann Colloquium*.

two more participants at the founding meeting of the MPS in Rappard and Robbins).[39]

Apart from containing two towering figures of Italian political and intellectual history and the Spanish lodestar of conservative European thought, this list includes, with Robbins, one of the main protagonists of the early years of the MPS, and, with Rist, one of the most influential figures in relevant French and international academic as well as financial affairs. With Huizinga and Rappard, the list of invitees also includes two members of the ICIC's Executive Committee from Geneva (which, as a matter of fact, also acted as the governing body of the IIIC).[40] Rappard was the director of the League's Mandate Section and co-director of the Graduate Institute of International Studies.[41] The second co-director was Paul Mantoux, who was also director of the League's Political Section and father of the WLC participant, Etienne Mantoux.

One member of the ICIC's Executive Committee, José Castillejo, actually did make it to Paris. When reading the verbatim protocol of the WLC, one wonders why he was such an outspoken, self-confident speaker. With a specialization in Roman law, his knowledge on economic matters or liberal thought was not his major professional asset. The answer may be that Castillejo, who had initiated the foundation (again through co-financing by government and Rockefeller funds) of the Spanish Instituto de Estudios Internacionales y Económicos in early 1931,[42] was a longstanding member of the ICIC's Executive Committee and possessed the highest institutional authority among the participants.[43] Tracy Kittredge, finally, was the Assistant Director of the Rockefeller Foundation's European Social Sciences Division office from 1931 to 1942 and participant at a number of ISCs. In 1919, Kittredge was a staff member of the Supreme Economic Council during the Paris Peace Conference.

---

39 Audier, *Le Colloque Lippmann*, 140.

40 biblio-archive.unog.ch/Dateien/CouncilDocs/C-3-1939_EN.pdf, 8.

41 Susan Pedersen, *The Guardians: The League of Nations and the Crisis of Empire* (Oxford: Oxford University Press, 2015). Pedersen stresses that beside the mandates, the most important and under-researched issue is the League's role in economic thought and policy-making.

42 José Castillejo, Letter to Ortega y Gasset, dated January 31, 1931, to which he attached a note explaining the organization and financing of the institute. See *Epistolario de José Castillejo, Vol. III, Fatalidad y Porvenir, 1913–1937* (Madrid: Editorial Castalia, 1999), 673–7.

43 Archives of the League of Nations, Geneva, Box R4000, 5B/25160/9508.

Almost all WLC participants came from within the existing transnational networks of the IIIC/ISC. This is true for Condliffe, who was hired
from the Institute of Pacific Relations to join the IIIC/ISC as rapporteur
and research manager (popping up everywhere in the correspondence
between Rockefeller and IIIC) in 1931. It is also true for Heilperin from
the Graduate Institute in Geneva and Castillejo from the ICIC. Bruce
Hopper was affiliated with Harvard, the Sorbonne and the Pacific
Institute as well. Both Mises and Hayek worked at two of the leading
research institutes supplying ideas to the IIIC. Marcel van Zeeland acted
probably more as a representative of his brother, Paul, Belgian prime
minister until 1937 and author of the "Van Zeeland Report" from
January 1938, around which Rougier would organize the next colloquium in 1939 (an occasion that received Lippmann's blessing and
congratulations,[44] but is otherwise hard to reconstruct empirically so
far). Marcel worked for the National Bank of Belgium (and later joined
the Bank for International Settlements).

The economists and philosophers Rüstow, Röpke, Mises, and Hayek
had all been associated with either the Rockefeller Foundation or the
League or both, as in the case of Röpke who received a large grant from
the foundation and whose business cycle theory was translated into
English on the League's initiative. Rüstow was Röpke's friend from
Istanbul, where they shared the experience of exile (and the privilege of
founding a whole social science faculty at Istanbul University). Mises
and Hayek worked at the two most prominent research institutions the
League had within the IIIC/ISC network, the Graduate Institute of
International Studies in Geneva and the LSE. They were also connected
by the Business Cycle Research Institute they had founded in Vienna
and whose expertise was drawn upon by the League.

Before turning to the thirteen French WLC participants, this
leaves Michael Polanyi, Stefan Possony, and Alfred Schütz. The latter
two had both attended Mises's private seminars in Vienna and were
in exile at the moment of the WLC. Both had also been recent authors
of studies related to the WLC's topic. Possony had written and
published on the war economy in 1938, whereas Schütz (who also
studied with Hans Kelsen and heard Max Weber in Vienna) was a
friend of Fritz Machlup and Erich Vögelin and had been in Paris

---

44 Walter Lippmann, Letter to Louis Rougier, October 28, 1938, Box R1, Fonds
Rougier, Château de Lourmarin.

since March 1938. Schütz was not an early macroeconomist, but an expert in epistemology inspired by von Mises and particularly phenomenologists like Edmund Husserl. Schütz's contributions to early neoliberal thought are within social theory and relate more to von Mises's *Human Action* and the theory of praxeology than to business cycle research.[45] By the late 1930s, Polanyi, the polymath older brother of Karl, had turned away from his core specialty in chemistry to the social sciences. At the time of the WLC, he was shooting his Rockefeller Foundation-funded film on *Unemployment and Money*. He had also been to the Soviet Union on several occasions in the 1930s, where he had seen the alternative to the liberal way and formed his opinion on both the kind of society he believed in and science's role for that society.[46]

The thirteen French participants can be dealt with in groups. First, there is a trio of brilliant young scholars: Raymond Aron, Etienne Mantoux, and Robert Marjolin. Aron had just defended his PhD in the spring of 1938. Fundamental for his connection to the IIIC was his relation to Celestin Bouglé. The latter was not only a member of the French National Committee for Intellectual Cooperation, but also an advisor for the League and regular participant (and outspoken discussant) at the IIIC/ISC annual conferences as the official delegate of the French government to the IIIC.[47] The second major academic figure of importance for Aron was Bouglé's good friend, Elie Halévy, who was a much admired, well-connected philosopher and historian specializing in economic and political thought and deeply devoted to the question as to how the circle of social justice and economic freedom might be squared. In fact, Halévy, who had died from heart disease in 1937, taught the young French WLC participants and they all were enthralled by his intellectual and human capacities.[48] In 1921, Bouglé founded the Centre

45 See Alfred Schütz, *Der sinnhafte Aufbau der sozialen Welt: Eine Einleitung in die verstehende Soziologie* (Vienna: J. Springer, 1932); Ludwig von Mises, *Human Action: A Treatise on Economics* (New Haven: Yale University Press, 1949), 24 and 100, actually builds on Schütz.

46 See Michael Polanyi, "USSR Economics: Fundamental Data, System and Spirit," *The Manchester School* 6, no. 2 (December 1935): 67–88.

47 IIIC, *Second Study Conference on the State and Economic Life*, 416.

48 Robert Marjolin, *Le travail d'une vie. Mémoirs 1911–1986* (Paris: Robert Laffont, 1986), 54. Halévy's 1936 lectures on the 'age of tyranny' were particularly formative for Aron, Marjolin, and Mantoux. See Halévy's posthumously published work (prefaced by Bouglé), *L'Ère des tyrannies. Etudes sur le socialisme et la guerre* (Paris: Gallimard, 1938).

de Documentations Sociales (CDS) at the École Normale Supérieure, to which he was deputy director. Aron joined the CDS while he wrote his PhD on the philosophy of history in relation to social theory, specifically on Max Weber, Emile Durkheim, Wilhelm Dilthey, and German thought more specifically. Aron's PhD was representative of early neoliberal epistemology in many ways and particularly close to Popper's strong critique of "historicism."[49]

Critical of a liberal paradigm rooted in laissez-faire and in a philosophy of history based on the interpretation of the concept of nature, Aron, perfectly in tune with fellow early neoliberals (see Martin Beddeleem's contribution to this volume), argued for a conscious development of values on which society might be built as a consequence of the critique of earlier liberal epistemologies and understandings of the science of history.[50] The CDS was the perfect place for this kind of research and it is another good example of the funding strategy Rockefeller had at the time. Initially financed by the banker Albert Kahn, Rockefeller took over the CDS's financial support following the financial crisis of 1929. The grant allowed the employment of research assistants, and the foundation had certain ideas regarding the nature of the research to be carried out at the center. Sociology had been identified by Rockefeller as one of the disciplines able to develop "methods for social control" and he was particularly supportive of research in the vein of "inductive sociology."[51]

Etienne Mantoux was recognized among the circles of early neoliberals as a highly promising scholar, mostly through his essay on Keynes's claim that Germany could not pay back the reparations demanded after the First World War. He argued the opposite (as did others among the early neoliberal economists, especially Rueff and Heilperin).[52] Educated at Sciences Po in Paris as a student of Halévy's,

---

See also Ludovic Frobert, "Elie Halévy's First Lectures on the History of European Socialism," *Journal of the History of Ideas* 68, no. 2 (2007): 329–53.

49   Karl Popper, *The Poverty of Historicism* (London: Routledge, 1957).

50   Aron, *Introduction à la philosophie de l'histoire*.

51   See Marcel Fournier, *Marcel Mauss: A Biography* (Princeton: Princeton University Press, 2006), 293.

52   Etienne Mantoux, *La paix calomniée ou les conséquences économiques de M. Keynes* (Paris: Gallimard, 1946). Mantoux died in April 1945. His work, posthumously published, was immediately translated as *The Carthaginian Peace or the Economic Consequences of Mr Keynes* (Oxford: Oxford University Press, 1946), and then just as immediately praised by fellow early neoliberals in a string of reviews for academic journals.

whom he admired and visited privately on a regular basis, he moved to London in the mid-1930s to study with Harold Laski and Hayek at the LSE.

Marjolin worked as chief assistant for Charles Rist's research institute at the time of the colloquium. Rist was certainly among the intellectual influences on Marjolin, who was otherwise inspired in his economic thinking by both Keynes and Hayek as well as Knut Wicksell, Gunnar Myrdal, and John Hicks.[53] At the time of the WLC, Marjolin had just turned twenty-seven and he was already a specialist in macroeconomics and business cycle theory as well as the relation between socially conscious politics and liberal markets. He was in the midst of his PhD project, which was finally published in 1941.[54] He was a lifelong friend of Aron's with whom he claims to have been in full agreement intellectually.[55]

The second group of WLC participants from France were the industrialists. They were Louis Marlio, Marcel Bourgeois, Auguste Detœuf, and Ernest Mercier. Marlio, though working for the French energy industry, was likely the most academic among them and he also had a background in working for the League of Nations. He was entrusted with the mandate of becoming the first president of the Centre International d'Études pour la Rénovation du Libéralisme (CIRL) in 1939 following the WLC, and together with Baudin and Rüstow probably among the most enthusiastic champions of the term "neoliberalism."[56]

Detœuf, founder and long-term director of the French energy giant Alstom, had gained some intellectual profile through his activities within the interdisciplinary intellectual platform of the 1930s called Groupe x-crise. He had published a strong critique of capitalism and liberalism, not believing in their survival. Rougier sent him a copy of Lippmann's *Good Society* to convince him that there were still ways of redesigning liberalism and Detœuf joined the WLC as a

---

53   Marjolin, *Le travail d'une vie*, 52.

54   Robert Marjolin, *Prix, monnaie et production: Essai sur les mouvements économiques de longue durée* (Paris: Thèses, Universités de Paris, Faculté de droit, 1941), prefaced by Charles Rist.

55   Marjolin, *Le travail d'une vie*, 56.

56   Louis Marlio, "Le Néo-libéralisme," talk at CIRL in Paris, 1939, in *Les Essais. Cahiers bimestriels*, 86–108.

supporter of Lippmann's ideas—and a critic of Mises.[57] Ernest Mercier was connected to Marlio and Detœuf via Groupe x-crise, but even more via another platform called Redressement français, which Mercier had founded and for which he acted as president until 1932. It aimed at shaping and uniting the elite as well as educating the masses and running the country in a technocratic, corporative manner. Mercier was director of the Compagnie française du petrol (CFP), the predecessor of the French petroleum group Total. Marcel Bourgeois was connected to the French chemical industry, but was also co-founder of the Librairie de Mèdicis, the liberal French publishing house in which *The Good Society* appeared in French translation as *La Cité Libre* and where the WLC proceedings were published originally in 1939.[58]

The third group of French participants is characterized by their more senior academic status and by their connections to the League and its affiliated international organizations. They are Roger Auboin, Louis Baudin, Bernard Lavergne, André Piatier, Louis Rougier, and Jacques Rueff. Auboin had been appointed as General Manager of the Bank for International Settlements (BIS) in early 1938. Ever since its foundation in 1930, the Bank's representatives had been involved in meetings and dialogue with the League. In the mid-1930s, the BIS's economic advisor, Per Jacobsson, was present in the wider circle of actors following Rockefeller's Annecy conference from 1936 on business cycles and the concept of the world economy.[59]

Baudin was an internationally respected economist during the late 1930s, author of a memorandum for the IIIC, and among the more enthusiastic users of the term neoliberalism, the "basic idea" of which, he explained again after the war in 1953, "is the rescue of the human person."[60] He was affiliated to the Sorbonne and to the Geneva

---

57 See their discussions in Reinhoudt and Audier, *The Walter Lippmann Colloquium*. For Rougier's approaching of Detœuf, see also Box R1, Fonds Rougier, Château de Lourmarin.

58 See François Denord, "Aux origines du néo-libéralisme en France. Louis Rougier et le Colloque Walter Lippmann de 1938," *Le Mouvement Social* 195, no. 2 (2001): 9–34.

59 See the detailed description in Jérôme Wilson, *Robert Triffin. Milieux académiques et cénacles économiques internationaux 1935–1951* (Fond Camille Gutt: Editions Versant Sud), particularly chaper 2, "Naissance d'un économiste (1932–1935)."

60 Louis Baudin, *L'Aube d'un nouveau libéralisme* (Paris: Librairie de Médicis, 1953), 146.

Graduate Institute of International Studies as well as to the League, where he joined Oscar Morgenstern and Bertil Ohlin in a group of experts with the marvelously bulky name of the Committee of Economists to assist the Fiscal Committee in the Enquiry on the Behaviour of Tax Systems.[61]

Bernard Lavergne was again a Sorbonne graduate, a collaborator with Rist, and on friendly terms with Halévy, with whom he corresponded regularly.[62] Lavergne worked mainly on the field of cooperative movements and on the concept and role of the consumer.[63] In fact, the *co-opératif* was a particularly articulated idea (and also practice) in French economic thought. During IIIC/ISC meetings, Bouglé would make sure to enumerate the cooperative movement as one of the key examples for the possible coexistence of free markets with more socially controlled elements of the economy.[64]

André Piatier is a lesser known character who appears in the sources as a young expert who worked for the IIIC/ISC on the Danubian Economic Study, as an author of a memorandum for the 1939 conference, and at the WLC. He was also a Sorbonne graduate and the first secretary of the Paris-based International Institute of Public Finances that had been founded in 1937 (by the omnipresent William Rappard among others) on the initiative of Edgar Allix, the Dean of the Law Faculty at Paris University. When Allix died unexpectedly in mid-1938, Piatier, initially Allix's assistant, took over.[65]

The last actors to consider are Louis Rougier and Jacques Rueff. Both are key figures for the history of neoliberalism. Rougier has received more attention than Rueff from scholars thus far, mainly because he was the WLC's organiser. While he tarnished his image politically during the

---

61 biblio-archive.unog.ch/Dateien/CouncilDocs/C-3-1939_EN.pdf, 7.

62 For example, in 1936, Lavergne turned to Halévy in a handful of letters about his candidature for the Collège de France. See the Papers of Elie Halévy at the École Normale Supérieure, Box 7 (1930–37).

63 See, based on his PhD at the law faculty: Bernard Lavergne, *Le Régime coopératif. Etude général de la coopération de consommation en Europe* (Paris: Rousseau, 1908); *L'hégémonie du consommateur: vers une renovation de la science économique* (Paris: Presses Universitaires de France, 1958).

64 For France, he enumerated four strong powers to reckon with when shaping economic policies: "peasants, democrats, trade-unionists and co-operators." Célestin Bouglé, in League of Nations, *The State and Economic Life with Special Reference to International Economic and Political Relations* (Paris: IIIC, 1932), 46.

65 "IIPF History," at iipf.net.

war through his collaboration with the Vichy regime, he remained affiliated to the transnational network of economists.[66] Rougier reappeared
in the mid-1950s after he was allowed to resume teaching in France, and
participated in the discussion of neoliberalism at Oostende, Belgium, in
mid-September 1957, twenty years after the publication of Lippmann's
The Good Society.[67]

More important and influential intellectually and politically was
Rueff. A renowned expert on monetary issues, he was the mastermind
behind the change from the old to the new franc in 1960. He hammered
home the key message of early neoliberalism throughout—that the price
mechanism needs to be in place as the decisive element indicative of a
liberal society, yet that this price mechanism may well live in peaceful
coexistence with certain forms of state intervention (of a liberal kind)
and even tariffs.[68] In addition, he was also immensely active as a policy-
maker and within international organizations. And of course, he was
well known as Charles de Gaulle's economic advisor and as an ardent
advocate of the gold standard.

For the League, Rueff served (together with, again, Morgenstern
and Ohlin) as a member of the Special Delegation of the Financial
and Economic Committees for the Study of Economic Depressions.
He continued his political work as a strong supporter of European
integration and as the first president of UNESCO's International
Council for Philosophy and Humanistic Studies, where, in conversation with colleagues from other disciplines and with more global
origins he repeated his most influential message about the price
mechanism's role in safeguarding civilization, and continued to reflect
deeply on the very role and function of core concepts for societies and
their interrelations.[69] While his clarity and strong convictions in this
area qualified him for membership in the Mont Pèlerin Society, it was

---

66 See his *Mission Sectète à Londres. Les Accords Pétain-Churchill* (Geneva: Les
Editions du Cheval Ailé, 1946).

67 *Travaux du Colloque International du Libéralisme Economique* (Brussels: Editions
du Centre Paul Hymans, 1957), 279–93, where he would continue to separate
"neoliberalism" from "liberalism of strict observance."

68 See Rueff's interventions in Reinhoudt and Audier, *The Walter Lippmann
Colloquium* and perhaps most importantly in *L'Ordre Social* (Paris: Librairie de Médicis,
1949) and *Épitre aux Dirigistes* (Paris: Gallimard, 1949).

69 UNESCO Archive. See for example the "Report of the Meeting of the Committee
on the Philosophical Analysis of Fundamental Concepts," May 3–7, 1949, Paris, Box
CISHP 1, UNESCO/PHS/12.

his capacity in the field of macroeconomics *avant la lettre* that qualified him for the League's roster of economists and the WLC in the first
place.

Embedding Early Neoliberals into the Origins of "Macro-Dynamic Economics"

Jacques Rueff's connections to the League of Nations were shared by
many of those present in Paris in 1938. From the beginning of its existence, the League had looked for expertise in what Ragnar Frisch had
baptized "macro-dynamic" economics. The Norwegian economist was
the first laureate of the Nobel Memorial Prize for Economics in 1969
(see Philip Mirowski's contribution to this volume). In the early 1930s
he served as director of the University Institute of Economics in Oslo,
which had been funded by "generous grants" of the Rockefeller
Foundation together with a Norwegian source, A/S Norsk Varekrig.[70]
As he explained in 1933:

> When we approach the study of the business cycle with the intention
> of carrying through an analysis that is truly dynamic and determi-
> nate . . ., we are naturally led to distinguish between two types of
> analyses: the micro-dynamic and the macro-dynamic types. The
> micro-dynamic analysis is an analysis by which we try to explain in
> some detail the behaviour of a certain section of the huge economic
> mechanism . . . The macro-dynamic analysis, on the other hand, tries
> to give an account of the fluctuations of the whole economic system
> taken in its entirety.[71]

For the League, the "whole economic system" was indeed global, and
among the general crowd of experts in "dynamic economics" a number
of early neoliberals had their share in shaping the League's policies—
until the intervention of a certain Mr. Keynes. Apart from the League,
the growing transnational breed of "macro-dynamic" economists found
an academic home in the Econometric Society that was founded in late

---

70 Ragnar Frisch, "Propagation Problems and Impulse Problems in Dynamic
Economics," *Publications of the University Institute of Economics*, no. 3 (1933), 1–35.
    71 Ibid., 2.

1930 by the same Ragnar Frisch, with Joseph Schumpeter, Keynes, and Rueff as founding fellows.[72] The Econometric Society continued to serve UNESCO as a consultative organization once the IIIC had been dismantled and UNESCO became its successor.

Early neoliberal forms of macro analysis were fundamentally different to that of Keynes's *General Theory* and to other spin-offs of the new discipline at the time, for example that of Schumpeter.[73] Keynes's focus on crisis amendment—the "bust" side of the business cycle—is diametrically opposed to how early neoliberals approached business cycles. For them, the policies steering the boom are what matters. Intervention needs to act on the framework for growth, and not be based on urgent social needs when the crisis has hit. At the same time, they also acknowledged some of Keynes's ideas, particularly the insight that a purely monetary policy to prevent deflation would not be enough in cases of deep depression. The "how" of the policy then mattered and was disputed.[74] Notwithstanding their objections to the emerging mainstream, early neoliberals were part of the transnational team of experts providing models of business cycle analysis for Geneva. In fact, looking at the WLC participants once again, expertise in early forms of macroeconomics (back then still a rather indistinct field far from the mathematically based models of econometrics today) is what unites the majority of the economists present in Paris.

Austrian business cycle theory was developed by Hayek and Mises in the 1920s, and Hayek's main contribution to the field came out soon after.[75] It argues, in a nutshell, that the reason for any crisis of capitalism lies not in the moment and context of crisis itself. Treatment should be for the boom, not for the bust. Crises, in this shorthand, become malformations of mishandled growth processes and responsibility for them can thus be laid at the doorsteps of politics. As a result of such a position (which Hayek revised throughout the 1930s after a spate of criticism),

---

72 See the memo by Frisch and Schumpeter at www.dev.econometricsociety.org.

73 John Maynard Keynes, *General Theory of Employment, Interest, and Money* (London: Macmillan, 1936); Joseph Schumpeter, *Business Cycles: A Theoretical, Historical, and Statistical Analysis of the Capitalist Process* (New York, Toronto, and London: McGraw-Hill Co., 1939).

74 See "Between Mises and Keynes: An Interview with Gottfried von Haberler," *Austrian Economics Newsletter* 20, no. 1 (Spring 2000), at mises.org.

75 F. A. Hayek, *Prices and Production* (London: Routledge, 1931).

those suffering from economic crises would be left without any support until markets rebalance and new employment emerges. Beside more obvious critics of such a position, such as fellow macroeconomist and welfare theorist John Hicks,[76] even Milton Friedman later criticized Austrian business cycle theory for its apparent prescription of letting "the bottom drop out of the world."[77]

In 1927, the Österreichisches Institut für Konjunkturforschung (Austrian Institute for Business Cycle Research) began its work with Hayek as director and Mises as *spiritus rector*. In its early stages, the institute was financed by the latter's contacts at the Chamber of Commerce in Vienna, the Austrian National Bank and the Railway Federation. Later, it received support from the Rockefeller Foundation and became one of a string of funded business cycle institutes across Europe, which formed a Standing Committee of Business Cycle Institutes with Charles Rist as its president.[78]

From the pioneering work of the Swedish economists Carl Gustav Cassel (the intellectual pioneer of the rediscovered Purchasing Power Parity paradigm particularly influential in the 1920s at the League[79]) and Knut Wicksell to Gottfried Haberler's League-commissioned writing on business cycles, the League actively attracted research-based policy recommendations. The Business Cycle Institute's approach, besides the leading Swedish economists of the time, informed the League's approach to Central and Eastern Europe in the 1930s. Haberler had moved on from Hayek's original position, but as a member of Mises's Vienna circle and an employee of the Business Cycle Institute, he was never far away. The Business Cycle Institute became particularly important for the League during the Danubian Economic Study project, a large-scale comparison of Danubian countries east of Austria that was proposed to the League by the institute in 1934 and took off after the 1935 meeting of the ISC in Copenhagen. The Business Cycle Institute then also formally applied to the ISC in

76 John Hicks, "The Hayek Story," in *Critical Essays in Monetary Theory* (Oxford: Clarendon Press, 1967), 203–15.

77 Milton Friedman, "Mr. Market," *Hoover Digest* 1999/1, at hoover.org.

78 Neil de Marchi, "League of Nations Economists and the Ideal of Peaceful Change in the Decade of the 'Thirties,'" in: Craufurd D. Goodwin, *Economics and National Security: A History of their Interaction*, Duke University Press, 1991. Series: History of Political Economy Annual Supplement (Book 23), 143–78, 149.

79 Gustav Cassel, "Abnormal Deviations in International Exchanges," *The Economic Journal* 28 (1918): 413–15.

March 1936 to become an "indirect member," represented via the official Austrian representative, the *Konsularakademie*, the leading diplo-
matic school with an international student body that served as the
IIIC's main research hotspot in the field of international studies in
Austria.[80]

Early "macro-dynamic" economics, which included business cycle
analysis along with statistics as major methods in the 1930s, was also
linked to the ISC when the Rockefeller Foundation agreed to support
the Danubian Economic Study, and was included within the "Peaceful
Change" study cycle from 1935 to 1937. At the second study group
meeting, held in Paris, results needed to be reported.[81] The Danubian
Economic Study was directed by Oscar Morgenstern, who had
succeeded Hayek as the director of the Business Cycle Institute when
the latter left for the LSE in 1931. Morgenstern shared a methodological uneasiness towards statistical data with Hayek, whose first
publications were in this field, recalling the "fuzziness" of both the
data and the theory that go into business cycle analysis.[82] But as
business cycle research was prominent with the League otherwise,
Morgenstern became a member of the League's Committee of
Statistical Experts.[83]

The Danubian Economic Study stirred the interest of economists
interested in business cycle theory—or, as the Rockefeller Foundation
put it, in "the problem of cyclical and structural change"—and was
connected to the network of business cycle institutes coordinated by
Rist. In the spring of 1937, preparing for the Paris conference, the
prolongation of the grant was further discussed and the interest of
economists like Wilhelm Röpke and John Bell Condliffe—who would
later participate at the WLC—was noted by Rockefeller.[84] Röpke was
brought into the League's rank of experts because his work on business
cycle theory had made him an internationally recognized expert in the
field. The translation from Röpke's German original (1931) got

---

80 See the Rockefeller Foundation Archive, RG1, S100, Box 110, Folder 1002, and
particularly the internal letter from Tracy Kittredge, dated December 10, 1935.

81 See International Studies Conference, *Peaceful Change: Procedures, Populations,
Raw Materials, Colonies* (IIIC: Paris, 1938), 214-57.

82 Oskar Morgenstern, *International Financial Transactions and Business Cycles*
(Princeton: Princeton University Press, 1959), 10.

83 biblio-archive.unog.ch/Dateien/CouncilDocs/C-3-1939_EN.pdf, 6.

84 RG1, S100, Box 110, Folder 1002, see proposed resolution from January 12,
1937.

underway on the initiative of the League's Ragnar Nurkse and was finally published in 1936, the year of the Annecy conference on international economy.[85] At the conference, Röpke was given the task of initiating research on "postwar agrarian and industrial protectionism."[86] He carried out the research under the auspices of the Graduate Institute in Geneva from 1937 onward. He then applied for funding at the Rockefeller Foundation to realize the study in the best possible manner. In March 1938, a group of experts had been charged by Rockefeller to review Röpke's proposal. They met at the Paris-based Institut de Recherche Economiques et Sociales directed by Rist on 19 March and decided that the project deserved funding. Röpke was granted $60,000.[87] Members of the board judging Röpke's proposal belonged to the permanent committee of *Instituts de conjuncture* (business cycle institutes) mentioned above. Among them were Charles Rist, John Condliffe, and William Rappard. Indeed, the business cycle part of the story brings the WLC in touch with the ISC and Rockefeller once more. Not only were WLC participants and invitees found within the deeper trenches of the funding network and at the *Instituts de conjuncture*, but they had also been to the 1936 Annecy conference. Mises, Röpke, and Condliffe participated both in Annecy and in Paris in 1938. Rappard, Rist, and Robbins were at least invited to Paris and participated in Annecy.[88]

The short story of the business cycle theory and its connection to both early neoliberalism and the League shows that those early neoliberals who were in Paris for the WLC were, among other things, experts in the emerging field of what Frisch had called "macro-dynamic" economics and dealt with empirical and theoretical efforts to get a grip on the global economy. This was spot-on in terms of the focus of the League's interest. When looking at the list of participants and invitees of the WLC one can already find Condliffe, Hayek, Marjolin, Mantoux, Mises, Rist, Röpke, and Rappard involved in business cycle analysis. All of them were invited to join the WLC, though not all of them managed to attend.

85   Wilhelm Röpke, *Cycles and Crises* (London: W. Hodge, 1936), iv.

86   See the preface in Wilhelm Röpke, *International Economic Disintegration* (London: W. Hodge, 1942).

87   Charles Rist, Letter to Tracy B. Kittredge, dated March 9, 1938, IIIC Archives, Folder K.1.3.

88   See De Marchi, "League of Nations Economists," 149–50.

Conclusion

Reading the Walter Lippmann Colloquium in the context of its time shows that it did not fall from the sky in the summer of 1938 as the first seed of a robust and unchanging worldview of what would later become an ever-growing ideological flora in the Mont Pèlerin Society. It shows that neoliberalism was entrenched from the beginning in transnational elite networks whose goal was (and still is) to define ideas of normative statehood and liberal governance able to keep politics within its "proper limits" while making sure that nation-states share an ideological DNA without being identical.[89]

Early neoliberals were fully aware of the scale of their project. They were making states and economies. Their ambitions were never small but they had the confidence of their proximity to powerful political and financial sources. Because of this awareness they can be thought of as normative actors fully aware of their very norm making. The liberal variety of the "good society" had to be shaped and molded like any other society. Conscious of their fundamental work, they built the ideological elements of neoliberal language and discourse.

Early neoliberalism was embedded in the transnational networks of expertise emerging in the 1930s in a number of ways. It was embedded institutionally through the League of Nations, its consultative bodies of the ICIC and the IIIC, and was particularly inspired by the ISC, linked to and developed in dialogue with the newly forming discipline of international studies. In the latter, it was embedded also conceptually, building its ideological semantics alongside the general trends in international law, political theory, and international relations. Despite later characterizations of Karl Polanyi and neoliberals as ideological and methodological opposites, the institutional focus of early neoliberals even suggested the embedding of the economy in a sense reminiscent of Polanyi. Of course, Karl Polanyi argued for different forms of embedding, and early neoliberals were clearly in favor of retaining land, labor, and capital as commodities (the root cause of capitalism's crisis according to Polanyi),[90] but they were also acutely aware that nation-states were here to stay and that national

---

89 Carl J. Friedrich, "The Political Thought of Neo-Liberalism," *The American Political Science Review* 49, no. 2 (1955), 509–25, 525.

90 Karl Polanyi, *The Great Transformation* (New York: Farrar and Rinehart, 1944).

economies had to be embedded politically and socially to fit in with other national economies on a global economic playing field. The Agenda of Liberalism was their proposal to reach such an international order.

Furthermore, early neoliberalism found nourishment in the theories of business cycle analysis, understood as a research program on cyclical and structural economic change. In general, ideas of normative statehood—the need to build states in certain ways in order to guarantee economic success and with it internal peace—began to thrive within the League's institutional network as answers were sought to questions emerging both from European state-building after the unravelling of empires in Central, Eastern and South-Eastern Europe and from the Mandate System that needed to define how former colonies might reach full independence.[91]

A number of early neoliberals who participated at the WLC continued their careers within global elite networks. Rueff became the first director of UNESCO's International Council for Philosophy and Humanistic Studies. Marjolin became the first director of the OEEC. Auboin continued as general director of the BIS until 1958. Yet new questions arise. For if neoliberalism was already deeply entrenched in global governance networks, why was there a need for the MPS in the first place? One answer is that the embedding enacted with the postwar reconstruction, the Bretton Woods institutions, the UN, and the early European integration process was not the kind of embedded liberalism early neoliberals wholeheartedly supported.[92] While their ideas were mainstream in the late 1930s, they were marginal by 1945. Bretton Woods' fixed but adjustable exchange rates, the dominance of Keynesian macroeconomics, and the increasing limitation of the price mechanism's scope by welfare state practices and various plans within the European reconstruction process might have motivated some early neoliberals to purify their doctrine and to gather their strength in the MPS (see Matthias

---

91 See Antony Anghie, *Imperialism, Sovereignty and the Making of International Law* (Cambridge: Cambridge University Press, 2007); Quinn Slobodian, *Globalists: The End of Empire and the Birth of Neoliberalism* (Cambridge, MA: Harvard University Press, 2018).

92 John Gerard Ruggie, "International Regimes, Transactions, and Change: Embedded Liberalism in the Postwar Economic Order," *International Organization* 36, no. 2 (1982): 379–415.

Schmelzer's contribution to this volume), while others remained powerful policy-makers, for example Marjolin, and tolerated a more pragmatic approach. Yet this purification must be seen as one of many possible outcomes of the original Agenda of Liberalism from 1938, not as an ironclad inevitability. Seeing the Walter Lippmann Colloquium in context reveals the importance of a more globally oriented conceptual history that is aware of institutional conditions and possibilities. We must locate the origins of neoliberalism within a contested field of thought rather than track a putatively pure essence. Neoliberalism was born in dialogue with other views and should be studied in such a way too.

8

What Comes After Bretton Woods?
Neoliberals Debate and Fight
for a Future Monetary Order

Matthias Schmelzer

Who killed Bretton Woods?[1] Scholars have yet to deliver a final verdict on the question of how and why we moved from an age of fixed but adjustable exchange rates and capital controls designed by John Maynard Keynes and others in 1944 to that of flexible rates and free capital movements in which we still live—a shift that proved fundamental for the neoliberal counter-revolution at large. After the Great Depression and well into the 1960s, most economists and policy-makers saw free markets for international capital and currency flows as too destabilizing for a robust and well-functioning capitalism. The neoliberals around the Mont Pèlerin Society (MPS) disagreed and the Bretton Woods order was a deep thorn in their side. In fact, they saw capital and exchange controls as one of the most fundamental threats not only to the market system but to Western civilization itself.

For all their consternation, neoliberals remained in the minority on matters of international monetary order until the early 1970s, when the hemorrhaging of gold from US coffers and what policy-makers saw as the persistent overvaluation of the dollar drove Richard Nixon's administration to seek drastic solutions, culminating in the closure of the gold window and beginning the move to floating exchange rates. In 1982, Milton Friedman famously observed that when a "crisis occurs, the

---

1 For helpful comments on earlier versions of this chapter, I want to thank in particular Quinn Slobodian, but also Dieter Plehwe, Harmut Kaelble, and Alexander Nützenadel.

actions that are taken depend on the ideas that are lying around." The
goal was "to develop alternatives to existing policies, to keep them alive
and available until the politically impossible becomes politically
inevitable."[2] Friedman illustrated his key dictum by reference to the
breakdown of Bretton Woods: "Such a crisis arose in 1971. If the alternative of floating exchange rates had not been fully explored in the
academic literature . . . it is not clear what solution would have been
adopted."[3]

The neoliberal campaign to end the Bretton Woods system of "embedded liberalism" was an example of Friedman's strategy in action and
offers one of the earliest and most comprehensive examples of successful
neoliberal policy entrepreneurship in academic, political, and business
circles.[4] How did Friedman and other neoliberal economists become
influential? What did "keeping options available" mean in practice?
Alongside US national interests, scholars have highlighted the importance of the ideological outlook of key decision-makers of the Nixon
administration in the decision to dismantle Bretton Woods. They have
pointed to the influence of individuals like Herbert Stein, Paul
McCracken, William Fellner (all members of the Council of Economic
Advisers), Gottfried Haberler (head of Nixon's Task Force on US Balance
of Payments Policies), and Milton Friedman.[5] These economists,
together with their academic and think tank networks, were able to
place their interpretations, arguments, and strategies within the Nixon
administration and to portray flexible exchange rates as an attractive
resort for US policy-makers in times of balance of payments crisis.

Less often observed is the shared membership of almost all of these
individuals within the Mont Pèlerin Society and their participation in

2 Milton Friedman, *Capitalism and Freedom* (Chicago: University of Chicago Press,
1982), ix.

3 Milton Friedman and Rose D. Friedman, *Two Lucky People: Memoirs* (Chicago:
University of Chicago Press, 1998), 220.

4 John Gerard Ruggie, "International Regimes, Transactions, and Change:
Embedded Liberalism in the Postwar Economic Order," *International Organization* 36,
no. 2 (1982): 379–415.

5 See for example Carol M. Connell, *Reforming the World Monetary System: Fritz
Machlup and the Bellagio Group* (Abingdon: Routledge, 2013); Eric Helleiner, *States and
the Reemergence of Global Finance: From Bretton Woods to the 1990s* (Ithaca: Cornell
University Press, 1994); Robert Leeson, *Ideology and the International Economy: The
Decline and Fall of Bretton Woods* (New York: Palgrave Macmillan, 2004); John S. Odell,
US International Monetary Policy: Markets, Power, and Ideas as Sources of Change
(Princeton: Princeton University Press, 1982).

debates about the future of monetary order within the MPS that stretched back to the 1940s. Whereas neoliberalism is often presented as an internally consistent and unified ideology, the case of monetary order belies this impression. While the final message may have been that "there is no alternative," debates took place first about what that one policy option was, to which there is no alternative. Indeed, the rather complicated, arcane, and seemingly technical question of the international monetary system was the most controversial and divisive among organized neoliberals in the postwar decades. It resulted in the longest and most contentious internal controversy between two fundamentally opposed camps that dominated many of the yearly MPS meetings in the postwar period and threatened to split the emerging neoliberal international in the course of the 1960s. Thus, even as it documents a considerable policy victory, this chapter shows that neoliberals did not always speak with a single voice. Although unified around the need to free international movements of capital, investment, and money, neoliberals could not agree at first on the specific nature of the alternative to the Bretton Woods order.

The controversy pitted the proponents of the gold standard led by Ludwig von Mises, Wilhelm Röpke, and F. A. Hayek against advocates of floating exchange rates, most saliently Milton Friedman, Fritz Machlup, and Gottfried Haberler. The advocates of flexible exchange rates eventually prevailed. In the long run, they argued, floating currency markets would establish market discipline for national monetary and fiscal policy because there would be limits to using devaluation as an easy way to address a lack of competitiveness. And by pushing for "independent" central banks that followed set rules rather than relying on democratic decision-making, monetarists could also control the money supply, thus keeping it within strict limits and limiting the inflation they saw as caused by escalating social demands for state spending.

After the neoliberal advocates of floating rates won out in the internal debates, they launched a remarkable transnational campaign aimed at convincing key decision-makers and experts of the merits of such a post-Bretton Woods order. The campaign was carried out by both academics and experts from financial institutions. MPS members were prominent in the coordination of the campaign, which involved a concerted communication strategy and sweeping publication efforts on both sides of the Atlantic. It also relied on the organization of the era's most influential academic conference series on monetary questions aimed at economists, central bankers, and the private banking community. When the Bretton Woods system was on the verge of collapsing in the early 1970s, the flexible exchange rate discourse coalition had built up a powerful international alliance ready with an alternative. It exerted influence through key expert and advisory posts in the Nixon administration, which finally ended the gold parity of the US dollar in 1971 and did not return to a fixed exchange rate regime at the global level thereafter. If not the primary culprits in the death of Bretton Woods, the neoliberals were enthusiastic accomplices in its euthanasia.

From the Classical Gold Standard to Bretton Woods: The Historical Context

While opinions within the neoliberal thought collective of the MPS converged on most issues, the question of the monetary system proved an exception. In his insider's history of the MPS, Max Hartwell observed that the only two topics that sparked continuous controversies were the gold standard and the related question of "fixed versus flexible exchange rates."[6] At the 1984 conference in Cambridge, John Davenport could still draw "a laugh by observing that the original Pèlerinians could agree on everything save the subjects of God and gold."[7] Why was the money question so important? The first obvious point is that the neoliberals were not alone in their interest. Questions about monetary order, the stability of international trade, and the balance of payments were among the most relevant and broadly discussed issues in the transatlantic policy community from the 1950s to the 1970s.[8] However, a more specific reason helps illuminate the relationship of the emerging neoliberal thought collective to questions of democracy and freedom.

The gold standard—the liberal economic order that shaped the first phase of globalization between 1871 and 1914, lasted until the outbreak of the First World War, and was resuscitated in the interwar

---

6 Max Hartwell, *A History of the Mont Pèlerin Society* (Indianapolis: Liberty Fund, 1995), xvii; see also 114, 119.

7 Greg Kaza, "The Mont Pèlerin Society's 50th Anniversary," *The Freeman* 47, no. 6 (June 1997), https://archive.li/4RBCN.

8 Harold James, *International Monetary Cooperation since Bretton Woods* (New York: Oxford University Press, 1996).

period—was fundamentally anti-democratic. To enable free international capital flows at an astonishingly high level—around 1900 at a similar level to the year 1990 in proportional terms—this system of fixed exchange rates and gold backing posed strict limits to domestic economic policies.[9] Karl Polanyi has given a moving description of what this meant for working people and the poor: if the balance of payments, volatile international capital markets, and the stabilization of exchange rates demanded domestic restraint, then high unemployment and falling wages were condoned.[10] As stated in a standard textbook, the "stability of exchange rates relied on the submission of national economic policies under the diktat of balance of payments adjustment."[11]

Barry Eichengreen has demonstrated how this monetary system of the gold standard grew increasingly dysfunctional with the rise of democracies, strong trade unions, and the rise to prominence of interventionist and (proto-)Keynesian theories and state practices around the world. Under these new circumstances, governments had a hard time aligning their monetary policies solely to stabilize the necessary amount of gold and defend the currency peg when demands such as full employment and economic growth were gaining in importance.[12] The gold standard broke down during the First World War, and all efforts to reinstall a gold exchange standard during the 1920s—that is, all attempts to contain the political power of trade unions and voting people—failed due to a lack of harmonization between central banks, protectionist capital controls, and a new social balance of power.[13] In reaction to the widely perceived failure of laissez-faire policies leading to the Great Depression, governments around the world enacted new policies, including extensive social programs, new forms of government

---

9 Barry Eichengreen, *Golden Fetters: The Gold Standard and the Great Depression, 1919–1939* (New York: Oxford University Press, 1992).

10 Karl Polanyi, *The Great Transformation* (New York: Farrar & Rinehart, 1944).

11 Rolf Caspers, *Zahlungsbilanz und Wechselkure* (Munich und Wien: Oldenbourg Verlag, 2002).

12 Eichengreen has argued that the main conditions underpinning the functioning of the gold standard were that voting rights were limited, workers' parties and trade unions were weak, wages and prices were highly flexible, and there was a willingness to accept high unemployment. See Barry Eichengreen, *Globalizing Capital: A History of the International Monetary System* (Princeton: Princeton University Press, 1996).

13 Matt Hampton, "Hegemony, Class Struggle and the Radical Historiography of Global Monetary Standards," *Capital & Class* 30, no. 2 (2006): 131–64; Maurice Obstfeld and Alan M. Taylor, *Global Capital Markets: Integration, Crisis, and Growth* (Cambridge: Cambridge University Press, 2004), 37.

intervention and tariffs, and abandoning the gold standard, thus destroying "economic liberalism for half a century."[14]

When a new international economic order for the postwar period
was crafted at the Bretton Woods conference in 1944, the agreement was
based on a widely held consensus that rejected both the gold standard
and free-floating exchange rates in favor of a prioritization of domestic
policy goals—most importantly full employment—and the need for
widespread capital controls. The mainstream rejection of the two options
discussed by the neoliberals demonstrates how far their views were from
the economic consensus in the mid-twentieth century and is thus worth
explaining at some length.

Circa 1945, the belief in automatically equilibrating market forces
and the dangers of government controls of capital movements was
widely regarded as historically obsolete. Henry Dexter White, leader of
the US delegation to the conference, argued characteristically that objections to interference with capital and gold movements were "hangovers
from a Nineteenth Century economic creed, which held that international economic adjustments, if left alone, would work themselves out
towards an 'equilibrium' with a minimum of harm to world trade and
prosperity."[15] In an influential publication from the League of Nations,
Ragnar Nurkse explained the dominant professional opinion of the time
that "international monetary policy [should] conform to domestic
social and economic policy and not the other way round."[16]

The rejection of floating exchange rates was equally strong, in particular because the short experience of run-away inflation in the 1920s were
interpreted as causally responsible for the Great Depression. Economists
argued against the dangers of competitive devaluation and speculative,
destabilizing capital movements. Nurkse captured the *Zeitgeist* when he
wrote that "if there is anything that the inter-war experience has clearly
demonstrated, it is that paper currency exchanges cannot be left free to
fluctuate." To do, he continued, "would almost certainly result in

14   Eric J. Hobsbawm, *Age of Extremes: The Short Twentieth Century, 1914–1991*
(London: Abacus, 1995), 94–5.

15   Cited in J. Keith Horsefield et al., *The International Monetary Fund 1945–1965:
Twenty Years of International Monetary Cooperation* (Washington: International
Monetary Fund, 1969), vol. 3, 64.

16   Ragnar Nurkse, *International Currency Experience: Lessons of the Inter-War
Period* (Princeton: League of Nations Publications Department, 1944), 230.

chaos."[17] Thus the belief underpinning the Bretton Woods system was that the stability of the international monetary and trade order could only be guaranteed through fixed exchange rates, which had to be managed by central banks—with the support of the International Monetary Fund (IMF)—and through deliberate interventions in currency markets.

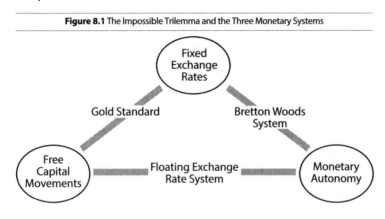

Figure 8.1 The Impossible Trilemma and the Three Monetary Systems

Rejecting both the discipline of the gold standard and the instability of floating exchange rates, the international gathering of policy-makers at Bretton Woods established a monetary system that combined two policy goals: on the one hand, enabling sovereign, autonomous, and democratic economic policies aimed at full employment; and on the other hand, fixed but adjustable exchange rates that were pegged to the US dollar, which in turn had a gold parity (gold exchange standard coupled with IMF assistance). The dominant opinion at Bretton Woods was that strict capital controls were needed to make democratic domestic fiscal and monetary policies compatible with fixed exchange rates, and "almost every analyst" regarded "control of capital movements for unlimited time" as a precondition for the restoration of stable international trade.[18]

As indicated by the impossible trilemma developed much later, according to which governments can only realize two out of the three policy goals of fixed exchange rates, free capital movements, and monetary autonomy, the Bretton Woods system sacrificed free capital movements (see Figure 8.1).[19] At the time, this was not perceived as a sacrifice by most economists and politicians. On the contrary, governments were even invited to control all international capital movements.[20] Accordingly, the postwar decades developed into the period with the densest capital controls in the history of international capitalism.[21]

It was precisely the matter of capital controls that neoliberal promoters of the gold standard and floating exchange rates saw as the key threat to a liberal order. Two recurring points can be regarded as fundamental axioms of neoliberal monetary thought: First, the rejection of any form of currency and capital controls. Second, the attempt to use automatic market mechanisms to impede or roll back democratic (and Keynesian) economic policies and thus reintroduce fiscal and monetary restraint. While the rejection of government controls was generally constitutive of liberal worldviews—and the pathos behind these arguments for freedom within the Cold War context can hardly be overlooked—capital controls were of particular concern for neoliberals. Hayek highlighted the special status of international currency controls in one of the founding documents of neoliberalism, *The Road to Serfdom*.[22] He argued that currency controls demonstrated best his main argument that government controls of the economy or "planning" led to slavery. He wrote that government controls of foreign exchange are "the decisive advance on the path to totalitarianism and the suppression of individual liberty. It is, in fact, the complete delivery of the individual to the tyranny of the state, the final suppression of all means of escape—not merely for the rich, but for everyone."[23] In a similar vein, Friedman argued in *Capitalism and Freedom* that exchange controls are the "most serious threat to freedom in the US" and, even more fundamentally, that "the most effective way to convert a market economy into an authoritarian economic society is to start by imposing direct controls on foreign

19 The trilemma was originally formally developed in the early 1960s by Fleming and Mundell. More recent accounts include Obstfeld and Taylor, *Global Capital Markets*; James, *International Monetary Cooperation*.

20 Helleiner, *States*, 49. See also Eichengreen, *Globalizing Capital*, 93–135.

21 Jörg Huffschmid, *Politische Ökonomie der Finanzmärkte* (Hamburg: VSA-Verlag, 2002), 117; Obstfeld and Taylor, *Global Capital Markets*.

22 F. A. Hayek, *The Road to Serfdom* (Chicago: University of Chicago Press, 1944). Short biographies of all the MPS economists discussed in this paper can be found in Matthias Schmelzer, *Freiheit für Wechselkurse und Kapital. Die Ursprünge neoliberaler Währungspolitik und die Mont Pèlerin Society* (Marburg: Metropolis, 2010), 217–25.

23 Hayek, *The Road to Serfdom*, 92.

exchange."[24] Friedman and Haberler argued that controls "congeal the blood of capitalism,"[25] could lead to the abandonment of the market system,[26] and, in von Mises's words, even to the "demise of Western civilization."[27]

It reveals much about the neoliberal notion of freedom that they saw the most powerful threat to the freedom of individuals and to Western civilization as such in the government regulation of foreign exchange, that is, in regulations instituted in an effort to enhance economic stability and general welfare, which posed little restriction on those not engaged in international investment and trade. Yet for the MPS, these controls were a key threat, and its internal debates and external advocacy thus revolved around the question of which monetary system could make controls for capital and foreign exchange superfluous or even impossible.[28]

Alongside capital controls, Bretton Woods established an international framework for the domestic interventionist policies of the Fordist regime of "embedded liberalism." One could argue that this was the international institutionalization of what Hayek had criticized as "monetary nationalism" since the 1930s—the idea that an autonomous and democratic monetary policy was possible within the boundaries of nation-states.[29] Keynesianism and monetary nationalism were "built into the international postwar order," Hayek claimed in his only publication on these questions during the Bretton Woods era.[30] In the view of Hayek and many of his colleagues from the MPS, the Bretton Woods system practically forced governments on a path of inflationary and

24 Friedman, *Capitalism and Freedom*, 57.

25 In Milton Friedman and Robert Roosa, *The Balance of Payments: Free Versus Fixed Exchange Rates* (Washington: American Enterprise Institute, 1967), 82f.

26 Fritz Machlup, "Three Concepts of the Balance of Payments and the so-called Dollar Shortage," *The Economic Journal* 60 (March 1950), 46–68.

27 Ludwig von Mises, *The Theory of Money and Credit* (New Haven: Yale University Press, 1954), 434.

28 Philip Mirowski, "Postface: Defining Neoliberalism," in *The Road from Mont Pèlerin*, ed. Philip Mirowski and Dieter Plehwe (Cambridge, MA: Harvard University Press, 2009), 417–55.

29 F. A. Hayek, *Monetary Nationalism and International Stability* (London: Longmans, Green and Co., 1937).

30 F. A. Hayek, "Bemerkungen über die Funktion von Währungsreserven und den Begriff der internationalen Liquidität," in *Was mit der Goldwährung geschehen ist. Ein Bericht aus dem Jahre 1932 mit zwei Ergänzungen* (Tübingen: J. C. B. Mohr, 1965), 31–4. See also Mises, *Theory of Money*, 434.

expansionist monetary policy, which in turn leads to an expansion of the state apparatus and increases the danger of collectivist and totalitarian developments.[31]

Rather than a global order that allowed for national-economic experimentation and expansion, neoliberals aimed at turning the causal chain around and establishing an international monetary order that would force societies onto a market-liberal and anti-inflationary path. The key question that shaped the neoliberal debates for the coming quarter century was posed by Hayek at the founding meeting of the MPS: "how can monetary policy be automatic, and outside the range of politics?"[32] The classical solution to the twin neoliberal demands of free capital flows and automatic market mechanisms to roll back democratic economic policies had been the gold standard. Yet, after 1945, neoliberals launched an intense and enduring debate, in which the classical solution was criticized as unrealistic and was increasingly displaced by another proposal—that of floating exchange rates.

'Pèlerinians Could Agree on Everything Save God and Gold': The Internal Debates in the Postwar Decades

To properly understand the debates among neoliberals about alternative international monetary systems it is key to situate them in the general intellectual climate of the postwar decades. Even amid a prevailing mood of skepticism towards market forces, the price system, and liberalized and deregulated capital markets, the gold standard and flexible exchange rates were rejected particularly strongly. This situation lasted well into the 1960s.[33] The gold standard was widely regarded as an outdated artifact of the past and was only supported by an extremely small minority of economists—estimates suggest well below 1 percent. One advocate of the gold standard, MPS member Murray Rothbard,

---

31   See F. A. Hayek, "Opening Address to Mont Pèlerin Conference, 1947," Liberaal Archief, Ghent, MPS-files (henceforth LA). After the collapse of Bretton Woods, Hayek started to advocate for free banking through competitive currencies, thus overcoming the government monopoly on the creation and printing of money. F. A. Hayek, *Denationalization of Money* (London: IEA, 1976).

32   Hartwell, *A History of the Mont Pèlerin Society*, 37.

33   Leeson, *Ideology and the International Economy*, 20; Odell, *US International Monetary Policy*, 22.

described the situation in 1962 aptly: "now [the gold standard] is considered an absurd anachronism, a relic of a tribal fetish."[34]

In a similar vein, floating exchange rates were almost universally dismissed and ignored, as summarized by US economist Richard Cooper: "Initially Friedman was nearly alone in his views. Most contemporary economists favored fixed exchange rates and feared the instabilities that flexible exchange rates might bring, or reveal."[35] Until the 1960s, one historian has argued, "it was widely accepted both by academic and IMF economists that floating exchange rates were a species of law-breaking behavior."[36] This skeptical view was even more pronounced among politicians and businesspeople than among economists. With the exception of France under de Gaulle in the 1960s, who invoked the gold standard idea, and Canada's experience with its floating currency during the 1950s, both were entirely ignored. Within this rather hostile intellectual climate that dismissed both the gold standard and floating exchange rates, the community of organized neoliberals strove to find agreement on a solution to the challenges posed by the existing international monetary order of Bretton Woods.

In the beginning, the neoliberals were almost all gold bugs. At the founding MPS conference in 1947, nearly every participant agreed that the reintroduction of the classical gold standard with liberalized capital movements would be the monetary system consistent with the core values of the new society, while flexible exchange rates were regarded as Keynesian, nationalist, and unstable. Yet there was dissent even at this first conference as the renowned Princeton economist Frank Graham presented the idea of a "Commodity Reserve Standard" as a preferable alternative to the gold standard.[37] Graham died in 1949 and could not continue the project further, but it was taken up by Milton Friedman, whose arguments for flexible exchange rates developed in the years following the foundation of the MPS bore a clear resemblance to those

---

34 Murray N. Rothbard, "The Case for a Genuine Gold Dollar," in *In Search of a Monetary Constitution*, ed. Leland Yeager (Cambridge, MA: Harvard University Press, 1962), 94.

35 Richard N. Cooper, "Exchange Rate Choices," Conference Series, Federal Reserve Bank of Boston (June 1999), 103. See also Milton Friedman, Edward M. Bernstein, Milton Gilbert, "Discussion," *The American Economic Review* 55, no. 1/2 (1965), 183; Friedman and Roosa, *Balance*, 133.

36 Anthony M. Endres, *Great Architects of International Finance: The Bretton Woods Era* (London and New York: Routledge, 2005), 9.

37 Schmelzer, *Freiheit für Wechselkurse und Kapital*, 76–8.

of Graham.[38] Friedman formulated his position in a memorandum written as part of his service as an advisor to the OEEC, in which he made the provocative suggestion that the German balance of payments problem would be solved by floating the deutsche mark—a suggestion that received little sympathy from German authorities. Completed after the MPS conference in 1950, his seminal article on "the case for flexible exchange rates" was published in 1953.[39]

In the following years, Friedman, supported by the German economists and former gold standard advocates Friedrich Lutz and Albert Hahn, developed his argument for floating exchange rates, which was discussed at various MPS conferences. In particular, he argued that while the gold standard would function fully automatically in principle and would guarantee "freedom of political control" under the prevalent social and political circumstances, it was questionable whether governments would stick to the rules.[40] He defended the stability of flexible exchange rates through a twofold argument. On the one hand, he reinterpreted the historical experiences of the 1920s by focusing on the "underlying instability of economic conditions." On the other hand, he criticized the idea of destabilizing currency speculations theoretically, arguing that profitable speculations could actually stabilize the system.[41]

Both sets of arguments—that the gold standard advocates relied on unrealistic assumptions and that flexible exchange rates are a viable and stable alternative—came to shape the debate in the coming decades and were repeated time and again by Friedman and other disciples of floating exchange rates. In many cases, these were combined with an insistence on domestic monetarism as the "logical" counterpart strategy that also aimed at demarcating this policy set from the Keynesian proposals for flexible rates, promoted most notably by James Meade.[42]

By the mid-1950s, advocates of floating seem to have won over the two "American Austrians," Gottfried Haberler and Fritz Machlup, both

38 Leeson, *Ideology and the International Economy*; Anthony M. Endres, "Frank Graham's Case for Flexible Exchange Rates: A Doctrinal Perspective," *History of Political Economy* 40, no. 1 (January 1, 2008): 133–62.

39 Milton Friedman, "The Case for Flexible Exchange Rates," in *Essays in Positive Economics* (Chicago: University of Chicago Press, 1953), 157–203.

40 Milton Friedman, "Commodity Reserve Money," 1950, LA.

41 Ibid.; Friedman, "The Case for Flexible Exchange Rates," 177.

42 Friedrich Lutz, "Comment," 1950, LA; Friedman, "The Case for Flexible Exchange Rates," 158; James Meade, *The Balance of Payments* (Oxford: Oxford University Press, 1951).

former students of von Mises and advocates of the gold standard who became key protagonists in the neoliberal crusade for floating exchange rates. They were joined by others from the German tradition of the Freiburg school of ordoliberalism, including Friedrich Lutz and Fritz Meyer.[43] At the discussions within the MPS, however, the position remained unpopular. As reported from the 1957 meeting in St. Moritz, "the advocates of flexible exchange rates [were a] minority" and were "accused of monetary nationalism by Prof. Heilperin."[44]

Nonetheless, ever more MPS economists converted to floating exchange rates, partly convinced by the arguments of their peers, partly by real world events such as rising inflation in West Germany and US balance of payments problems. Among these converts was Ludwig A. Hahn, a West German economist, stock trader, and banker, who used his private financial success to gain authority in monetary debates and introduced the argument of "imported inflation" due to rigid exchange rates in hard currency countries such as the Federal Republic.[45] Similarly, the German ordoliberal and former student of Walter Eucken, Fritz Meyer, changed his opinion in the early 1950s and promoted flexible exchange rates as a member of the Federal Republic's government expert advisory board (*Sachverständigenrat*) from 1954 onward.[46] Another example of conversion was the Yale economist William Fellner, another Central European émigré, and a key protagonist of the transnational debates of the 1960s and later a member of Nixon's Council of Economic Advisers.[47]

43 Gottfried Haberler, *Currency Convertibility* (Washington: AEI, 1954); Schmelzer, *Freiheit für Wechselkurse und Kapital*, 88–90. On Machlup see in particular Connell, *Reforming the World Monetary System*.

44 *Neue Zürcher Zeitung*, September 16, 1957, 10.

45 Ludwig A. Hahn, "Autonomous Monetary Policy and Fixed Exchange Rates," 1957; Ludwig A. Hahn, "Gold-Revaluation and Dollar-Devaluation?" 1960, LA; Jan-Otmar Hesse, "Some Relationships between a Scholar's and an Entrepreneur's Life: The Biography of L. Albert Hahn," *History of Political Economy* 39 (2007): 215–33.

46 "Sachverständigenrat zur Begutachtung der gesamtwirtschaftlichen Entwicklung," *Jahresgutachten 1964/65* (1964), reprinted 1994 by Schmidt Periodicals GmbH, Bad Feilnbach; Fritz W. Meyer, "Die internationale Währungsordnung im Dienste der stabilitätspolitischen Grenzmoral und die Möglichkeiten einer Reform," in *25 Jahre Marktwirtschaft in der Bundesrepublik Deutschland*, ed. Dieter Cassel et al. (Stuttgart: Fischer, 1972), 283–96.

47 William Fellner, *Amerikanische Erfahrungen mit der Lohninflation in den Fünfziger Jahren* (Tübingen: J. C. B. Mohr, 1962); William Fellner, "On Limited Exchange-rate Flexibility," in *Maintaining and Restoring Balance in International Payments*, ed. William Fellner et al. (Princeton: Princeton University Press, 1966), 111–22. See also James N. Marshall, *William J. Fellner. A Bio-Bibliography* (Westport: Greenwood Press, 1992).

Some new MPS members also joined the camp of flexible exchange rate advocates, most importantly the following: Egon Sohmen, who was influenced by his mentors Machlup, Haberler, and Fellner, and played a key role at the international level in making floating acceptable through conferences, public talks, and political networking;[48] James Buchanan, student of Friedman and Frank Knight in Chicago and founder of the Virginia School for Political Economy, who helped publicize Friedman's dictum inside the MPS and beyond;[49] and Leland B. Yeager, the co-founder (with James M. Buchanan) of the neoliberal Virginia School, who became crucially important for the academic formalization and dissemination of Friedman's arguments, in particular through his 1966 textbook.[50] Finally, an internal dispute within the MPS about the policy outlook of the society—the so-called Hunold-Hayek crisis in 1960—led to the exclusion from the MPS of some key promoters of the gold standard, most importantly Wilhelm Röpke and Alexander Rüstow.[51]

The controversy pitting advocates of gold against those of floating rates came to a head at the longest-ever discussion at MPS general meetings, in 1961 in Turin, which crystallized the internal dynamics and key arguments.[52] Some elements are worth highlighting. Firstly, many speakers emphasized that the neoliberals' inability to agree on these basic questions was a "shame," and that this "embittered controversy" within the neoliberal camp had given "help and encouragement to a common enemy."[53] Conflicts should be dealt with internally, participants argued, while in the

---

48   Egon Sohmen, *Flexible Exchange Rates: Theory and Controversy* (Chicago: University of Chicago Press, 1961).

49   James M. Buchanan, "Staatliche Souveränität, nationale Planung und wirtschaftliche Freiheit," *Ordo* 14 (1963): 249–58. The article is a published version of a talk given at an MPS meeting. Thanks to Quinn Slobodian for this reference. See also *Washington Post*, May 19, 1967, D9.

50   Leland B. Yeager, *International Monetary Relations: Theory, History, and Policy* (New York: Harper & Row, 1966).

51   Bernhard Walpen, *Die offenen Feinde und ihre Gesellschaft. Eine hegemonietheoretische Studie zur Mont Pèlerin Society* (Hamburg: VSA-Verlag, 2004), 131–51.

52   At least thirteen men gave presentations, among them as supporters of the gold standard Michael Heilperin, Philip Cortney, Jacques Rueff, Henry Hazlitt, Alexander Loveday, Hans Sennholz, and Arthur Kemp; and the advocates of flexible exchange rates Friedman, Lutz, Machlup, Hahn, and Hans Ilau. It is the only general meeting of which an audio recording exists, which makes a detailed analysis possible.

53   Cortney in MPS, "Audio Recordings of the General Meeting 1961," 1961, available at brunoleoni.it.

public they should aim at emphasizing the commonalities.[54] Yet in the debate, discrediting the opposing neoliberal position was the dominant strategy. Promoters of flexible exchange rates argued that a gold standard was plainly impossible "in the face of the strengthened political power of trade unions."[55] For their part, gold standard promoters accused their opponents of basing their arguments on the unrealistic assumption that monetary policy could function in a stable and anti-inflationary fashion without the discipline of a gold-based monetary system.[56]

Far from being a single-minded homogeneous bloc, the neoliberal thought collective was deeply divided. Both camps argued that only their proposal would enable free flows of capital and that their opponents' position was not compatible with liberal core values and was thus secretly supporting dirigiste and collectivist policies.[57] A split in the gold standard camp developed when they could not agree if the gold price would need to be substantially raised (a position fervently promoted by Philip Cortney, Heilperin, and Rueff), or whether such a move would lead to inflationary disaster (as argued by Arthur Kemp and others around the US think tank Economists' National Committee on Monetary Policy).

The controversy continued through the 1960s but support for the gold standard option eroded steadily, particularly after the 1965 MPS meeting in Stresa. Haberler and Machlup acted as key mediators in the debate by dissecting assumptions, and offering arguments, counter-arguments, and logical conclusions. Their attempts at diplomacy were only partially successful. After the 1965 meeting, debates over the proper monetary order ultimately dissolved longstanding friendships, including that of Mises and Machlup, who had been a close friend of both Mises and his wife since the Vienna years, and that of Mises and Haberler, who had acted as the witness at Mises's wedding in Geneva.[58] Even Friedman's attempt at the 1968 meeting to resolve the controversy by presenting a "list of propositions agreed to by both proponents and

---

54 Arthur Kemp, "The International Monetary Order," 1961, LA.

55 Ilau in MPS, "Audio Recordings"; Fritz Machlup, "International Liquidity and International Money Creation," 1961, LA.

56 Michael Heilperin, "Monetary Reform in an Atlantic Setting," 1961; Hans Sennholz, "From Dollar Gap to Dollar Glut," 1961, LA.

57 Friedman in MPS, "Audio Recordings"; Kemp, "International Monetary Order."

58 Fritz Machlup, "Ludwig von Mises: The Academic Scholar Who Would Not Compromise," *Wirtschaftspolitische Blätter* 28, no. 4 (1981), 13.

opponents of free exchange rates" failed to reconcile the fundamentally incompatible positions.[59]

How can we explain the depth of feeling inspired by the monetary issue? The question of generational differences offers some clues. Looking at age cohorts, one finds that the gold standard was promoted primarily by economists born before 1900, who had experienced not only the functioning classical gold standard but, more importantly, the catastrophic experiences with floating exchange rates in the 1920s, and who had been socialized before Keynesianism began to shape the discipline of economics.[60] Economists born in the first decade of the twentieth century constitute a saddle group, advocating the gold standard until the 1950s or early 1960s before shifting to flexible exchange rates.[61] Younger economists born after 1910 and socialized during the height of Keynesianism and interventionism tended to promote floating rates almost exclusively, which they regarded as more realistic in the face of prevailing circumstances.[62]

The combination of young advocates and converts from the middle generational cohort meant that floating exchange rates emerged over time at the MPS meetings as the privileged neoliberal proposal for a new international monetary system. By providing a space to debate and largely work through entrenched divisions, the meetings helped build a transnational elite network of advocates for flexible exchange rates that can be characterized as an epistemic community following Peter Haas's definition: an advocacy coalition with shared normative assumptions and principles (all of which were also shared within the entire MPS), shared causal beliefs, shared notions of validity (both widely diverging from the gold standard camp), and, finally, "a common policy enterprise."[63]

59 Milton Friedman, "Free vs Fixed Exchange Rates. List of propositions agreed to by both proponents and opponents of free exchange rates," 1968, LA. For a detailed analysis of all MPS meetings in this period see Schmelzer, *Freiheit für Wechselkurse und Kapital*, 74–118.

60 This group includes Ludwig von Mises (born 1981), Henry Hazlitt (1894), Philip Cortney (1895), Jacques Rueff (1896), Otto Veit (1898), Wilhelm Röpke (1899), F. A. Hayek (1899), William Hutt (1899). A younger exception was Michael Heilperin (1909).

61 Gottfried Haberler (1900), Friedrich Lutz (1901), Fritz Machlup (1902), William Fellner (1905), Fritz Meyer (1907).

62 George Stigler (1911), Milton Friedman (1912), Enoch Powell (1912), Paul McCracken (1915), Herbert Stein (1916), Herbert Giersch (1921), Leeland B. Yeager (1923), Arnold Harberger (1924), Egon Sohmen (1930).

63 Peter M. Haas, "Introduction: Epistemic Communities and International Policy Coordination," *International Organization* 46, no. 1 (1992): 3; Schmelzer, *Freiheit für Wechselkurse und Kapital*, 118–27.

The defeat of the proposal to return to the nineteenth-century model of the gold standard offers strong evidence that neoliberalism itself was and is not simply the return of laissez-faire or classical liberalism reborn but a genuinely novel response to changed circumstances. Yet even here the process of creating a common internal opinion was not absolute. As later developments demonstrated, the losing side remained relevant in debates on a monetary union in Western Europe (which was similarly divisive in neoliberal circles) and in discussions about currency boards and dollarization in the Global South. Thus, the debate over monetary order demonstrates both the existence of divergent epistemic communities within the thought collective of the MPS, and also the fact that their commitment to a set of core values still held the group together.[64] It offers an insight into neoliberal thought as a doctrine in a constant process of becoming, not emerging from whole cloth in founding texts of the movement but constantly reworked according to shifting conditions.

Conferences, Think Tanks and the Nixon Administration: Freedom Fighters in Action

When Milton Friedman published his article calling for flexible exchange rates in 1953, fewer than 5 percent of economists worldwide shared his opinion; by the end of the 1960s, approximately 90 percent of economists did, and they were joined by powerful figures within government and the banking community.[65] The early neoliberal debates and later campaign to promote flexible exchange rates thus laid the epistemological and organizational groundwork for the end of Bretton Woods. During the 1960s and early 1970s, the campaign manifested an astonishing degree of activity and became one of the early high points of neoliberal influence.[66] The organizational background of the protagonists of the agenda within the

---

64 Dieter Plehwe, "Transnational Discourse Coalitions and Monetary Policy: Argentina and the Limited Powers of the 'Washington Consensus,'" *Critical Policy Studies* 5, no. 2 (2011), 127–48; see also Dieter Plehwe, "Neoliberal Thought Collectives: Integrating Social Science and Intellectual History," in *Sage Handbook of Neoliberalism*, ed. Damien Cahill, Melinda Cooper, Martijn Konings, and David Primrose (Los Angeles: Sage, 2018).

65 Schmelzer, *Freiheit für Wechselkurse und Kapital*, 96.

66 Connell, *Reforming the World Monetary System*; Schmelzer, *Freiheit für Wechselkurse und Kapital*, 129-96.

MPS is key to understanding the breadth and coordination of their activities. These included a large series of lectures, academic and journalistic articles, pamphlets and books, public calls in daily newspapers, public debates and appearances in the media, and international conferences in all Western countries, all targeting not only the general public but, more importantly, academics, private bankers, and politicians.

The origin of the collective effort to push for flexible exchange rates can be dated to 1963, when an international reform debate took off after a series of publications by Robert Triffin, and the policy-makers of the large industrialized countries initiated a fundamental study on the international monetary system at that year's IMF meeting. The study, they argued, was to be written by government economists, since academics in their view could not agree on anything, and it should be based on the consensus that the fundamental structure of fixed exchange rates and the established gold price should remain the foundation for future arrangements.[67] This sparked the ambition of a group of academics around Machlup, Fellner, and Triffin to organize what became the Bellagio conferences to regain authority for academics in these debates and, equally important but largely overlooked in the literature, to broaden the scope of the debate by integrating both flexible exchange rates and the gold standard as two of four options discussed.[68]

Charles Kindleberger later labeled this a "new industry": "the holding of conferences on the international monetary system by academic economists with an occasional admixture of central and commercial bankers."[69] Neoliberals were the prime motors of the new industry. From the wealth of conferences that followed, three are regarded as the most important ones of the postwar era: The Bellagio conferences by the Group of 32 economists in 1963 and 1964; the Bellagio conferences that followed from 1964 onward, targeted at a dialogue between economists, central bankers, and politicians; and the Bürgenstock conferences in 1969, which were aimed mainly at international private bankers and

67 Fritz Machlup and Burton Malkiel, eds, *International Monetary Arrangements: The Problem of Choice. Report on the Deliberations of an International Study Group of Thirty-two Economists* (Princeton: Princeton University Press, 1964), 5.

68 Ibid.; Connell, *Reforming the World Monetary System*; Carol M. Connell and Joseph Salerno, eds, *Monetary Reform and the Bellagio Group: Selected Letters and Papers of Fritz Machlup, Robert Triffin and William Fellner*, 5 vols (London: Taylor & Francis Group, 2014).

69 Charles Kindleberger, "Review of Mundell/Swoboda," *Journal of International Economics* 1 (1971), 127–40, here 127.

business representatives.[70] MPS members not only initiated and organized all of these conferences, they also dominated in personnel and content, comprising eight of the thirty-two participants of the Bellagio conference, four out of fourteen central economists of the following conferences with politicians, and eight out of seventeen economists at the Bürgenstock conference. The only economists that participated in all three conference series—except the Chicagoan Harry Johnson—were all MPS members: Machlup, Haberler, Fellner, and Lutz.[71] While not present in person at all conferences, Friedman played a key role as the uncompromising "extremist."[72]

Though not in the majority, neoliberals were especially influential because, as initiators, keynote speakers, and organizers, they held key positions and, in contrast to the other participants, acted as an organizationally networked epistemic community. These "'vital few' in the great battle for ideas" were supported by an entire network of MPS economists and politicians, all promoting free capital movements and exchange rates with similar arguments at these conferences and beyond, who could be characterized as "the many disciples."[73] This group included Rómulo Ferrero, Eugenio Gudin, Arnold Harberger, Bertrand de Jouvenel, Wolfgang Kasper, Paul McCracken, Allan Meltzer, Frank W. Paish, Herbert Stein, George Stigler, and Thomas F. Johnson. Other key institutions in spreading the gospel of flexible exchange rates were the International Finance Section at Princeton University headed by Machlup, which held many key conferences, and the Economics Department at the University of Chicago, where Friedman, Johnson, Stigler, Meltzer, and Stein taught. These were joined by think tanks such as the American Enterprise Institute (AEI), the Institute of Economic Affairs in Britain, and the Walter Eucken Institute in West Germany.[74]

---

70 Connell, *Reforming the World Monetary System*; Endres, *Great Architects*, 7; Leeson, *Ideology and the International Economy*, 48; Odell, *US International Monetary Policy*, 92, 182.

71 The only other organized group of economists was the Brookings Institution. At the first Bellagio conference, only one economist from Brookings participated. At the Bürgenstock conference only two did. Economists participating at two of the key conferences were Egon Sohmen (MPS), Robert Triffin, Walter Salant, Jürg Niehans, Alexandre Lamfalussy, and Peter B. Kenen.

72 *New York Times*, May 23, 1971.

73 Hartwell, *A History of the Mont Pèlerin Society*, 228.

74 See Schmelzer, *Freiheit für Wechselkurse und Kapital*, for more details of their respective activities in publishing pamphlets, holding seminars and conferences, organizing debates, etc.

The importance of these conferences, the related publicity work, and the follow-up process with politicians, central bankers, and the private sector during the rest of the 1960s cannot be overestimated. In this endeavor, the neoliberal promoters organizationally connected through the MPS played a key role. As summarized by Triffin: "These discussions undoubtedly initiated a slow but radical evolution in the thinking of our official colleagues, preparing them at least for the decisions that were finally forced upon them by the events rather than as a deliberate choice many years later in 1971 and 1973."[75]

The involvement of MPS economists in these conferences was an explicit expansion of the neoliberal project into wider circles. It was also a remarkable translation of private authority into public power pre-dating the rise of conservative think tanks in the 1980s. The approach foreshadowed later practices. As Machlup explained at a monetary symposium held at the American Enterprise Institute in 1965, if politicians were "unwilling to discuss, let alone adopt" flexible exchange rates, their advocates should not fall into a "ten-year period of inaction but, instead, should get busy teaching the politicians," because they "lag behind in their intellectual development."[76] Similarly, Friedman argued that there were two possibilities for introducing floating exchange rates: either during a serious economic crisis—but only if it was academically recognized and decision-makers had been made accustomed to it—or in the first month after a new cabinet of the opposing party was installed. Only three years later, Friedman wrote a memorandum to this effect to Nixon.[77] As scholars have documented, the influence of MPS economists culminated with the Nixon administration and its 1971 decision to unilaterally abandon gold parity and introduce freely floating exchange rates. The policy of floating exchange rates, argued first as a minority position not only within the economic mainstream but even within the neoliberal camp, became reality. A process of persuasion

75 Robert Triffin, "The Impact of the Bellagio Group on International Reform," in *Breadth and Depth in Economics. Fritz Machlup—The Man and His Ideas*, ed. Jacob S. Dreyer (Lexington: Lexington Books, 1978), 145–58; Marshall, *William J. Fellner*; Schmelzer, *Freiheit für Wechselkurse und Kapital*.

76 Fritz Machlup, "International Monetary Systems and the Free Market Economy," in *International Payments Problems. A Symposium Sponsored by the American Enterprise Institute for Public Policy Research* (Washington: AEI, 1966), 153–76, here 159f.

77 Milton Friedman, "Discussion," in *International Payments Problems. A Symposium*, 87–90. For more on this mode of policy-making see Naomi Klein, *The Shock Doctrine: The Rise of Disaster Capitalism* (New York: Penguin, 2007), 75–106.

which emerged contentiously among neoliberals helped redefine the monetary order of the world.

Conclusion

In his book on the decline and fall of Bretton Woods, Robert Leeson argued that intellectuals, economists, and academics "behaved 'as if' they were members of a coordinated coalition pressing for flexible exchange rates."[78] An analysis of these persons in their organizational context within the MPS makes the thesis plausible. Indeed, the key economists involved in the process of propagating floating exchange rates were almost all members of a transnational neoliberal network who debated theories and strategies at the regular MPS meetings and who collaborated closely in popularizing their vision for taming democracy and liberalizing capital.

While the decision to dismantle the Bretton Woods system cannot be directly attributed to neoliberals, their internal debates and, more importantly, their advocacy paved the way and thus proved to be a necessary condition. By disseminating the idea of flexible exchange rates assiduously, they helped to shift the terrain of the feasible. It is telling that Hayek saw something similar in the 1930s demise of the gold standard. As he argued in 1932, the fact that "the otherwise so conservative leaders of central banks drifted from the traditional rules of monetary policy with relatively light hearts must be attributed to the influence of new ideas of currency policy propagated by academics."[79] One might argue by analogy that the departure from the rules of Bretton Woods can also be ascribed to the influence of new monetary ideas propagated by transnationally connected neoliberals, ideas which gained wide prominence during the 1960s.

What were the long-term effects of the success of the neoliberal argument? Floating exchange rates largely became the global norm in the following decades, with the remarkable exception of Western Europe. Here, a diverging neoliberal conception became influential through the

---

78 Leeson, *Ideology and the International Economy*, 2.

79 F. A. Hayek, "Was der Goldwährung geschehen ist," in *Was mit der Goldwährung geschehen ist. Ein Bericht aus dem Jahre 1932 mit zwei Ergänzungen* (Tübingen: J. C. B. Mohr, 1965), 7.

increasing power of the West German Bundesbank and the creation of the European Monetary System—an experiment which continues to divide neoliberal opinion internally.[80] Most importantly, the more widespread adoption of flexible exchange rates became the central precondition for the rapid liberalization of global capital movements and thus the explosion of financial markets, which have been adequately described as the lever of the neoliberal counter-revolution in the coming decades.[81]

The adoption of this new order, where speculation and so-called hot money flows became the rule and not the exception, produced the conditions for the financialized hyper-globalization that has helped exacerbate ever-expanding chasms of economic inequality across much of the world and brought the global economic order to the brink of collapse in 2008. Understanding historically how new paradigms, initially contested, became the new normal is essential to an alertness about how new forms of commonsense are being created today. Unraveling internal debates such as those over monetary order also offers a prophylactic against attributing to neoliberals superhuman or unrealistic levels of internal consistency, party discipline, or foresight. Indeed, part of the efficacy of the neoliberal strategy must be seen in the flexible two-step process outlined here: the MPS offers first a space for fiery internal debate then a base for unified mobilization.

80 Kathleen R. McNamara, *The Currency of Ideas: Monetary Politics in the European Union* (Ithaca: Cornell University Press, 1998); Emmanuel Mourlon-Druol, *A Europe Made of Money: The Emergence of the European Monetary System* (Ithaca: Cornell University Press, 2012).

81 Helleiner, *States*; Huffschmid, *Politische Ökonomie*; Obstfeld and Taylor, *Global Capital Markets*.

9

The Neoliberal Ersatz Nobel Prize

Philip Mirowski[1]

People must have their heroes; or as Thomas Carlyle put it, "Universal History, the history of what man has accomplished in this world, is at bottom the History of the Great Men who have worked here."[2] Trends in historiography have intermittently warmed and chilled to this proposition since 1840, but it should be obvious that much of the general public continue to prefer to understand their hopes, their worldviews, and their complex personal doctrinal commitments through the biographies of exemplary thinkers. The great mass of people prefer to signal their fealties by testifying their allegiance to a few heroic personages, be they a religious guru, a movie star, a politician, or, in some cases, a 'public intellectual'. Historians who pander to the bottomless market for biographies of politicians and key intellectuals understand this implicitly. Heroes have always served as placeholders for ideas; none more so than in the case of economics.

Here we engage in a bit of old-fashioned, fine-grained institutional history to describe the role and meaning of the Bank of Sweden Award in Economic Sciences in Honor of Alfred Nobel, often mistakenly referred to as the "Nobel Prize in Economics." That nominal confusion alone should signal that something odd has been going on in this instance; but the role of the neoliberal thought collective (NTC) in this

1 I am very grateful to Gabriel Soderberg, Quinn Slobodian, and Beatrice Cherrier for their help on archival issues.
2 Thomas Carlyle, "On Heroes, Hero-worship, and the Heroic in History," at gutenberg.org.

story is something almost universally overlooked.[3] Indeed, I shall argue that this ersatz Nobel Prize has been a very effective component of the neoliberal toolkit for constructing an alternative regime of truth, particularly with regard to the public face and the content of the economic orthodoxy, and their place in it. Because the NTC has understood the integral role of hero-worship in the construction of public understanding of ideas, their intervention in this particular case helps us understand how neoliberal concepts have become established as the generic commonsense wisdom of the early twenty-first century.

The Real Nobel Prizes

People who know next to nothing about science and literature and care even less are still aware of the Nobel Prizes: they are regularly cited in most contemporary cultures as the ultimate act of recognition of worth and intellectual consequence. When Alfred Nobel died in December 1896, he left the bulk of his considerable fortune to institute *five* prizes annually to those who:

> shall have conferred the greatest benefit on mankind. The said interest shall be divided into five equal parts, which shall be apportioned as follows: one part to the person who shall have made the most important discovery or invention within the field of physics; one part to the person who shall have made the most important chemical discovery or improvement; one part to the person who shall have made the most important discovery within the domain of physiology or medicine; one part to the person who shall have produced in the field of literature the most outstanding work of an idealistic tendency; and one part to the person who shall have done the most or best work for fraternity among nations, for the abolition or reduction of standing armies and for the holding and promotion of peace conferences.[4]

---

3 But not completely. I must acknowledge Avner Offer and Gabriel Soderberg, *The Nobel Factor* (Princeton: Princeton University Press, 2016), which does touch on the subject. I should admit here I was originally a member of that project team, but decided to resign when I grew dissatisfied with the way the politics of the Prize was being dealt with by Offer. Indeed, much of the historical detail herein overlaps with that in their book; this paper is an attempt to set down my version of the events surrounding the Prize.

4 Alfred Nobel's will, quoted in Robert Marc Friedman, *The Politics of Excellence* (New York: Times Books, 2001), 13–14.

He further stipulated that the physics and chemistry prizes would be awarded by the Swedish Academy of Sciences, the medicine prize by the Karolinska Institute in Stockholm, the literature prize by the Swedish Academy, and the peace prize by a committee elected by the Norwegian Parliament. According to the most perceptive historian of the prizes, Robert Marc Friedman, for the first few decades the prizes did not enjoy the global significance they have today. There were issues of 'internal' politics—for instance, the perceived tendency to award certain prizes to Swedes who were not perceived by outsiders as quite up to world standards[5]—as well as 'external' politics—such as the storm of controversy and shame whipped up by the award of the chemistry prize in 1919 to Fritz Haber, who had been responsible for poison gas research in World War I.[6] This seemed precisely the bellicose heritage (of the source of the bequest in dynamite and other war industries) which Nobel's prizes were intended to erase. There was also the question of the Swedish capacity to continue activating the prizes through the disruption of World War II, and no prize in any category was awarded from 1940–42. Although the sums of prize money were substantial, it is fair to say that, with the exception of the physics prize, the Nobels were predominantly considered more of parochial Scandinavian significance in those early decades.

Friedman dates the elevation of the prizes in public esteem to the period immediately following World War II, especially in the United States.[7] This timing corresponds to the destruction of German science, the military assumption of science policy in the US, and the fascination with the role of science in the Cold War.[8] Under these dramatic shifts, Sweden sought to realign itself relative to the new world hegemons; the league tables turned definitively in America's favor; this was the period when Nobels were widely promoted to the general public as the canonization of the heroes exemplifying what was best in the human race. It is often said that the Nobels are awarded for achievements, not to *people*; but both Alfred Nobel's own will and the ceremony surrounding the modern prizes suggest otherwise. What all and sundry now expect every November is the deliverance of a

---

5 See, for instance, ibid., 56ff.

6 Ibid., 111–15.

7 Ibid., 251ff.

8 On the importance of this watershed for US science, see Philip Mirowski, *ScienceMart* (Cambridge, MA: Harvard University Press, 2011), Chapter 3.

new slate in the pantheon of heroes, based upon Romantic overtones of genius-kissed individuals.

The Nobels have been promoted as a pristine indicator of what is true and virtuous in human intellectual endeavor; but of course, they are no such thing. They are, rather, another human device constructed to shore up a regime of human veridiction. As Friedman has written:

> There are no grounds, based on history, for assuring the laureates constitute a unique population of the very best in science; even less so, to impute to them, as a class, the status of genius . . . The oft-repeated claim that the prize's prestige has reflected the skill of the Royal Swedish Academy of Sciences in picking the right winners simply does not hold up to inspection.[9]

That is the considered opinion of the premier historian of the actual Nobels in the natural sciences. So, what can it portend for the existence of an *ersatz* Nobel Prize, one instituted sixty-eight years after the real prizes, explicitly constructed to bask in the reflected glory of the real Nobels? The ersatz prize grew out of an inception that was so controversial that the Nobel Foundation went out of its way to insist that *no more new Nobels* would ever be countenanced by the Foundation into the future.[10] What was so very embarrassing that it warranted this spasm of manic repression? That is the question explored in the rest of this chapter.

---

9 Friedman, *The Politics of Excellence*, 267.

10 "Every now and then there are proposals to establish additional Nobel Prizes, for example in Mathematics or Environmental science. The foundation as well as the prize juries have rejected such requests. They consider themselves bound by the testament, wondering what it would lead to if new Nobel Prizes or equivalents were created . . . However, this principle has been departed from on one occasion, regarding the prize in economics. This prize must not be treated as a Nobel Prize and is for this reason titled Prize in Economic Sciences in Memory of Alfred Nobel . . . There was considerable doubt among the Nobel committees about accepting the prize. Propaganda activities were intense, especially from the Governor of the Central Bank, Per Åsbrink . . . The prize in economics has continued in causing controversy." Lars Gyllensten (former chairman of the Nobel Foundation), *Minnen, bara minnen* (Stockholm: Albert Bonniers förlag, 2000), 281 (translated from Swedish). See also Agneta Levinovitz and Nils Ringertz, eds, *The Nobel Prize: The First 100 Years* (London: Imperial College Press, 2001).

The Bank of Sweden Goes Rogue

There are only two academic sources in English which hint that there might be something mildly fishy about the Bank of Sweden Prize. The first is by Assar Lindbeck,[11] and was intended as a defense of the prize; but there is buried within it a single clause, stating that there existed "a certain skepticism towards the new prize idea among some natural scientists in the Academy." This glancing acknowledgment signals something that is absent, something significant, something that is central to an understanding of Lindbeck's own definitive role in stabilizing the prize. We shall deal with Lindbeck's central contribution shortly. The other intervention was by Yves Gingras,[12] who came at the prize from the opposite stance. In a short paper, he indicated that we should stare intently at the Bank of Sweden as a major protagonist in the inception of the prize, and that the process needed to be understood in terms of the effects it was intended to produce: "this prize does not exist: and moreover, . . . this so-called 'Nobel prize' is an extraordinary case study in the successful transformation of economic capital into symbolic capital, a transformation which greatly inflates the symbolic power of the discipline of economics in the public mind."[13]

Neither paper bothered to explore these hints further, and this is all the more striking given the stretch of time that has elapsed since their publications. A little extra digging in the original sources reveals a narrative far more twisted than anything either commentator had hinted at. The name of the prize is the first clue: the story should begin with the history of the Swedish Riksbank.

This is not the place to become excessively embroiled in the economic history of Sweden, yet a modicum of monetary history is a necessary prerequisite for understanding the prize. The place to start is to recognize one fact that set the Riksbank apart from other European central banks in the early twentieth century: The Swedish central bank was entirely owned by the Swedish state. The reigning government appointed the chair of the court of directors, while the Parliament elected the remaining six directors. In its attempts to set monetary policy after

11 Assar Lindbeck, "The Prize in Economic Science in Memory of Alfred Nobel," *Journal of Economic Literature* 23 (1985): 38.

12 Yves Gingras, "Nobel by Association: Beautiful Mind, Non-existent Prize," Open Democracy, October 23, 2002, opendemocracy.net.

13 Ibid.

World War I, the bank was repeatedly overruled by Parliament.[14] One
should not infer that there was a political option of pure central bank
independence anywhere else in the developed world prior to the 1970s;
rather, different central banks enjoyed varying degrees of being tethered
to their respective governments. Until the 1930s, the belief held sway
that the 'gold standard' rendered any policy independence unnecessary;
yet the Bank of England had managed to carve out a modicum of room
for maneuver on the grounds that it maintained a private ownership
status. The repeated breakdown of the gold standard up to the Great
Depression certainly raised the possibility that central banks might
perform some more active management role. In any event, there was
almost no theoretical tradition of a 'public interest' for such banks to
serve; mostly, they regarded themselves as guarantors of the interests of
their private domestic banks, not as the protagonists of some sort of
abstract 'macroeconomic policy' informed by economists. Indeed, the
shift to a doctrine of the political imperative of central bank independence only dates from the 1980s.[15]

The Riksbank began to chafe at the fetters imposed by its Swedish
parliamentary masters after World War II. With the appointment of the
new central bank governor in 1955, Per Åsbrink, the bank welcomed a
turncoat from the reigning Social Democratic Party who would skill-
fully assert bank prerogatives in what the modern Riksbank calls on its
own website the "interest rate coup" of 1957.

The details of the coup would be an unnecessary distraction;[16] suffice
it to say that Åsbrink persuaded his Board to raise the discount rate in
1957 by 1 percent without first notifying its nominal owner, the government. A political crisis for the Social Democratic Party ensued; Åsbrink's
right-hand economist Erik Lindahl countered that there was no place
for political meddling in monetary policy, as did the younger economist
Erik Lundberg, and both argued that the central bank should be subject

---

14   See Martin Eriksson, "A Golden Combination: The Formation of Monetary
Policy in Sweden after WWI," *Enterprise & Society*, no. 16 (2015): 556–79.

15   See, for instance, James Forder, "Why is Central Bank Independence so Widely
Approved?" *Journal of Economic Issues*, no. 39 (2005): 843–65. Forder directly relates
this to the enhanced status of the economics profession, which ties nicely into our own
narrative.

16   But see Gabriel Soderberg, "Constructing Invisible Hands: Market Technocrats
in Sweden 1880–2000," *Acta Universitatis Upsaliensis (Uppsala Studies in Economic
History)* 98 (2013). Much of the narrative detail of the following three paragraphs is
derived from this source.

to a regimen of depoliticization. In Swedish history, this is often portrayed as the first salvo in a full-blown attack on the economic policies of the left-wing Social Democratic Party in the postwar period. For various reasons, the government did not opt to punish Åsbrink, and he was allowed to remain as Riksbank governor.

The successful interest rate coup strengthened Åsbrink's hand politically, but it also had a further unintended consequence. The period following 1957 was one of prosperity for Sweden; with the higher interest rates came substantially enhanced profits for the central bank in the subsequent years, on the order of 20–40 million USD per year. These growing surpluses themselves became a further bone of contention between the bank and its nominal owner, the government. The bank conceded it was obliged to hand over some fraction of the surplus to the Treasury, but insisted privately that it should control the remainder itself, arguing that it was better situated to decide how and when it should be expended. Again, the Social Democrats countered that the Board did not possess the official discretion to make such a call. The Riksbank peremptorily settled the issue by publicly asserting the creation of a Jubilee Fund for research to celebrate the impending tercentenary of the bank in 1968. Some Members of Parliament were shocked to hear of the plan initially through newspaper and radio outlets, since they had not been previously approached to approve such a fund; others complained that the Riksbank was recklessly behaving as though it were a "state within a state," something that was not remotely permitted in its charter. Nevertheless, over strenuous objections, the Parliament voted to approve the proposed fund in April 1962. The bank then proceeded to build itself a new black granite fortress with some of the funds, and contemplated how to allocate another moiety to "research."

The Bank of England had commissioned a scholarly history of the institution for its 250th birthday; but Åsbrink had far more grandiose plans for the Riksbank' s birthday celebration in 1968, which involved an even more audacious power play than the interest rate coup or the Jubilee Fund. While the bank publicly explored the subsidized publication of a number of commissioned books on economics, Åsbrink began to sound out some key players behind the scenes about the possibility of a dedicated Nobel Prize for Economics organized and funded by the bank. No other political actor at the time thought that such a prize was anything other than a delusion, not to mention a remotely sensible way to spend the revenues accruing to the bank from its restrictive monetary policies. The real Nobels, after all, had been the consequence of a private bequest. Lindbeck, then a professor at the Stockholm School of Economics and a formal advisor to the bank since 1964, reports that he was approached by Åsbrink in 1967 or early 1968 to evaluate the possibility of such a prize funded entirely by the Riksbank out of the surplus. Because it might be unseemly for the chairman of the Riksbank to go skulking about surreptitiously laying the groundwork for such a prize with absolutely no prior political mandate whatsoever, Lindbeck was enlisted as a go-between for Åsbrink and the Nobel Foundation. Lindbeck consulted the chair of the Nobel Foundation, Nils Ståhle, and its financial advisor, Jacob Wallenberg; but the latter felt that adding another Nobel was out of the question. After intense negotiations, a 'compromise' was reached: the bank could fund a 'different' prize that nevertheless looked suspiciously like a real Nobel; that is, a parallel ersatz prize; a "Bank of Sweden Prize in Economic Science in Memory of Alfred Nobel." It was just a slight inconvenience that Alfred Nobel would be spinning in his grave.

Something about the "celebration" did not smell quite right; but the ever-entrepreneurial Åsbrink once more revealed his disdain for rules and protocol, in a manner almost as despotic and high-handed as in the previous cases of the interest rate coup and the Jubilee Fund. In short, the Riksbank bureaucracy resorted to deception and worse in order to steamroller the prize. Almost all the stakeholders were opposed in 1968: the Foundation to some extent, the Nobel family, the existing Nobel infrastructure, and the Parliament. The first trick was to usher the interests arrayed against the prize into an abrupt ambush. While still negotiating in secret, the bank announced the prize's existence in the press as a fait accompli—two weeks before the agreement was signed with the Nobel Foundation on May 14, 1968! Some of the principals were thus shamed into compliance by not allowing the dispute over an illicit conspiracy to go public. Also, Åsbrink used his regulatory leverage over the Foundation to get them to agree; existing tax rules prevented the Foundation from investing in certain securities, which was causing the endowment to be hemmed in; the bank got the rules applying to the Foundation's capital management changed in their favor.[17]

The second trick involved neutralizing the Nobel family. In 2010, Peter Nobel issued the following statement:

17 Gabriel Soderberg, Email to author, November 22, 2010.

What was the position of the Nobel family? Three days before the meeting of April 26, the then director of the Nobel Foundation, Nils Ståhle, met two members of the family and telephonically talked with a third one. Their position was that "it should not become like a sixth Nobel Prize," but that if the economics prize could be kept clearly separate from the Nobel Prizes then it might be an acceptable idea. On May 10, Ståhle and the president of the Nobel Foundation, von Euler, visited the family's eldest, Martha Nobel, then 87 years old—with severely impaired hearing but intellectually in good form. They obtained her written approval of the economics prize "under given conditions," namely that the new prize in all official documents and statements should be kept separated from the Nobel prize, and called the "prize in economic science in memory of Alfred Nobel." In a telephonic conversation with a nephew, Martha Nobel said that the whole thing was prearranged and impossible to oppose, so that one could only hope that they would keep their pledge that no confusion with the real Nobel prize should occur. There was no approval from the Nobel family as a whole. We were informed only much later.[18]

Peter Nobel has stated in public this was an unparalleled example of successful trademark infringement; but it was also much more. Members of the organizations formally tasked with judging the real Nobels were left in the dust as the steamroller passed by. A few notables, such as Professor Sten Friberg, rector of the Karolinska Institute, attempted to speak out in opposition, but to no avail. The bank's third trick was to extend the strong-arm tactics to its nominal owner, the Swedish state. The Riksbank had wandered very far off reservation by mounting this full-court press to create an ersatz Nobel; some sort of approval was required. A special committee pointed out that the bank's charter limited it to running a banking service, a printing press, and production of bank paper; anything else would require special legislation. A bill was rushed through Parliament, and *votes were held with no public debate whatsoever*.[19] On April 11, 1969 the first chamber voted 79 in favor, 20 against

18 Jorge Buzaglo, "The Nobel Family Dissociates itself from the Economics Prize," Real-World Economics Review Blog (October 22, 2010). There is also some unconfirmed information that government officials used some tax problems suffered by Martha Nobel to make her an offer she couldn't refuse.

19 Gabriel Soderberg, Email to author, June 24, 2013. Parenthetically, Assar Lindbeck ("The Prize", 38) misreports the final government sanction as occurring on January 1969. One therefore expects he is a less than reliable source for the timeline concerning these events.

and 18 abstaining; on April 16, the second chamber voted 152 in favor, 28 against and 28 abstaining. With this last obstacle removed, it became possible for the Riksbank to construct a Nobel which resembled as much as possible as the real thing.

This attempt to render the prize "close but not identical to the real Nobels" was engineered directly by the bank, *not* by any of the other stakeholders. Lindbeck's published statement that "the Procedures for the choice of the winner of the economics prize are the same as for the original Nobel prizes" is therefore not strictly correct.[20] If it were true, that would violate the terms of the original agreement that it could not be put on a thoroughgoing equivalent footing with the real Nobels. It is true that the bank managed to get the date of the award to be identical with the other Nobels—December 10—and guaranteed that the Bank of Sweden Prize be bestowed in the very same ceremony as the real Nobels. Outward conformity tends to mask the small but telling ways that signal the ersatz character of the Bank of Sweden Prize. One small sign is that the Bank of Sweden medal, reproduced in Figure 9.1, is of a somewhat different design than the other real Nobel medals.

Figure 9.1. The Sveriges Riksbank Prize Medal

Far more importantly, the constitution of the prize committee did not parallel that of the other real Nobels. Alfred Nobel's will stipulated that the prize committees be chosen and staffed for the natural science

---

20   Ibid., 45.

Nobels by the designated Royal Academies. There was no Royal Swedish Academy of Economics, so presumably this meant that, if it truly mimicked the real science Nobels, the prize would have to be controlled by the Royal Academy of Sciences. However, it seems in retrospect that the bank itself was active in constituting the original Economics prize committee. For instance, one key player in the narrative, Assar Lindbeck, was *not* a member of the Royal Swedish Academy of Sciences when appointed to the committee; according to his own vita, that did not occur until 1971. Another member, Ragnar Bentzel, was not inducted until 1972. Much of this suggests Academy membership being bestowed as an afterthought to being appointed to the Bank of Sweden committee, to hide the flouting of the rules. Since the composition of the prize committee plays a dominant role in our subsequent narrative, this divergence from the real Nobels was not an insignificant detail. The bank, having gone to such great lengths to institute the prize, was not going to simply withdraw altogether from the stipulation of what sort of economists would benefit from it, at least at the outset.

The insistent question for the historian is why Åsbrink, Lindbeck, and a few others would sail so close to the wind merely for the sake of blowing a hefty sum of public money on a prize for *economists*. (Public choice theory would later suggest they should have simply embezzled it instead.) The contemporary PR campaign by the Riksbank was fulsome in its evocation of enhanced prestige for Sweden, but given the prospective recipients were economists, this seems a rather thin justification. Åsbrink was himself frequently challenged as to the rationale for such a prize, and was dogmatically unapologetic:

> I do not find it particularly difficult to motivate the new prize. The domain, that is the object of economic science, is if anything central and important for all people and all societies around the world. Would anyone claim that the advances in this area are less important or less pressing than advances for instance in medicine, physics or chemistry? I can certainly understand if anyone thinks that these things cannot be compared, or even if someone finds that other circumstances, for instance the difficulties in separating politics and science in this particular area, make it problematic to award a prize in economics. But I would still like to believe that the economic science

today is so developed and established as a scientific discipline, that
such caveats cannot be decisive.[21]

Our protagonist gets close to the deep structure of the politics of the
prize, but cannot state the obvious. Few people in 1968 would have
conceded that economics, as it was then constituted, enjoyed an intellectual stature commensurate with medicine, physics, or chemistry.
However, the purpose of the prize was not to 'recognize' that fact, but
rather, to conjure the appearance of similar stature by fronting a prize
that closely mimicked existing prizes that did enjoy that esteem in the
mind of the public. *The purpose of the prize was to elevate the stature of
the economics profession, not to acknowledge its already hallowed status.*
Economics was supposed to look like a science to spectators, and the
prize was just one means for the makeover. But that seems to beg the
question: Why did Åsbrink do it?

Cast your eye back over our brief history, and you will discover that
Åsbrink, Lindbeck, Lindahl, and Lundberg were all part of a school of
thought that was convinced that the Social Democrats and the so-called
'Swedish model' were threatening the economic stability of Sweden, that
the distinctive social welfare state that it represented in the minds of
foreigners should be curtailed and cut back, and that one immediate way
to achieve that end was to render the central bank more independent
from its nominal owner, the Swedish state. But that would involve basing
the independence of the bank upon the untrammeled rule of experts
such as themselves, freed from the fetters of political subordination. In
1968, most Swedes would not have acquiesced in the credo that creden-
tialed economists just naturally knew better than the man in the street
how to run the economy without any democratic input. Therefore, it was
in the interest of the Swedish Riksbank to indirectly promote the discipline of economics as a vibrant and successful science, so that the general
public would eventually come to defer to its expertise, and let the central
bank get along and run things unencumbered, the way it saw fit.

Indeed, conveniently, the fortified economics profession turned its
macroeconomic cadres to explicitly argue for the *necessity* of an independent central bank as a prerequisite for rational monetary policy in
the 1970s and 1980s. But in a 'virtuous' (or vicious?) cycle, central banks

---

21 Per Åsbrink, Letter to Gez Holzer, dated May 27, 1968. Correspondence of Per
Åsbrink, Bank of Sweden Archive.

began to hire vast phalanxes of economists as part of their staffs, and, increasingly, even as their governors. After all, the purpose of 'independence' was to actualize expertise. Thus professional economists enjoyed new paths to power unencumbered by political accountability, and the central banks in turn devoted resources to enhancing economists' intellectual credibility. As Forder has pointed out, "The idea of central bank independence and the doctrines surrounding it contribute in significant ways to the standing and self-esteem of the economics profession."[22] Any macroeconomic failures can be blamed on the misdeeds of outsiders, with their tainted political interventions, while the economists deem themselves absolved of all blame. One observes this dynamic in recent exculpatory memoirs of the main protagonists of the erstwhile Great Recession. This symbiotic dependence certainly paid off for the Swedish Riksbank, which managed to attain full political independence from democratic accountability in 1999.

But, returning to the 1960s, we observe that the Nobel dynamic in Sweden existed to promote a certain species of economics, not all possible versions of economics indiscriminately. The legitimate profession had to be constrained to a sharply circumscribed intellectual ambit. This is another fact to which Åsbrink, Lindbeck, and Lundberg could not openly admit. Lindbeck, in his retrospective offered to an American audience, made the smarmy comment that the ideological perspectives of the prizewinners "have, of course, been neglected."[23] It was imperative that the Swedish committee for the ersatz Nobel evade the very thing that outsiders suspected all along was definitely a major consideration. As Lindbeck continued, "Has the selection committee viewed the award as a chance to influence the direction of new research in economics? The answer is definitely no."[24]

These protests are themselves another 'supplement', marking out another willful silence concerning the most important aspect of the Bank of Sweden Prize—and the Memory of Alfred Nobel has nothing to do with that.

---

22 Forder, "Why is Central Banking Independence so Widely Approved?" 854. See also Philip Mirowski, *Never Let a Serious Crisis Go to Waste* (London: Verso, 2013), 204–23.

23 Lindbeck, "The Prize," 51.

24 Ibid., 55.

The Mont Pèlerin Connection

It is an error to think that the Nobel Prizes effortlessly represent the distillation of the historical hive mind of the invisible college of scientists distributed across the world; if that were the case, one could simply distribute awards according the highest citation counts and h-indexes, and do away with the rigmarole of nomination rules, committees and consultations, plus the elaborate press briefings and PR that surround the event. Both disciplinary dynamics and local context matter, and never more so than with the Bank of Sweden Prize.

There were two major trends that played out in the first few decades of the Bank of Sweden Prize with regard to selectivity concerning prizeworthy economics: one that was obvious, and another that was obscured to a substantial degree. The obvious trend was the reorientation of the Swedish community away from their earlier pre-World War II focus on European schools of economic thought, and in particular Germanic sources, to home in on American economics as the new standard of orthodoxy. Whereas the interwar Swedish scene had been neoclassical in some Wicksellian sense, it soon became apparent that the versions of neoclassical economics being forged in postwar America were deemed to be the wave of the future, at least when it came to much of the Swedish profession.

Many of the founder generation, such as Lindbeck himself, had spent time at US universities soaking up the novel idioms and research practices, in preparation for producing publications in English for American journals.[25] There was a suspicion that Sweden lagged behind in mathematical technique, and perhaps even econometric sophistication, although Herman Wold had enjoyed an international reputation in the latter field. It was therefore foreordained that after the very first prize in 1969 was bestowed upon the Norwegian Ragnar Frisch and the Dutch Jan Tinbergen, the American dominance of the prize hardened rapidly into an unabated trend. It was the rare recipient from thenceforth who did not study at US institutions, or else hold a position sometime during their life at an American university, no matter what their country of birth.

American orthodox neoclassical economics was deemed world benchmark economics by the Bank of Sweden Prize committee, and this

---

25 Lindbeck himself studied at Yale with a Rockefeller fellowship, and was then a visiting Assistant Professor at the University of Michigan in 1958.

had very profound consequences for the trajectory of economics in Europe. In the 1950s and '60s there were still scattered home-grown schools of economic thought in various countries that generally published the bulk of their research in their home language; some, such as the French regulation school or the Italian neo-Ricardians, were openly hostile to the American version of neoclassical economics. Marxian economics was ensconced behind the Iron Curtain. There were even reputable Brits such as the Cambridge Keynesians who were very skeptical concerning the American ascendancy.[26] Not only did none of these groups ever merit a Bank of Sweden Prize in the opinion of the Swedes; but the prize served to sanction the displacement of the cutting edge of economics in Europe from indigenous traditions to a narrow (and sometimes tone-deaf) construction of the American economic orthodoxy. In some instances, the purge was brutal and quick;[27] but more frequently it took decades of replacing older faculty with young-sters who had read the writing on the wall. Perhaps European econo-mists would have intellectually knelt to the hegemon in any event in the absence of the prize; but one suspects the local politics might have played out very differently.

It is the second, far less visible, trend that will take up the rest of this chapter. It is not at all clear that, initially, the Bank of Sweden *consciously* sought to elevate the American orthodoxy to *primus inter pares* as a major consequence of its ersatz prize; but a case can be made that they did seek to skew the prize, and therefore the economics profession, in a far more neoliberal direction than would have been expected in the late 1960s. Thus, the prize provided a fulcrum which permanently moved the Overton Window.

The intimate relations of the neoliberals of the early Mont Pèlerin Society with the pinnacles of European high finance is a history which still remains to be written in sufficient detail. Max Hartwell, the insider historian of the MPS, admits that the money to fund the first meeting in April 1947 came from the William Volker Fund to support the American side, and, somewhat more vaguely, a subvention "provided by Albert Hunold, who raised the money from Swiss sources," which

---

26 Paul Samuelson actually nominated Joan Robinson: Letter to Assar Lindbeck, dated February 14, 1977, Paul Samuelson's Papers, Box 4, File "Nobel Nominating Committee," Perkins Library, Duke University.

27 For the situation at Humboldt University in Berlin, see Till Duppe, "Economic Science in Berlin," *Studies in the History and Philosophy of Science*, no. 51 (2015): 22–32.

paid for the European expenses.[28] One can understand Hartwell's circumspection when one realizes it was largely Swiss banking and finance interests that lavishly subsidized the early Mont Pèlerin meetings. Indeed, it appears Hayek's first proposal for a new organization to rethink liberalism occurred at a reception thrown for him by Swiss banking and industrial interests in Zurich, November 1945.[29] For many, the Swiss banks had been caught out playing both sides of the gold street during World War II, and were especially concerned to plead their ideological purity to counter the skepticism of the victorious allies. With the encouragement of Hunold, they were brought around to the notion that by supporting the political and intellectual plans of Hayek they would demonstrate their unstinting opposition to any form of socialism. The reason the first meeting took place on the slopes of Mont Pèlerin is that it was funded largely in Swiss Francs, primarily from Credit Suisse, the United Bank of Switzerland (UBS), and the insurance companies Swiss Re and Zurich Assurances.[30] Hunold had worked for Credit Suisse from 1945–47, and was able to keep returning to the well for further subventions in support of the MPS, to the tune of largely funding three more meetings (1949, 1953, and 1957) out of Swiss funds.[31] So the MPS were lucky in their Swiss patrons; but there was another, possibly more consequential aspect to the Swiss Connection. The Swiss banks were also the wellspring of support for a transnational organization of central bankers in the aftermath of World War II. The Bank for International Settlements (BIS), a private coordination institution for central bankers dating from 1930, was another instrument enabling Swiss banks to reintegrate themselves into the postwar global financial system.[32]

Far from serving as a mere clearinghouse, the BIS also became a source of intellectual arguments to be spread to other member banks and their countries. Hence, the BIS turned out to be an important conduit for neoliberal ideas and neoliberal support in the period of the

---

28   Max Hartwell, *A History of the Mont Pèlerin Society* (Indianapolis: Liberty Fund, 1995), 26.

29   Ibid., 30.

30   See Yves Steiner, "Les riches amis suisses du néolibéralisme. De la debacle de la revue Occident à la Conférence du Mont Pèlerin d'avril," *Traverse*, no. 1 (2007).

31   See Hartwell, *A History of the Mont Pèlerin Society*, 67.

32   For the history, see Kazuhiko Yago, *The Financial History of the Bank for International Settlements* (London: Routledge, 2013); Adam LeBor, *Tower of Basel* (New York: Public Affairs, 2013).

1930s through the 1950s throughout Europe. For instance, the second general manager of the BIS, Roger Auboin, was an MPS member who maintained close contacts with Swiss banks, and had attended the Lippman Colloquium in 1938. Other members of the BIS included Marcus Wallenberg, brother of Jacob Wallenberg (encountered in the previous section as a Nobel conspirator). But more relevant to our current narrative, the first Chair of the BIS, the Swede Per Jacobsson, found the ideas of MPS figures such as Fritz Machlup, Wilhelm Röpke, and Walter Eucken to be incisive expressions of the versions of economics which underwrote his agenda for 'sound money'.[33] Although Jacobsson left the BIS in 1956 to helm the International Monetary Fund, one of his main legacies was the ongoing support of his primary Swedish protégé, Per Åsbrink.

To document these links in detail more research is required, but nevertheless, there is sufficient indication that there was a *sub rosa* Swiss Connection to the Swedish central bank, and it was consistent with the ideals of the Mont Pèlerin Society. The Swedish bankers were second only to the Swiss in dealing with Nazi funds, and so they too required an ideological clean bill of health after the war.[34] The neoliberal thought collective eventually seemed to provide them with a sterling postwar doctor's scrip forswearing any whiff of collectivism, if not a completely clean bill of health.

Returning to our original observation, Per Åsbrink had surrounded himself at the Riksbank with economist advisors who were hostile in varying degrees to the then-dominant "Swedish model" of the welfare state; these were naturally the sorts of economists that the central bank would have been inclined to have on its roster of advisors, given its recent political contretemps with the Social Democrats. Perhaps the most outspoken of the bank cabal's attitudes towards the rest of the Swedish economics profession has been Assar Lindbeck: in his impressions in retrospect, Swedish economists

> were on their way in Sweden to put the market out of play from the beginning of the 70s to the early 90s . . . Beginning in the mid-90s, we introduced a new, rule-based economic policy with an independent

33 See Yago, *Financial History*, 44ff., and Offer and Soderberg, *The Nobel Factor*, 81–8.
34 See LeBor, *Tower of Basel*.

Riksbank, limits for allowable budget deficit, and a new budget process in which one first determines expenditure levels before starting negotiations on how much money the various activities should be assigned. We have therefore achieved fiscal discipline and an independent Riksbank in combination with deregulation.[35]

The bank cabal included Lindbeck, Lundberg, and Bentzel, in conjunction with Bertil Ohlin, leader of the People's Party, the main opposition to the Social Democrats from the right in that era; they were all mobilized to bring about a set of rollbacks of the Swedish welfare state, objectives which were achieved by the 1990s.[36]

Hence it was the great good fortune of the NTC in 1969 to have either *actual MPS members or their overt sympathizers* conveniently available to be plucked from the Riksbank stables to staff the early ersatz Nobel committee, essentially hand-picked by Åsbrink in the first instance. Far from conforming to some bland notion of "ideological balance," the Bank of Sweden Prize committee had one actual MPS member on board from its inception until 1995, and during the early years was majority dominated by neoliberal economists. For the first six years they were in the majority—which will shortly go some distance in explaining the contentious 1974 prize—and thereafter were represented primarily by Assar Lindbeck, who had an outsized influence on deliberations in the key years from 1974 to 1994. Since that period, their representation has been diminished, and this has had a pronounced effect on the track record of the prize. We can summarize the trend as follows:

1. The award bestowed upon Friedrich Hayek in 1974 was the first, and perhaps the greatest coup of the MPS and the neoliberal thought collective in the history of the ersatz Nobel. This was recognized as such at the time.

---

35   Quoted in Lars Nordbakken, "Interview with Assar Lindbeck," 2012, minervanett. no. Lars Nordbakken is himself a member of the MPS. One of the main targets in the 1970s was Rudolf Meidner's "solidarity wage policy."

36   "The social democrats had obviously lost their political hegemony in the 1990s and 2000s [in Sweden]." Lennart Erixon, *The Economic Policy and Macroeconomic Performance of Sweden in the 1990s and 2000s* (Bingley: Emerald House, 2011), 285. Ohlin's politics were apparently influenced by his encounter with Hayek's *Road to Serfdom*.

2. Beginning in 1974, the MPS had the most extraordinary run of favorable prizes, extending over two decades. Seven awards in total went to MPS members in this period.

3. The consequence of these two trends was the marked expansion of the proportion of neoliberal winners (a category larger than simply MPS members) relative to the cumulative population of total winners. The proportion of neoliberal winners rose from 11 percent in 1974 to 38 percent in 1993.

4. MPS members had far fewer winners from 1994 forwards. The only additional member was Vernon Smith in 2002. This slowdown corresponds to Assar Lindbeck's removal from the committee in 1994, as well as the last actual MPS member cycling off the committee.

5. However, the flow of new neoliberal additions to the prize has been such that the neoliberal representation of the cumulative stock of winners has remained around 38–40 percent since 1993.

6. While the ersatz Nobel has never experienced a *majority* of neoliberals in its cumulative stock of laureates, the selection committee has guaranteed that neoliberalism enjoys a stable proportional representation in the supposed "best of the orthodoxy." This is the second major coup of the MPS with regard to the Bank of Sweden Prize.

Before we deal with the actual sequence of prizes and vexed questions of ideological definition, it is critical to note just how unlikely it would have been that any exclusive club consisting of roughly 300 or so members worldwide during the period under consideration would manage to capture such an outsized proportion of Bank of Sweden Prizes.[37] Conveniently, we have one of the members of the selection committee himself admitting the very same thing in, of all things, an address to the MPS: "There seems to be an overrepresentation in the Nobel Prize Hall of Fame of the MPS group. [Milton] Friedman indicates some kind of political bias against an outspoken Marxist

---

37 Some authors have noticed this—e.g. Thomas Karier, *Intellectual Capital* (New York: Cambridge University Press, 2010), 14—but are never sufficiently curious to explore it further.

economist when it comes to not awarding the prize. But is there a corresponding positive bias in favour of the other camp?"[38] Furthermore, the
neoliberal thought collective has not been shy in trumpeting this
extraordinary set of events. As Max Hartwell, the designated historian
of MPS put it: "A main reason for the heightened public profile of the
Society was the awarding of the Nobel Prize in economics to seven of its
members between 1974 and 1991 . . . There is no doubt that the Nobel
Prizes, with their worldwide recognition, strengthened the status of the
Society."[39]

All and sundry treat this as some sort of marvelous confirmation that
the Swedish Prize committee miraculously manages to power through
all the noise and flummery of "irrelevant" considerations to an objective
valuation of the truth in economics; but of course, there is another more
historically accurate and ultimately more insightful explanation of these
events. It consists of the combination of some elements of pure historical contingency, along with other actions of the most direct and
unabashed intentionality. The dose of contingency came in the form of
the Swiss Connection to the Swedish central bank, the audacity of Per
Åsbrink in pursuing an ersatz Nobel, and the alliance of convenience
between Åsbrink and a set of Swedish economists bent upon rolling
back the Swedish welfare state. Of course, Swedes harboring those sorts
of political ambitions would tend to be familiar with many of the neoliberal protagonists of the MPS in the late 1960s, and indeed would include
in their number a few actual MPS members. Once those stochastic
preconditions were baked into place, the subsequent sequence of events
was more or less due to premeditated planned agendas.

The outsized representation of MPS in the ersatz Nobel was a direct
consequence of Per Åsbrink creating the nascent Swedish Prize committee from scratch, and then accessing the same cabal of right-leaning
Swedish economists and Riksbank consultants who had helped him get
the ersatz Nobel off the ground to staff its bureaucratic structure. These
scholars, consisting of Assar Lindbeck, Erik Lundberg, and Ragnar
Bentzel, with the tacit cooperation of Bertil Ohlin, sought to bolster the
intellectual credibility of their program by initially making the prize

38 Ingemar Ståhl, "The Prize in Economic Science and Maurice Allais," Paper
presented to MPS meeting, 1990, 2. Not unexpectedly, in the next sentence the author
goes on to deny the very thing he has brought to our attention.
39 Hartwell, *A History of the Mont Pèlerin Society*, 160. This is confirmed in Lanny
Eberstein, *Chicagonomics* (New York: St. Martin's Press, 2015), 135.

seem "apolitical" for the first five years, only then to embark on a number of awards (including one to Ohlin himself) designed to make the hard-right MPS appear as a legitimate orthodox component of world economics. In other words, they laid the groundwork for the program described by Lindbeck: "fiscal discipline and an independent Riksbank in combination with deregulation," and subsequently pursued by the Riksbank.

So far, this might seem an excessively parochial Swedish story: intellectual fortifications summoned to reinforce one side of a local political battle. But by construction, the ersatz Nobel was intended to have international repercussions as well. First, there was the reorientation of global "orthodoxy" to the new American normal, which meant a commitment to a formal understanding of the centrality of the Walrasian system of equilibrium as constituting the heart of economics, which in turn accounted for the initial prizes bestowed upon Paul Samuelson, Kenneth Arrow, Wassily Leontief, Tjalling Koopmans, and that most Walrasian of Brits, John R. Hicks. The problem faced by the early committee was that this "new postwar orthodoxy" represented by the above roster was pretty uniformly dismissive of the MPS cadre in the 1960s, to the extent of an intransigent unwillingness to allow most of them into the tent named "orthodox economics." The Nobel committee did end up with a lopsided emphasis on American economics, but they also forced the issue of reconciliation of these two imperatives through a decisive set of awards in 1974–77, as described in the next section.

Another objective of the ersatz Nobel in the 1970s was therefore to *raise the level of scientific credibility of the MPS* within the postwar economics profession. That is why Lindbeck's subsequent denial that "the selection committee viewed the award as a chance to influence the direction of new research in economics" is utterly unavailing, once one examines the historical record in greater detail.[40] The general level of denial in this respect (usually paired with an unwillingness to acknowledge the ersatz status of the economics "Nobel") has spread throughout much of the modern economics profession, especially after the history of economic thought has been summarily banished from orthodox economics departments worldwide. It has gotten so bad that even Nobel laureates can spout the most misleading rubbish, secure in the conviction that no one will ever call them out on their ignorance:

---

40 See Lindbeck, "The Prize," 55.

So far as I know, the MPS never produced and distributed an agreed public statement of its program. Outside the economics profession, it was invisible.

The MPS was no more influential inside the economics profession. There were no publications to be discussed. The American membership was apparently limited to economists of the Chicago School and its scattered university outposts, plus a few transplanted Europeans. "Some of my best friends" belonged. There was, of course, continuing research and debate among economists on the good and bad properties of competitive and noncompetitive markets, and the capacities and limitations of corrective regulation. But these would have gone on in the same way had the MPS not existed.[41]

Some Episodes on the Road to a Neoliberal Economics

The historical materials to support the thesis of this chapter are partly available from scattered sources in the history of economics, and partly hidden in the archives of the Swedish Academy, subject to a fifty-year embargo. The evidence in this chapter is derived in part from the archives of the Mont Pèlerin Society, partly from the archives of selected Bank of Sweden Prize laureates, and partly from the publications of the neoliberal thought collective itself. From the MPS, we have a number of members discussing the track record and significance of the prize at various meetings. There is the revealing talk by Ingemar Ståhl in 1990 that we have already quoted. There was also a regional conclave of the MPS in Stockholm in 2009; not only did Assar Lindbeck address that meeting on the defeat of the "Swedish model" (although it appears Lindbeck never did assume formal MPS membership), but Ståhl presided over a session devoted to the lessons to be derived from the track record of the prize. The MPS has always displayed an unapologetic fascination with the ersatz Nobel, as one might expect from its curious inception. And then there is the issue of the larger archive of the Neoliberal Thought Collective.

I can anticipate that some readers might feel uneasy with the notion of neoliberalism as a coherent intellectual movement, thus it would be prudent to give some account of the selection principles behind Table

---

41 Robert Solow, "Hayek, Friedman and the Illusions of Conservative Economics," *New Republic*, November 16, 2012.

9.1, which constitutes a central piece of evidence supporting the arguments of this chapter.

Table 9.1. Neoliberal Winners of the Bank of Sweden Prize in Economics

Year	Prizewinner	Mont Pèlerin	Joint	Cumulative Percent
1974	Friedrich Hayek	Yes	Yes	11
1976	Milton Friedman	Yes		16
1977	Bertil Ohlin		Yes	21
1979	Theodore Schultz		Yes	25
1982	George Stigler	Yes		26
1986	James Buchanan	Yes		26
1988	Maurice Allais	Yes		33
1990	Merton Miller		Yes	32
1991	Ronald Coase	Yes		34
1992	Gary Becker	Yes		37
1993	Douglass North		Yes	38
1995	Robert Lucas			36
1997	Robert Merton		Yes	38
	Myron Scholes		Yes	38
1999	Robert Mundell			38
2001	Michael Spence		Yes	36
2002	Vernon Smith	Yes	Yes	37
2004	Fynn Kydland		Yes	38
	Edward Prescott		Yes	38
2005	Robert Aumann			37
2006	Edmund Phelps			38
2007	Eric Maskin		Yes	40
2009	Elinor Ostrom			39
2010	Christopher Pissarides		Yes	40
2011	Thomas Sargent		Yes	39
2013	Robert Shiller		Yes	39
	Eugene Fama		Yes	39

What does it mean to be a neoliberal economist? I think most can agree that membership in the MPS serves as a fairly non-contentious litmus test, but that would be too limited, since it would only account for eight of our roster of twenty-seven Bank of Sweden laureates in the years 1969–2013. One consideration which factors into this statistic is the observation that, while the MPS was once the core furnace of intellectual white heat in forging new ideological principles in the first four decades of its existence, its centrality to the neoliberal project has diminished as we approach the present, and its intellectual heat has cooled appreciably. In effect, the level of practical success of neoliberal politics has resulted in the core now being primarily populated by affluent people who view membership as a status symbol, another Davos to inscribe on the social calendar, rather than joining a hand-picked crew of innovative thinkers cloistered away in intense debate and subtle disputation.

The neoliberal thought collective is far more likely to be found nowadays in the outer rings of its dedicated institutional structures, in the numerous think tanks, news outlets, tied academic units, NGOs and shell foundations which litter the political landscape. Here is one telling example. Although the laureates Thomas Sargent, Douglass North, and Michael Spence have never been MPS members, they have enjoyed extended tenure as Hoover Institution Fellows, which in some ways is far more indicative of their modern political and intellectual commitments. This is one class of information that has been factored into the creation of the neoliberal roster in Table 9.1. Beyond that, it should be conceded that there exists no engraved catechism of tenets which one could check off in evaluating the published work of any economist in question. A certain level of specialized knowledge of the careers of those involved must provide an inescapable backdrop to the attribution of neoliberal commitments. For instance, much of the popular press still mistakenly thinks that Robert Shiller is some species of left-liberal economist, at least in part due to his evocation of certain strains of behavioral economics, and his warnings of the instability of the mortgage market in the run-up to the Great Recession. However, one need only read his extensive works to realize that he subscribes to most of the major tenets of a neoliberal theory of finance.[42]

Nevertheless, the reader need not depend entirely upon the discernment of authors such as myself to assign the laureates to neoliberal categories. The neoliberal thought collective has been so fascinated by the ersatz Nobel and its implications that they themselves have devoted substantial resources to taking the ideological temperature of each and every prize winner. In effect, neoliberals strive to have summary box scores, in order to gauge whether or not, from their vantage point, they are winning, and by how much. Conveniently, there exists a journal issued by the Koch-funded Mercatus Institute at George Mason University called *Econ Journal Watch*, which itself devoted a 450+ page issue[43] in 2013 to testing the

---

42 See Mirowski, *Never Let a Serious Crisis Go to Waste*, 353–5.

43 See Daniel Klein, "Special Issue: The Ideological Migration of the Economics Laureates," *Econ Journal Watch*, no. 10 (2013): 218–682. Honestly, I cannot understand those who rail against the notion of the neoliberal thought collective as a phantasm born of a 'conspiracy theory', when one observes the exorbitant amounts of money and effort

neoliberal mettle of each and every individual Bank of Sweden prizewinner up to that point. While not agreeing in every case with its political verdicts—for instance, it is derived entirely from readily available published sources, and makes no effort to tap archives—it provides a good first pass at the classification embodied in our Table 9.1. As in so many other cases of the political sociology of science, one finds that it was the NTC that managed to get there first.

With those considerations out of the way, we will conclude this chapter with two episodes from the history of the Bank of Sweden Prize which capture to varying degrees the myriad ways the prize has served to further the neoliberal project.

The 1974 Prize Awarded to Friedrich Hayek and Gunnar Myrdal

As mentioned, the early Swedish Prize committee was heavily stacked with neoliberal sympathizers, but from 1970–73 it set out to elevate the American neoclassical orthodoxy as the gold standard for what it would henceforth consider cutting-edge world economics. After having established this as its primary mandate, it then abruptly revealed an alternative agenda with the 1974 prize, awarded to Friedrich Hayek and Gunnar Myrdal. Thus began a practice, which would surface again a few more times, of bestowing a joint award to economists asserting A and not-A, respectively, while keeping a straight poker face. Clearly something like this had never happened in the real Nobels for the natural sciences, and it was perceived as an outlandish departure from standard operating procedure at the time.

Forty years later, it is perhaps difficult to recapture just how preposterous this award seemed to most contemporary economists. It seemed that the Swedes had just abnegated their own prior definition of orthodoxy, because it was apparent that almost no one in the American profession considered Hayek qualified as an economist back in 1974. I

---

and *organization* that have been poured into the monitoring and commentary on intellectual trends in the modern world in order to rate and intervene in their political valence, as exemplified in this instance. For another instance out of George Mason, see Peter Boettke, Alexander Fink, and Daniel Smith, "The Impact of Nobel Prize Winners in Economics: Mainline vs. Mainstream," *American Journal of Economics and Sociology*, no. 71 (2012): 1219–49.

defer here to one of the previous laureates, himself struck by the gracelessness of the award:

> in the 1974 common rooms of Harvard and MIT, the majority of the inhabitants there seemed not to know the name of this new laureate [Hayek]. By contrast, the following year I was in Stockholm to celebrate the 75th anniversary of the original five Nobel Prizes, it was my vague impression that the Royal Swedish Academy electors paid greater deference to Hayek than to their own native son Myrdal.[44]

To telegraph the scene to those not aware of Hayek's biography, he began his career as an Austrian economist attempting to argue against government attempts to offset business cycles, and continued to do so at the LSE long after the 1929 crash. There he was attacked by the Keynesians in the later 1930s and by Gunnar Myrdal for serious errors in his version of monetary theory.[45] Hayek was deeply disheartened by the chorus of disdain, as well as the failure of his next book *The Pure Theory of Capital*, and turned away from the genre of "economic theory" altogether in favor of philosophy, publishing his popular book on politics, *The Road to Serfdom* (1944). At that point he was condemned to the status of being "not an economist," particularly in the American context; so much so that he was denied a position in the University of Chicago economics department, although he was hired to the Committee on Social Thought in 1950.[46]

This long period of wandering in the wilderness of intellectual banishment would have been the first thing to have struck insiders back then about the 1974 prize. Hayek had "lost" status, because he could no longer participate in "scientific economics." Hence it would seem all the more striking to an outsider like Samuelson that such deference was shown to Hayek in Stockholm, beyond that towards native son Myrdal. Some would say that Myrdal himself had also drifted away from economics in the interim, to something akin to sociology with his work on American segregation and Indian development

---

44 Paul Samuelson, "A Few Remembrances of Friedrich von Hayek," *Journal of Economic Behaviour and Organization*, no. 69 (2009): 1.

45 See Bruce Caldwell, *Hayek's Challenge* (Chicago: University of Chicago Press, 2004), 178ff.

46 Ibid., 297.

problems. Yet it was their diametrically opposed politics which drew the most strident commentary.

The contempt for Myrdal was intense within the MPS thought collective. As P. T. Bauer wrote to Hayek, "I can well understand your feelings about being bracketed with Myrdal. If you had waded through 2300 pages of *Asian Drama* (as I did), you would feel this even more. Myrdal's and Tinbergen's Nobel Prizes tell us quite a lot about the state of economics. But we must try not to be trapped in a feeling analogous to that of guilt by association."[47]

After the prize was announced, there were all sorts of criticisms of the aberrant behavior of the Bank of Sweden committee; they were forced to defend their choice over and over again. Indeed, the Hayek/Myrdal pairing remained the most controversial award until the 1994 prize bestowed upon John Nash, which caused such a hubbub that the prize committee was itself reconstituted by the Royal Swedish Academy.[48] The complaints about the 1974 prize occurred in public and in private. One particularly plangent example was Assar Lindbeck's response to Paul Samuelson's request for clarification:

> The background for the Hayek-Myrdal prize was that the committee was eager to 'finish' the backlog as soon as possible, which resulted in a number of shared prizes during the seventies. That specific prize reflected perhaps, to some extent, also Erik Lundberg's sense of humor! But more seriously, both H. and M. were pioneers in aggregate analysis of output fluctuation by the concepts of aggregate saving and aggregate investment. Both later turned to broader issues of the relations between institutions, economic mechanisms, and political processes. The fact that they came up with contrary policy prescriptions was not regarded by the committee as an obstacle for the prize.[49]

This gloss was widely perceived as implausible. No one in the American orthodoxy would have considered either Hayek or Myrdal part of the 'backlog' of orthodox economists to be cleared; almost no one would

47 Bauer, Letter to Hayek, dated August 18, 1975, Box 11, Folder 33, Hayek Papers, Hoover Institution.

48 See Sylvia Nasar, *A Beautiful Mind* (New York: Simon & Schuster, 1998).

49 Assar Lindbeck, Letter to Paul Samuelson, dated February 3 1989, Paul Samuelson Archives, Box 4, File: "Nobel Nominating Committee," Perkins Library, Duke University.

have deemed that either Hayek or Myrdal had made any lasting contribution to orthodox macroeconomics, as it stood in 1974.[50] And the
notion that the prize was in any sense a "joke" bordered on offensive.

Perhaps the person most disturbed by the prize was its other recipient. Although he did not decline the award, remorse soon set in, and
Myrdal went public a few times in subsequent years suggesting he
should have renounced it.[51] He openly questioned the pairing of two
such diametrically opposed thinkers in the interests of "balance." In a
widely reprinted article, he suggested the award to Milton Friedman in
1976 had finally made him see what was really going on. Economics was
not a science like those celebrated by the other Nobels; due to the
"confused admixture of science and politics, the awarding of a Nobel
Prize in economic science will commonly be conceived as a political act
of the Academy. This, of course, is what has happened in the case of
Milton Friedman." His proposal was that the Royal Academy divest
itself of the Bank of Sweden Prize, "an opinion of mine . . . shared by
many members of the Academy and not only by natural sciences."
Perhaps he felt prudence dictated leaving out how his own remorse at
having cooperated with Åsbrink in the late 1960s to get the prize instituted in the first place was also eating away at him.

A case can be made that Hayek was equally in the dark when it came
to comprehension of the subtle tactics of the award committee.
Unexpectedly, Hayek had the nerve to denounce the Bank of Sweden
Prize in his acceptance speech:

> Yet I must confess that if I had been consulted whether to establish a
> Nobel Prize in economics, I should have decidedly advised against it.
> One reason was that I feared that such a prize, as I believe is true of
> the activities of some of the great scientific foundations, would tend to
> accentuate the swings of scientific fashion. This apprehension the
> selection committee has brilliantly refuted by awarding the prize to
> one whose views are as unfashionable as mine are. I do not yet feel

---

50 That is why I do not find creditable the secondhand claim by David Laidler that
in a conversation between Erik Lundberg and Herbert Giersch in 1973 they had claimed
that Myrdal was perceived as being at the top of the queue, and then they had to find
someone else for "balance." See Robert Leeson, ed., *Hayek: A Collaborative Biography*
(Basingstoke: Palgrave Macmillan, 2013), 72.

51 The rest of this paragraph is derived from Gunnar Myrdal, "The Nobel Prize in
Economic Science," *Challenge* (March–April 1977): 50–2.

equally reassured concerning my second cause of apprehension. It is that the Nobel Prize confers on an individual an authority which in economics no man ought to possess.[52]

At first sight, it may seem that Hayek's denunciation (but note well—combined with acceptance) of the prize might seem to contradict the major thesis of this chapter: How could the Riksbank award be skewed to promote the MPS and its doctrines when its most famous member was so disparaging about the functions of the prize at the award ceremony? Here, I think, it becomes necessary to insist once again that neoliberalism and the NTC cannot be reduced to the utterances of Hayek alone.[53] However brilliant Hayek may have been, he was distinctly inferior in his understanding of the sociology of the economics profession than many other members of the NTC, as the quote from Hartwell above implicitly indicates. If he really believed the ersatz Nobel was so deleterious for economic thought, then he should have practiced what he preached and renounced the prize. I think it plain that the wisdom of Lundberg, Lindbeck, and the others ultimately won out: all agree Hayek's stock as an economist began its recovery with the bestowal of the Bank of Sweden Prize. And, validating NTC wisdom, Hayek is second-most cited laureate in the *other* Bank of Sweden Prize lectures, just after Kenneth Arrow.[54]

There has grown up an urban legend that Myrdal was inevitably in line for a prize, but that the Swedes disliked him to such an extent that they paired him with Hayek to forever make his life (and legacy) miserable. One might think that credible if one restricted one's gaze solely to that single prize, but the evidence gathered herein about the longer term suggests otherwise. The rival interpretation is that the committee consisting of one MPS member plus three neoliberals tipped their hand as to their second project in the Bank of Sweden Prize: to lend public credibility to the Mont Pèlerin Society in particular and the neoliberal

52   Friedrich Hayek, Nobel Banquet Speech, Dec. 10, 1974, at: https://www.nobelprize.org/prizes/economic-sciences/1974/hayek/speech/
53   This is a case I have been making repeatedly. See Philip Mirowski and Dieter Plehwe, eds, *The Road from Mont Pèlerin: The Making of the Neoliberal Thought Collective* (Cambridge, MA: Harvard University Press, 2009), and Mirowski, *Never Let a Serious Crisis Go to Waste.*
54   See David Skarbeck, "F. A. Hayek's Influence on the Nobel Prize Winners," *Review of Austrian Economics*, no. 22 (2009): 109–12.

project in general, by inserting targeted awards intercalated with those
to the American orthodoxy. The committee could never have bestowed
the award on Hayek alone, since that would have put the kibosh on the
prize for good; the purely political character of such a singleton would
have left no grounds for plausible deniability. So they paired him with
Myrdal to disguise what would soon become a striking run of single-
person prizes to MPS members. The prize committee was willing to put
up with a modicum of grief concerning the Hayek/Myrdal prize, because
it broke the global ice dam which had frozen out the MPS from the
realm of legitimate economic discourse since World War II. The ploy
worked like a charm for Hayek; numerous historians have commented
that his 'rehabilitation' as an economist dates from the 1974 prize.
Myrdal experienced no such similar rehabilitation, and soon realized he
had been a cat's paw for the neoliberals on the committee. By 1976, with
the prize going to Milton Friedman, and to Bertil Ohlin in 1977, Myrdal
finally saw the writing on the wall. The Bank of Sweden Prize was being
driven by two different and conflicting agendas, or at least so it seemed
in the 1970s: promote the American hegemony, and promote the MPS
and neoliberal arguments. True success would arrive when neoliberal
orthodox economists had become so commonplace that no one would
think to make an issue of them any longer.

Other Economics Prizes Abandoned

So far we have approached the ersatz Nobel almost exclusively from the
vantage point of the Swedes, but another way to gauge the significance
and influence of the prize is to briefly examine its consequences from
the side of its main beneficiaries, viz., the American economics orthodoxy. Lindbeck's disavowal that the prize did not affect the subsequent
direction of research can be directly refuted by looking at what happened
to *other* economist prizes in the American context.

In retrospect, Hayek was essentially correct in his diagnosis that
high-profile prizes tend to accentuate swings in scientific fashion, and
confer authority on certain heroic figures, in order to imperfectly
telegraph what certain professional organizations deem to be exemplary
lines of inquiry worthy of emulation. The way we have related the story
so far tends to portray the dynamic as the Swedes single-handedly
performing this function, but that would be too narrow a construction

of events. Some insist that the Swedes on the committee attended closely to the advice of early American winners for their selection of choices of subsequent laureates, but the archival record equally reveals a certain modicum of perplexity concerning the motives of the Swedish committee on the part of past laureates. One example can be found in the later correspondence of Paul Samuelson:

> All who count in Cambridge, Massachusetts, regretted that a Krugman-Helpman award was not given. Same was lamented that no gold medal for George Dantzig or Peter Diamond. (Just why Lewis, Schultz, Buchanan, Stone or North scored, we'll never know. Who said life is fair?) There were too many single-person prizes. In 1970, better than a Samuelson award would have been an Arrow-Hicks-Samuelson award. Hayek-Friedman would have been better than Hayek-Myrdal and Friedman.[55]

Outside of that little bit of faux-modesty, and some MIT home-team bias, this correspondence reveals that many Americans believed they knew better than their Swedish colleagues whom and what should be elevated in the public mind as exemplary performances in cutting-edge economics. So the question naturally arises: Why did they not just give out their own prizes instead? The surprising answer is: they did, for a while, but then opted to defer to the Swedes in the early 1980s.

Most contemporary economists are familiar with the John Bates Clark medal, awarded to the *American* economist under forty who is judged to have made a significant contribution to economics; but, significantly, most are unaware that the American Economic Association (AEA) instituted *two* prizes in 1947. One was the Clark medal, and the other was the now-defunct Francis Amasa Walker medal, depicted in Figure 9.2. Originally, the two awards were conceived as a complementary package after World War II; so, it is all the more telling that in less than four decades the package was torn asunder.

---

55 Paul Samuelson, Letter to Stanley Fischer, dated December 24, 2008, Box 31, Paul Samuelson Papers, Perkins Library, Duke University. This is more evidence that the MIT School never really understood the role and importance of the Mont Pèlerin Society in postwar economics orthodoxy. See Samuelson to Fischer, January 6, 1997: "My generation were mostly scared of Milton. I knew his potential but never envied or admired him."

Figure 9.2. Francis Amasa Walker Medal

The Walker medal, named after the Association's first president, Francis Amasa Walker, was inaugurated in 1947 by the AEA, and was to be awarded every five years "to the living American economist who in the judgment of the awarding body has during his career made the greatest contribution to economics." The Walker Prize was instituted at an interesting juncture in the history of American economics. It is now widely conceded that in the interwar period there was no dominant orthodoxy regnant in the American context.[56] Yet, with stunning alacrity, American economics became unusually homogeneous over the next three decades. Since, by construction, the Walker Prize would be bestowed in retrospective recognition of an entire career, that necessarily dictated that many of the initial winners would have made their mark in an earlier era, and in idioms other than the nascent postwar orthodoxy, which was only recently becoming narrowly neoclassical and substantially more mathematical than anything that had come before. (The Clark medal had no similar problem: Its first recipient in 1947 was none other than Paul Samuelson.) So, curiously, the Walker medal was awarded to a number of individuals who would come to be deemed "not real economists" by the congealing postwar orthodoxy. The record of the Walker Prize (see Table 9.2) is illustrative

---

56 See the papers in Malcolm Rutherford and Mary Morgan, eds, *From Interwar Pluralism to Postwar Neoclassicism: 1998 Supplement to vol. 30, History of Political Economy* (Durham, NC: Duke University Press, 1998).

of the problem. The first two winners—Mitchell and Clark—were figureheads of the Institutionalist School of economics; this school had come under vicious attack by the Walrasian advocates of high-tech mathematical economics in what became known as the "Measurement without Theory" controversy in the late 1940s.[57] By the 1970s, the school was essentially kaput in formal economics departments in the US. The next Walker winner, Frank Knight, was being disparaged by his colleagues as a philosopher, not an economist, as early as the 1950s. The next two winners—Viner and Hansen—while certainly closer to the postwar neoclassical orthodoxy, would have been regarded as too retrograde and literary to resonate with the newly adopted self-conception of the skills and demeanor of the professional American economist by 1960. So although the American economics profession came equipped with a high-profile prize, it was not so clear that it was performing the all-important function of elevating the new model of exemplary performance to iconic status.

Table 9.2. Walker Medal Awards
1947—Wesley Clair Mitchell, 1874–1948
1952—John Maurice Clark, 1884–1963
1957—Frank H. Knight, 1885–1972
1962—Jacob Viner, 1892–1970
1967—Alvin H. Hansen, 1887–1975
1972—Theodore W. Schultz, 1902–1998
1977—Simon Kuznets, 1901–1985

The historian Beatrice Cherrier has drawn our attention to the fact that both AEA prizes, the Clark and Walker medals, faced criticism and challenge in the first decades of their existence.[58] Perhaps unexpectedly, the Clark medal came in for some disparagement as being too narrow, too theoretical, insufficiently elevating empirical work, and not adequately concerned with public policy. The discontent came to a head at the 1958 AEA meeting, where there was a proposal to mint another medal to highlight the empirical and public policy side of economics, to be named the Wesley Clair Mitchell medal. In the executive committee meeting, a motion was proposed to either pair the Clark medal with the

---

57 On the Measurement without Theory controversy, see Mirowski, "The Measurement Without Theory Controversy: Defeating Rival Research Programs by Accusing Them of Naive Empiricism," *Economies et Sociétés*, Serie Oeconomia, no. 11 (1989): 65–87.

58 See Beatrice Cherrier, "The Wesley Clair Mitchell Medal: The AEA Award that Never Came to Be," Institute for New Economic Thinking, November 11, 2015, ineteconomics.org.

new Mitchell medal, or else discontinue the Clark medal altogether. Some of the membership began to chafe at the "all must have prizes" argument, and controversy broke out about the whole idea of having formal prizes of any stripe sponsored by the AEA. The executive committee refused to respond to the hubbub, but that did not signify that the difficulties were in any sense mitigated.

The stalwarts of the AEA could have had no way of knowing that the resolution of the impasse would be conveniently provided by the Bank of Sweden in the 1960s. As we have argued, due to their own geopolitical and intellectual imperatives, the Swedish committee had decided to privilege the *nouvelle vague américaine* as the future of economics. This became practically apparent by the later 1970s, as did the principle that no other schools of thought than an American neoclassicism or an MPS neoliberalism would ever be graced with a call from Stockholm. Furthermore, it was obvious that the Bank of Sweden ersatz Nobel drew far more press attention and commentary than either the Clark or Walker prizes. As Ståhl said to the MPS in 1990: "it is a good thing for a scientific society to have something like a Nobel Prize . . . The contest character, the secrecy around the selection procedure and the final luxurious prize award ceremony and banquet are necessary ingredients in this public relations connection."[59] It did not take long for the greybeards of the AEA to realize they had made some grievous mistakes with their trophy bestowal when it came to promoting the image of the economics profession among the larger public. Clearly the Swedes had something to teach them concerning pomp and circumstance, but they also brought a clarity to the PR project which was seriously lacking in the existing array of professional prizes in America.

The first lesson was: do not name your prize after someone who could not in all good conscience himself be portrayed as exemplifying the virtues that the prize is intended to extol. In this instance, however important Francis Amasa Walker had been in the nineteenth-century context,[60] he could by no stretch of the imagination be refurbished as

---

59 Ståhl, "The Prize."

60 Walker had been brigadier general at age twenty-four for the Army of the Potomac during the Civil War, superintendent of the US Census at thirty, one of the first presidents of the Massachusetts Institute of Technology (MIT), president of the American Statistical Association (ASA) and the first president of the American Economic Association. He was also an economics professor at Yale and head of the statistical bureau of the US Treasury.

an American neoclassical economist *avant la lettre*. This point was made rather brutally in the 1980s by that arbiter of all things orthodox in the history of economics, Robert Solow.[61] The second lesson was: never give the prize to avatars of schools more or less opposed to the outlines of the postwar neoclassical orthodoxy. The Walker medal was wrong-footed from the starting line, bestowing eminence on figures such as Wesley Clair Mitchell, J. M. Clark, and Frank Knight. Only late in the game did the AEA medal begin going to people whom the Swedes would come to acknowledge as members in good standing of the new model orthodoxy: Theodore Schultz and Simon Kuznets. But there persisted the nagging issue of the unseemly prior track record.

Having learned their lesson from the Swedes, the AEA took the startling tack of quietly discontinuing the Walker medal in 1982. It is often said that the ersatz Nobel rendered the Walker medal obsolete, but rarely has it been spelled out exactly what this means. The purpose of the ersatz Nobel was to elevate certain strains of economic thought above their competitors; those strains were an Americanized version of Walrasianism and an MPS-inspired neoliberalism. If the two strains found a stilted hybrid at the University of Chicago, then all the better for Chicago and its global reputation. The Swedes were forward-looking, realizing they were intervening to bring about an outcome that had not yet become a global standard: English-inflected American orthodoxy, tricked out to resemble the natural sciences, with a dollop of neoliberal political theory. The American prizes, by contrast, had been sadly backward-looking; therefore, it was the better part of valor to simply retire the Walker medal with little fanfare.

Conclusion

The role of prizes deserves to be taken more seriously in an expansive social epistemology. Prizes serve to inform and structure the internal dynamics of an intellectual field like economics; and equally, they play an important part in the validation of the doctrines of the field amongst the larger public. But in this case, there is a further consideration that is frequently overlooked. Because epistemology is so very

---

61 Robert Solow, "What Do We Know that Francis Amasa Walker Didn't?" *History of Political Economy* 19, no. 2 (1987), 183–89.

central to neoliberalism, they were well poised to take advantage of
the opportunity created by the rogue behavior of the Bank of Sweden
to upgrade their standing in the postwar economics profession,
through occupation of the newly formed Prize committee, and the
elevation of MPS members to the exalted status of 'winners of the
Nobel Prize'.

PART FOUR

NEOLIBERAL INFLUENCE BEYOND REAGAN, THATCHER, AND PINOCHET

10

How the Neoliberal Think Tank Went Global: The Atlas Network, 1981 to the Present

Marie-Laure Djelic and Reza Mousavi

Since the late 1970s, neoliberalism has transformed the world. It has impacted the structures and strategies of firms and organizations—whether private, public, or not-for-profit.[1] It has influenced policy-making at national and transnational levels.[2] It has transformed our private lives and our very sense of self.[3] The idea of a market society has become performative in the Austinian sense.[4] Yet not all ideas that circulate become performative—only those that are framed, carried, adopted, appropriated, enacted, and institutionalized successfully. Despite the many studies of neoliberalism as a doctrine and way of life, scholars have yet to explain fully how this particular set of ideas was translated into institutions and practices with a global reach.

---

1 E. Vaara, J. Tienari, and J. Laurila, "Pulp and Paper Fiction: On the Discursive Legitimation of Global Industrial Restructuring," *Organization Studies* 27, no. 6 (2006). E. Girei, "NGOs, Management and Development: Harnessing Counter-Hegemonic Possibilities," *Organization Studies* 37, no. 2 (2016).

2 L. Baccaro and C. Howell, "A Common Neoliberal Trajectory: The Transformation of Industrial Relations in Advanced Capitalism," *Politics & Society* 39, no. 4 (2011). S. Böhm, M. C. Misoczky, and S. Moog, "Greening Capitalism? A Marxist Critique of Carbon-Markets," *Organization Studies* 33, no. 11 (2012). H. Buch-Hansen and A. Wigger, "Revisiting Fifty Years of Market-Making: The Neoliberal Transformation of European Competition Policy," *Review of International Political Economy* 17, no. 1 (2010).

3 C. Graham, "The Calculation of Age," *Organization Studies* 35, no. 11 (2014). M. Lazzarato, *The Making of the Indebted Man* (Cambridge, MA: MIT Press, 2012).

4 J. L. Austin, *How to Do Things with Words* (Oxford: Oxford University Press, 1962).

This chapter contributes to our understanding of this institutionalization process by exploring the role of a singular organization, the Atlas Network.[5] Founded in 1981, Atlas played a strategic role as an architect organization in the transnational liberal constellation. In this chapter, we follow the development of Atlas as it constructed and expanded a broad network of neoliberal think tanks across the world. We delve into the mechanisms that turned it into the hub organization of a dense transnational community of neoliberal think tanks. From a network of fifteen think tanks in nine countries in the mid-1980s, Atlas now brings together 457 'partner organizations' in ninety-six countries. In the meantime, the organization's operating budget has gone from $150,000 to over $15 million. Over three decades, Atlas self-consciously refined and diffused an organizational blueprint for public opinion and policy influence to win what it often called "the war of ideas."[6]

More than any other single organization, Atlas was responsible for the globalization of the neoliberal think tank model. By tracking a history surprisingly neglected by scholars to date, we can better understand the durability of neoliberal policy networks. Unaffected by political and administrative changeovers, these networks have embedded over time a particular ideology and sets of policy imaginaries in many countries around the world. By focusing on *geographical reach, modes of enlisting, mechanisms for diffusion,* and *strategies of stabilization,* this chapter shows how Atlas has fostered the spread of a transnational organizational architecture to structure and uphold the diffusion and institutionalization of neoliberalism. Ideas matter, but they need institutions in order to travel as well as to survive and embed themselves into policies. Our exploration of Atlas offers a view of neoliberalism in motion.

---

5 Founded in 1981 as the Atlas Economic Research Foundation, the organization was renamed the Atlas Network in 2011. Henceforth in this chapter, we will refer to it using the shorter 'Atlas'. In the footnotes, references to *Atlas Highlights*, 1987–2015 (entirely downloaded in 2015, all available upon request) are made in the following way: AtlasH (YEAR), and when there are several issues that year we add a (Winter), b (Spring), c (Summer), d (Fall). For example: AtlasH (1995c) corresponds to Atlas Highlights Summer of 1995. References to the *Atlas Investor Report Special Year-in-Review*, 2001–2013 (entirely downloaded in 2014, all available upon request) are made in the following way: AtlasIR (YEAR).

6 Colleen Dyble, ed., *Taming Leviathan: Waging the War of Ideas around the World* (London: Institute of Economic Affairs, 2008).

At the Creation: The Origins of Atlas

Atlas was incorporated in July 1981. The founder, Sir Antony Fisher, had created the Institute of Economic Affairs (IEA) in London in 1955, which played a pivotal role in spreading neoliberal ideology within British public opinion, policy, and political circles in the 1970s and 1980s.[7] The success of the IEA meant that Fisher was invited to launch sister organizations in Canada and the US and soon became a "think tank entrepreneur."[8] In the late 1970s, Fisher was ready to take the next step—to create an organization with the mission to "litter the world with free-market think tanks."[9] In 1979, he sought formal endorsement from key neoliberal luminaries—Margaret Thatcher, F. A. Hayek, and Milton Friedman, writing "A letter from you . . . expressing your confidence in the effectiveness of a proliferation of the IEA idea would be immensely valuable."[10]

Securing the support of this trio allowed Fisher to raise funds and incorporate Atlas. The objective of the new organization was to push for and help the seeding, staffing, and coaching of neoliberal think tanks across the world to "influence public sentiment" and in the process "make legislation possible."[11] Initially located in San Francisco, Atlas started small with a budget of $150,000. Early donors were the Sarah (Mellon) Scaife Foundation, Fisher's second wife Dorian, and private philanthropists from the US and Canada.[12] The budget was stable at around $2 million from 1995 to 2005. From that point, it increased rapidly—reaching over $15 million in 2016.[13] When Fisher died in 1988, the new director, John Blundell, moved the organization to George Mason University in Fairfax, Virginia, already the home of the Center for the Study of Public Choice since 1983 and the Mercatus Center founded in 1980. In 1991, Alejandro

---

7   C. Muller, "The Institute of Economic Affairs: Undermining the Post-war Consensus," *Contemporary British History* 10, no. 1 (1996). D. Yergin and J. Stanislaw, *The Commanding Heights* (New York: Touchstone, 1998).

8   G. Frost, *Antony Fisher: Champion of Liberty* (London: Profile Books, 2008).

9   R. Cockett: *Thinking the Unthinkable* (London: HarperCollins, 1994), 307.

10   A. Fisher, Letter to Friedrich Hayek, dated December 31, 1979, Box 4, Folder 1, Document 80, Friedrich von Hayek's Papers, Hoover Institution, Stanford University.

11   A. Fisher, Atlas Presentation and Promotion Video, 1985, youtube.com.

12   A. Chafuen, "Atlas Economic Research Foundation Early History," chafuen.com.

13   Atlas, "Annual Report 2016," atlasnetwork.org.

Chafuen took over Atlas and remained president and CEO until 2009.[14] Since 2009, Chafuen has kept the role of president while Brad Lips, a former equity research analyst on Wall Street who joined Atlas in 1998, took over as CEO. In 2011, the Atlas Economic Research Foundation was renamed the Atlas Network— underscoring its increasing organizational density and keeping pace with trends in the *Zeitgeist* of management, marketing, and academia, where everything is or becomes a 'network'.

In 1982, Atlas brought together fifteen think tanks from nine countries. Today, as shown in Figure 10.1 and as indicated on its website, the network boasts a "global network of more than 450 free-market organizations in over 90 countries."

Figure 10.1 Number of Think Tanks Added to/Dropped from the Atlas Network

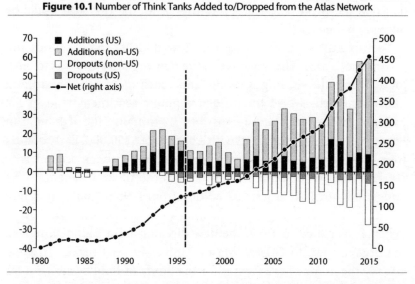

Think tanks are not "member" but "partner" organizations; together they make up a broad transnational network with Atlas as the hub. Atlas was created to institutionalize the process of helping start up new think tanks. And it has played that role, being a catalyst through the years for the setting up and the stabilization of many such organizations. More than half of the think tanks are located in North America and Europe but, as Figure 10.2 shows, the network has a global presence. We identify two distinct but complementary periods in the development of Atlas.

---

14 Chafuen joined the MPS in 1980 and the Atlas team in 1985.

During the fledgling years (1981 to 1995), the survival and legitimacy of the organization depended on its capacity to expand the network. The period of expansion and maturity started in earnest in the mid-1990s (1996–2015). Atlas then became an attractor organization and partner organizations needed it more than it needed them.

Figure 10.2 Global Reach of the Atlas Network in 2015

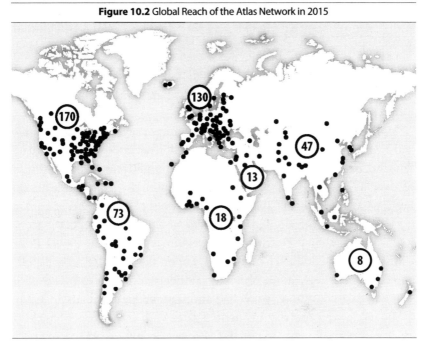

Geographical Reach: From Controlled Expansion to Global Ambition

When Atlas was incorporated in the early 1980s, Fisher had personal connections with all the existing think tanks, most of which he had helped to create. They shaped an emergent neoliberal constellation around Atlas. As it was then an organization with limited resources and capabilities, Fisher and his team implemented a geographically controlled expansion, starting with the American continent. By 1981, thanks in part to Fisher's activism during the 1970s, the neoliberal think tank was already becoming an identifiable organizational category in North America. Along with the rise of "Reaganomics," this made the US fertile soil for Atlas. By 1995, there were already 122 think tanks in the Atlas network and sixty-nine were based in North America (see Figure 10.3).

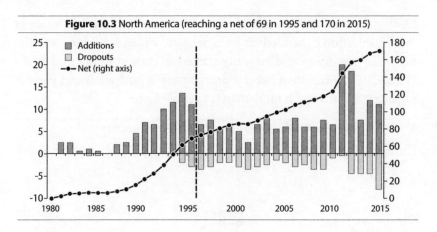

Figure 10.3 North America (reaching a net of 69 in 1995 and 170 in 2015)

In the 1980s, Latin America was also an important target region. Chile had been an early laboratory for neoliberal ideas and policies. Augusto Pinochet had called upon a local group of Chicago-trained economists to propose a radically different economic program.[15] By 1976, the "Chicago Boys" were in control of Chilean economic policy.[16] Hayek and Friedman traveled to Chile, consulting with and encouraging this team of pioneers. In the process, they bestowed their legitimacy as recent Nobel Prize winners (in 1974 and 1976 respectively) upon the new economic experiment and, indirectly, on the brutal dictatorial government of Pinochet.

Economic conditions were bad throughout Latin America in the 1980s. Following the rise in interest rates with the Volcker Shock in 1979, and officially initiated by the Mexican default in 1982, debt crises wreaked havoc in the region. For Atlas, however, this "lost decade" carried a promise and created a window of opportunity for the dissemination and application of neoliberal ideas. It was in this context that Fisher met Alejandro Chafuen, a young Argentinian economist and member of the Mont Pèlerin Society (MPS). Chafuen joined Atlas in 1985 to create the Direction of Latin American Affairs. The focus on Latin America resulted in a rapid expansion of the network in that part of the world. Figure 10.4 shows that a total of twenty-five Latin American think tanks were integrated between 1981 and 1995—not all of which have survived.

---

15 J. G. Valdes, *Pinochet's Economists* (Cambridge: Cambridge University Press, 1995).

16 Atlas, "Chile's Economic Transformation: Planting the Seed of Ideas (Part One)," 2012, youtube.com.

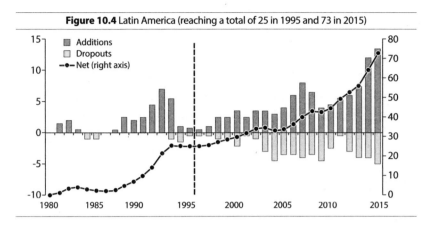

Figure 10.4 Latin America (reaching a total of 25 in 1995 and 73 in 2015)

Speaking at the 28th Atlas International Workshop in Istanbul in 1996, Deepak Lal, economist and MPS member, rejoiced that "the intellectual battle was being won."[17] The fall of the Berlin Wall, the acceleration of globalization, and the impact of the Pinochet, Thatcher, and Reagan "revolutions" meant that ever more regions of the world were targets of neoliberal proselytism. The time was ripe for Atlas, with around 120 think tanks in its "family," to expand its international ambitions. Letting the American continent develop on existing dynamics, Atlas turned to those regions where the network was non-existent or weak—Asia, Europe (West and East), and Africa. After 2001, Atlas also targeted the Middle East, trying to reach the Muslim world. The increasing international reach of Atlas was reflected in the structure of its annual reports—starting in 2004, there were dedicated pages for each region. In 2008, Atlas also changed its website name from atlasUSA.org to atlasnetwork.org.

One new focus was Asia. In the mid-1990s, Atlas's footprint in the continent was limited, with a notable exception in the Hong Kong Centre for Economic Research founded in 1987 by Y. C. Richard Wong with the help of Atlas. In the early 1990s, Atlas combined its expertise with the resources of the German Friedrich Naumann Foundation (FNF), which had a presence in China. Together, they organized a workshop in Beijing in 1995. The Atlas team took this opportunity to explore China, Hong Kong, and India.[18] In India, Chafuen met Barun Mitra, a "science writer" with whom he had been

---

17 AtlasH (1996d): 2.
18 AtlasH (1995b).

in written contact. Mitra founded a think tank in New Delhi the following year, the Liberty Institute, and remained an important contact for Atlas in South Asia. Other workshops and forums were organized in Asia, particularly after 2002, and generated a base of contacts for Atlas in China, Japan, South Korea, Malaysia, Mongolia, India, Pakistan, Philippines, and Vietnam. Some of these contacts came to Fairfax, Virginia and, with the help of Atlas, established their own institutes. They also over time created a regional network of support and resource sharing.[19] Figure 10.5 shows the expansion of the network, from a net of seven institutes in 1995 to fifty-five today in Asia/Pacific.

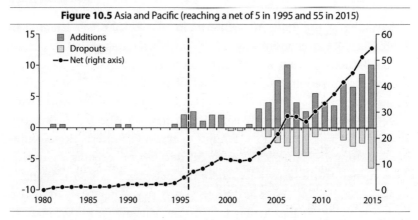

Figure 10.5 Asia and Pacific (reaching a net of 5 in 1995 and 55 in 2015)

Another new site of attention was Europe. Europe had historically been Atlas's worst disappointment—Western Europe being "mired in heavy regulation and taxation" and Eastern Europe lacking "a strong rule of law."[20] Understanding that Europe was not welcoming to the neoliberal "think tank culture," Atlas leaders decided to enter through academia. Atlas helped the pro-market teaching and research efforts of some European scholars while also encouraging them to establish free market think tanks. From the mid-2000s, Atlas organized regional gatherings in Europe to boost resource sharing and collaboration among the fledgling institutes and isolated academic centers. The hope was also to bridge the East-West divide. The efforts paid off in the new millennium. The European network quadrupled after 2000 (Figure 10.6). Numbers went from a net of nine institutes in 2000 to

19 AtlasH (2006a).
20 AtlasH (2000a).

forty-nine today in Eastern Europe and from thirteen to eighty-one in Western Europe.

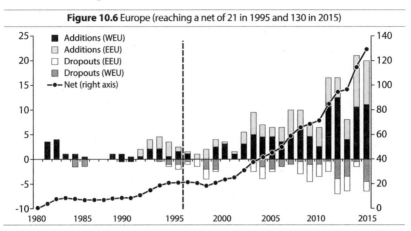

Figure 10.6 Europe (reaching a net of 21 in 1995 and 130 in 2015)

Even more than Europe, "Atlas' most challenging and untapped markets" have been Africa and the Middle East.[21] In 2000, the network only had two associated institutes in Africa: IEA Ghana and the Free Market Foundation in South Africa. There was a double difficulty— finding motivated champions and convincing donors. Things slowly started to change, however, when James Shikwati, from Kenya, contacted Atlas in 2001 announcing that he was keen on creating a think tank.[22] The International Policy Network (a British institute run by Linda Whetstone, Fisher's daughter) funded his trip and that of Thompson Ayodele, from Nigeria, to the 5th anniversary of the Liberty Institutes in India in 2001.[23] Having shown their commitment by launching Kenya's (Inter Regional Economic Network) and Nigeria's (Institute for Public Policy Analysis) first neoliberal think tanks, both were invited to Fairfax for a month in 2002. Subsequent trips to Uganda, Rwanda, Burundi, Tanzania, Zambia, Zimbabwe, Botswana, South Africa, and Lesotho helped identify other interesting and committed contacts.

The Middle East proved more challenging still. Despite outreach attempts, Atlas's success in finding local institute leaders has been limited. Today, its presence there is mostly through local-language websites. Figure 10.7 shows that Atlas's network in Africa and the Middle East expanded from a net of 4 think tanks in 2000 to 31 in 2015.

---

21 AtlasH (2004b).

22 AtlasIR (2002): 5.

23 AtlasH (2001c).

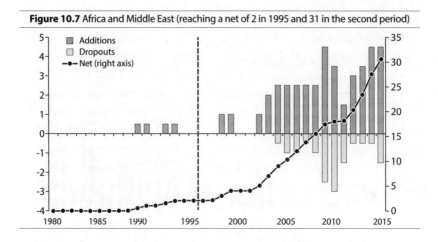

Figure 10.7 Africa and Middle East (reaching a net of 2 in 1995 and 31 in the second period)

Modes of Enlisting: From ad hoc Identification to Organized Outreach

Finding individuals willing to subscribe to and champion the cause was a necessary first step to diffusing the think tank model. Initially, the identification of those potential champions was mostly ad hoc—happening through the mobilization of direct and indirect personal networks. In the US, Fisher could rely on his own personal connections to identify the new generation of think tank leaders. In Latin America, however, his personal contacts were limited. Hence he used indirect mechanisms. First he leveraged his contacts within the MPS, of which he had been a member since 1954. When Hayek or Friedman traveled to South America and met interesting prospects, they connected them with Fisher. This was how, for example, Fisher met Hernando de Soto. Fisher spurred de Soto, a Peruvian economist trained in Switzerland, to create his home country's first think tank—the Instituto Libertad y Democracia (ILD) in 1981. When Chafuen joined Atlas in 1985 and started to mobilize his personal network, scouting efforts in Latin America intensified.

The identification and mobilization of prospective foot soldiers also happened through the organization of workshops. The first workshop took place in 1983, in Vancouver, Canada, and by 1995, Atlas had organized twenty-five. Annual workshops were organized in connection with MPS meetings. This allowed Atlas to piggyback on MPS intellectual resources, renowned members being invited as speakers. The proximity of both events was an attraction for liberal champions from around the world even if the doors of the core were closed; invitation to the Atlas workshop did not carry a parallel invitation to the MPS meeting. These workshops were small (around 100 participants) and co-organized with local affiliate think tanks. This made it easier to attract local participants and gave local think tanks and their leaders legitimacy and visibility.

The workshops had several objectives: to share information and best practices; to discuss key policy issues with particular consideration for concrete realizations; and to showcase the work of think tanks to foundations and corporate officers.[24] The workshops also proved useful to identify new contacts. Hence, Fisher and Chafuen soon organized regional variants, starting with Latin America, to bolster Atlas's projects there. The first regional workshop took place in Jamaica in 1987 and was followed by seven more in Latin America before 1995 (see Table 10.1).

Table 10.1. Atlas International Workshops, 1981–1995

	Main Workshops	Latin America Regional Workshop	Other Workshops
1983	Vancouver, Canada		
1984	Cambridge, UK		
1985	Sidney, Australia		
1986	St Vincent, Italy		
1987	Indianapolis, Indiana, US	Montego Bay, Jamaica	
1988	Herndon, Virginia, US	Caracas, Venezuela	
1989	Christchurch, New Zealand	Sao Paulo, Brazil	
1990	Herndon, Virginia, US	Antigua, Guatemala Guadalajara, Mexico	Munich, Germany Moscow, Russia
1991	Herndon, Virginia, US	Punta del Este, Urugay	
1992	Cuernavaca, Mexico	Guayaquil, Ecuador	
1993	Herndon, Virginia, US	Santa Cruz, Bolivia	Stockholm, Sweden
1994	East Sussex, UK		
1995	Philadelphia, Pennsylvania, US		Beijing, China

Regional workshops were smaller (around forty participants). The objective was to champion the think tank-model and to "provide support and advice to regional free-market policy institutes."[25] One of the speakers at the Jamaica meeting, Walter Williams, economics professor at George Mason University, was impressed by what he heard. He introduced Chafuen to Gordon St. Angelo, from the Lilly Endowment. This marked the beginning of one of Atlas's strongest "financial ties."[26] In 1990, Lilly Endowment Inc. provided Atlas with a three-year grant to

24 AtlasH (1989).
25 AtlasH (1990b): 3.
26 Chafuen, "Atlas Economic Research Foundation Early History."

expand its activities in Latin America. This helped significantly with the local seeding of new think tanks.

As the Atlas organizational network expanded, the search for and development of motivated champions could no longer be accommodated by occasional field trips and targeted workshops. Atlas hence fostered the systematic formalization, organization, and branding of its outreach efforts. With a view to systematize and formalize its outreach and scouting efforts, it also created the Atlas International Freedom Corps (IFC) in 2003, as "the free market alternative to Peace Corps."[27] Through the *discovery* arm of IFC, Atlas dispatched senior members of the network to "scout for intellectual entrepreneurs in difficult parts of the world."[28] The potential "freedom fighters" thus identified could be invited to Atlas, as part of IFC's *visiting fellow* arm. The fellowships, from several weeks to a few months, allowed newcomers to "learn about think tanks," prepare for their think tank entrepreneur role and develop a sense of belonging to the Atlas "family."[29] The fellows then often became themselves effective "scouts." In the first half of 2000s, Atlas financed five missionary trips to Asia and Africa and hosted thirty-three visiting fellows from Latin America, Europe, Asia, and Africa. These efforts accelerated the expansion of the network and fostered the integration of a core of connected think tanks across different regions of the world.

By the late 2000s, each arm of the IFC became a full-fledged program. In 2009, the Cato Institute transferred its internationalization service to Atlas. Tom Palmer, from Cato, became Vice-President for International Programs at Atlas, absorbing the discovery arm of the IFC. Palmer soon became the symbolic figure of Atlas's missionary and discovery activities. He worked with a team of native speakers (in a dozen languages) and deployed an outreach and discovery strategy for challenging regions. Classic texts were translated and distributed and new material produced and shared through web platforms tailored for a given language.[30] The platforms also organized essay contests and relayed information on initiatives like Freedom Schools or university tours. This online strategy implied "aggressive branding and integration of programs around a website."[31]

Another strategy targeted academia. Initially, Atlas scorned universities

---

27   AtlasIR (2003): 13.
28   AtlasIR (2003): 13.
29   AtlasIR (2003): 13.
30   AtlasH (2009a).
31   AtlasH (2009a): 3.

as "ideological monopolies of the Left."[32] Vocal in its contempt, it constructed itself as an alternative to academia, contributing to "un-politicized" public policy "based on sound science."[33] The realization, however, that "many cultures of the world [had] not yet fully embraced the think tank model" imposed a pragmatic reorientation.[34] A key actor here was Leonard Liggio, law professor at George Mason, and veteran of the Institute of Humane Studies, who joined Atlas in 1994. In 1999, the John Templeton Foundation gave Liggio and Atlas a grant to target academia. The International Freedom Project (IFP) financed through this grant aimed at planting "seeds of truth" in academia outside North America.[35] The plan was to fund university professors (ranging from \$10,000 to \$40,000) to develop free market courses and invite prominent guest lecturers. Between 1999 and 2002, Atlas funded sixty-eight courses in twenty-seven countries, an estimated 1,500 students being reached.[36] Although this program ended in 2002, Sir John Templeton (investor, philanthropist, friend of Fisher, and longtime MPS member) remained an important funder of Atlas, underwriting various initiatives through his Foundation.

In the mid-2000s, Atlas broadened its academic ambitions. Through the Teach Freedom Initiative (TFI), Atlas helped a select group of professors to sponsor speakers, craft workshops, and find adequate fellowships and internships for their students. Through TFI, Atlas organized conferences to showcase the contributions of free market oriented academic centers—hoping to help along their ultimate transformation into think tanks.[37] The Fund for the Study of Spontaneous Orders (FSSO) was oriented to research designed to support and reward academic scholarship in the tradition of Austrian methodological individualism. Underwritten by an anonymous donor, FSSO held annual conferences and granted fellowships (\$10,000) to young scholars and life-time achievement awards (\$50,000) to scholars "whose work exemplifies the ideals of the Fund."[38]

---

32 AtlasIR (2002): 14.
33 AtlasH (1995b): 2.
34 AtlasH (2000a): 3.
35 AtlasH (2001c): 7.
36 AtlasIR (2002). The potential was even more significant as there were around 100 applications per year.
37 AtlasIR (2005): 26.
38 AtlasH (2003b): 2.

By the late 2000s, these initiatives had lost momentum. Whether due to limited returns on investment or to Liggio's bad health, the focus on academia receded. This happened as Palmer rose to prominence. Palmer had close ties with Students for Liberty (SFL) networks, which brought together graduates of the Institute for Humane Studies Koch Summer Fellowship Program. In the new approach, academia was bypassed and scorn returned: *What Your Professors Won't Tell You* was the subtitle of a series of books edited by Palmer and distributed by SFL. Academic hierarchies were being bypassed and college students became direct targets.

Mechanisms of Diffusion: From Tailored Interventions to Standardized Processes

The early expansion of Atlas was rapid but controlled and geographically bounded. The Atlas network grew from eight members in 1981 to 122 in 1995. In the next twenty years the network would be nearly multiplied by four. In these two periods, Atlas deployed tools of intervention that were fitted to the specificities of the network and context.

Initially, Atlas fostered diffusion through practical "venturing" actions. Having identified individual foot soldiers, it worked to empower them by helping them materially and coaching them directly. Atlas then made sure to keep in contact, with a double objective—to stabilize the think tank locally and to tighten its integration into the transnational neoliberal community. When the Atlas team met motivated individuals, it was ready to finance exploratory trips. In 1988, it thus financed one trip to India and two to Ghana. Shyam Kamath, a young economics professor from California State University, and Parth Shah, a PhD student, went to India. Kamath had already mobilized potential donors and the objective of the trip was to find "the right individuals to manage and run the institute locally."[39] Charles Mensah, PhD candidate in economics at George Mason, organized the trips to Ghana. "Incorporation, finding premises, recruiting a board of directors, and seeking financial support were all on his agenda."[40] The Indian trip only bore fruit in 1997 when Shah returned to India to found the Centre for

39 AtlasH (1988a): 3.
40 AtlasH (1989): 4.

Civil Society. The African trips proved rapidly successful: IEA Ghana was created in 1989 in a country governed by the military.

As Fisher had underscored, "one of the difficulties in setting up an institute is to raise the money in the first place, because usually business-men don't know what it's all about."[41] Atlas could help through "provision of seed money, which could mean an instant start."[42] Altas's first invest-ment was in a French institute—the Institut Economique de Paris.[43] In the US, Fisher put high hopes in John Goodman, a PhD graduate in econom-ics from Columbia. In 1983, with a starting grant of $20,000, Goodman launched the National Center for Policy Analysis (NCPA) in Dallas, Texas.[44] In Latin America, Fisher supported de Soto in establishing ILD. Many other fledgling institutes received seed money from Atlas in that period—in Iceland, Australia, Italy, Spain, Latin and North America, and, in the early 1990s, in Russia, Romania, and the Czech Republic.[45]

Initially, Fisher used his personal contacts to raise funds for this purpose. As Atlas and its role became more visible, established foundations contrib-uted structured grant packages. We mentioned above the Lilly Endowment grant with a focus on Latin America. Other foundations followed—Smith Richardson, Sarah Scaife, Carthage—as well as anonymous donors.[46] This successful fundraising—"revenues doubled in 1989 . . . donors continue to respond magnificently"—was a powerful accelerator and allowed Atlas to rapidly expand its network.[47] It also meant that Atlas could diversify the nature of financial assistance—from only "seed money" to a menu of start-up, project, visiting, or conference attendance grants.[48]

Beyond financial assistance, Atlas also provided one-on-one coach-ing to help institutes develop in unique contexts. The idea was to relay "the experience of the [IEA]" and other first generation think tanks to "advise an ever-growing family of institutes."[49] Initially, this took the

41   A. Fisher, "Letter to a Businessman in Jamaica, 1981," extracts available on chafuen.com.

42   Ibid.

43   A. Fisher, "Pourquoi l'Institute of Economic Affairs?" Speech at the Inauguration of the Institut Economique de Paris, September 29, 1982, Liberté économique et progrès social, no. 46–7 (October 1983).

44   Chafuen, "Atlas Economic Research Foundation Early History."

45   AtlasH (1990a), AtlasH (1992a).

46   AtlasH (1988a), AtlasH (1988b), AtlasH (1990b).

47   AtlasH (1989d): 4.

48   AtlasH (1991b), AtlasH (1992c), Atlas (1993a).

49   AtlasH (1987b): 2.

form of personal visits by Fisher. As de Soto later recalled, for example: "It was on the basis of his vision that we designed the structure of the ILD. He then came to Lima and told us how to structure the statutes, how to plan our goals, how to build the foundation, what to expect in the short and long term."[50]

Fisher did the same for most think tanks created before his death.[51] Building on his experience, he had a clear framework in mind.[52] First, a think tank should stay out of politics and focus instead on building influence. Hence, key targets were the media and policy influencers even more than policy-makers. Second, think tanks should stay away from governmental or political financing. Hence foundation and private funding were privileged. Third, think tanks should work like businesses. While Fisher was singularly active, other staff members soon got involved by helping write the bylaws of new institutes, constitute boards of directors (often with Atlas trustees or team members), develop budget plans, and initiate research and publishing projects.

Workshops, particularly regional ones, also played an important role in relaying the think tank model. The 1988 workshop in Venezuela, for example, proposed seminars on "all aspects of founding, funding and running an institute."[53] In 1990, the structuring, funding, and organizing of institutes were also discussed at length in a regional meeting in Moscow.[54] In the early 1990s, the evolution towards the professionalization and managerialization of think tanks started in earnest. Private models and templates were transferred to the nonprofit think tanks to ensure efficiency and accountability to funders. In November 1991, the Heritage Foundation organized a workshop on "Fundraising in the New Policy Environment," where Atlas was represented. The workshop was "devoted to the importance of developing clear organizational missions, devising better methods of marketing products and services and refining donor relations."[55]

As the number of initiatives and targeted countries increased rapidly in the 1990s, diffusion mechanisms had to be rethought. Indirect and mediated forms of influence came to complement direct interaction and

---

50 T. Mitchell, "The Work of Economics: How a Discipline Makes its World," *European Journal of Sociology* 46 (2005).

51 Frost, *Antony Fisher.*

52 Chafuen, "Atlas Economic Research Foundation Early History."

53 AtlasH (1988a).

54 AtlasH (1990b).

55 AtlasH (1992a): 4.

communication. Initially, Atlas had provided seed money in an ad hoc manner to "worthy" think tanks. From the early 2000s, it moved to distribute general purpose funds through grant competitions. Think tanks filled out a six-page grant application, accessible from the website. Atlas organized the review and selection. Most of the grants went to non-US think tanks (around 85 percent between 2004 and 2013). Grant competitions meant that Atlas could have leverage on and steer the agenda of network members. Whereas initially it had to persuade think-tank leaders to engage with certain debates, through grant competitions it could nudge them towards the issues it deemed important. Atlas set up, for example, a grant competition to foster private solutions to health and welfare issues. Thirty institutes were awarded this grant ($10,000) between 2002 and 2004. Grant programs multiplied over the years (see Table 10.2). Start-up, Student Project, and Video Production grants were created alongside the standard General grant. New topical short-term grant competitions also emerge regularly—they currently include a "Liberating Enterprise to Advance Prosperity Grant" for think tanks outside North America who want to work on improving the regulatory environment in their countries, and an "Illiberalism Grant" designed to help think tanks who are involved in combating new forms of authoritarianism and statism.[56]

Table 10.2. Atlas Grants in Recent Years

Year	Amount	Number of recipients	Number of countries
2010	$2,575,000	–	–
2011	$3,110,000	–	–
2012	$3,515,000	147	57
2013	$4,042,000	–	62
2014	$4,340,000	177	67

Source: Atlas' annual reports

The first phase of coaching had built upon the experience of veterans of the think tank world. Early on, though, Fisher had thought of making the rules for think tank creation and development explicit. In 1983, he circulated a fifty-page text—*Some Do's and Don'ts for Public Policy Institutes*. The Atlas team worked to refine and make these recommendations more explicit—producing "recipe books," modular "management toolkits," and ultimately a blueprint that became accessible through

56 Grants and Awards, atlasnetwork.org.

the website in 2000.[57] The blueprint covered many dimensions. There were start-up guidelines—how to select a name; how to write bylaws; how to define the mission and set up a proper governance. There were functioning guidelines—how to organize everyday activities; how to remain independent from government and political parties; how to conduct market analysis. And finally, there were development guidelines—how to raise funds; how to find and work with authors; how to market and sell ideas; how to project competence and expertise.[58] In addition to the blueprint, sample documents were collated—bylaws, three-year action plans, detailed planning for an annual dinner, operation budgets. With the development of the internet, the blueprint morphed into a directory of links to material produced by Atlas and major think tanks.

After 2000, with an increasingly dense network, Atlas restructured its international operations to create regional sub-networks.[59] Regional networks were an attempt to deal with the difficult question of local inscription. They proved effective in facilitating collaboration, fostering synergies among local institutes, and "hooking" new contacts to the cause. Building upon an initiative of the Heritage Foundation, Atlas encouraged local institutes to establish regional resource banks to foster regional networking and coalition building. The African Resource Bank was launched in 2003, the Asian and Eastern European ones in 2004. In the late 2000s, a few successful think tanks were upgraded as Atlas "satellites" to act as regional gatekeepers and relays. The idea was to push some of Atlas's discovery, organizing, and training operations downstream.[60]

Strategies of Stabilization: From Network Consolidation to Community Integration

Initially, most of the resources and activities deployed by Atlas targeted the diffusion of the think tank model. Soon, however, Fisher and the Atlas team realized the importance of longer-term objectives—ensuring the survival of individual think tanks and fostering their

---

57 Atlas, "Guidelines, Suggestions, and Ideas for Public Policy Institutes, 2000," web.archive.org.

58 Ibid.

59 AtlasIR (2009).

60 AtlasIR (2009): 9.

integration into a larger (neoliberal) community. An important challenge during the first period was to create a sense of belonging and to
sustain mobilization around a common project. Atlas deployed different mechanisms in that direction. One effective mechanism was to
invite think tank leaders to Fairfax. The Lilly Endowment grant made
it possible to bring Latin American leaders for periods of six months,
allowing real immersion. The program was small but its alumni
became influential in the Latin American neoliberal landscape and
retained strong ties with Atlas. Dora de Ampureo set up the Instituto
Ecuatoriano de Economia Politica (IEEP) in 1992 and joined the MPS
in 2000. Rocio Guijarro Saucedo became the executive director of
CEDICE, a Venezuelan think tank with strong ties to Atlas. Similarly,
in the 1990s, Atlas invited Eastern Europeans. Daniel Stancu, Executive
Director of the Liberty Institute in Romania, Leslaw Kuzaj of the
Cracow Industrial Society, Poland, and Jiri Schwartz of the Liberal
Institute in Prague, Czechoslovakia, came for several months. This
allowed them to strengthen links with Atlas and other institutes in the
broad Washington region.[61]

The broad diffusion of intellectual products and the circulation of a
small group of so-called freedom intellectuals were also effective mechanisms to strengthen connections between Atlas, think tanks, and the
core of the neoliberal community (the MPS). Initially, a handful of
neoliberal luminaries did the rounds, including Hayek, Friedman, James
Buchanan, and Henri Lepage. Soon, however, the circle expanded to
include leaders from older think tanks—Lord Ralph Harris from the
IEA, Michael Walker from the Fraser Institute, Ed Crane from the Cato
Institute, de Soto from the ILD, and Goodman from the NCPA.[62] Atlas
was the connector—putting "freedom intellectuals" and local think
tanks in contact and financing the trips.

Atlas also fostered the diffusion of intellectual products across the
network, including books, reports, memos, and videos. Convinced
that "the widespread availability of pro-market books is a critical
element in communicating the principles of a free society," Atlas
financed translations of the classics of liberalism, including books by
Adam Smith, Hayek, Buchanan, and Friedman.[63] The corpus evolved

---

61 AtlasH (1990a), AtlasH (1992a).
62 AtlasH (1987b), Atlas (1988a), Atlas (1989d), Atlas (1994c).
63 AtlasH (1988a).

through time and Atlas also helped translate and diffuse texts produced by members of associated institutes, including de Soto, Goodman, and many others. In the 1990s, those texts championed private and market solutions with a particular focus on healthcare, welfare, and environmental issues.[64]

Showcasing the concrete results and successes of institutes made it possible to foster a sense of pride and belonging and heighten the perception of an urgent shared project. There were two main channels— the *Atlas Highlights* newsletter and the workshops. *Atlas Highlights* identified concrete initiatives, "showing how the institutes in the Atlas network are redefining the boundaries of 'politically impossible' policies worldwide."[65] For example, the strategies by which Atlas and associated think tanks have weighed in on the healthcare and climate change debates since the mid-1980s were given prominence.[66] The newsletter also relayed information on the "Better Government Contests"—a 1991 initiative of the Pioneer Institute in Boston that rapidly spread throughout the network. Soliciting "citizen plans to cut government spending," these contests mobilized government representatives who promised implementation.[67]

Workshops created further opportunities for the presentation, discussion, and showcasing of concrete realizations. During the Indianapolis workshop in 1987, speakers were to "address a particular facet of [their] work and its consequences." In that context, John Goodman discussed "The role of the new think tank: How privatizing came to the White House."[68] The showcasing of realizations took another dimension with the first edition, in 1990, of the Fisher Memorial Award Competition for Best Publications. The award honored institutes that published "a book, report, monograph, or study that in the opinion of the judges made the greatest contribution to the public understanding of the free economy."[69] A list of winners, from 1990 to 1995, presented in Table 10.3 below, included essays in both English and Spanish on topics ranging from "free market environmentalism" to "families without fathers."

64 AtlasH (1991–94) all issues.
65 AtlasH (1988a).
66 AtlasH (1989–94) all issues.
67 AtlasH (1992b).
68 AtlasH (1987b).
69 AtlasH (1989d): 1.

Table 10.3. Fisher Memorial Award Competition, 1990–1995

Year	Title	Author	Think Tank
1990	1st. The Other Path 2nd.The Economic Consequences of Immigration 3rd. Advertising and the Market Process	H. De Soto J. Simon R. Ekelund & D. Saurman	ILD, Peru Cato Institute, Washington PRI, San Francisco
1991	1st. Economics and the Environment 2nd. Welfare State or Constitutional State 3rd. Work and Welfare in Massachusetts 3rd. Para Combatir la Pobreza 3rd. Taxation and the Elderly	W. Block (ed) S. Ratnapala J. O'Neill T. Castaneda J. Goodman et al.	Fraser Institute, Canada CIS, Australia Pioneer Institute, Boston CEP, Chile NCPA, Texas
1992	1st. Free Market Environmentalism 2nd. International Telecommunications in Hong Kong 3rd. Social Security in Venezuela	T. Anderson & D. Leal M. Mueller C. Sabino & J.E. Rodriguez	PRI & PERC, Montana Hong Kong CER CEDICE, Venezuela
1993	1st. Drug Policy and Decline of American Cities 2nd. Patient Power 3rd. Families without Fatherhood 3rd. The Heated Debate	S. Staley J. Goodman and G. Musgrave N. Dennis & G. Erdos R. Balling Jr	UPRI, Dayton, Ohio NCPA, Texas IEA, London PRI, San Francisco
1994	1st. The Loss of Virtue 1st. Property Rights and the Limits of Democracy 2nd. Federalism and Free Trade 3rd. Grand Theft and Petty Larceny 3rd. Out of Work	D. Anderson C.K. Rowley (ed) J.L. Migue M. Pollot R. Vedder & L. Gallaway	Social Affairs Unit, London Locke Institute, Virginia IEA, London PRI, San Francisco Independent Institute, CA
1995	1st. Public Goods and Private Communities 2nd. Las Tareas de Hoy 2nd. Perpetuating Poverty 3rd. Separating Schools and States 3rd. Beyond Politics	F. Foldvary C. Larroulet (ed) D. Bandow & I. Vasquez S. Richman W. Mitchell & R. Simmons	Locke Institute, Virginia Libertad y Desarollo, Chile Cato Institute, Washington Future Freedom Foundation, VA Independent Institute,, CA

While diffusion work remained important after 1995, the proliferation of think tanks meant that Atlas increasingly had to focus on the challenge of integrating the broader "Atlas family." Flagship events were adapted to the needs of the new era in both content and form. First, the content of the workshops shifted from a focus on policy issues and promotion of the think tank model to discussions of strategies and the sharing of best practices for managing think tanks. Second, the form changed too. In 2001, the Atlas Liberty Forum, held every year in the US (and recently always in New York), replaced roving international workshops. Initially, Atlas workshops had always coincided with the annual meetings of the MPS and the Heritage Foundation Resource Bank in what were "three jam-packed days of free-market networking and programs." This aggregation of events could hook newcomers "overwhelmed by the magnitude of the vibrant American movement."[70] As Atlas became ever more central in the neoliberal constellation, it turned the Liberty Forum into a stand-alone event highly attractive in itself. In 2003, 150 participants came from twenty-six countries while the 2014 forum brought 600 participants from fifty-nine countries. In parallel, Atlas developed the practice of co-sponsoring events in different parts of the world. Many workshops were thus organized—including regional Liberty Forums in Asia, Africa, and Europe. These contributed to the development and even more to the stabilization of the Atlas network.

As that network became increasingly dense, Atlas spent more time and resources showcasing the impact of institutes. The newsletter remained an important outlet, going from an average of eight to twenty pages. In 2002, Atlas started to publish annual investor reports that also became a tool for showcasing success. The newsletter and investor reports featured long pieces on aspiring think tank entrepreneurs, successful or promising new institutes and best or innovative practices. The new format, lively and filled with stories and anecdotes, gave a "personal touch," avoiding the impersonality that could come with a growing network.[71]

Showcasing and recognition took another turn in 2003 when the John Templeton Foundation underwrote a $2 million pledge to finance the Atlas's Templeton Freedom Awards (TFA). Every year Atlas could award, during the Liberty Forum, two prizes of $10,000 each in eight categories—Free Market Solutions to Poverty, Social Entrepreneurship, Ethics and Values, Student Outreach, Initiative in Public Relations, Innovative Media Award, University-based Centers, and Young Think Tanks. In 2013, the Templeton Religion Trust took over, granting each year a single $100,000 grand prize recognizing

70 AtlasIR (2004): 4.
71 AtlasIR (2013): 1.

"exceptional think tank achievement."[72] New awards have been launched over the years. Recognizing specific achievements, these awards come with monetary rewards and are handed out during official events. They celebrate individuals and organizations but they also serve to integrate the network around its common project and common successes.

Towards the end of the 2000s, particularly with the arrival of Tom Palmer, Atlas started to take advantage of its dense network to encourage cooperation between institutes on the co-production and co-diffusion of contents. Atlas commissioned co-authored "snack box" books featuring plain-language essays promoting free market ideology. The authors include celebrated figures in the network such as Nobel Laureate Mario Vargas Llosa, famous CEOs or journalists, but also young "liberty champions" from around the world. Atlas monitors the writing, translation, and distribution of these books and other produced contents (videos, blog posts . . .) through its designated outreach channels, including local language websites, organized liberty tours, summer schools, and seminars.

While Atlas was involved from the start in the development of "think-tank entrepreneurs," training efforts were only institutionalized in the late 2000s. The Atlas Leadership Academy (ALA), announced in 2008, was formalized in 2012. The idea was to offer a "thorough education in the fundamentals of think tank management."[73] The ALA proposes various training modules tailored to different stages of maturity—from beginner online courses and webinars, regional schools, onsite leadership training courses, mentoring programs, all the way to the recently launched Atlas Think Tank MBA (TTMBA). Online courses explore the basics of starting and running a think tank, while the onsite two-week TTMBA covers all stages of think tank development (strategic and program planning, fundraising, branding, marketing, communication, evaluation). A new mentorship program matches "high potentials" with successful veterans for nine-month, one-on-one correspondence and meetings. Completing twelve credits leads to graduation from ALA. Becoming an alumnus has perks—"access to a community of leaders, stakeholders, and benefactors, in addition to eligibility to

72 AtlasIR (2013): 15.
73 AtlasIR (2008): 4.

compete in the annual Think Tank Shark Tank competition (a project pitching competition) to win a $25,000 project grant," as listed on the Atlas website. Table 10.4 below shows the rapid increase in the number of people going through the ALA.

Table 10.4. ALA Training and Graduates

Year	Number of people who received training (number of countries)	Number of ALA graduates (number of countries)
2011	213	–
2012	450	8
2013	622	25
2014	1000 (90)	34 (25)

The objective of the ALA is to "apply sound business practices" to the domain of influence building and public policy shaping.[74] As such its training programs progress from basic ideas about the free market to practical business skills:

> Freedom is our business: we believe that using the best business methods is the key to advancing the ideas and the policies of freedom. Accordingly, Atlas teams plan strategically, seek the highest value added, engage in competitor analysis, brand our products and use the most suitable marketing techniques to encourage our target markets to "consume" our products, and measure our successes (and our failures).[75]

By the 2010s, the think tank model, born in England in 1955 with the IEA, had become a formalized and explicit blueprint, a modularized solution, and an object for global diffusion and emulation.

Conclusion

The case of the Atlas Network helps us understand how the neoliberal think tank model went global. Its history illustrates the deployment of a structural, material, and organizational architecture that helped create the conditions for certain ideas to spread, have an influence, and

---

74 AtlasIR (2008): 5.
75 AtlasIR (2010): 13.

ultimately become potentially performative. Atlas was instrumental not only in the construction and densification of the network but also in the institutionalization through time of the well-delineated organizational template of the modern (neoliberal) think tank. From 1981 to the present, Atlas has been the linchpin of the organizational deployment, diffusion, and activation of neoliberal ideas. It became a "diffusor and connector" organization—a transnational architect organization. Through a systematic exploration of the public archives of Atlas, we have traced the impact of its activities on the construction and increasing density, through time, of what we call, with Hayek, a "second-hand dealer" organizational circle in the transnational architecture of neoliberalism.[76]

Some of the changes in this evolution reflected scale effects. As the network expanded, Atlas had to reassess its tools and practices and move from a craft-like to a mass process. Other changes were connected to evolving legitimacy. Initially, Atlas and its few associated think tanks were marginal organizations. They had no chance of recognition from better-established producers and diffusors of knowledge like universities. Their strategy was to play up the position of the outcast and insist on their own singularity. Over time, however, Atlas gained centrality and legitimacy in the transnational neoliberal community, and think tanks became locally institutionalized. As a consequence, a significant evolution took place. Instead of scorning academia, Atlas and the think tanks aspired to and embraced academic legitimacy. This happened first through the co-optation of academics sympathetic to the cause as well as through think tank leaders acquiring academic credentials, usually a PhD in economics.

In a later phase, Atlas and the think tanks distanced themselves from and bypassed professors to directly target college and university students. Today, they have appropriated the tools and some of the regalia of academia; they do "scientific" research and even deliver "diplomas" through their own Academy. Achieving legitimacy through association with mainstream academia seems less necessary; Atlas and the think tanks have become legitimate entities in their own right. A related set of changes was connected to broader societal trends towards managerialization. Like most nonprofit and voluntary sector organizations across

---

76 F. A. Hayek, "Intellectuals and Socialism," *The University of Chicago Law Review* 16, no. 3 (1949).

the world in that period, Atlas and the think tanks have been influenced by managerial ideas and practices.[77]

While the starting point of this chapter was that ideas matter, we have not focused on the nature of those ideas per se. Instead we illuminated the conditions in which ideas can be made to matter. Ideas do not float nor do they do things by themselves. They are championed, carried, inscribed organizationally and institutionally, fought over, appropriated, and interpreted. Only then can they come to have an impact. This chapter has shown the performance of the conditions necessary for ideas to have an impact transnationally—a performance, in large part, comprising organization building, network creation, and community integration. The deployment of an organizational architecture is a necessary precondition for the influence of ideas. Only through the careful work of reconstructing lines of funding, organizing, network building, and influence framing can we understand the globalization of neoliberalism as a coherent body of thought and of self-conscious policy activism.

77   H. Hwang and W. Powell, "The Rationalization of Charity: The Influences of Professionalism in the Non-Profit Sector," *Administrative Science Quarterly* 54, no. 2 (2009). F. Maier, M. Meyer, and M. Steinbereithner, "Nonprofit Organizations Becoming Business-Like: A Systematic Review," *Nonprofit and Voluntary Sector Quarterly* 45 (2016).

11

Think Tank Networks of German Neoliberalism: Power Structures in Economics and Economic Policies in Postwar Germany

Stephan Pühringer

Economics itself (that is the subject as it is taught in universities and evening classes and pronounced upon in leading articles) has always been partly a vehicle for the ruling ideology of each period as well as partly a method of scientific investigation.

Joan Robinson[1]

The debate about the political and social impact of "economic imaginaries"[2] is not a new one. As early as 1936 John Maynard Keynes pointed out that "the ideas of economists and political philosophers . . . are more powerful than is commonly understood. Indeed, the world is ruled by little else."[3] F. A. Hayek, one of Keynes's early opponents, added the caveat that "economists have this great influence only in the long run and indirectly."[4] Many scholars have explored the political impact of economic ideas and specific schools of economic thought particularly in times of politico-economic crisis. Peter Hall emphasizes

---

1 Joan Robinson, *Economic Philosophy* (London: Watts, 1962), 7.

2 Bob Jessop, "Cultural Political Economy and Critical Policy Studies," *Critical Policy Studies* 3, no. 3–4 (2010); Bob Jessop, "Recovered Imaginaries, Imagined Recoveries: A Cultural Political Economy of Crisis Construals and Crisis-Management in the North Atlantic Financial Crisis," in *Before and Beyond the Global Economic Crisis: Economics, Politics and Settlement*, ed. Mats Benner (Cheltenham: Edward Elgar Publishing, 2013).

3 John Maynard Keynes, *The General Theory of Employment, Interest and Money* (London: Macmillan, 1936), 383.

4 F. A. Hayek, *Economic Freedom* (Oxford: Blackwell, 1991), 37.

the impact of economic ideas as a "guiding principle" for politics, and others stress the role of actors or institutions in the process of the transmission of economic ideas into politics.[5]

Questions about the political and social influence of economics became more pointed in the aftermath of the Global Financial Crisis (GFC) of 2007–8. On the level of economic policy, against the political background of the Cold War and then especially after the breakdown of Keynesian economics in the 1970s, the reference to the economic imaginaries of free markets and the free market mechanism served as the theoretical frame for promoting neoliberal policies of deregulation, privatization, and austerity. Although the GFC could have induced a paradigm shift in the field of economic policy, the dominance of neoliberal policies does not seem to be contested. Colin Crouch has described this persistence as the "strange non-death of neoliberalism," while Mark Blyth has warned of the social and societal consequences of austerity policies.[6]

There has been special attention paid to the role of Germany in the context of the European crisis. Some scholars have focused on the (new) hegemonic position of Germany as the central actor in European economic crisis policies—with, e.g., the Fiscal Compact, the eurozone crisis or the European Stability Mechanism (ESM)—due to its economic power and its status as principal creditor.[7] Others have suggested that the European post-crisis economic policies reflect a "return of ordoliberalism" or even an "ordoliberal transformation" or "ordoliberalization of Europe."[8] Some observers have detected the "long shadow of

---

5   Peter A. Hall, ed., *The Political Power of Economic Ideas: Keynesianism Across Nations* (Princeton: Princeton University Press, 1989); Sebastiaan Princen and Femke van Esch, "Paradigm Formation and Paradigm Change in the EU's Stability and Growth Pact," *European Political Science Review* 8, no. 03 (2016). Daniel Hirschman and Elizabeth P. Berman, "Do Economists Make Policies? On the Political Effects of Economics," *Socio-Economic Review* 12, no. 4 (2014).

6   Colin Crouch, *The Strange Non-death of Neoliberalism* (Cambridge: Polity, 2013); Mark Blyth, *Austerity: The History of a Dangerous Idea* (Oxford: Oxford University Press, 2013).

7   Simon Bulmer and William E. Paterson, "Germany as the EU's Reluctant Hegemon? Of Economic Strength and Political Constraints," *Journal of European Public Policy* 20, no. 10 (2013).

8   Thomas Biebricher, "The Return of Ordoliberalism in Europe: Notes on a Research Agenda," *i-lex. Scienze Giuridiche, Scienze Cognitive e Intelligenza artificiale Rivista quadrimestrale*, on-line: www.i-lex.it, no. 21 (2014); Brigitte Young, "German Ordoliberalism as Agenda Setter for the Euro Crisis: Myth Trumps Reality," *Journal of*

ordoliberalism" in German economic policies, claiming that especially in the field of macroeconomic policy ordoliberalism can be perceived as the "basis of German economic thinking."[9] Such claims have been contested by different scholars (Wigger, etc.), inter alia pointing to the limits of an exclusive focus on the Freiburg School of ordoliberals in German neoliberalism.

Yet little work has been done to establish what the networks of ordoliberalism—or, more precisely, German neoliberalism—have been since 1945 and what role they played in German economic policy. This chapter provides evidence that German neoliberal thought had a persistent and strong impact on German economic policy in the postwar period up to the financial and economic crisis policies of 2008 and after. It begins with a reflection on German neoliberalism as a central component in the common neoliberal thought collective, before introducing the category of a "performative footprint of economists" (PFP) in order to operationalize the "external," non-academic influence of economists. It then highlights the close connections of ordoliberal economists with politics in relation to three important phases, or turning points, in German politico-economic history. The final section uses the PFP methodology to show the persistent dominance of German neoliberalism in German economic policy after World War II compared to Keynesian networks.

Ordoliberalism as Part of the Neoliberal Thought Collective

The debate about a possible revival of ordoliberalism after the crisis requires defining it against what is often called "American neoliberalism," i.e. the Chicago School of Milton Friedman, Gary Becker, and others associated with today's mainstream economic approach of Chicago-style neoclassical economics, in particular. Foucault set the stage by arguing for a "political rationality" of ordoliberalism distinct

---

Contemporary European Studies 22, no. 3 (2014); Thomas Biebricher, "Europe and the Political Philosophy of Neoliberalism: Critical Exchange on Neoliberalism and Europe," *Contemporary Political Theory* 12, no. 4 (2013).

9   Sebastian Dullien and Ulrike Guérot, "The Long Shadow of Ordoliberalism: Germany's Approach to the Euro Crisis," *European Council on Foreign Relations Policy Brief*, 2012: 2.

from American neoliberalism.[10] Nevertheless, American neoliberalism and German ordoliberalism are both based on a free market ideology, where the functionality of the free market mechanism depends on processes of political engineering.[11] In 1982, Ver Eecke had already used the term neoliberalism to describe both German ordoliberalism and American monetarism.[12] Due to their similar preference for a strong state, whose important but exclusive task is the establishment and reestablishment of market mechanisms or the market economy, Thomasberger labeled the neoliberal project "planning for the market."[13]

The ambivalent role of the state in the ordoliberal version of neoliberalism is present in founding thinker Walter Eucken's definition of the principles of economic policy. The first principle, Eucken argues, is that "the policy of the state should be focused on dissolving power groups or at limiting their functioning." The second principle dictates that "the politico-economic activity of the state should focus on the regulation of the economy, not on the guidance of the economic process."[14] Whereas the first principle stresses the need for a strong state for political engineering (*Ordnungspolitik*), the second (regarding *Prozesspolitik*) stresses avoiding interventionist policies against the market mechanism. Ordoliberalism advocated influencing the rules of the game, not the process.

Although there are some differences between German ordoliberalism and American neoliberalism, especially concerning their policy implications, both can be assigned to a common neoliberal thought collective in light of the participation of figures from both schools of thought in the Mont Pèlerin Society (MPS) founded in 1947.[15] Mirowski

---

10 Biebricher, "The Return of Ordoliberalism in Europe."

11 Werner Bonefeld, "Freedom and the Strong State: On German Ordoliberalism," *New Political Economy* 17, no. 5 (2012); Walter O. Ötsch, Stephan Pühringer, and Katrin Hirte, *Netzwerke des Marktes: Ordoliberalismus als Politische Ökonomie* (Wiesbaden: Springer VS, 2017).

12 Wilfried v. Eecke, "Ethics in Economics: From Classical Economics to Neo-liberalism," *Philosophy & Social Criticism* 9, no. 2 (1982).

13 See Claus Thomasberger, "'Planung für den Markt' versus 'Planung für die Freiheit': Zu den stillschweigenden Voraussetzungen des Neoliberalismus," in *Der neoliberale Markt-Diskurs: Ursprünge, Geschichte, Wirkungen*, ed. Walter O. Ötsch and Claus Thomasberger, (Marburg: Metropolis-Verl., 2009).

14 Walter Eucken, *Grundsätze der Wirtschaftspolitik* (Bern: Francke, 1952), 334, translation in Blyth, *Austerity*, 143.

15 Philip Mirowski, "The Political Movement that Dared not Speak its own Name: The Neoliberal Thought Collective Under Erasure," *Institute for New Economic Thinking*

argues that in the initial era of the neoliberal thought collective in the 1940s ordoliberalism was one of the three important strands, alongside Austrian economics and Chicago School neoclassical economics. He further points out that the neoliberal thought collective can be understood in analogy to a Russian doll, with the MPS at its center and a set of heterogeneous institutions and think tanks around it. The MPS and its annual meetings offered a protected place for intellectual exchange and confrontation between scholars from these different strands of neoliberal thought.

This characterization is shared by participants themselves. MPS member Joachim Starbatty, a central actor in German neoliberal networks and head of the think tank Aktionsgemeinschaft Soziale Marktwirtschaft, defined the MPS as the "organizational expression of neoliberalism" ("der organisatorische Ausdruck").[16] He argues further that ordoliberalism should be seen as the "German variety of neoliberalism." With this self-declaration by one of Germany's most prominent ordoliberals in mind, it is safe to define a "network of German neoliberalism" organized in think tanks and institutions around the MPS. In what follows, I define the "German neoliberal network" as comprised of think tanks or institutions in which at least one of the founding or leading members is also a member of the MPS.[17]

The second main justification for interpreting ordoliberalism as an integral part of the neoliberal thought collective is based on the strong personal connections of main ordoliberal scholars with leading neoliberal thinkers, and even more explicitly on the role of Friedrich Hayek as a figure linking several sites of neoliberal thought. Hayek was the leading scholar of the third generation of the Austrian School of Economics, the

---

Working Paper Series, no. 23 (2014); Philip Mirowski and Dieter Plehwe, eds, *The Road from Mont Pèlerin: The Making of the Neoliberal Thought Collective* (Cambridge, MA: Harvard University Press, 2009). I will use the definition of the neoliberal thought collective offered by Mirowski "to refer to this multilevel, multiphase, multisector approach to the building of political capacity to incubate, critique, and promulgate ideas." Philip Mirowski, *Never Let a Serious Crisis Go to Waste: How Neoliberalism Survived the Financial Meltdown* (London: Verso, 2013), 44.

16 Joachim Starbatty, "Ordoliberalismus," in *Geschichte der Nationalökonomie*, ed. Otmar Issing (Munich: Vahlen, 1994), 251.

17 See Dieter Plehwe and Bernhard Walpen, "Between Network and Complex Organization: The Making of Neoliberal Knowledge and Hegemony," in *Neoliberal Hegemony: A Global Critique*, ed. Dieter Plehwe, Bernhard Walpen, and Gisela Neunhöffer (London: Routledge, 2006).

main opponent of John Maynard Keynes in the 1930s at the London School of Economics (along with founding MPS member Lionel Robbins), and a faculty member at the University of Chicago from 1948 to 1962. He also had close connections with ordoliberals (and later also with MPS members) such as Walter Eucken, Wilhelm Röpke, and Alexander Rüstow already in the 1930s.[18] In 1962 Hayek was appointed professor of economics at the University of Freiburg and became head of the Walter Eucken Institute. Furthermore, he contributed continuously to ordoliberal publications and was a founding editor of the ordoliberal journal *Ordo*. In the *Quarterly Journal of Economics* in 1960, Henry Oliver stated that "in a sense he [Hayek] serves as their [the ordoliberals] leading political theorist."[19] In a similar vein Knut Borchardt stresses the similarities between ordoliberal scholars and Hayek, especially in their emphasis on the role of law, the institutional framework, and the common political will to establish and preserve capitalism.[20] No less a figure than Alfred Müller-Armack, one of the most politically active ordoliberal scholars in Germany from the 1950s to the 1970s, who also coined the term "social market economy," denoted Hayek, together with Eucken, Franz Böhm, Röpke, and Rüstow, as a pioneer of the ordoliberal "theory of economic order" (*Wirtschaftsordnungstheorie*).[21]

Nevertheless, many ordoliberal scholars stress the heterogeneity of different strands of the neoliberal thought collective or even of ordoliberalism itself,[22] which can, perhaps, be explained by the rather negative image of American "deregulatory" neoliberalism in European political debates. Although many of the European crisis policies signify ordoliberal conceptions, there are those (e.g. Feld et al.) who stress that the

---

18 Ralf Ptak, *Vom Ordoliberalismus zur sozialen Marktwirtschaft: Stationen des Neoliberalismus in Deutschland* (Opladen: Leske und Budrich, 2004); Ekkehard A. Köhler and Stefan Kolev, "The Conjoint Quest for a Liberal Positive Program: 'Old Chicago,' Freiburg and Hayek," *HWWI Research Paper*, no. 109 (2011); Stefan Kolev, Nils Goldschmidt, and Jan-Otmar Hesse, "Walter Eucken's Role in the Early History of the Mont Pèlerin Society," *Freiburg Discussion Papers on Constitutional Economics*, no. 02 (2014).

19 Henry Oliver, "German Neoliberalism," *The Quarterly Journal of Economics* 74, no. 1 (1960): 119.

20 See Knut Borchardt, "Die Konzeption der Sozialen Marktwirtschaft in heutiger Sicht," in *Zukunftsprobleme der sozialen Marktwirtschaft*, ed. Otmar Issing (Berlin: Duncker & Humblot, 1981).

21 Ptak, *Ordoliberalismus*.

22 See, e.g., Viktor Vanberg, "The Freiburg School: Walter Eucken and Ordoliberalism," *Freiburg Discussion Papers on Constitutional Economics*, no. 11 (2004).

influence of ordoliberal thought is often overestimated and that the policies implemented in the aftermath of the 2007–8 crisis should, instead, be characterized as "pragmatic." However, while European measures to stabilize the European Currency Union certainly have not followed an orthodox ordoliberal script one can still observe a kind of metamorphosis of hegemonic neoliberal economic imaginaries, indicating a shift inside the neoliberal thought collective from American deregulatory neoliberalism, especially in the context of financial markets, to more restrained markets in an ordoliberal framework.[23] As Jamie Peck put it, the ordoliberal political project seems to be "back in favour."[24]

While the diagnosis of a revival or a comeback of ordoliberalism or German neoliberalism in economic policy might hold in the European or maybe even the international context, in the next section I will argue that it is misleading to claim such a "return thesis" for Germany. Although ordoliberalism as an independent economic theory might, in fact, have been "marginalized and thus forgotten,"[25] the infrastructures of German neoliberalism, such as politico-economic think tanks, political institutions, and economic research institutes, remained an influential vehicle for the discursive hegemony of German neoliberalism in German economic policies.

The Performative Footprint as a Measurement of the External Influence of Economists

Many of the empirical findings presented in the next two sections stem from a research project on the history of German economics after World War II, supported by the Hans-Böckler-Foundation.[26] In this project we analyzed the evolution of economics in Germany on two levels. First, we compiled a database of about 800 professors of economics at German universities from 1954 to 1994. The database consisted of biographical

---

23 See Biebricher, "Europe and the Political Philosophy of Neoliberalism."

24 Jamie Peck, *Constructions of Neoliberal Reason* (Oxford: Oxford University Press, 2010), 275.

25 Biebricher, "Europe and the Political Philosophy of Neoliberalism."

26 These results have partly been published in Ötsch et al., *Netzwerke des Marktes* and Stephan Pühringer, "The success story of ordoliberalism as guiding principle of German economic policy," in *Ordoliberalism. Law and the rule of economics*, ed. Josef Hien, Christian Joerges (Oxford: Hart Publishing, 2018).

details of the economists, particularly about their academic career trajectories as well as their academic background, i.e. place, date, and supervisors of their doctoral thesis and professorial thesis or habilitation (their "second book"). We also researched other academic and external activities of the economists, in particular their policy involvement as political actors or advisors or their memberships in economic think tanks. Second, we developed the measure of a "Performative Footprint" (PFP) for these 800 economists, as a means to measure the potential impact of economists or specific economic thought collectives on politics and society, thereby going far beyond the narrow range of academic rankings. The potential influence of economists is presented in five categories of internal and external influence. Whereas the first two (academic productivity and academic re-productivity) focus on inner-academic influence, the other three (political advice, political actor, and public presence) take into account the political and societal efficacy of "economic imaginaries." In a further step, a social network analysis approach was applied in order to highlight personal and institutional relations in a politico-economic framing, focusing especially on the role of think tanks.

The three external influence coefficients relevant for this chapter are the media coefficient, the political actor coefficient and the political advice coefficient. Each combines several variables of potential influence in its specific fields. The media coefficient measures the presence of economists (hits for each person) in leading German newspapers and magazines over the whole period analyzed. The media coefficient builds on a weighted average of hits per person in electronic archives, by construing individual reference archives in order to control for different academic life spans. The political actor coefficient operationalizes positions in political institutions (Bundesbank, ministries, Bundestag, political parties, monopoly commission), according to the specific position and the length of time it is occupied, using a classification scheme (see appendix). The political advice coefficient operationalizes positions in economic policy advice institutions like the German Council of Economic Experts (GCEE), the scientific advisory boards of the German ministries of finance and economics, and economic research institutes.

History of German Neoliberalism in Economic Think Tank Networks

The roots of German neoliberalism date back to the Freiburg School, built around Walter Eucken, Franz Böhm, and Leonhard Miksch in the 1920s and 1930s, and Alexander Rüstow and Wilhelm Röpke, two German economists in close personal contact with Eucken.[27] At the level of economic theory, the central aim of these early ordoliberal scholars was to attack the "ruins of the German Historical School,"[28] which manifested in the idea of the foundation of the "Theoretical Club of Ricardians." Rüstow suggested also inviting Austrian economists such as Hayek, Haberler, Machlup, and Mises into this club.[29] Beyond the personal contacts of ordoliberals with Hayek and later proponents of the Chicago School, Köhler and Kolev also stress the similarities in the research agendas concerning monetary policy in Freiburg and Chicago in the 1930s, particularly in the work of Eucken's pupils Friedrich Lutz and Henry Simons, teacher of Milton Friedman and progenitor of the Chicago School of Economics.[30] Eucken furthermore played a central role in the foundation of the MPS, as evidenced in the fact that Hayek delegated the right to propose German members for the MPS to Eucken.[31]

Infrastructures of German Neoliberalism in the Early Federal Republic of Germany

Although this academic exchange was interrupted in 1933 with the Nazi takeover, which forced Röpke and Rüstow to emigrate to Turkey, both

27 Jan-Otmar Hesse, *Wirtschaft als Wissenschaft: Die Volkswirtschaftslehre in der frühen Bundesrepublik* (Frankfurt am Main: Campus Verlag, 2010); Hauke Janssen, *Milton Friedman und die "monetaristische Revolution" in Deutschland* (Marburg: Metropolis-Verl., 2006).

28 Rüstow in a letter to Eucken dated 24.1.1927, cited in Janssen, *Friedman*, p. 104.

29 Hayek retrospectively remarked that this group of Ricardians was the only active and influential circle of economists fighting for a "free economy" before 1933. F. A. Hayek, "Die Wiederentdeckung der Freiheit—Persönliche Erinnerungen," in *Produktivität, Eigenverantwortung, Beschäftigung: Für eine wirtschaftspolitische Vorwärtsstrategie*, ed. VDM 31 (Cologne: Deutscher Instituts-Verlag, 1983), 12.

30 Köhler and Kolev, "The Conjoint Quest."

31 Kolev et al., "Walter Eucken," 6; for a detailed analysis of early German neoliberal economists see Max Bank, "Stunde der Neoliberalen? Politikberatung und Wirtschaftspolitik in der Ära Adenauer," PhD Diss, University of Cologne, 2013.

the university of Freiburg and the circle around Eucken in particular remained core centers of economic research in Germany.[32]

The strong academic influence was manifested in the successful academic reproduction of the Freiburg School and especially of Eucken's students. Figure 11.1 shows German professors of economics whose doctoral theses and/or habilitation theses were supervised by Eucken. Although

Figure 11.1 Walter Eucken as Academic Teacher

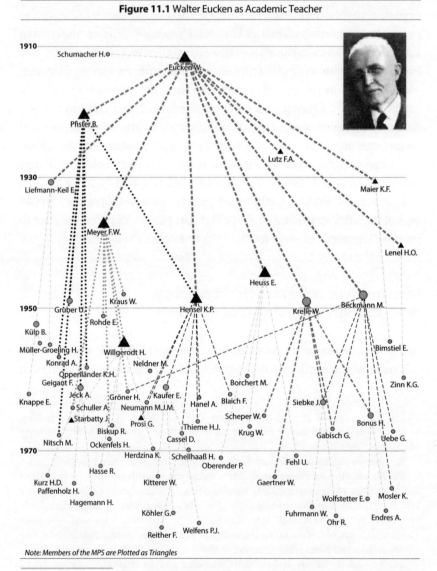

Note: Members of the MPS are Plotted as Triangles

---

32   Walter O. Ötsch and Stephan Pühringer, "Marktradikalismus als Politische Ökonomie," *ICAE Working Paper Series*, no. 38 (2015).

Eucken died rather young at the age of fifty-nine, during a research visit at the LSE (to which he had been invited by Hayek), he was one of the most successful "producers of pupils" in the history of German economics.[33] After the successful reproduction of the first generation of the Freiburg School (Eucken supervised at least eleven pupils who were later to become professors of economics at German universities), Eucken's pupils (in particular, Bernhard Pfister, Karl Paul Hensel, and Fritz Walter Meyer, all of whom later became members of the MPS) proved to be very successful academic supervisors, too. Beside the academic influence on the course of German economic history in and immediately after World War II, ordoliberal economists were continuously engaged in giving policy advice to the Nazi regime but were also, especially in the 1940s, in contact with the "conservative opposition" to that regime.[34] During the 1940s the "Arbeitsgemeinschaft Erwin von Beckerath" served as a meeting point for ordoliberals, their main objective being to discuss and develop the economic order for postwar Germany.

The engagement of German neoliberal economists in policy advice continued after the capitulation of Germany in 1945 and resulted in a strong dominance of ordoliberal economists in the two very influential scientific advisory boards of the ministries of finance and economics[35] (see Figure 11.2), as well as in the central role of Ludwig Erhard in the adoption of the "currency reform," which was later discursively framed as the starting point for the German economic miracle.[36]

In addition to having a direct influence on German postwar politics, ordoliberal economists were closely connected to the international networks of the neoliberal thought collective. Four of Eucken's advisees

33 Stephan Pühringer, "The Success Story of Ordoliberalism as Guiding Principle of German Economic Policy," in *Ordoliberalism: Law and the Rule of Economics*, ed. Josef Hien and Christian Joerges (Oxford: Hart Publishing, 2018).

34 See Ptak, *Ordoliberalismus*; Nils Goldschmidt, ed., *Wirtschaft, Politik und Freiheit: Freiburger Wissenschaftler und der Widerstand* (Tübingen: Mohr Siebeck, 2005); Daniela Rüther, "Freiburger Nationalökonomen auf dem Weg in den Widerstand," *Historisch-Politische Mitteilungen*, no. 10 (2003).

35 The Keynesian economist Erich Schneider even labeled the influence of German neoliberals like Wilhelm Röpke during the 1950s and early 1960s a "dictatorship of the liberals." Hesse, *Wirtschaft als Wissenschaft*, 126.

36 See Bank, "Stunde der Neoliberalen?," for a detailed analysis, particularly of the role of German neoliberals on the advisory board of the ministry of economics.

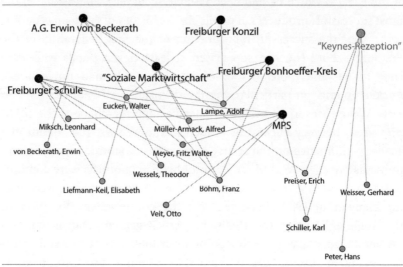

Figure 11.2 Continuity of German Neoliberal Networks After World War II

(Pfister, Maier, Hensel, and Lutz) were early members of the MPS already in the 1940s, and seven of the ten advisees indicated in Figure 11.1 later became members of the MPS. Moreover, up to the third and fourth generation after Eucken one can find core proponents of the German neoliberal network, including Hans Willgerodt, Manfred J. M. Neumann, Joachim Starbatty, and Peter Oberender.

Rather than subsuming the different groups of German neoliberals under one Freiburg School, we can follow Ptak who speaks of a confluence of three different strands of thought with a shared political will: first, the Freiburg School with Eucken, Böhm, and Miksch; second, the "sociological wing" of ordoliberalism with Rüstow and Röpke; and third, a group of practitioners consisting of Ludwig Erhard and the longstanding editor of the newspaper *Frankfurter Allgemeine Zeitung*, Erich Welter. Alfred Müller-Armack could be ascribed to the second and third strands of ordoliberalism.[37] The

37   Ptak, *Ordoliberalismus*, 17. Kolev distinguishes between the ordoliberalism of the Freiburg School and Rüstow and Röpke, and the "German neoliberalism" of Müller-Armack and Erhard: Ştefan Kolev, "F. A. Hayek as an Ordo-liberal," *HWWI Research Paper*, no. 5 (2010). Hesse doubts that there is one homogeneous ordoliberal school: Jan-Otmar Hesse, "Der Mensch des Unternehmens und der Produktion. Foucaults Sicht auf den Ordoliberalismus und die 'Soziale Marktwirtschaft,'" *Studies in Contemporary History*, no. 3 (2006).

personal and institutional relations of Walter Eucken and other early German neoliberals show that German neoliberalism had a central presence in the field of economic policy-making and policy advice, and the economics discipline itself, in the early Federal Republic of Germany.

Infrastructures of German Neoliberalism During the Monetarist Turn in Germany

A second episode in German economic history indicating the continuous political influence of economists organized around the infrastructure of German neoliberalism was the period of the "monetarist turn" in the early 1970s after a short period of "German Keynesianism" in the late 1960s.[38] Janssen analyzed the "counter-revolution in German monetary theory"—i.e. the theoretical debate among German economists about Milton Friedman's monetarist theory—and found that fifteen, mainly young, German economists introduced monetarism into German economics. He concluded that "the revolt of the thirty-somethings," especially from 1970 to 1976, initiated the monetarist anti-Keynesian revolution in German economics.[39] This initiative resulted in the monetarist turn of the German Bundesbank, which was the first central bank worldwide to introduce monetarist money supply targeting as suggested by Friedman.[40] Figure 11.3 shows the numerous connections of economists active in

---

38   Harald Hagemann, "Ordoliberalism, the Social Market Economy, and Keynesianism: Germany After 1945," in *Liberalism and the Welfare State: Economists and Arguments for the Welfare State*, ed. Roger Backhouse, Bradley W. Bateman, Tamotsu Nishizawa, and Dieter Plehwe (Oxford: Oxford University Press, 2017). The era of "German Keynesianism" was short; the "brief Keynesian experiment" ended in 1972 with the resignation of Schiller as minister of economics and finance. See Jeremy Leaman, *The Political Economy of Germany under Chancellors Kohl and Schröder: Decline of the German Model?* (New York: Berghahn Books, 2009), 7.

39   For details see Karl Brunner, ed., *Proceedings of the First Konstanzer Seminar on Monetary Theory and Monetary Policy* (Berlin: Duncker und Humblot, 1972).

40   See, e.g., Herbert Giersch, Karl-Heinz Paqué, and Holger Schmieding, eds, *The Fading Miracle: Four Decades of Market Economy in Germany* (Cambridge: Cambridge University Press, 1992); Rudolf Richter, *Deutsche Geldpolitik 1948–1998 im Spiegel der zeitgenössischen wissenschaftlichen Diskussion* (Tübingen: Mohr Siebeck, 1999).

Figure 11.3 The Academic Roots of the Proponents of the Monetarist Turn in Germany

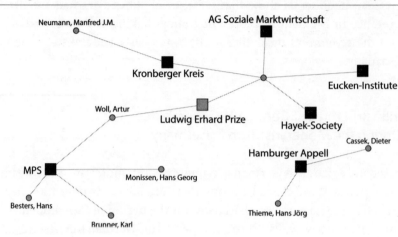

the monetarist revolution to the German neoliberal thought collective.[41]

The empirical result partly contradicts Feld et al., who claim that there is no common ground between monetarism and ordoliberalism.[42] At least in the common infrastructure of German neoliberalism, there are connections on both personal and institutional levels.

The persistence of the influence of economists organized around the infrastructure of German neoliberalism can, furthermore, be empirically shown in terms of academic advisor-advisee relationships. As indicated in Figure 11.4, there are many connections between the protagonists of the monetarist turn (as advisees) and the core early German neoliberal economists (as academic advisors), such as Eucken, Hensel, Welter, and Müller-Armack.

41 The seven actors not plotted in Figure 11.3—and thus according to our methodological approach not part of the German neoliberal network organized around think tanks and institutions—are Volbert Alexander, Emil-Maria Claassen, Ernst Dürr, Werner Ehrlicher, Hans-Edi Loef, Jürgen Siebke, and Manfred Willms.

42 Lars P. Feld, Ekkehard A. Köhler, and Daniel Nientiedt. "Ordoliberalism, Pragmatism and the Eurozone Crisis: How the German Tradition Shaped Economic Policy in Europe," CESifo Working Paper, no. 5368 (2015).

Figure 11.4 Economists in German Neoliberal Networks During the Monetarist Turn in Germany

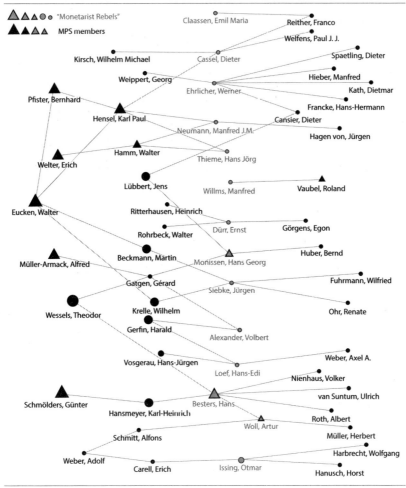

Alongside the group of fifteen "monetarist rebels," the monetarist turn of the Bundesbank was also supported by the German Council of Economic Experts (GCEE), which argued similarly for a Friedman-oriented money supply target in its annual economic report.[43] After a paradigm shift in the GCEE from a Keynesian to a supply-oriented policy in the early 1970s[44]—initiated mainly by MPS member Herbert

43   Janssen, *Friedman*; GCEE, *Jahresgutachten: Mut zur Stabilisierung* (Stuttgart: Kohlhammer, 1973).

44   Schmelzer even doubts whether there was a Keynesian dominance in the GCEE. Matthias Schmelzer, *Freiheit für Wechselkurse und Kapital: Die Ursprünge neoliberaler Währungspolitik und die Mont Pèlerin Society* (Marburg: Metropolis-Verl., 2010), 110.

Giersch and later his advisee Gerhard Fels in the run-up to the monetar-
ist turn of the Bundesbank—at least three out of five members of the
GCEE were organized in German neoliberal networks (Norbert Kloten,
Olaf Sievert, and Armin Gutowski).

The influence of German neoliberalism in the Bundesbank and later
also in the ECB has manifested itself at both a theoretical and a personal
level over several decades.[45] Alesina and Grilli, for instance, stress that
"the institutional design of the ECB is more similar to that of the
Bundesbank than to any other central bank of the Eurozone."[46]
Furthermore, central actors in the Bundesbank, e.g. Otmar Issing, Hans
Tietmeyer, Axel Weber, and Jens Weidmann, are linked to the network
of German neoliberalism through both their academic background and
their membership in neoliberal think tanks. At a speech at the Euro
Finance Week in Frankfurt, Jürgen Stark, the former president of the
Bundesbank and ECB executive board member stressed that the work of
Eucken had been "a constant source of inspiration throughout my
career."[47]

The Influence of German Neoliberalism
During the Neoliberal Turn

A third episode in German economic history in which the influence
of economists organized around the infrastructures of German
neoliberalism is even more clear is in the period of the "neoliberal
turn" in Germany in the early 1980s.[48] Leaman, for instance, argues
that despite several indicators of continuity, "1982 can still be seen as
a very significant marker in the history of Germany's political economy . . . because it ushered in a period in which there was a gradual

---

45   Richter, *Deutsche Geldpolitik.*

46   Alberto Alesina and Vittorio Grilli, *The European Central Bank: Reshaping
Monetary Politics in Europe* (Cambridge, MA: National Bureau of Economic Research,
1991), 13.

47   Jürgen Stark, "Monetary, Fiscal and Financial Stability in Europe: Speech at the
11th Euro Finance Week in Frankfurt, 18 November 2008," ecb.europa.eu.

48   The term might be misleading when compared to the "neoliberal turn" in the US
or the UK; see Martin Werding, "Gab es eine neoliberale Wende? Wirtschaft und
Wirtschaftspolitik in der Bundesrepublik Deutschland ab Mitte der 1970er Jahre,"
Vierteljahrshefte für Zeitgeschichte 56 (2008). Nevertheless market-oriented social and
economic policies also gained importance in Germany in the 1980s.

but inexorable shift in the quality of economic policy decisions, the ideological paradigm within which they were consistently framed and the global context within which national, regional and global institutions operated."[49] In 1981, economics minister Otto Graf Lambsdorff (Free Democratic Party, FDP) published a seminal paper entitled "Manifesto of the Market Economy: Concept for a Policy to Overcome Weak Growth Performance and Reduce Unemployment"— the so-called *Lambsdorff Paper*—where he stressed that the government interfered too much in the free market and suggested radical labor market reforms, strict budget consolidation, and deregulation policies.

Alongside Lambsdorff, Otto Schlecht—who was already in the ministry of economics under Erhard and Tietmeyer, and would later become president of the Bundesbank and one of the main initiators of the neoliberal advocacy think tank Initiative for New Social Market Economy (INSM) in 2000[50]—was responsible for the paper. Together with Tietmeyer he authored the memorandum for Otto Graf Lambsdorff. The Lambsdorff Paper marked the end of the social-liberal coalition in Germany and especially of the (Keynesian) economic concept of macroeconomic management (*Globalsteuerung*). It can therefore be interpreted as inaugurating a politico-economic paradigm shift. From the perspective of economic policy advice, the paper can be seen in the tradition of the GCCE annual report of 1973/74, indicating a monetarist turn, and the 1976/77 report, arguing for a supply-side-orientation of economic policy.[51]

The common politico-economic objective of these reform documents reflects the institutional and personal connections of the members of the Kronberger Kreis think tank. The Kronberger Kreis was founded in December 1981 as scientific advisory board to the Frankfurter Institut

---

49   Leaman, *The Political Economy of Germany*, 5.

50   See, for instance, Christoph Butterwegge, "Rechfertigung, Maßnahmen und Folgen einer neoliberalen (Sozial-)Politik," in *Kritik des Neoliberalismus*, ed. Christoph Butterwegge, Bettina Lösch, and Ralf Ptak (Wiesbaden: VS Verlag für Sozialwissenschaften, 2008), 135–213; Rudolf Speth, *Die politischen Strategien der Initiative Neue Soziale Marktwirtschaft* 96 (Dusseldorf: Hans-Böckler-Stiftung, 2004).

51   Lars P. Feld, "Zur Bedeutung des Manifests der Marktwirtschaft oder: Das Lambsdorff-Papier im 31. Jahr," *Zeitschrift für Wirtschaftspolitik* 62, no. 3 (2013); GCEE, *Vierzig Jahre Sachverständigenrat: 1963–2003* (Wiesbaden: Statistisches Bundesamt, 2003).

(later, Stiftung Marktwirtschaft) by the economist and editor of the magazine *Wirtschaftswoche*, Wolfram Engels, and the entrepreneur Ludwig Eckes. The Kronberger Kreis was organized on the model of a modern American think tank with the objective of influencing public opinion and politico-economic discourse through "organized events, publications, individual policy advice, concrete actions as well as formulated legislative texts."[52] The initial goal of the Kronberger Kreis was to develop a market-oriented politico-economic program for the next Bundestag elections in 1984. After the publication of the Lambsdorff Paper and the end of the social-liberal coalition—later labeled the "ordopolitical awakening of Germany" by executive board member of the Stiftung Marktwirtschaft, Michael Eilfort—the Stiftung Marktwirtschaft and the Kronberger Kreis successfully influenced the public debate with position papers and short statements.[53]

Over the next decades, under both Chancellors Helmut Kohl and Gerhard Schröder, members of the Kronberger Kreis[54] held core positions in or had close ties to central German economic policy institutions, e.g. the ministry of economics (Eekhoff), the Bundesbank (Issing, Neumann), governmental commissions (Möschel, Donges, Raffelhüschen), and the monopoly commission (Möschel, von Weizsäcker, Hellwig, Haucap). Moreover, members of the Kronberger Kreis were very active as economic policy advisors in the GCEE as well as in the scientific advisory boards of the ministries of finance and economics. Referring to the multi-dimensional political and public influence of these economists (see also the PFP-coefficients in Table 11.1), as well as their dense connections in the network of German neoliberalism, Ptak describes the Kronberger Kreis as "an influential market-radical elite network."[55]

---

52   Stiftung Marktwirtschaft, "Mehr Mut zum Markt ...," Geo.net IT GmbH, stiftung-marktwirtschaft.de.

53   Michael Eilfort, "Begüßung," in *25 JAHRE Stiftung Marktwirtschaft und Kronberger Kreis*, ed. Stiftung Marktwirtschaft (Berlin, 2007), 9.

54   Most members of the Kronberger Kreis are economists; some are also legal scholars, which is another similarity to the early Freiburg School.

55   Ralf Ptak, "Grundlagen des Neoliberalismus," in Butterwegge et al., *Kritik des Neoliberalismus*, 79.

Table 11.1. Performative Footprint of Members of the Kronberger Kreis (Percentages Shown)[56]

Name	Media coeff.	Policy advice coeff.	Policy actor coeff.	Acad. repr. coeff.	Acad. pr. coeff.
Wolfgang Franz	1.02	3.60	0.00	0.48	0.83
Olaf Sievert	0.42	3.54	1.17		
Armin Gutowski	0.45	1.75	0.00		
Juergen Donges	0.23	1.25	0.00	0.12	
Carl Christian von Weizsäcker	0.52	0.56	3.50		0.52
Gerhard Fels	0.28	0.54	0.00		0.36
Otmar Issing	1.02	0.51	3.50	2.35	0.80
Martin Hellwig	0.22	0.28	4.21		1.15
Wolfgang Stützel	0.51	0.18	0.12	0.03	0.40
Wolfram Engels	0.71	0.00	0.00		
Walter Hamm	0.11	0.00	0.00		
Hans Willgerodt	0.09	0.00	0.00		0.36

An analysis of the Performative Footprint (PFP) of the Kronberger Kreis economists supplies further empirical evidence for the think tank's major impact on the course of German economic policy during the last decades. The immediate influence of the Kronberger Kreis, which also indicates the close ideological connection between the intention of the Lambsdorff Paper and the think tank, is reflected in a quote from Otto Lambsdorff's speech on the occasion of the 25th anniversary of its foundation: "I think I simply copied from the Kronberger Kreis; this was the easiest way because it was always right."[57]

The Long Shadow of German Neoliberalism in Economics

In order to highlight the central position of institutions like the Kronberger Kreis among politically and publicly influential economists, I undertook further social network analysis of its members as well as members of other institutions of the German neoliberal thought collective. This was based on an institutional analysis of the multiple positions occupied by economists in institutions and think tanks (e.g. as founder, active member, participant in the advisory board or in an expert

---

56 Due to limitations of data sources the PFP is only calculated for economists who were already professors at German universities by 1996. For the social network analysis all members of the Kronberger Kreis are included.

57 Otto G. Lambsdorff, in *25 JAHRE Stiftung Marktwirtschaft und Kronberger Kreis*, 37–45.

Figure 11.5 Kronberger Kreis as the Central Node in German Neoliberal Networks of Economists

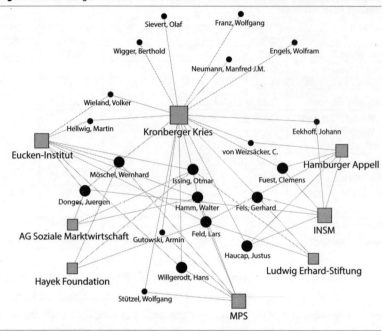

committee). I also searched for economists with positions in Keynesian, union-linked, or economic-alternative think tanks or institutions in order to highlight a potential countervailing power of economists. While the procedure for assigning institutions to the German neoliberal thought collective is standardized (essentially, involving a connection to the MPS[58]), the definition of a "Keynesian-Alternative thought collective" is based on a broad range of politico-economic institutions.

The thesis of an infrastructural continuity of German neoliberalism among economists can be proven in three steps. First, twenty-two economists with a high or medium media coefficient score in their think-tank networks. Twelve out of those twenty-two (55 percent) are linked via the network of German neoliberalism, with the MPS (five connections) and the Kronberger Kreis and the Hayek-Stiftung/Gesellschaft (the Hayek Foundation or Society) (each with three connections) holding central positions. In contrast, one economist with a medium media coefficient score is connected to the union-linked Böckler Foundation, which in contrast to the neoliberal thought collective could be termed a Keynesian-Alternative thought collective.

---

58   See also Plehwe and Walpen, "Between Network and Complex Organization."

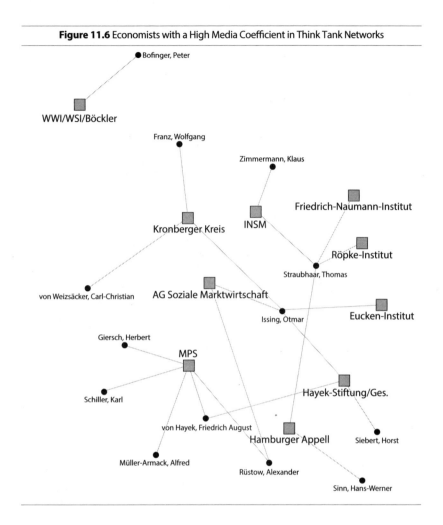

Figure 11.6 Economists with a High Media Coefficient in Think Tank Networks

Second, among the forty economists with a high or medium policy advice coefficient, eleven economists (28 percent) are connected via a network of German neoliberalism, and again only one economist is connected to a Keynesian thought collective. In the network of influential policy advisers, the AG Soziale Marktwirtschaft, the Kronberger Kreis, and the Initiative for New Social Market Economy (INSM) are the nodes with the highest degree of centrality. On a personal level, Jürgen Donges and Christian Watrin (president of the MPS from 2000–2) hold the position of important interlocking directorates.

In a third and final step, the result of a personal and institutional network analysis of German economists in my sample with at least a "medium" influence in at least two PFP coefficients is provided.

Figure 11.7 Economists with a High Economic Policy Advice Coefficient in Think Tank Networks

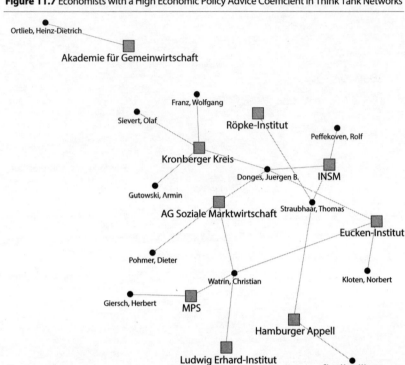

Figure 11.8 again demonstrates the uneven politico-economic power structure among German economists. On the one hand in the bottom and center there is a group of fifteen out of twenty-eight economists (54 percent), connected in a dense network of German neoliberal think tanks and institutions and thus part of a German neoliberal thought collective. On the other hand, as mentioned earlier, Peter Bofinger, who is tellingly often termed by the media the "last Keynesian," is connected to the union-linked Böckler Foundation as part of a Keynesian-Alternative thought collective.

The analysis of the political and public influence of German economists with professorships in economics from 1954 to 1995 reflects a very uneven power structure in favor of neoliberals. Both the detailed analysis of economists with a high media presence or central policy advice positions, and the overall analysis of influential economists in all five coefficients of the PFP, highlight that the majority of economists with an influence on politics and the public can be assigned to the German neoliberal thought collective. While there also exists a network of economists

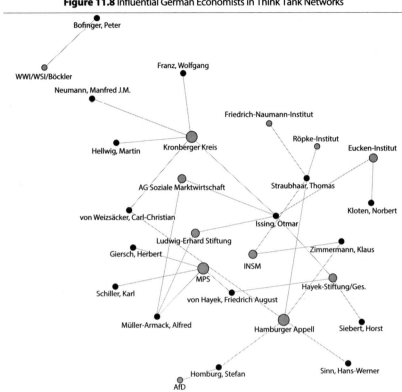

Figure 11.8 Influential German Economists in Think Tank Networks

organized in a Keynesian-Alternative thought collective, indicating a poten-tial countervailing power in politico-economic discourses, the network analyses show that this group is in a marginalized minority position.

Conclusion

This chapter has examined the ideological and politico-economic power structures of German economics since World War II. Using the concept of a German neoliberal thought collective organized around the Mont Pèlerin Society, I first highlighted the connections between ordoliberal-ism and other early strands of neoliberalism on a personal as well as on an institutional level. Second, I introduced the methodology of a performative footprint of economists in order to conceptualize the academic, political, and public impacts of economic thought and of individual economists.

Building on this twofold theoretical and methodological basis, the chapter showed that economists organized in a German neoliberal thought collective had a formative impact on the course of German economic policies. Beginning with the foundation of the Federal Republic in the late 1940s, and later during the "monetarist turn" of the Bundesbank in the 1970s and the "neoliberal turn" in economic politics in the early 1980s, economists connected to the infrastructures of German neoliberalism had key positions which allowed them to influence economic policies.

Beside these concrete examples of the impact of the infrastructures of German neoliberalism on the history of economic politics in Germany, the chapter provided personal and institutional network analyses of a sample of 800 post-World War II German economics professors. The main conclusion drawn from these analyses is that, among the group of economists with a high media presence or important positions in policy advice, or even in economic organizations such as the Bundesbank or governmental authorities, a majority can be assigned to the German neoliberal thought collective. In contrast, only a small minority of "influential" economists is connected to the Keynesian-Alternative thought collective. Therefore one can conclude that a densely connected infrastructure of German neoliberalism, organized around neoliberal economists, think tanks, policy advice institutions, and economic research institutes, has over many decades exercised a formative influence on German economic policies.

Table 11.2. Classification Scheme for the Operationalization of Political Coefficients of the PFP

Category	Weighting Factor	Ministry of Economy/Finanance	Other Ministries	German Federal Statistical Office	Parliament	Monopoly Commission/ Cartel Authority	German/European Central Bank	International Economic Institutions
0	32	minister/chancellor						
1	16	state secr.	state sec/minist.			chair/vice chair	president/chief econ.	
2	8	head of dep.	head of dep.	head of econ/finance department	head of econ/ finance committee	member	board member	head of econ/finance dep.
3	4	scientific staff	scientific staff	leading position in dep.	MP	scientific staff	leading position in regional cent. Bank	leading position in dep.
4	1	scientific staff		scientific staff	scientific staff		scientific staff	scientific staff

Category	Weighting Factor	Governing Party	Opposition Party	Other Political Positions	Economic Research Institutes	Advocacy Groups (Unions, Employers Ass.)	Scientific Advisory Board in BMWi/BMF	German Council of Economic Experts
0	32							
1	16							chair/vice chair
2	8	party leader			president	leading position	chair	member
3	4	spokesman on econ/finance	party leader	leading positions in econ/finance	head of department	spokesman on econ/finance	vice chair	scientific staff
4	1	scientific staff	spokesman on econ/finance	others			member	

Note: For the calculation of the coefficient positions in the institutions are weighted according to their categories and then multiplied by the years economists held these positions. Adequate positions in a German state or abroad lead to a downward-shift in the categories.

About the Contributors

Martin Beddeleem is an historian of early neoliberalism who focuses on its theory of science, currently a post-doctoral researcher at Aarhus University.

Melinda Cooper is a professor of sociology at Australian National University working in the broad areas of social studies of finance, neoliberalism and new social conservatisms.

Marie-Laure Salles-Djelic is a professor of sociology and Dean of the School of Management and Innovation at Sciences Po Paris and the incoming director of the Graduate Institute of International and Development Studies in Geneva.

Rüdiger Graf is an historian at the Leibniz Center for Contemporary History Potsdam (ZZF) where he heads the department of the history of economic life.

Philip E. Mirowski is Carl E. Koch Professor of Economics and Policy Studies and the History and Philosophy of Science at University of Notre Dame.

Reza Mousavi is an assistant professor of management at IESEG School of Management working in the areas of social studies of technology and online social movements.

Edward Nik-Khah is a professor of economics focused on the history of economics at Roanoke College.

Dieter Plehwe is a political scientist with a focus on neoliberalism and think tank networks at the Center for Civil Society Research at the WZB Berlin Social Science Center.

Stephan Pühringer is an economist focusing on the performativity of economic thought and power structures in economics, currently working at the Institute for Comprehensive Analysis of the Economy (ICAE) at the University of Linz.

Matthias Schmelzer is an economic historian and climate activist. He works at the department of Sociology at Friedrich-Schiller-University Jena and at the Laboratory for New Economic Ideas in Leipzig.

Hagen Schulz-Forberg is an associate professor of global and European history at Aarhus University.

Quinn Slobodian is an associate professor of history at Wellesley College.

Bibliography

Aaronson, Mark Neal. "Representing the Poor: Legal Advocacy and Welfare Reform during Reagan's Gubernatorial Years." *Hastings Law Journal* 64 (2013): 933–1119.

Akerlof, George A. et al. "The Copyright Term Extension Act of 1998: An Economic Analysis." (May 2002), at www.brookings.edu.

Alesina, Alberto, and Vittorio Grilli. *The European Central Bank: Reshaping Monetary Politics in Europe*. Cambridge, MA: National Bureau of Economic Research, 1991.

Alstott, Anne. "Neoliberalism in US Family Law: Negative Liberty and Laissez-Faire Markets in the Minimal State." *Law and Contemporary Problems* 77, no. 4 (2014): 25–42.

Ambrosius, Gerold. *Der Staat als Unternehmer: Öffentliche Wirtschaft und Kapitalismus seit dem 19. Jahrhundert*. Göttingen: Vandenhoeck & Ruprecht, 1984.

Anderson, Terry. *The Movement and the Sixties*. New York: Oxford University Press, 1995.

Anghie, Antony. *Imperialism, Sovereignty and the Making of International Law*. Cambridge: Cambridge University Press, 2007.

Aron, Raymond. *Introduction à la philosophie de l'histoire*. Paris: Gallimard, 1986 [1938].

Audier, Serge. *Néo-libéralisme(s). Une archéologie intellectuelle*. Paris: Grasset, 2012.

Austin, J. L. *How to Do Things with Words*. Oxford: Oxford University Press, 1962.

Baccaro, L., and C. Howell. "A Common Neoliberal Trajectory: The Transformation of Industrial Relations in Advanced Capitalism." *Politics & Society* 39, no. 4 (2011): 521–63.

Bachelard, Gaston. *The New Scientific Spirit*. Boston: Beacon Press, 1984.

Bandow, Doug. "Totalitarian Global Management: The UN's War on the Liberal International Economic Order." *Cato Institute Policy Analysis*, no. 61 (1985).

Bank, Max. "Stunde der Neoliberalen? Politikberatung und Wirtschaftspolitik in der Ära Adenauer." PhD Diss, University of Cologne, 2013.

Baudin, Louis. *Free Trade and Peace*. Paris: IIIC, 1939.

Baudin, Louis. *L'Aube d'un nouveau libéralisme*. Paris: Librairie de Médicis, 1953.

Becker, Gary S. "Irrational Behavior and Economic Theory." *Journal of Political Economy* 70, no. 1 (1962): 1–13.

Becker, Gary S. *A Treatise on the Family*. Cambridge, MA: Harvard University Press, 1993 [1981].

Becker, Gary S. *The Economics of Life: From Baseball to Affirmative Action to Immigration, How Real-World Issues Affect Our Everyday Life*. New York: McGraw Hill Education, 1998.

Bell, Daniel. *The Coming of Post-Industrial Society: A Venture in Social Forecasting*. New York: Basic Books, 1973.

Benko, Robert P. "Intellectual Property Rights and the Uruguay Round." *The World Economy* 11, no. 2 (1988): 217–32.

Berelson, Bernard R. "Behavioral Sciences." In *International Encyclopedia of the Social Sciences*, Vol. 2, ed. David Sills and Robert K. Merton. New York: Macmillan, 1968, 41–5.

Bernal, John Desmond. *The Social Function of Science*. London: Routledge, 1939.

Biebricher, Thomas. "Europe and the Political Philosophy of Neoliberalism: Critical Exchange on Neoliberalism and Europe." *Contemporary Political Theory* 12, no. 4 (2013): 338–75.

Biebricher, Thomas. "The Return of Ordoliberalism in Europe: Notes on a Research Agenda." *Scienze Giuridiche, Scienze Cognitive e Intelligenza artificiale* 21 (2014).

Blank, David, and George Stigler. *The Demand and Supply of Scientific Personnel*. New York: NBER, 1957.

Bleemer, Zachary, Meta Brown, Donghoon Lee, and Wilbert van der Klaauw. *Debt, Jobs, or Housing: What's Keeping Millennials at Home?* Federal Reserve Bank of New York Staff Reports, November 1, 2014, at www.newyorkfed.org.

Blumenberg-Lampe, Christine, and Norbert Kloten. *Der Weg in die soziale Marktwirtschaft: Referate, Protokolle, Gutachten der Arbeitsgemeinschaft Erwin von Beckerath 1943–1947*. Stuttgart: Klett-Cotta, 1986.

Blyth, Mark. *Austerity: The History of a Dangerous Idea*. Oxford: Oxford University Press, 2013.

Boettke, Peter, Alexander Fink, and Daniel Smith. "The Impact of Nobel Prize Winners in Economics: Mainline vs. Mainstream." *American Journal of Economics and Sociology*, no. 71 (2012): 1219–49.

Böhm, Franz. *Die Ordnung der Wirtschaft als geschichtliche Aufgabe und rechtssschöpferische Leistung.* Stuttgart and Berlin: Kohlhammer, 1937.

Böhm, S., M. C. Misoczky, and S. Moog. "Greening Capitalism? A Marxist Critique of Carbon-Markets." *Organization Studies* 33, no. 11 (2012): 1617–38.

Boldrin, Michele, and David K. Levine. *Against Intellectual Monopoly.* Cambridge: Cambridge University Press, 2008.

Bonefeld, Werner. "Freedom and the Strong State: On German Ordoliberalism." *New Political Economy* 17, no. 5 (2012): 633–56.

Bonefeld, Werner. *The Strong State and the Free Economy.* London: Rowman & Littlefield, 2017.

Borchardt, Knut. "Die Konzeption der Sozialen Marktwirtschaft in heutiger Sicht." In *Zukunftsprobleme der sozialen Marktwirtschaft,* ed. Otmar Issing. Berlin: Duncker & Humblot, 1981, 33–53.

Bouckaert, Boudewijn. "What Is Property?" *Harvard Journal of Law & Public Policy* 13 (1990): 775–816.

Bowman, Sam. "Coming out as Neoliberals." *Adam Smith Institute Blog,* October 11, 2016.

Boyer, John. *A Twentieth-Century Cosmos: The New Plan and the Origins of General Education at Chicago.* Chicago: The College of the University of Chicago, 2007.

Brandes, Sören. "'Free to Choose': Die Popularisierung des Neoliberalismus in Milton Friedmans Fernsehserie (1980/90)." *Zeithistorische Forschungen/ Studies in Contemporary History* 12, no. 3 (2015): 526–33.

Brenner, Neil. "Building 'Euro-Regions': Locational Politics and the Political Geography of Neoliberalism in Post-Unification Germany." *European Urban and Regional Studies* 7, no. 4 (2000): 319–45.

Brenner, Neil, Jamie Peck, and Nik Theodore. "New Constitutionalism and Variegated Neo-Liberalization." In *New Constitutionalism and World Order,* ed. Stephen Gill and A. Claire Cutler. New York: Cambridge University Press, 2014, 126–42.

Brooks, Roger A. "At the UN, a Mounting War on Patents." *The Heritage Foundation Backgrounder,* no. 215 (October 4, 1982).

Brooks, Roger A. "Multinationals: First Victim of the UN War on Free Enterprise." *The Heritage Foundation Backgrounder,* no. 227 (November 16, 1982).

Brown, Wendy. "Neo-Liberalism and the End of Liberal Democracy." *Theory & Event* 7, no. 1 (2003).

Brown, Wendy. *Undoing the Demos: Neoliberalism's Stealth Revolution.* New York: Zone Books, 2015.

Brunner, Karl, ed. *Proceedings of the First Konstanzer Seminar on Monetary Theory and Monetary Policy*. Berlin: Duncker und Humblot, 1972.

Buch-Hansen, H., and A. Wigger. "Revisiting Fifty Years of Market-Making: The Neoliberal Transformation of European Competition Policy." *Review of International Political Economy* 17, no. 1 (2010): 20–44.

Buchanan, James M. *The Public Finances*. Homewood, Illinois: Richard D. Irwin, Inc. 1960.

Buchanan, James M. "Staatliche Souveränität, nationale Planung und wirtschaftliche Freiheit." *Ordo* 14 (1963): 249–58.

Buchanan, James M. "The Samaritan's Dilemma." In *Altruism, Morality, and Economic Theory*, edited by E. S. Phelps, 71–85. New York: Russell Sage Foundation, 1975.

Buchanan, James M. "Methods and Morals in Economics: The Ayres-Knight Discussion." In *Science and Ceremony: The Institutional Economics of C. E. Ayres*, edited by W. Breit and J. William Patton Culbertson, 163–74. Austin: University of Texas Press, 1976.

Buchanan, James M., and Yong J. Yoon. "Symmetric Tragedies: Commons and Anticommons." *Journal of Law and Economics* 43 (2000): 1–13.

Bukharin, N. I., ed. *Science at the Cross-Roads*. London: Frank Cass & Co., 1971.

Bulmer, Simon, and William E. Paterson. "Germany as the EU's Reluctant Hegemon? Of Economic Strength and Political Constraints." *Journal of European Public Policy* 20, no. 10 (2013): 1387–1405.

Burgin, Angus. *The Great Persuasion: Reinventing Free Markets Since the Depression*. Cambridge, MA: Harvard University Press, 2012.

Butterwegge, Christoph, Bettina Lösch, and Ralf Ptak, eds. *Kritik des Neoliberalismus*. Wiesbaden: VS Verlag für Sozialwissenschaften, 2008.

Buzaglo, Jorge. "The Nobel Family Dissociates itself from the Economics Prize." Real-World Economics Review Blog, October 22, 2010, at https://rwer. wordpress.com.

Caldwell, Bruce. *Hayek's Challenge*. Chicago: University of Chicago Press, 2004.

Capps, Patrick. *Human Dignity and the Foundations of International Law*. Oxford: Hart, 2009.

Caspers, Rolf. *Zahlungsbilanz und Wechselkurse*. Munich and Vienna: Oldenbourg Verlag, 2002.

Cassel, Gustav. "Abnormal Deviations in International Exchanges." *The Economic Journal* 28 (1918): 413–15.

Castillejo, José. Letter to Ortega y Gasset, January 31, 1931. In *Epistolario de José Castillejo, Vol. III, Fatalidad y Porvenir 1913–1937*. Madrid: Editorial Castalia, 1999, 673–7.

Cato Institute, *Cato Handbook for Congress: Policy Recommendations for the 108th Congress*. Washington, DC: Cato Institute, 2003.

Centre International d'études pour la rénovation du libéralisme. "Le néo-libéralisme." Inaugural Discussion on March 8, 1939. Reprinted in *Les Essais. Cahiers bimestriels*. Nancy: Didry and Varcollier, 1961, 86–108.

Chafuen, Alejandro. "Atlas Economic Research Foundation Early History," at www.chafuen.com.

Chandler, Alfred D. *Strategy and Structure: Chapters in the History of the American Industrial Enterprise*. Cambridge, MA: MIT Press, 1962.

Chappell, Marisa. *The War on Welfare: Family, Poverty, and Politics in Modern America*. Philadelphia: University of Pennsylvania Press, 2010.

Cherrier, Beatrice. "The Wesley Clair Mitchell Medal: The AEA Award that Never Came to Be." Institute for New Economic Thinking, November 11, 2015, at ineteconomics.org.

Cockett, Richard. *Thinking the Unthinkable*. London: HarperCollins, 1994.

Coen, Deborah R. *Vienna in the Age of Uncertainty: Science, Liberalism, and Private Life*. Chicago: University of Chicago Press, 2007.

Cohen, Jean L. *Regulating Intimacy: A New Legal Paradigm*. Princeton: Princeton University Press, 2004.

Condliffe, John Bell. *International Collaboration in the Study of International Relations*. Paris: IIIC, 1930.

Connell, Carol M. *Reforming the World Monetary System: Fritz Machlup and the Bellagio Group*. London and New York: Routledge, 2013.

Connell, Carol M., and Joseph Salerno, eds. *Monetary Reform and the Bellagio Group: Selected Letters and Papers of Fritz Machlup, Robert Triffin and William Fellner*, 5 vols. London: Taylor & Francis Group, 2014.

Coontz, Stephanie. *The Way We Never Were: American Families and the Nostalgia Trap*. New York: Basic Books, 2000.

Cooper, Melinda. *Family Values: Between Neoliberalism and the New Social Conservatism*. New York: Zone Books, 2017.

Cooper, Richard N. "Exchange Rate Choices." Conference Series, Federal Reserve Bank of Boston (June 1999): 99–136.

Crouch, Colin. *Post-Democracy*. London: Polity, 2004.

Crouch, Colin. *The Strange Non-Death of Neoliberalism*. Cambridge: Polity, 2011.

Crowther-Heyck, Hunter. *Herbert A. Simon: The Bounds of Teason in Modern America*. Baltimore: Johns Hopkins University Press, 2005.

Crowther, M. A. "Family Responsibility and State Responsibility in Britain before the Welfare State." *The Historical Journal* 25, no. 1 (1982): 131–45.

Crozier, Michel, Jōji Watanuki, and Samuel P. Huntington. *The Crisis of*

Democracy: Report on the Governability of Democracies to the Trilateral Commission. New York: University Press, 1975.

Cutler, A. Claire. *Private Power and Global Authority: Transnational Merchant Law in the Global Political Economy.* New York: Cambridge University Press, 2003.

Davies, William. "Economics and the 'Nonsense' of Law: The Case of the Chicago Antitrust Revolution." *Economy and Society* 39, no. 1 (2010): 64–83.

Davies, William. *The Limits of Neoliberalism: Authority, Sovereignty and the Logic of Competition.* Thousand Oaks: SAGE, 2014.

Davis, Aeron, and Catherine Walsh. "Distinguishing Financialization from Neoliberalism." *Theory, Culture & Society* 34, no. 5–6 (2017): 27–51.

Davis, Martha F. *Brutal Need: Lawyers and the Welfare Rights Movement, 1960–1971.* New Haven: Yale University Press, 1993.

Denord, François. "Aux origines du néo-libéralisme en France. Louis Rougier et le Colloque Walter Lippmann de 1938." *Le Mouvement Social* 195, no. 2 (2001): 9–34.

Denord, François. *Néo-libéralisme version française. Histoire d'une idéologie politique.* Paris: Demopolis, 2007.

de Marchi, Neil. "League of Nations Economists and the Ideal of Peaceful Change in the Decade of the 'Thirties.'" In *Economics and National Security*, ed. Craufurd D. Goodwin. Durham, NC: Duke University Press, 1991, 143–78.

Dewey, Thomas E. L. "At WIPO, New Threats to Intellectual Property Rights." *The Heritage Foundation Backgrounder*, no. 51 (September 11, 1987).

Diamond, Arthur. "Measurement, Incentives, and Constraints in Stigler's Economics of Science." *European Journal of the History of Economic Thought* 12, no. 4 (2005): 635–61.

Director, Aaron. "The Parity of the Economic Market Place." *Journal of Law and Economics* 7 (1964): 1–10.

Doering, Detmar. "'Sozialdarwinismus' Die unterschwellige Perfidie eines Schlagwortes." *Eigentümlich Frei* 2, no. 6 (1999): 200–2.

Drahos, Peter, and John Braithwaite. *Information Feudalism.* London: Earthscan, 2002.

Dullien, Sebastian, and Ulrike Guérot. "The Long Shadow of Ordoliberalism: Germany's Approach to the Euro Crisis." *European Council on Foreign Relations Policy Brief*, 2012.

Duménil, Gérard, and Dominique Lévy. *The Crisis of Neoliberalism.* Cambridge, MA: Harvard University Press, 2011.

Dunn, Bill. "Against Neoliberalism as a Concept." *Capital & Class* 41, no. 3 (2017): 435–54.

Düppe, Till. "Economic Science in Berlin." *Studies in the History and Philosophy of Science*, no. 51 (2015): 22–32.

Dyble, Colleen, ed. *Taming Leviathan: Waging the War of Ideas around the World*. London: Institute of Economic Affairs, 2008.

Eagleton-Pierce, Matthew. *Neoliberalism: The Key Concepts*. London: Routledge, 2016.

Ebenstein, Alan. *Friedrich Hayek: A Biography*. New York: St. Martin's Press, 2001.

Ebenstein, Lanny. *Chicagonomics*. New York: St. Martin's Press, 2015.

Edwards, Lee. *The Power of Ideas: The Heritage Foundation at 25 Years*. Ottawa, IL: Jameson Books, 1997.

Eecke, Wilfried v. "Ethics in Economics: From Classical Economics to Neo-liberalism." *Philosophy & Social Criticism* 9, no. 2 (1982): 146–67.

Eichengreen, Barry. *Golden Fetters: The Gold Standard and the Great Depression, 1919–1939*. New York: Oxford University Press, 1992.

Eichengreen, Barry. *Globalizing Capital: A History of the International Monetary System*. Princeton: Princeton University Press, 1996.

Eilfort, Michael. "Begrüßung." In *25 JAHRE Stiftung Marktwirtschaft und Kronberger Kreis*, ed. Stiftung Marktwirtschaft. Berlin, 2007, 6–9.

Endres, Anthony M. *Great Architects of International Finance: The Bretton Woods Era*. London and New York: Routledge, 2005.

Endres, Anthony M. "Frank Graham's Case for Flexible Exchange Rates: A Doctrinal Perspective." *History of Political Economy* 40, no. 1 (2008): 133–62.

Epstein, Richard. *Principles for a Free Society*. New York: Basic Books, 1998.

Eriksson, Martin. "A Golden Combination: The Formation of Monetary Policy in Sweden after WWI." *Enterprise & Society*, no. 16 (2015): 556–79.

Erixon, Lennart. "The Economic Policy and Macroeconomic Performance of Sweden in the 1990s and 2000s." In *The Nordic Varieties of Capitalism*, ed. Lars Mjøset. Bingley: Emerald House, 2011, 265–330.

Eucken, Walter. *Grundsätze der Wirtschaftspolitik*. Bern: Francke, 1952.

Fang, Marina. "Born Amidst '60s Protests, Kalven Report Remains Controversial." *The Chicago Maroon*, February 21, 2013, at http://chicago-maroon.com.

Feld, Lars P. "Zur Bedeutung des Manifests der Marktwirtschaft oder: Das Lambsdorff Papier im 31. Jahr." *Zeitschrift für Wirtschaftspolitik* 62, no. 3 (2013): 227–43.

Feld, Lars P., Ekkehard A. Köhler, and Daniel Nientiedt. "Ordoliberalism, Pragmatism and the Eurozone Crisis: How the German Tradition Shaped Economic Policy in Europe." CESifo Working Paper, no. 5368 (2015).

Fellner, William. *Amerikanische Erfahrungen mit der Lohninflation in den fünfziger Jahren*. Tübingen: J. C. B. Mohr, 1962.

Fellner, William. "On Limited Exchange-rate Flexibility." In *Maintaining and Restoring Balance in International Payments*, ed. William Fellner et al. Princeton: Princeton University Press, 1966, 111–22.

Feulner, Edwin J. "Waging and Winning the War of Ideas." *The Heritage Lectures*, no. 84 (1986).

Fisher, Antony "Letter to a Businessman in Jamaica, 1981." Extracts available on www.chafuen.com.

Fisher, Antony "Pourquoi l'Institute of Economic Affairs ?" Speech at the Inauguration on the Institut Economique de Paris, September 29, 1982. *Liberté économique et progress social*, no. 46–7 (October 1983).

Fisk, Catherine L. "Knowledge Work: New Metaphors for the New Economy." *Chicago-Kent Law Review* 80 (2005): 839–72.

Fleming, Peter. *The Death of Homo Economicus: Work, Debt and the Myth of Endless Accumulation*. London: Pluto Press, 2017.

Foray, Dominique. *Economics of Knowledge*. Cambridge, MA: MIT Press, 2004.

Forder, James. "Why is Central Bank Independence so Widely Approved?" *Journal of Economic Issues*, no. 39 (2005): 843–65.

Foucault, Michel. *The Birth of Biopolitics: Lectures at the Collège de France, 1978–1979*, ed. Frédéric Gros. London: Palgrave Macmillan, 2008.

Foucault, Michel. *The Courage of Truth*. New York: Picador, 2011.

Fourcade, Marion. "The Construction of a Global Profession: The Transnationalization of Economics." In *The Economics of Economists*, ed. Jack Vromen and Alessandro Lantieri. Cambridge: Cambridge University Press, 2014, 25–76.

Fournier, Marcel. *Marcel Mauss: A Biography*. Princeton: Princeton University Press, 2006.

Franke, Katherine. "Becoming a Citizen: Reconstruction Era Regulation of African American Marriages." *Yale Journal of Law and the Humanities* 11 (1999): 251–309.

Frantz, Roger. "Frederick Hayek's Behavioral Economics in Historical Context." In *Hayek and Behavioral Economics*, ed. Roger Frantz. Basingstoke: Palgrave Macmillan, 2013, 1–34.

Fredona, Robert, and Sophus A. Reinert, "The Harvard Research Center in Entrepreneurial History and the Daimonic Entrepreneur." *History of Political Economy* 49, no. 2 (2017): 268–314.

Freeden, Michael. *Ideologies and Political Theory: A Conceptual Approach*. Oxford: Oxford University Press, 1996.

Friedman, Milton. "Neo-Liberalism and its Prospects." *Farmand* (February 1951): 1–4.

Friedman, Milton. "The Case for Flexible Exchange Rates." In *Essays in Positive Economics*. Chicago: University of Chicago Press, 1953, 157–203.

Friedman, Milton. "Discussion." In *International Payments Problems. A Symposium Sponsored by the American Enterprise Institute for Public Policy Research*. Washington, DC: American Enterprise Institute, 1966, 87–90.

Friedman, Milton. "The Methodology of Positive Economics (1953)." In *Essays in Positive Economics*, ed. Milton Friedman. Chicago: University of Chicago Press, 1966, 3–46.

Friedman, Milton. "'Free' Education." *Newsweek*, February 14, 1967: 86.

Friedman, Milton. *Capitalism and Freedom*. Chicago: University of Chicago Press, 1982.

Friedman, Milton. "Mr. Market." *Hoover Digest*, no. 1 (1999).

Friedman, Milton, Edward M. Bernstein, Milton Gilbert. "Discussion." *The American Economic Review* 55, no. 1/2 (1965): 178–88.

Friedman, Milton, and Robert Roosa. *The Balance of Payments: Free Versus Fixed Exchange Rates*. Washington, DC: American Enterprise Institute, 1967.

Friedman, Milton, and Rose Friedman. *Capitalism and Freedom*. Chicago: University of Chicago Press, 1962.

Friedman, Milton, and Rose D. Friedman. *Two Lucky People: Memoirs*. Chicago: University of Chicago Press, 1998.

Friedman, Robert Marc. *The Politics of Excellence*. New York: Times Books, 2001.

Frisch, Ragnar. "Propagation Problems and Impulse Problems in Dynamic Economics." *Publications of the University Institute of Economics*, no. 3 (1933): 1–35.

Frisch, Ragnar, and Joseph Schumpeter, "Memo," at www.dev.econometricsociety.org.

Frobert, Ludovic. "Elie Halévy's First Lectures on the History of European Socialism." *Journal of the History of Ideas* 68, no. 2 (2007): 329–53.

Frost, Gerald. *Antony Fisher: Champion of Liberty*. London: Profile Books, 2008.

Gallie, Walter Bryce. "Essentially Contested Concepts." *Proceedings of the Aristotelian Society* 56 (1955–6): 167–98.

GCEE. *Jahresgutachten: Mut zur Stabilisierung*. Stuttgart: Kohlhammer, 1973.

GCEE. *Vierzig Jahre Sachverständigenrat: 1963–2003*. Wiesbaden: Statistisches Bundesamt, 2003.

Gideonse, Harry. "Changing Issues in Academic Freedom in the United States

Today." *Proceedings of the American Philosophical Society* 94, no. 2 (1950): 91–104.

Gideonse, Harry. "Academic Freedom: A Decade of Challenge and Clarification." *Annals of the American Academy of Political and Social Science* 301, no. 1 (1955): 75–85.

Giersch, Herbert. "Das Beste aus beiden Welten: Planung und Preismechanismus." *Weltwirtschaftliches Archiv*, no. 69 (1952): 216–31.

Giersch, Herbert. "The Role of Entrepreneurship in the 1980s." *Kiel Discussion Papers* (August 1982).

Giersch, Herbert. "The Age of Schumpeter." *The American Economic Review* 74, no. 2 (1984): 103–9.

Giersch, Herbert, "Eurosclerosis: The Malaise that Threatens Prosperity." *Financial Times*, January 8, 1984: 9.

Giersch, Herbert. "Anmerkungen zum weltwirtschaftlichen Denkansatz." *Weltwirtschaftliches Archiv* 125, no. 1 (1989): 1–16.

Giersch, Herbert, Karl-Heinz Paqué, and Holger Schmieding. *The Fading Miracle: Four Decades of Market Economy in Germany*. Cambridge: Cambridge University Press, 1992.

Gigerenzer, Gerd, and Reinhard Selten, eds. *Bounded Rationality: The Adaptive Toolbox*. Cambridge, MA: MIT Press, 2001.

Gilad, Benjamin, and Stanley Kaish, eds. *Handbook of Behavioral Economics: Behavioral Microeconomics*. Greenwich, CN: Jai Press, 1986.

Gill, Stephen, and A. Claire Cutler, eds. *New Constitutionalism and World Order*. New York: Cambridge University Press, 2014.

Gingras, Yves. "Nobel by Association: Beautiful Mind, Non-existent Prize." *Open Democracy*, 23 October, 2002, at www.opendemocracy.net.

Girei, E. "NGOs, Management and Development: Harnessing Counter-Hegemonic Possibilities." *Organization Studies* 37, no. 2 (2016): 193–212.

Godin, Benoît. "The Knowledge Economy: Fritz Machlup's Construction of a Synthetic Concept." *Project on the History and Sociology of S&T Statistics Working Paper*, no. 37 (2008).

Goldschmidt, Nils. "Alfred Müller-Armack and Ludwig Erhard: Social Market Liberalism." *Freiburg Discussion Papers on Constitutional Economics*, 04/12 (2004).

Goldschmidt, Nils, ed. *Wirtschaft, Politik und Freiheit: Freiburger Wissenschaftler und der Widerstand*. Tübingen: Mohr Siebeck, 2005.

Goodwin, Craufurd D. *Walter Lippmann: Public Economist*. Cambridge, MA: Harvard University Press, 2014.

Gorlin, Jacques J. "US Industries, Trade Associations, and Intellectual Property Lawmaking." *Cardozo Journal of International Comparative Law* (2002): 5–11.

Governor of California (Ronald Reagan). California's Blueprint for National Welfare Reform: Proposals for the Nation's Food Stamp and Aid to Families with Dependent Children Programs. Sacramento, CA: Office of the Governor, 1974.

Graf, Rüdiger, and Kim Christian Priemel. "Zeitgeschichte in der Welt der Sozialwissenschaften. Legitimität und Originalität einer Disziplin." *Vierteljahrshefte für Zeitgeschichte* 59, no. 4 (2011): 479–508.

Graham, C. "The Calculation of Age." *Organization Studies* 35, no. 11 (2014): 1627–53.

Gray, John. *Hayek on Liberty.* New York: Routledge, 1984.

Großmann, Johannes. *Die Internationale der Konservativen: Transnationale Elitenzirkel und private Außenpolitik in Westeuropa seit 1945.* Munich: Oldenbourg, 2014.

Gwartney, James, and Robert Lawson. "The Concept and Measurement of Economic Freedom." *European Journal of Political Economy* 19 (2003): 405–30.

Haas, Peter M. "Introduction: Epistemic Communities and International Policy Coordination." *International Organization* 46, no. 1 (1992): 1–35.

Haberler, Gottfried. *Currency Convertibility.* Washington, DC: American Enterprise Institute, 1954.

Haberler, Gottfried. "Between Mises and Keynes: An Interview with Gottfried von Haberler." *Austrian Economics Newsletter* 20, no. 1 (2000), at https://mises.org.

Hacohen, Malachi Haim. "Karl Popper, the Vienna Circle, and Red Vienna." *Journal of the History of Ideas* 59, no. 4 (1998): 711–34.

Hagemann, Harald. "Capitalist Development, Innovations, Business Cycles and Unemployment: Joseph Alois Schumpeter and Emil Hans Lederer." *Journal of Evolutionary Economics* 25, no. 1 (2015): 117–31.

Hagemann, Harald. "Ordoliberalism, the Social Market Economy, and Keynesianism: Germany after 1945." In *Liberalism and the Welfare State: Economists and Arguments for the Welfare State*, ed. Roger Backhouse, Bradley W. Bateman, and Tamotsu Nishizawa. Oxford: Oxford University Press, 2017, 57–74.

Halévy, Elie. *L'Ère des tyrannies. Études sur le socialisme et la guerre.* Paris: Gallimard, 1938.

Hall, Daniel, ed. *The Frustration of Science.* New York: Arno Press, 1975.

Hall, Peter A., ed. *The Political Power of Economic Ideas: Keynesianism Across Nations*. Princeton: Princeton University Press, 1989.

Hamilius, Jean Pierre. "Intellektuelle und Unternehmer." In *Der Unternehmer im Ansehen der Welt*, ed. Günter Schmölders. Bergisch Gladbach: Lübbe, 1971, 156–71.

Hampton, Matt. "Hegemony, Class Struggle and the Radical Historiography of Global Monetary Standards." *Capital & Class* 30, no. 2 (2006): 131–64.

Hanke, Steve H., and Stephen J. K. Walters. "Economic Freedom, Prosperity, and Equality: A Survey." *Cato Journal* 17, no. 2 (1997): 117–46.

Hansen, Drew D. "The American Invention of Child Support: Dependency and Punishment in Early American Child Support." *Yale Law Journal* 108, no. 5 (1999): 1123–53.

Hardin, Garrett. "The Tragedy of the Commons." *Science, New Series* 162, no. 3859 (1968): 1243–8.

Hardin, Garrett. "Lifeboat Ethics: The Argument Against Helping the Poor." *Psychology Today* 8, (1974): 38–43.

Hardin, Garrett, and John Baden, eds. *Managing the Commons*. San Francisco: W. H. Freeman and Company, 1977.

Harper, Floyd A., Henry Hazlitt, Leonard Read, Gustavo R. Velasco, and F. A. Hayek, eds. *Toward Liberty: Essays in Honor of Ludwig von Mises*. Menlo Park: Institute for Humane Studies, 1971.

Hartwell, Max. *A History of the Mont Pèlerin Society*. Indianapolis: Liberty Fund, 1995.

Harvey, David. *A Brief History of Neoliberalism*. New York: Oxford University Press, 2005.

Haubrichs, Wilhelm. "Laudatio." In *An den Grenzen der Belastbarkeit: Festschrift für Günter Schmölders zum 75. Geburtstag*, ed. Wilhelm Haubrichs. Frankfurt am Main: Knapp, 1978, 7–10.

Haus, Jasmina. *Förderung von Unternehmertum und Unternehmensgründungen an deutschen Hochschulen*. Lohmar: Josef Eul Verlag, 2006.

Hayek, F. A. *Prices and Production*. London: Routledge, 1931.

Hayek, F. A. *Monetary Nationalism and International Stability*. London: Longmans, Green and Co., 1937.

Hayek, F. A. *The Road to Serfdom*. Chicago: University of Chicago Press, 1944.

Hayek, F. A. *Individualism and Economic Order*. Chicago: University of Chicago Press, 1948.

Hayek, F. A. "Wahrer und falscher Individualismus." *Ordo* 1 (1948): 19–55.

Hayek, F. A. "Intellectuals and Socialism." *The University of Chicago Law Review* 16, no. 3 (1949): 417–33.

Hayek, F. A. "Kinds of Order in Society." *New Individualist Review* 3, no. 2 (1964): 457–66.

Hayek, F. A. *Was mit der Goldwährung geschehen ist. Ein Bericht aus dem Jahre 1932 mit zwei Ergänzungen.* Tübingen: J. C. B. Mohr, 1965.

Hayek, F. A. *Rules and Order: A New Statement of the Liberal Principles of Justice and Political Economy. Law, Legislation, and Liberty. Vol. 1.* London: Routledge & Kegan Paul, 1973.

Hayek, F. A. *Denationalization of Money.* London: American Enterprise Institute, 1978.

Hayek, F. A. *New Studies in Philosophy, Politics, Economics and the History of Ideas.* Chicago: University of Chicago Press, 1978.

Hayek, F. A. "Die Wiederentdeckung der Freiheit—Persönliche Erinnerungen." In *Produktivität, Eigenverantwortung, Beschäftigung: Für eine wirtschaftspolitische Vorwärtsstrategie*, ed. VDM 31. Cologne: Deutscher Instituts-Verlag, 1983, 9–22.

Hayek, F. A. *The Fatal Conceit: The Errors of Socialism.* Chicago: University of Chicago Press, 1988.

Hayek, F. A. *Economic Freedom.* Oxford: Blackwell, 1991.

Hayek, F. A. *The Fortunes of Liberalism: Essays on Austrian Economics and the Ideal of Freedom.* Chicago: University of Chicago Press, 1992.

Hayek, F. A. *Socialism and War.* Chicago: University of Chicago Press, 1997.

Hayek, F. A. *Studies on the Abuse and Decline of Reason.* Chicago: University of Chicago Press, 2010.

Hayek, F. A. *The Constitution of Liberty.* Chicago: University of Chicago Press, 2011 [1960].

Hayek, F. A. "The Overrated Reason." *Journal of the History of Economic Thought* 35, no. 2 (2013): 239–56.

Hazlett, Thomas. "Interview of George Stigler." *Reason* (January 1984): 44–8.

Heilperin, Michael. *Les aspects monétaires du problèmes des matières premières.* Paris: IIIC, 1937.

Heilperin, Michael. *International Monetary Organisation.* Paris: IIIC, 1939.

Heise, Arne, and Sebastian Thieme. "The Short Rise and Long Fall of Heterodox Economics in Germany after the 1970s: Explorations in a Scientific Field of Power and Struggle." *Journal of Economic Issues* 50, no. 4 (2016): 1105–30.

Helleiner, Eric. *States and the Reemergence of Global Finance: From Bretton Woods to the 1990s.* Ithaca: Cornell University Press, 1994.

Herbener, Jeffrey M., Hans-Hermann Hoppe, and Josef T. Salerno. "Introduction to the Scholarly Edition." In Ludwig von Mises, *Human Action. The Scholarly Edition.* Auburn: Ludwig von Mises Institute, 1998, iv–xxiv.

Herbst, Ludolf. *Der Totale Krieg und die Ordnung der Wirtschaft: Die Kriegswirtschaft im Spannungsfeld von Politik, Ideologie und Propaganda 1939–1945.* Stuttgart: Deutsche Verlags-Anstalt, 1982.

Hesse, Jan-Otmar. "Der Mensch des Unternehmens und der Produktion. Foucaults Sicht auf den Ordoliberalismus und die 'Soziale Marktwirtschaft.'" *Studies in Contemporary History,* no. 3 (2006): 291–6.

Hesse, Jan-Otmar. "Some Relationships between a Scholar's and an Entrepreneur's Life: The Biography of L. Albert Hahn." *History of Political Economy* 39 (2007): 215–33.

Hesse, Jan-Otmar. *Wirtschaft als Wissenschaft: Die Volkswirtschaftslehre in der frühen Bundesrepublik.* Frankfurt am Main: Campus Verlag, 2010.

Hesse, Jan-Otmar. "Wissenschaftliche Beratung der Wirtschaftspolitik." In *Das Bundeswirtschaftsminsterium in der Ära der sozialen Marktwirtschaft,* ed. Werner Abelshauser. Berlin: De Gruyter, 2016, 390–482.

Hessen, Boris. "The Social and Economic Roots of Newton's 'Principia.'" In *Science at the Cross-Roads,* ed. N. I. Bukharin. London: Frank Cass & Co., 1971, 147–211.

Heukelom, Floris. "Three Explanations for the Kahneman-Tversky Programme of the 1970s." *The European Journal of the History of Economic Thought* 19, no. 5 (2012): 797–828.

Heukelom, Floris. *Behavioral Economics: A History.* Cambridge: Cambridge University Press, 2014.

Hicks, John. "The Hayek Story." In *Critical Essays in Monetary Theory.* Oxford: Clarendon Press, 1967, 203–15.

Hien, Josef. "The Ordoliberalism That Never Was." *Contemporary Political Theory* 12, no. 4 (2013): 338–75.

Hill, Gladwin. "Reagan Defeated on Tuition Plans: Regents Vote, 14–7, to Bar Fees at the University." *New York Times,* September 1, 1967: 13.

Hirschman, Daniel, and Elizabeth P. Berman. "Do Economists Make Policies? On the Political Effects of Economics." *Socio-Economic Review* 12, no. 4 (2014): 779–811.

Hobsbawm, Eric J. *Age of Extremes: The Short Twentieth Century, 1914–1991.* London: Abacus, 1995.

Hopkins, Frederick G. "Some Chemical Aspects of Life." *Nature* 132, no. 3332 (1933): 381–94.

Horsefield, J. Keith et al., *The International Monetary Fund 1945–1965: Twenty Years of International Monetary Cooperation,* Vol. 3. Washington, DC: International Monetary Fund, 1969.

Huffschmid, Jörg. *Politische Ökonomie der Finanzmärkte*. Hamburg: VSA-Verlag, 2002.

Hwang, H., and W. Powell. "The Rationalization of Charity: The Influences of Professionalism in the Non-Profit Sector." *Administrative Science Quarterly* 54, no. 2 (2009): 268–98.

Iriye, Akira. *Cultural Internationalism and World Order*. Baltimore: The Johns Hopkins University Press, 2000.

Jackson, Ben. "At the Origins of Neo-Liberalism: The Free Economy and the Strong State, 1930–1947." *The Historical Journal* 53, no. 1 (2010): 129–51.

Jackson, Ben. "Freedom, the Common Good, and the Rule of Law: Lippmann and Hayek on Economic Planning." *Journal of the History of Ideas* 73, no. 1 (2012): 47–68.

Jackson, Ben, and Mark Stears, eds. *Liberalism as Ideology: Essays in Honour of Michael Freeden*. Oxford: Oxford University Press, 2012.

James, Harold. *International Monetary Cooperation since Bretton Woods*. New York: Oxford University Press, 1996.

James, Harold. *Making the European Monetary Union*. Cambridge, MA: Belknap Press of Harvard University Press, 2012.

Janssen, Hauke. *Milton Friedman und die 'monetaristische Revolution' in Deutschland*. Marburg: Metropolis-Verl., 2006.

Jarvie, Ian C. *The Republic of Science: The Emergence of Popper's Social View of Science 1935–1945*. Atlanta: Rodopi, 2001.

Jessop, Bob. "Cultural Political Economy and Critical Policy Studies." *Critical Policy Studies* 3, no. 3–4 (2010): 336–56.

Jessop, Bob. "Recovered Imaginaries, Imagined Recoveries: A Cultural Political Economy of Crisis Construals and Crisis-Management in the North Atlantic Financial Crisis," in *Before and Beyond the Global Economic Crisis: Economics, Politics and Settlement*, ed. Mats Benner. Cheltenham: Edward Elgar, 2013, 234–54.

Joas, Hans. *Die Entstehung der Werte*. Frankfurt am Main: Suhrkamp Verlag, 1999.

Johns, Adrian. "Intellectual Property and the Nature of Science." *Cultural Studies* 20, no. 2–3 (2006): 145–64.

Kalven, Jamie. "Unfinished Business of the Kalven Report." *The Chicago Maroon*, November 28, 2006, at http://chicagomaroon.com.

Kapczynski, Amy. "Intellectual Property's Leviathan." *Law and Contemporary Problems* 131 (2014): 131–45.

Karier, Thomas. *Intellectual Capital*. New York: Cambridge University Press, 2010.

Kaza, Greg, "The Mont Pèlerin Society's 50th Anniversary." *The Freeman* 47, no. 6 (June 1997).

Kelsen, Hans. *General Theory of Law and State*. Cambridge, MA: Harvard University Press, 1949.

Kelsen, Hans. *Pure Theory of Law*. Berkeley: University of California Press, 1969 [1934].

Kerr, Clark. *The Gold and the Blue: A Personal Memoir of the University of California, 1949–1967*, Vol. 1. Berkeley: University of California Press, 2001.

Keynes, John Maynard. *The General Theory of Employment, Interest and Money*. London: Macmillan, 1936.

Kiesling, Lynne. "The Knowledge Problem." In *The Oxford Handbook of Austrian Economics*, ed. Peter J. Boettke and Christopher J. Coyne. New York: Oxford University Press, 2015, 45–64.

Kindleberger, Charles. "Review of Mundell/Swoboda." *Journal of International Economics* 1 (1971): 127–40.

Kinsella, N. Stephan. *Against Intellectual Property*. Auburn: Ludwig von Mises Institute, 2008.

Kirzner, Israel, "Methodological Individualism, Market Equilibrium, and Market Process." *Il Politico* 32 no. 1 (1967): 787–98.

Kirzner, Israel. "Entrepreneurship and the Market Approach to Development." In *Toward Liberty: Essays in Honor of Ludwig von Mises*, ed. Floyd A. Harper et al. Menlo Park: Institute for Humane Studies, 1971, 194–208.

Kirzner, Israel. *Competition and Entrepreneurship*. Chicago: University of Chicago Press, 1973.

Kirzner, Israel, "The Primacy of Entrepreneurial Discovery." In *Prime Mover of Progress*, ed. Arthur Seldon. London: Institute of Economic Affairs, 1980.

Klaes, Matthias, and Esther-Mirjam Sent. "A Conceptual History of the Emergence of Bounded Rationality." *History of Political Economy* 37, no. 1 (2005): 27–59.

Klaus, Václav. "Mont Pèlerin Society Speech in Korea," 2017, at www.montpelerin.org.

Klein, Daniel. "Special Issue: The Ideological Migration of the Economics Laureates." *Economic Journal Watch*, no. 10 (2013): 218–682.

Klein, Naomi. *The Shock Doctrine: The Rise of Disaster Capitalism*. New York: Penguin, 2007.

Köhler, Ekkehard A., and Stefan Kolev. "The Conjoint Quest for a Liberal Positive Program: 'Old Chicago,' Freiburg and Hayek." *HWWI Research Paper*, no. 109 (2011).

Kolev, Stefan. "F. A. Hayek as an Ordo-liberal." *HWWI Research Paper*, no. 5 (2010).

Kolev, Stefan, Nils Goldschmidt, and Jan-Otmar Hesse. "Walter Eucken's Role in the Early History of the Mont Pèlerin Society." *Freiburg Discussion Papers on Constitutional Economics*, no. 02 (2014).

Kornbluh, Felicia. *The Battle for Welfare Rights*. Philadelphia: University of Pennsylvania Press, 2007.

Koselleck, Reinhart. *Critique and Crisis: Enlightenment and the Pathogenesis of Modern Society*, Cambridge MA: MIT Press, 1988.

Koselleck, Reinhart. *Futures Past: On the Semantics of Historical Time*. New York: Columbia University Press, 2004.

Koselleck, Reinhart. *Sediments of Time: On Possible Histories*. Stanford: Stanford University Press, 2018.

Koskenniemi, Martti. "International Law and Hegemony: A Reconfiguration." *Cambridge Review of International Affairs* 17, no. 2 (2004): 197–218.

Koskenniemi, Martti. "International Law as Political Theology: How to Read *Nomos der Erde?*" *Constellations* 11, no. 4 (2004): 492–511.

Kresge, Stephen, and Leif Wenar, eds. *Hayek on Hayek: An Autobiographical Dialogue*. London: Routledge, 1994.

Krippner, Greta R. *Capitalizing on Crisis: The Political Origins of the Rise of Finance*. Cambridge, MA: Harvard University Press, 2012.

Kronberger Kreis. *Dismantling the Boundaries of the ECB's Monetary Policy Mandate: The CJEU's OMT Judgement and its Consequences*. Berlin: Stiftung Marktwirtschaft, 2016.

Landes, William M., and Richard A. Posner. *The Economic Structure of Intellectual Property Law*. Cambridge, MA: Belknap Press of Harvard University Press, 2003.

Langlois, Richard N. "From the Knowledge of Economics to the Economics of Knowledge: Fritz Machlup on Methodology and on the 'Knowledge Society'." *Research in the History of Economic Thought and Methodology* 3 (1985): 225–35.

Laqua, Daniel. "Transnational Intellectual Cooperation, the League of Nations, and the Problem of Order." *Journal of Global History* 6, no. 2 (2011): 223–47.

Lavergne, Bernard. *Le Régime coopératif. Etude général de la coopération de consommation en Europe*. Paris: Rousseau, 1908.

Lavergne, Bernard. *L'hégémonie du consommateur: vers une renovation de la science économique*. Paris: Presses Universitaires de France, 1958.

Lavoie, Don. "The Market as a Procedure for Discovery and Conveyance of Inarticulate Knowledge." *Comparative Economic Studies* 28 (1986): 1–19.

Lazzarato, Maurizio. *The Making of the Indebted Man*. Cambridge, MA: MIT Press, 2012.

League of Nations. *The State and Economic Life with Special Reference to International Economic and Political Relations*. Paris: IIIC, 1932.

League of Nations. *A Record of a Second Study Conference on the State and Economic Life*. Paris: IIIC, 1934.

League of Nations. *National Committees on Intellectual Co-operation*. Geneva, 1937.

Leaman, Jeremy. *The Political Economy of Germany under Chancellors Kohl and Schröder: Decline of the German Model?* New York: Berghahn Books, 2009.

Lebaron, Frederic. "Nobel Economists as Public Intellectuals." *International Journal of Contemporary Sociology*, no. 43 (2006): 87–101.

LeBor, Adam. *Tower of Basel.* New York: Public Affairs, 2013.

Leeson, Robert. *Ideology and the International Economy: The Decline and Fall of Bretton Woods*. New York: Palgrave Macmillan, 2004.

Leeson, Robert. *Hayek: A Collaborative Biography.* Basingstoke: Palgrave Macmillan, 2013.

Lenel, Hans Otto. "Alexander Rüstows wirtschafts- und sozialpolitische Konzeption." *Ordo* 37 (1986): 45–58.

Levinovitz, Agneta, and Nils Ringertz. *The Nobel Prize: The First 100 Years.* London: Imperial College Press, 2001.

Lewin, Peter. "Review: Dina Kallay, the Law and Economics of Antitrust and Intellectual Property." *Review of Austrian Economics* 18, no. 3–4 (2005): 343–4.

Lewin, Peter. "Creativity or Coercion: Alternative Perspectives on Rights to Intellectual Property." *Journal of Business Ethics* 71 (2007): 441–55.

Lincoln, Bruce. "Address to the University Senate." October 15, 2008.

Lindbeck, Assar. "The Prize in Economic Science in Memory of Alfred Nobel." *Journal of Economic Literature*, no. 23 (1985): 37–56.

Lippmann, Walter. *An Inquiry into the Principles of the Good Society*. Boston: Little, Brown & Co., 1937.

Lippmann, Walter. *Die Gesellschaft freier Menschen*. Bern: A. Francke, 1945.

Lippmann, Walter. *The Good Society.* New Brunswick: Transaction Publishers, 2005.

Longchamp, Olivier, and Yves Steiner. "The Contribution of the Schweizerisches Institut für Auslandsforschung to the International Restoration of Neoliberalism (1949–1966)." Paper presented to the EBHA conference, Geneva, 2007.

Lundberg, Erik. "The Rise and Fall of the Swedish Model." *Journal of Economic Literature*, no. 23 (1985): 1–36.

Machlup, Fritz. "Three Concepts of the Balance of Payments and the so-called Dollar Shortage." *The Economic Journal* 60 (March 1950), 46–68.

Machlup, Fritz. *An Economic Review of the Patent System*. Washington, DC: United States Government Printing Office, 1958.

Machlup, Fritz. "Patents and Inventive Effort." *Science* 133, no. 3463 (1961): 1463-6.

Machlup, Fritz. *The Production and Distribution of Knowledge in the United States.* Princeton: Princeton University Press, 1962.

Machlup, Fritz. "In Defense of Academic Tenure." *AAUP Bulletin* 50, no. 2 (1964): 112-24.

Machlup, Fritz. "International Monetary Systems and the Free Market Economy." In *International Payments Problems: A Symposium Sponsored by the American Enterprise Institute for Public Policy Research.* Washington, DC: American Enterprise Institute, 1966, 153-76.

Machlup, Fritz. *Knowledge and Knowledge Production. Knowledge, Its Creation, Distribution, and Economic Significance, Vol. 1.* Princeton: Princeton University Press, 1980.

Machlup, Fritz. "Ludwig von Mises: The Academic Scholar Who Would Not Compromise." *Wirtschaftspolitische Blätter* 28, no. 4 (1981): 6-14.

Machlup, Fritz. *The Economics of Information and Human Capital. Knowledge, Its Creation, Distribution, and Economic Significance, Vol. 3.* Princeton: Princeton University Press, 1984.

Machlup, Fritz, and Burton Malkiel, eds. *International Monetary Arrangements: The Problem of Choice. Report on the Deliberations of an International Study Group of Thirty-two Economists.* Princeton: Princeton University Press, 1964.

Machlup, Fritz, and Edith Penrose. "The Patent Controversy in the Nineteenth Century." *The Journal of Economic History* 10, no. 1 (1950): 1-29.

Macmillan, Harold. *Reconstruction: A Plea for a National Policy.* London: Macmillan, 1933.

McNamara, Kathleen R. *The Currency of Ideas: Monetary Politics in the European Union.* Ithaca: Cornell University Press, 1998.

Magnusson, Lars, and Bo Stråth. *A Brief History of Political Economy: Tales of Marx, Keynes and Hayek.* Cheltenham: Edward Elgar, 2016.

Maier, F., M. Meyer, and M. Steinbereithner. "Nonprofit Organizations Becoming Business Like: A Systematic Review." *Nonprofit and Voluntary Sector Quarterly* 45 (2016): 64-86.

Mair, Peter. *Ruling the Void: The Hollowing of Western Democracy.* New York: Verso, 2013.

Mandelker, Daniel R. "Family Responsibility under the American Poor Laws I." *Michigan Law Review* 54, no. 4 (1956): 497-532.

Mandelker, Daniel R. "Family Responsibility under the American Poor Laws II." *Michigan Law Review* 54, no. 5 (1956): 607-32.

Mannheim, Karl. *Man and Society in an Age of Reconstruction*. New York: Harcourt, Brace & Co., 1940.

Mantoux, Etienne. *La paix calomniée ou les conséquences économiques de M. Keynes*. Paris: Gallimard, 1946.

Mantoux, Etienne. *The Carthaginian Peace or the Economic Consequences of Mr. Keynes*. Oxford: Oxford University Press, 1946.

Marginson, Simon. *Education and Public Policy in Australia*. Cambridge: Cambridge University Press, 1993.

Marion, Mathieu. "Une philosophie politique pour l'empirisme logique?" *Philosophia Scientiae* CS 7 (2007): 181–216.

Marjolin, Robert. *Prix, monnaie et production: Essai sur les mouvements économiques de longue durée*. Paris: Thèses, Universités de Paris, Faculté de droit, 1941.

Marjolin, Robert. *Le travail d'une vie. Mémoirs 1911–1986*. Paris: Robert Laffont, 1986.

Marlio, Louis. "Le Néo-libéralisme." *Les Essais. Cahiers bimestriels*. Nancy: Didry and Varcollier, 1961, 86–108.

Marshall, James N. *William J. Fellner. A Bio-Bibliography*. Westport: Greenwood Press, 1992.

Marwick, Arthur. "Middle Opinion in the Thirties: Planning, Progress and Political 'Agreement.'" *The English Historical Review* 79, no. 311 (1964): 285–98.

Mason, Mary Ann. *From Father's Property to Children's Rights: The History of Child Custody in the United States*. New York: Columbia University Press, 1994.

May, Christopher. *A Global Political Economy of Intellectual Property Rights: The New Enclosures?* London: Routledge, 2000.

Mayer, Anna-K. "Setting up a Discipline, II: British History of Science and 'the End of Ideology,' 1931–1948." *Studies in History and Philosophy of Science* 35, no. 1 (2004): 41–72.

Mayer, Jane. *Dark Money: The Hidden History of the Billionaires Behind the Rise of the Radical Right*. New York: Doubleday, 2016.

Meade, James. *The Balance of Payments*. Oxford: Oxford University Press, 1951.

Medema, Steven. "A Case of Mistaken Identity: George Stigler, 'The Problem of Social Cost' and the Coase Theorem." *European Journal of Law and Economics* 31, no. 1 (2011): 11–38.

Melnick, R. Shep. *Between the Lines: Interpreting Welfare Rights*. Washington, DC: Brookings Institution Press, 1994.

Merges, Robert P. "One Hundred Years of Solicitude: Intellectual Property Law, 1900–2000." *California Law Review* 88, no. 6 (2000): 2187–240.

Mettler, Suzanne. *Degrees of Inequality: How the Politics of Higher Education Sabotaged the American Dream*. New York: Basic Books, 2014.

Meyer, Fritz W. "Die internationale Währungsordnung im Dienste der stabilitätspolitischen Grenzmoral und die Möglichkeiten einer Reform." In *25 Jahre Marktwirtschaft in der Bundesrepublik Deutschland*, ed. Dieter Cassel et al. Stuttgart: Fischer, 1972, 283–96.

Meyer, Fritz W., and Hans O. Lenel, "Vorwort." *Ordo. Jahrbuch für die Ordnung von Wirtschaft und Gesellschaft* 5 (1953): ix.

Mirowski, Philip. "The Measurement Without Theory Controversy: Defeating Rival Research Programs by Accusing Them of Naive Empiricism." *Economies et Sociétés*, Serie Oeconomia, no. 11 (1989): 65–87.

Mirowski, Philip. *Machine Dreams: Economics Becomes a Cyborg Science*. Cambridge: Cambridge University Press, 2002.

Mirowski, Philip. *ScienceMart*. Cambridge, MA: Harvard University Press, 2011.

Mirowski, Philip. "Does the Victor Enjoy the Spoils?" *Journal of the History of Economic Thought*, no. 35 (2013): 1–17.

Mirowski, Philip. *Never Let a Serious Crisis Go to Waste: How Neoliberalism Survived the Financial Meltdown*. London: Verso, 2013.

Mirowski, Philip. "The Political Movement that Dared not Speak its own Name: The Neoliberal Thought Collective Under Erasure." *Institute for New Economic Thinking Working Paper Series*, no. 23 (2014).

Mirowski, Philip, and Dieter Plehwe, eds. *The Road from Mont Pèlerin: The Making of the Neoliberal Thought Collective*. Cambridge, MA: Harvard University Press, 2009.

Mirowski, Philip, and Edward Nik-Khah. *The Knowledge We Have Lost in Information: The History of Information in Modern Economics*. Oxford: Oxford University Press, 2017.

Mises, Ludwig von. *The Theory of Money and Credit*. New Haven: Yale University Press, 1954.

Mitchell, Timothy. "The Work of Economics: How a Discipline Makes its World." *European Journal of Sociology* 46 (2005): 297–320.

Mitchell, Timothy. "How Neoliberalism Makes Its World: The Urban Property Rights Project in Peru." In *The Road from Mont Pèlerin: The Making of the Neoliberal Thought Collective*, ed. Philip Mirowski and Dieter Plehwe. Cambridge, MA: Harvard University Press, 2009, 386–416.

Moresco, Emanuel. *Peaceful Change International Studies Conference, Vol. III, Colonial Questions and Peace*. Paris: IIIC, 1939.

Morgenstern, Oskar. *International Financial Transactions and Business Cycles*. Princeton: Princeton University Press, 1959.

Mourlon-Druol, Emmanuel. *A Europe Made of Money: The Emergence of the European Monetary System*. Ithaca: Cornell University Press, 2012.

Moyn, Samuel. *Christian Human Rights*. Philadelphia: University of Pennsylvania Press, 2015.

Moyn, Samuel, and Andrew Sartori, eds. *Global Intellectual History* (New York: Columbia University Press, 2015)

Moynihan, Daniel Patrick. "The Moynihan Report. The Negro Family: The Case for National Action." In *The Moynihan Report and the Politics of Controversy*, ed. Lee Rainwater and William L. Yancey. Cambridge, MA: MIT Press, 1967 [1966], 39–124.

Mullainathan, S., and Richard H. Thaler. "Behavioral Economics." In *International Encyclopedia of the Social & Behavioral Sciences*. Vol. 2, 1094–100.

Muller, Christopher "The Institute of Economic Affairs: Undermining the Post-war Consensus." *Contemporary British History* 10, no. 1 (1996): 88–110.

Mullins, Phil, and Struan Jacobs. "T.S. Eliot's Idea of the Clerisy, and its Discussion by Karl Mannheim and Michael Polanyi in the Context of J. H. Oldham's Moot." *Journal of Classical Sociology* 6, no. 2 (2006): 147–56.

Mumper, Michael. *Removing College Price Barriers: What Government Has Done and Why It Hasn't Worked*. Albany: SUNY Press, 1996.

Myrdal, Gunnar. "The Nobel Prize in Economic Science." *Challenge* (March-April 1977): 50 52.

Nadesan, Premilla. *Welfare Warriors: The Welfare Rights Movement in the United States*. London: Routledge, 2005.

Nasar, Sylvia. *A Beautiful Mind*. New York: Simon & Schuster, 1998.

Nicholls, Anthony J. *Freedom with Responsibility: The Social Market Economy in Germany, 1918–1963*. New York: Oxford University Press, 1994.

Nik-Khah, Edward. "Chicago Neoliberalism and the Genesis of the Milton Friedman Institute (2006–2009)." In *Building Chicago Economics*, ed. Robert Van Horn, Philip Mirowski, and Tom Stapleford. New York: Cambridge University Press, 2011, 368–88.

Nik-Khah, Edward. "George Stigler, the Graduate School of Business, and the Pillars of the Chicago School." In *Building Chicago Economics*, ed. Robert Van Horn, Philip Mirowski, and Tom Stapleford. New York: Cambridge University Press, 2011, 116–47.

Nik-Khah, Edward. "Neoliberal Pharmaceutical Science and the Chicago School of Economics." *Social Studies of Science* 44, no. 4 (2014): 489–517.

Nik-Khah, Edward. "What is 'Freedom' in the Marketplace of Ideas?" In *Neoliberalism and the Crisis of Public Institutions*, ed. Anna Yeatman.

Rydalmere, NSW: Whitlam Institute within Western Sydney University, 2015, 56–69.

Nik-Khah, Edward. "Neoliberalism on Drugs: Genomics and the Political Economy of Medicine." In *Routledge Handbook of Genomics, Health, and Society*, ed. Sahra Gibbon, Barbara Prainsack, Stephen Hilgartner, and Janelle Lamoreaux, New York: Routledge, 2018.

Nik-Khah, Edward, and Robert Van Horn. "Inland Empire: Economics Imperialism as an Imperative of Chicago Neoliberalism." *Journal of Economic Methodology* 19, no. 3 (2012): 259–82.

Nik-Khah, Edward, and Robert Van Horn. "The Ascendancy of Chicago Neoliberalism." In *The Handbook of Neoliberalism*, ed. Simon Springer, Kean Birch, and Julie MacLeavy. New York: Routledge, 2016, 27–38.

Nordbakken, Lars. Interview with Assar Lindbeck, 2012, at www.minervanett. no.

North, Douglass C. *Institutions, Institutional Change and Economic Performance*. New York: Cambridge University Press, 1990.

North, Douglass C. "A Recommendation on How to Intelligently Approach Emerging Problems in Intellectual Property Systems." *Review of Law & Economics* 5, no. 3 (2009): 1131–3.

Nurkse, Ragnar, *International Currency Experience: Lessons of the Inter-War Period*. Princeton: League of Nations Publications Department, 1944.

Nye, Mary Jo. *Michael Polanyi and His Generation: Origins of the Social Construction of Science*. Chicago: University of Chicago Press, 2011.

Obstfeld, Maurice, and Alan M. Taylor. *Global Capital Markets: Integration, Crisis, and Growth*. Cambridge: Cambridge University Press, 2004.

Ockenfels, Axel, and Abdolkarim Sadrieh, eds. *The Selten School of Behavioral Economics: A Collection of Essays in Honor of Reinhard Selten*. Berlin: Springer, 2010.

Odell, John S. *US International Monetary Policy: Markets, Power, and Ideas as Sources of Change*. Princeton: Princeton University Press, 1982.

Offer, Avner, and Gabriel Soderberg. *The Nobel Factor*. Princeton: Princeton University Press, 2016.

Oliver, Henry. "German Neoliberalism." *The Quarterly Journal of Economics* 74, no. 1 (1960): 117–49.

Oppermann, Thomas, and Jutta Baumann. "Handelsbezogener Schutz geistigen Eigentums ('TRIPS') im GATT: Ein neues Stück Weltmarktwirtschaft durch die GATT-Uruguay-Runde?" *Ordo* 44 (1993): 121–37.

Ostry, Jonathan D., Prakash Loungani, and Davide Furceri. "Neoliberalism: Oversold?" *Finance & Development* (June 2016): 38–41.

Ostry, Sylvia. "The Uruguay Round North-South Grand Bargain: Implications for Future Negotiations." In *The Political Economy of International Trade Law*, ed. Daniel M. Kennedy and James D. Southwick. New York: Cambridge University Press, 2002, 285–99.

Ötsch, Walter O., and Stephan Pühringer. "Marktradikalismus als Politische Ökonomie." *ICAE Working Paper Series*, no. 38 (2015).

Ötsch, Walter O., Stephan Pühringer, and Katrin Hirte. *Netzwerke des Marktes: Ordoliberalismus als Politische Ökonomie*. Wiesbaden: Springer VS, 2017.

Palmer, Tom G. "Intellectual Property: A Non-Posnerian Law and Economics Approach." *Hamline Law Review* 12, no. 2 (1989): 261–304.

Paqué, Karl-Heinz. "Die Welt als Kegel und Vulkan." In *Das Zeitalter von Herbert Giersch. Wirtschaftspolitik für eine offene Welt*, ed. Lars P. Feld, Karen Horn, and Karl Heinz Paqué. Tübingen: Mohr Siebeck, 2013, 53–64.

Pautz, Hartwig. "Revisiting the Think-tank Phenomenon." *Public Policy and Administration* 26, no. 4 (2011): 419–35.

Peck, Jamie. "Neoliberalizing States: Thin Policies/Hard Outcomes." *Progress in Human Geography* 25, no. 3 (2001): 445–55.

Peck, Jamie. *Constructions of Neoliberal Reason*. Oxford: Oxford University Press, 2010.

Peck, Jamie. "Foreword: The Nine Lives of Neoliberalism." In *Urban Political Geographies: A Global Perspective*, ed. Ugo Rossi and Alberto Vanolo. London: Sage, 2012, xiii–xvii.

Peck, Jamie. "Explaining (with) Neoliberalism." *Territory, Politics, Governance* 1, no. 2 (2013): 132–57.

Peck, Jamie, Nik Theodore, and Neil Brenner. "Neoliberalism Resurgent? Market Rule after the Great Recession." *The South Atlantic Quarterly* 111, no. 2 (Spring 2012): 265–88.

Pedersen, Susan. *The Guardians: The League of Nations and the Crisis of Empire*. Oxford: Oxford University Press, 2015.

Pemberton, Jo-Anne. "The Changing Shape of Intellectual Cooperation: From the League of Nations to UNESCO." *Australian Journal of Politics and History* 58, no. 1 (2012): 34–50.

Pernau, Margrit, and Dominic Sachsenmaier, eds. *Global Conceptual History: A Reader*. London: Bloomsbury, 2016.

Phillips-Fein, Kim. *Invisible Hands: The Making of the Conservative Movement from the New Deal to Reagan*. New York: W. W. Norton & Company, 2009.

Phillips-Fein, Kim. *Fear City: New York City's Fiscal Crisis and the Rise of Austerity Politics*. New York: Metropolitan, 2017.

Piatier, André. *Report on the Study of Exchange Control*. Paris: IIIC, 1939.

Pitofsky, Robert, ed. *How the Chicago School Overshot the Mark: The Effect of Conservative Economic Analysis on US Antitrust.* Oxford: Oxford University Press, 2008.

Plehwe, Dieter. "The Origins of the Neoliberal Economic Development Discourse." In *The Road from Mont Pèlerin,* ed. Philip Mirowski and Dieter Plehwe. Cambridge, MA: Harvard University Press, 2009, 238–79.

Plehwe, Dieter. "Transnational Discourse Coalitions and Monetary Policy: Argentina and the Limited Powers of the 'Washington Consensus.'" *Critical Policy Studies* 5, no. 2 (2011): 127–48.

Plehwe, Dieter. "'Alternative für Deutschland,' Alternativen für Europa?" in *Europäische Identität in der Krise? Europäische Identitätsforschung und Rechtspopulismusforschung im Dialog,* ed. Gudrun Hentges, Kristina Nottbohm, and Hans-Wolfgang Platzer. Wiesbaden: Springer VS, 2017, 249–69.

Plehwe, Dieter. "Neoliberal Thought Collectives: Integrating Social Science and Intellectual History." In *Sage Handbook of Neoliberalism,* ed. Damien Cahill, Melinda Cooper, Martijn Konings, and David Primrose. Los Angeles: Sage, 2018, 85–97.

Plehwe, Dieter, and Bernhard Walpen. "Between Network and Complex Organization: The Making of Neoliberal Knowledge and Hegemony." In *Neoliberal Hegemony: A Global Critique,* ed. Dieter Plehwe, Bernhard Walpen, and Gisela Neunhöffer. London: Routledge, 2006, 27–50.

Plehwe, Dieter, and Quinn Slobodian, "Landscapes of Unrest: Herbert Giersch and the Origins of Neoliberal Economic Geography." *Modern Intellectual History* 16, no. 1 (2019): 185–215.

Plickert, Philip. *Wandlungen des Neoliberalismus. Eine Studie zu Entwicklung und Ausstrahlung der 'Mont Pèlerin Society'.* Stuttgart: Lucius & Lucius, 2008.

Plickert, Philip. "Paternalisten." *Frankfurter Allgemeine Zeitung,* August 27, 2014.

Polanyi, Karl. *The Great Transformation.* New York: Farrar & Rinehart, 1944.

Polanyi, Michael. "USSR Economics: Fundamental Data, System and Spirit." *The Manchester School* 6, no. 2 (1935): 67–88.

Polanyi, Michael. "Congrès du palais de la découverte." *Nature* 140 (1937): 710.

Polanyi, Michael. *The Contempt of Freedom: The Russian Experiment and After.* London: Watts & Co., 1940.

Polanyi, Michael. "The Growth of Thought in Society." *Economica* VIII (1941): 428–56.

Polanyi, Michael. "Patent Reform." *The Review of Economic Studies* 11, no. 2 (1944): 61–76.

Polanyi, Michael. "The Republic of Science: Its Political and Economic Theory." *Minerva* 1 (1962): 54–74.

Polanyi, Michael. *The Logic of Liberty: Reflections and Rejoinders*. Indianapolis: Liberty Fund, 1998.

Polanyi, Michael. *The Tacit Dimension*. Chicago: University of Chicago Press, 2009.

Pooley, Jefferson. "A 'Not Particularly Felicitous' Phrase: A History of the 'Behavioral Sciences' Label." *Serendipities* 1 (2016): 38–81.

Pooley, Jefferson, and Mark Solovey. "Marginal to the Revolution: The Curious Relationship between Economics and the Behavioral Sciences Movement in Mid-Twentieth-Century America." *History of Political Economy* 42 (annual supplement) (2010): 199–233.

Popper, Karl. *Unended Quest: An Intellectual Autobiography*. London and New York: Routledge, 1992.

Popper, Karl. *The Poverty of Historicism*. London: Routledge, 2002 [1957].

Popper, Karl. *The Logic of Scientific Discovery*. London: Routledge, 2002 [1959].

Popper, Karl. *The Open Society and Its Enemies*. London: Routledge, 2013 [1945].

Posner, Richard A. *The Economics of Justice*. Cambridge, MA: Harvard University Press, 1981.

Posner, Richard A. *Sex and Reason*. Cambridge, MA: Harvard University Press, 1994.

Posner, Richard A. Law, *Pragmatism and Democracy*. Cambridge MA: Harvard University Press, 2003.

Posner, Richard A. "Why There Are Too Many Patents in America." *The Atlantic*, July 12, 2012.

Prasad, Monica. "The Popular Origins of Neoliberalism in the Reagan Tax Cut of 1981." *Journal of Policy History* 24, no. 3 (2012): 351–83.

Princen, Sebastiaan, and Femke van Esch. "Paradigm Formation and Paradigm Change in the EU's Stability and Growth Pact." *European Political Science Review* 8, no. 03 (2016): 355–75.

Ptak, Ralf. *Vom Ordoliberalismus zur Sozialen Marktwirtschaft: Stationen des Neoliberalismus in Deutschland*. Wiesbaden: VS Verlag für Sozialwissenschaften, 2004.

Ptak, Ralf. "Grundlagen des Neoliberalismus." In *Kritik des Neoliberalismus*, ed. Christoph Butterwegge, Bettina Lösch, and Ralf Ptak. Wiesbaden: VS Verlag für Sozialwissenschaften, 2008, 13–86.

Ptak, Ralf. "Neoliberalism in Germany: Revisiting the Ordoliberal Foundations of the Social Market Economy." In *The Road from Mont Pèlerin*, ed. Philip Mirowski and Dieter Plehwe. Cambridge, MA: Harvard University Press, 2009, 98–138.

Pühringer, Stephan. "The Success Story of Ordoliberalism as Guiding Principle of German Economic Policy." In *Ordoliberalism: Law and the Rule of Economics*, ed. Josef Hien and Christian Joerges. Oxford: Hart Publishing, 2018, 134–58.

Quadagno, Jill. *The Color of Welfare: How Racism Undermined the War on Poverty*. Oxford: Oxford University Press, 1994.

Radnitzky, Gerard. "An Economic Theory of the Rise of Civilization and Its Policy Implications: Hayek's Account Generalized." *Ordo* 38 (1987): 47–90.

Rand, Ayn. *Capitalism: The Unknown Ideal*. New York: Signet, 1967.

Reagan, Ronald. *The Creative Society: Some Comments on Problems Facing America*. New York: Devin-Adair Company, 1968.

Reder, Melvin. "Chicago Economics: Permanence and Change." *Journal of Economic Literature* 20, no. 1 (1982): 1–38.

Reich, Charles A. "Individual Rights and Social Welfare: The Emerging Legal Issues." *Yale Law Journal* 74, no. 7 (1965): 1245–57.

Reich, Charles A. "Social Welfare in the Public-Private State." *University of Pennsylvania Law Review* 114, no. 4 (1966): 487–93.

Reinhoudt, Jurgen, and Serge Audier. *The Walter Lippmann Colloquium: The Birth of Neo-Liberalism*. London: Palgrave, 2017.

Richter, Rudolf. *Deutsche Geldpolitik 1948–1998 im Spiegel der zeitgenössischen wissenschaftlichen Diskussion*. Tübingen: Mohr Siebeck, 1999.

Riemens, Michael. "International Academic Cooperation on International Relations in the Interwar Period: The International Studies Conference." *Review of International Studies* 37, no. 2 (2011): 911–28.

Rietzler, Katharina. "Experts for Peace: Structures and Motivations of Philanthropic Internationalism in the Interwar Years." In *Internationalism Reconfigured: Transnational Ideas and Movements between the World Wars*, ed. Daniel Laqua. London: I. B. Tauris, 2011, 45–65.

Riley, Stephen. *Human Dignity and Law: Legal and Philosophical Investigations*. Abingdon: Routledge, 2017.

Robbins, Lionel. *Economic Planning and International Order*. London: Macmillan and Co., 1937.

Robinson, Joan. *Economic Philosophy*. London: Watts, 1962.

Robinson, Joan. *Economic Heresies: Some Old-Fashioned Questions in Economic Theory*. London: Palgrave Macmillan, 1971.

Rodgers, Daniel T. *Age of Fracture*. Cambridge MA: Belknap Press of Harvard University Press, 2011.

Rodrik, Dani. "Rescuing Economics from Neoliberalism." *Boston Review*, November 6, 2017.

Rogge, Benjamin. *Can Capitalism Survive?* Indianapolis: Liberty Fund, 1979.

Röpke, Wilhelm. *Cycles and Crises.* London: W. Hodge, 1936.

Röpke, Wilhelm. *International Economic Disintegration.* London: W. Hodge, 1942.

Röpke, Wilhelm. *Civitas Humana. Grundfragen der Gesellschafts- und Wirtschaftsreform.* Zurich: Eugen Rentsch, 1944.

Röpke, Wilhelm. *Mass und Mitte.* Zurich: Eugen Rentsch, 1950.

Röpke, Wilhelm. *The Social Crisis of Our Time.* Chicago: University of Chicago Press, 1950 [1942].

Röpke, Wilhelm. *Jenseits von Angebot und Nachfrage.* Zurich: Eugen Rentsch, 1958.

Rose, Nikolas. "Still 'Like Birds on the Wire'? Freedom after Neoliberalism." *Economy and Society* 46, no. 3–4 (2017): 303–23.

Rothbard, Murray N. "The Case for a Genuine Gold Dollar." In *In Search of a Monetary Constitution,* ed. Leland Yeager. Cambridge, MA: Harvard University Press, 1962, 94–136.

Rothstein, Bo. "The Prize in Contravention of the Spirit of Nobel's Will," at http://rothstein.dinstudio.se.

Rueff, Jacques. *Épitre aux Dirigistes.* Paris: Gallimard, 1949.

Rueff, Jacques. *L'Ordre Social.* Paris: Librairie de Médicis, 1949.

Rougier, Louis. *La philosophie géométrique de Henri Poincaré.* Paris: Alcan, 1920.

Rougier, Louis. *Les paralogismes du rationalisme. Essai sur la théorie de la connaissance.* Paris: Alcan, 1920.

Rougier, Louis. "La mystique soviétique. Une scolastique nouvelle: le marxisme-léninisme." *La Revue de Paris* 41, no. 2 (1934): 600–29.

Rougier, Louis. "Une philosophie nouvelle: l'empirisme logique. A propos d'un congrès récent." *La Revue de Paris* 43, no. 1 (1936): 182–95.

Rougier, Louis. *Mission Secrète à Londres. Les Accords Pétain-Churchill.* Geneva: Les Editions du Cheval Ailé, 1946.

Rougier, Louis. "L'impossibilité scientifique du planisme économique." *Écrits de Paris* (January 1948): 32–41.

Rueff, Jacques. *From the Physical to the Social Sciences.* Baltimore, MD: The Johns Hopkins Press, 1929 [1922].

Ruger, William. *Milton Friedman.* London: Bloomsbury Academic, 2011.

Ruggie, John Gerard. "International Regimes, Transactions, and Change: Embedded Liberalism in the Postwar Economic Order." *International Organization* 36, no. 2 (1982): 379–415.

Rüstow, Alexander. "Paläoliberalismus, Kollektivismus und Neoliberalismus." In *Wirtschaft, Gesellschaft und Kultur. Festgabe für Alfred Müller-Armack,* ed. Franz Greiß and Fritz W. Meyer. Berlin: Duncker & Humblot, 1961, 61–70.

Rüther, Daniela. "Freiburger Nationalökonomen auf dem Weg in den Widerstand." *Historisch-Politische Mitteilungen*, no. 10 (2003): 77–94.

Rutherford, Malcolm, and Mary Morgan, eds. *From Interwar Pluralism to Postwar Neoclassicism*. Durham, NC: Duke University Press, 1998.

Sachverständigenrat zur Begutachtung der gesamtwirtschaftlichen Entwicklung. *Jahresgutachten 1964/65* (1964), reprinted 1994 by Schmidt Periodicals GmbH, Bad Feilnbach.

Saint-Paul, Gilles. *The Tyranny of Utility: Behavioral Social Science and the Rise of Paternalism*. Princeton: Princeton University Press, 2011.

Samuelson, Paul. "A Few Remembrances of Friedrich von Hayek." *Journal of Economic Behavior and Organization*, no. 69 (2009): 1–4.

Schildt, Axel. "'Die Kräfte der Gegenreform sind auf breiter Front angetreten': Zur konservativen Tendenzwende in den Siebzigerjahren." *Archiv für Sozialgeschichte* 44 (2004): 449–78.

Schiller, Karl, ed. *Reden zur Wirtschaftspolitik*. Bonn: Ministry of Economics, 1972.

Schmelzer, Matthias. *Freiheit für Wechselkurse und Kapital. Die Ursprünge neoliberaler Währungspolitik und die Mont Pèlerin Society*. Marburg: Metropolis-Verlag, 2010.

Schmitt, Alfons, and Günter Schmölders. *Außenwirtschaft und Außenhandelspolitik*. Leipzig: Bibliographisches Institut, 1939.

Schmölders, Günter. *Prohibition im Norden: Die staatliche Bekämpfung des Alkoholismus in den nordischen Ländern*. Berlin: Unger, 1926.

Schmölders, Günter. *Die Prohibition in den Vereinigten Staaten: Triebkräfte und Auswirkungen des amerikanischen Alkoholverbots*. Leipzig: C. L. Hirschfeld, 1930.

Schmölders, Günter. *Die Ertragsfähigkeit der Getränkesteuern: Vergleichende Übersicht über die Voraussetzungen der Alkoholbesteuerung im Deutschen Reich, in Großbritannien, Frankreich, der Schweiz, Dänemark und den Vereinigten Staaten; ein Beitrag zur deutschen Finanzreform*. Jena: Fischer, 1932.

Schmölders, Günter. *Steuermoral und Steuerbelastung*. Berlin: C. Heymann, 1932.

Schmölders, Günter. *Die Konjunkturpolitik der Vereinigten Staaten: Erfahrungen und Lehren der amerikanischen Kredit- und Währungspolitik im Kampfe gegen Krise und Konjunktur*. Leipzig: Akademie Verlags-Gesellschaft, 1934.

Schmölders, Günter. *Geld und Kredit: Probleme der Wirtschaftspolitik*. Leipzig: Bibliographisches Institut, 1938.

Schmölders, Günter. *Das Sparkapital in der gelenkten Volkswirtschaft: Wandlungen der Kreditorganisation.* Stuttgart: W. Kohlhammer, 1940.

Schmölders, Günter. *Wirtschaftslenkung als angewandte Wirtschaftswissenschaft: Festrede gehalten bei der Feier des Tages der nationalen Erhebung verbunden mit der feierlichen Immatrikulation für das Trimester 1941 am 29. Januar 1941.* Cologne: Oskar Müller Verlag, 1941.

Schmölders, Günter. *Die Steuerzahlerbewegung in Schweden.* Cologne: Finanzwissenschaftliches Forschungsinstitut, 1950.

Schmölders, Günter. *Allgemeine Steuerlehre.* Stuttgart: Humboldt-Verlag, 1951.

Schmölders, Günter. "Finanzpsychologie." *Finanz-Archiv/Public Finance Analysis,* New Series 133, no. 1 (1951–2): 1–36.

Schmölders, Günter. *Die große Steuerreform.* Bad Nauheim: Vita-Verlag, 1953.

Schmölders, Günter. "Ökonomische Verhaltensforschung." *Ordo. Jahrbuch für die Ordnung von Wirtschaft und Gesellschaft* 5 (1953): 203–44.

Schmölders, Günter. *Organische Steuerreform: Grundlagen, Vorarbeiten, Gesetzentwürfe.* Berlin: F. Vahlen, 1953.

Schmölders, Günter. "J. M. Keynes' Beitrag zur 'ökonomischen Verhaltensforschung.'" In *John Maynard Keynes als "Psychologe,"* ed. Günter Schmölders, Rudolf Schröder, and Hellmuth S. Seidenfus. Berlin: Duncker & Humblot, 1956, 7–24.

Schmölders, Günter. *Ökonomische Verhaltensforschung.* Cologne & Opladen: Westdeutscher Verlag, 1957.

Schmölders, Günter. *Das Irrationale in der öffentlichen Finanzwirtschaft: Probleme der Finanzpsychologie.* Hamburg: Rowohlt, 1960.

Schmölders, Günter. "Zur Psychologie der Vermögensbildung in Arbeiterhand." *Kyklos: International Review for Social Sciences* 15 (1962): 165–82.

Schmölders, Günter. "10 Jahre sozialökonomische Verhaltensforschung in Cologne." *Ordo. Jahrbuch für die Ordnung von Wirtschaft und Gesellschaft* 14 (1963): 259–73.

Schmölders, Günter. "Der Beitrag der Verhaltensforschung zur Theorie der wirtschaftlichen Entwicklung." In *Systeme und Methoden in den Wirtschafts- und Sozialwissenschaften: Erwin von Beckerath zum 75. Geburtstag,* ed. Norbert Kloten et al. Tübingen: Mohr, 1964, 363–85.

Schmölders, Günter. "Das neue Finanzwissenschaftliche Forschungsinstitut." In *Finanzwissenschaftliche Forschung und Lehre an der Universität zu Köln 1927–1967.* Berlin: Duncker & Humblot, 1967, 27–44.

Schmölders, Günter. "Der Staatsbürger als Steuerzahler: Wandlungen des Menschenbildes in Finanzwissenschaft und Steuerpraxis." *Finanz-Archiv/Public Finance Analysis* 27, no. 1–2 (1968): 121–38.

Schmölders, Günter. *Geldpolitik*. 2nd edition. Tübingen/Zürich: Mohr Siebeck, 1968.

Schmölders, Günter. "Sozialökonomische Verhaltensforschung." In *Wörterbuch der Soziologie*. Vol. 3, ed. Wilhelm Bernsdorf. Frankfurt am Main: Fischer-Taschenbuch-Verlag, 1968/69, 1036–7.

Schmölders, Günter. *Personalistischer Sozialismus: Die Wirtschaftsordnungskonzeption des Kreisauer Kreises der deutschen Widerstandsbewegung*. Cologne: Westdeutscher Verlag, 1969.

Schmölders, Günter. *Der Unternehmer im Ansehen der Welt*. Bergisch Gladbach: Gustav Lübbe Verlag, 1971.

Schmölders, Günter. *Der verlorene Untertan: Verhaltensforschung enthüllt die Krise zwischen Staatsbürger und Obrigkeit*. Dusseldorf: ECON, 1971.

Schmölders, Günter. *Einführung in die Geld- und Finanzpsychologie*. Darmstadt: Wissenschaftliche Buchgesellschaft, 1975.

Schmölders, Günter. *Die Inflation: Ein Kernproblem in Wirtschaft und Gesellschaft*. Paderborn: Schöningh, 1976.

Schmölders, Günter. "Erhards Denkschrift im Lichte neuer Dokumente über die Kriegsfinanzierung 1933–45." In *Kriegsfinanzierung und Schuldenkonsolidierung*, ed. Ludwig Erhard, Theodor Eschenburg, and Günter Schmölders. Frankfurt am Main: Propyläen-Verlag, 1977, xxiii–xxiv.

Schmölders, Günter. *Ursprung und Entwicklung der Steuerzahlerbewegung*. 2nd edition. Bad Wörishofen: Holzmann, 1977.

Schmölders, Günter. "A Visit to Santiago de Chile." *International Background 8*, no. 6 (1981): 183f.

Schmölders, Günter. *Der Wohlfahrtsstaat am Ende: Adam Riese schlägt zurück*. 3rd edition. Munich: Wirtschaftsverlag Langen-Müller/Herbig, 1983.

Schmölders, Günter. *Lebenserinnerungen: "Gut durchgekommen?"* Berlin: Duncker & Humblot, 1988.

Schmölders, Günter, and Burkhard Strümpel. *Vergleichende Finanzpsychologie: Besteuerung und Steuermentalität in einigen europäischen Ländern*. Wiesbaden: Akademie der Wissenschaften und der Literatur, 1968.

Schneider, Erich. "Fundamental Errors in Recent Anti-Keynesian Literature." *PSL Quarterly Review 6* (1953): 3–24.

Schorr, Alvin Louis. *Filial Responsibility in the Modern American Family*. US 96. *Department of Health, Education and Welfare, Division of Program Research*. Washington, DC: US Government Printing Office, 1960.

Schulman, Bruce J., and Julian E. Zelizer, eds. *Rightward Bound: Making America Conservative in the 1970s*. Cambridge, MA: Harvard University Press, 2008.

Schultz, Theodore W. "Investment in Human Capital." *The American Economic Review* 51, no. 1 (1961): 1–17.

Schultz, Theodore W. "Woman's New Economic Commandments." *Bulletin of the Atomic Scientists* XXVIII, no. 2 (1972): 29–32.

Schulz-Forberg, Hagen, ed. *A Global Conceptual History of Asia 1860–1940*. London: Pickering & Chatto, 2014.

Schulz-Forberg, Hagen. "Laying the Groundwork: The Semantics of Neoliberalism in the 1930s." In *Re-Inventing Western Civilisation: Transnational Reconstructions of Liberalism in Europe in the Twentieth Century*, ed. Hagen Schulz-Forberg and Niklas Olsen. Newcastle Upon Tyne: Cambridge Scholars Press, 2014, 13–39.

Schumpeter, Joseph. *Business Cycles: A Theoretical, Historical and Statistical Analysis of the Capitalist Process*. New York: McGraw Hill Co., 1939.

Schumpeter, Joseph. *Capitalism, Socialism, and Democracy*. New York: Harper & Brothers, 1942.

Schumpeter, Joseph Alois. *Theory of Economic Development: An Inquiry into Profits, Capital, Credit, Interest, and the Business Cycle*. London: Routledge 1984 (based on original material published by Harvard University Press, 1934).

Schütz, Alfred. *Der sinnhafte Aufbau der sozialen Welt: Eine Einleitung in die verstehende Soziologie*. Vienna: J. Springer, 1932.

Seidenfus, Hellmuth S. "Verhaltensforschung, sozialökonomische." In *Handwörterbuch der Staatswissenschaften*. Vol. 11, ed. Erwin v. Beckerath et al. Stuttgart: Fischer, 1961, 95–102.

Seldon, Arthur, ed. *The Prime Mover of Progress: The Entrepreneur in Capitalism and Socialism*. London: Institute of Economic Affairs, 1980.

Sell, Susan K. *Private Power, Public Law: The Globalization of Intellectual Property Rights*. Cambridge: Cambridge University Press, 2003.

Sent, Esther-Mirjam. "Behavioral Economics: How Psychology Made Its (Limited) Way Back into Economics." *History of Political Economy* 36, no. 4 (2004): 735–60.

Shammas, Victor L. "Burying Mont Pèlerin: Milton Friedman and Neoliberal Vanguardism." *Constellations* 25, no. 1 (2018): 117–32.

Shearmur, Jeremy. "Epistemology Socialized?" *ETC: A Review of General Semantics* 42, no. 3 (1985): 272–82.

Shenoy, B. R. "Das Bild vom Unternehmer in Indien." In *Der Unternehmer im Ansehen der Welt*, ed. Günter Schmölders. Bergisch Gladbach: Lübbe Verlag, 1971, 156–71.

Shils, Edward. "A Critique of Planning: The Society for Freedom in Science." *Bulletin of the Atomic Scientists* 3, no. 3 (1947): 80–2.

Shweder, Richard. "Protecting Human Subjects and Preserving Academic Freedom: Prospects at the University of Chicago." *American Ethnologist* 33, no. 4 (2006): 507–18.

Siebert, Horst. *The World Economy: A Global Analysis*. 3 edition. London: Routledge, 2007.

Simon, Herbert A. "Behavioral Model of Rational Choice." *Journal of Economics* 69 (1955): 99–118.

Simons, Henry. *A Positive Program for Laissez-Faire: Some Proposals for a Liberal Economic Policy*. Public Policy Pamphlet no. 15. Chicago: University of Chicago Press, 1934.

Singer, Jana B. "The Privatization of Family Law." *Wisconsin Law Review* 5 (1992): 1443–568.

Skarbeck, David. "F. A. Hayek's Influence on the Nobel Prize Winners." *Review of Austrian Economics*, no. 22 (2009): 109–12.

Slobodian, Quinn. *Globalists: The End of Empire and the Birth of Neoliberalism*. Cambridge, MA: Harvard University Press, 2018.

Soderberg, Gabriel. "Constructing Invisible Hands: Market Technocrats in Sweden 1880 2000." *Acta Universitatis Upsaliensis (Uppsala Studies in Economic History)* 98 (2013).

Sohmen, Egon. *Flexible Exchange Rates: Theory and Controversy*. Chicago: University of Chicago Press, 1961.

Solomon, G. T., and Fernald, L. W., Jr. "Trends in Small Business Management and Entrepreneurship Education in the United States." *Entrepreneurship Theory and Practice* 15 (1991): 25–39.

Solow, Robert M. "Technical Change and the Aggregate Production Function." *The Review of Economics and Statistics* 39 (1957): 312–20.

Solow, Robert M. "Technical Progress, Capital Formation, and Economic Growth." *The American Economic Review* 52 (1962): 76–86.

Solow, Robert. "What Do We Know that Francis Amasa Walker Didn't?" *History of Political Economy* 19, no. 2 (1987): 183–9.

Solow, Robert. "Hayek, Friedman and the Illusions of Conservative Economics." *New Republic*, November 16, 2012.

Speth, Rudolf. *Die politischen Strategien der Initiative Neue Soziale Marktwirtschaft* 96. Dusseldorf: Hans-Böckler-Stiftung, 2004.

Springer, Simon, Kean Birch, and Julie MacLeavy. "An Introduction to Neoliberalism." In *The Handbook of Neoliberalism*, ed. Simon Springer, Kean Birch, and Julie MacLeavy. New York: Routledge, 2016, 1–14.

Ståhl, Ingemar. "The Prize in Economic Science and Maurice Allais." Paper presented to MPS meeting, 1990.

Stahl, Jason. *Right Moves: The Conservative Think Tank in American Political Culture since 1945*. Chapel Hill: University of North Carolina Press, 2016.

Stanford, Jim, *Economic Freedom for the Rest of Us*, Halifax: Canadian Autoworkers Union, 1999, at http://www.csls.ca.

Starbatty, Joachim. "Ordoliberalismus." In *Geschichte der Nationalökonomie*, ed. Otmar Issing. Munich: Vahlen, 1994, 251–69.

Stark, Jürgen. "Monetary, Fiscal and Financial Stability in Europe: Speech at the 11th Euro Finance Week in Frankfurt, 18 November 2008," at www.ecb. europa.eu.

Steelman, Aaron. "Intellectual Property." In *The Encyclopedia of Libertarianism*, ed. Ronald Hamoy. London: Sage, 2008, 249–50.

Steiner, Yves. "Les riches amis suisses du néolibéralisme. De la débâcle de la revue Occident à la Conférence du Mont Pèlerin d'avril 1947." *Traverse*, no. 1 (2007): 114–26.

Stiftung Marktwirtschaft. *25 JAHRE Stiftung Marktwirtschaft und Kronberger Kreis*. Berlin: 2007.

Stiftung Marktwirtschaft. "Mehr Mut zum Markt," at www.stiftung-marktwirtschaft.de.

Stigler, George. *The Intellectual and the Market Place*. New York: Free Press of Glencoe, 1963.

Stigler, George. *Essays in the History of Economics*. Chicago: University of Chicago Press, 1965.

Stigler, George. "The Confusion of Means and Ends." In *Regulating New Drugs*, ed. Richard Landau. Chicago: University of Chicago Center for Policy Study, 1973, 10–19.

Stigler, George. "The Intellectual and His Society." In *Capitalism and Freedom: Problems and Prospects*, ed. Richard Selden. Charlottesville, VA: University Press of Virginia, 1975, 311–21.

Stigler, George. "Do Economists Matter?" *Southern Economic Journal* 42, no. 3 (1976): 347–54.

Streeck, Wolfgang. *Gekaufte Zeit. Die vertagte Krise des demokratischen Kapitalismus*. Berlin: Suhrkamp, 2013.

Streeck, Wolfgang. *Buying Time: The Delayed Crisis of Democratic Capitalism*. New York: Verso, 2014.

Sturn, Richard. *Varianten des Unternehmertums in der Österreichischen Schule*. Graz: GSC Discussion Paper no. 18, 2017.

Swoboda Peter. "Schumpeter's Entrepreneur in Modern Economic Theory." In *Schumpeter Centenary Memorial Lectures*, ed. Christian Seidl. Berlin: Springer, 1984, 17–28.

TenBroek, Jacobus. "California's Dual System of Family Law: Its Origin, Development, and Present Status: Part I." *Stanford Law Review* 16, no. 2 (1964): 257–84.

Thaler, Richard H., and Cass R. Sunstein. "Libertarian Paternalism." *The American Economic Review* 93, no. 2 (2003): 175–9.

Thaler, Richard H., and Cass R. Sunstein. *Nudge: Improving Decisions About Health, Wealth and Happiness.* London: Penguin Books, 2009.

Thomasberger, Claus. " 'Planung für den Markt' versus 'Planung für die Freiheit': Zu den stillschweigenden Voraussetzungen des Neoliberalismus." In *Der neoliberale Markt Diskurs: Ursprünge, Geschichte, Wirkungen*, ed. Walter O. Ötsch and Claus Thomasberger. Marburg: Metropolis, 2009, 63–96.

Travaux du Colloque International du Libéralisme Economique. Brussels: Editions du Centre Paul Hymans, 1957.

Tribe, Keith. "Liberalism and Neoliberalism in Britain, 1930–1980." In *The Road from Mont Pèlerin*, ed. Philip Mirowski and Dieter Plehwe. Cambridge, MA: Harvard University Press, 2009, 68–97.

Triffin, Robert. "The Impact of the Bellagio Group on International Reform." In *Breadth and Depth in Economics. Fritz Machlup—The Man and His Ideas*, ed. Jacob S. Dreyer. Lexington: Lexington Books, 1978, 145–58.

Turner, Fred. *From Counterculture to Cyberculture: Stewart Brand, the Whole Earth Network, and the Rise of Digital Utopianism.* Chicago: University of Chicago Press, 2006.

Tversky, Amos, and Daniel Kahneman. "Judgment Under Uncertainty: Heuristics and Biases." *Science* 185 (1974): 1124–31.

Tyfield, David. "Science, Innovation, and Neoliberalism." In *The Handbook of Neoliberalism*, ed. Simon Springer, Kean Birch, and Julie MacLeavy. New York: Routledge, 2016, 340–50.

University of Chicago Kalven Committee. "Report on the University's Role and Social Action." *University of Chicago Record* 1, no. 1 (1967).

Unternehmer und Bildung. Festschrift zum 60. Geburtstag von Ludwig Vaubel. Cologne: Westdeutscher Verlag, 1968. (Band 10 der Veröffentlichungen der Walter Raymond-Stiftung.)

Vaara, E., J. Tienari, and J. Laurila. "Pulp and Paper Fiction: On the Discursive Legitimation of Global Industrial Restructuring." *Organization Studies* 27, no. 6 (2006): 789–813.

Valdés, Juan Gabriel. *Pinochet's Economists.* Cambridge: Cambridge University Press, 1995.

Van Horn, Robert. "Reinventing Monopoly and the Role of Corporations: The Roots of Chicago Law and Economics." In *The Road from Mont Pèlerin*, ed.

Philip Mirowski and Dieter Plehwe. Cambridge, MA: Harvard University Press, 2009, 204–37.

Van Horn, Robert, and Matthias Klaes. "Intervening in Laissez-Faire Liberalism: Chicago's Shift on Patents." In *Building Chicago Economics: New Perspectives on the History of America's Most Powerful Economics Program*, ed. Robert Van Horn, Philip Mirowski, and Thomas A. Stapleford. New York: Cambridge University Press, 2011, 180–207.

Van Horn, Robert, and Philip Mirowski. "The Rise of the Chicago School of Economics and the Birth of Neoliberalism." In *The Road from Mont Pèlerin*, ed. Philip Mirowski and Dieter Plehwe. Cambridge, MA: Harvard University Press, 2009, 139–78.

Van Horn, Robert, and Ross Emmett. "Two Trajectories of Democratic Capitalism in the Post-War Chicago School: Frank Knight versus Aaron Director." *Cambridge Journal of Economics* 35, no. 5 (2014): 1443–55.

Vanberg, Viktor. "The Freiburg School: Walter Eucken and Ordoliberalism." *Freiburg Discussion Papers on Constitutional Economics*, no. 11 (2004).

Venugopal, Rajesh. "Neoliberalism as Concept." *Economy and Society* 44, no. 2 (2015): 165–87.

Walpen, Bernhard. *Die offenen Feinde und ihre Gesellschaft. Eine hegemonietheoretische Studie zur Mont Pèlerin Society.* Hamburg: VSA-Verlag, 2004.

Wang, Marian, Beckie Supiano, and Andrea Fuller, "No Income? No Problem! How the Government is Saddling Parents with College Loans They Can't Afford." Propublica, October 4, 2012, at www.propublica.org.

Weede, Erich. "Vertragen die alternden europäischen Sozialstaaten die Massenzuwanderung, die wir haben?" *Orientierungen zur Wirtschafts- und Gesellschaftspolitik*, no. 143 (2016): 54–66.

Werding, Martin. "Gab es eine neoliberale Wende? Wirtschaft und Wirtschaftspolitik in der Bundesrepublik Deutschland ab Mitte der 1970er Jahre." *Vierteljahrshefte für Zeitgeschichte* 56, no. 2 (2008): 559.

Whitehead, Mark, Rhys Jones, Rachel Howell, Rachel Lilley, and Jessica Pykett. "Nudging All Over the World: Assessing the Global Impact of the Behavioral Sciences on Public Policy," at https://changingbehaviours.files.wordpress.com.

Wible, James. *The Economics of Science.* New York: Routledge, 1998.

Wilson, Jérôme, and Robert Triffin. *Milieux académiques et cénacles économiques internationaux 1935–1951.* Fond Camille Gutt: Editions Versant Sud, 2015.

Wissenschaftlicher Beirat beim Bundesministerium der Finanzen, ed. *Organische Steuerreform: Bericht an den Herrn Bundesminister der Finanzen.* Bonn, 1953.

Witt, John Fabian. *The Accidental Republic: Crippled Workingmen, Destitute Widows, and the Remaking of American Law.* Cambridge, MA: Harvard University Press, 2004.

Wright, Carl M. "Memorandum on the Danubian Study Group." In *Peaceful Change*, 4 vol, ed. International Studies Conference. Paris: IIIC, 1939, 214–57.

Zeman, Ray. "Reagan Pledges to Squeeze, Cut and Trim State Spending: Reagan Pledges Strict Government Economy." *Los Angeles Times*, January 6, 1967: 1 and 20.

Zumbrun, Ronald A., Raymond M. Momboisse, and John H. Findley, "Welfare Reform: California Meets the Challenge." *Pacific Law Journal* 4 (1973): 739–85.